The Black Laws

Ohio University Press Series
on Law, Society, and Politics in the Midwest

SERIES EDITOR: PAUL FINKELMAN

STEPHEN MIDDLETON

The Black Laws

Race and the Legal
Process in
Early Ohio

Ohio University Press   Athens

Ohio University Press, Athens, Ohio 45701

© 2005 by Ohio University Press
www.ohio.edu/oupress

13 12 11 10 09 08 07 06 05   5 4 3 2 1

Jacket/cover image:
Addison White, a fugitive slave whose freedom was purchased in
part by the city of Mechanicsburg, Champaign County, Ohio.
Courtesy Ohio Historical Society.

Library of Congress Cataloging-in-Publication Data

Middleton, Stephen.
  The Black laws : race and the legal process in early Ohio / by Stephen Middleton.
    p. cm. — (Ohio University Press series on law, society, and politics in the Midwest)
  Includes bibliographical references and index.
  ISBN 0-8214-1623-5 (cloth : alk. paper) — ISBN 0-8214-1624-3 (pbk. : alk. paper)
  1. African Americans—Legal status, laws, etc.—Ohio—History. 2. Race discrimination—
Law and legislation—Ohio—History. 3. Race discrimination—Ohio—History. I. Title.
II. Series.

  KF0411.5.A34M53 2006
  342.7308'73—dc22

                                                                    2005024836

For Alexander J. De Grand

CONTENTS

PREFACE AND ACKNOWLEDGMENTS

The research for this book was extensive, and I spent more years engaged in this project than I care to admit. I accumulated many debts with friends, colleagues, and the staffs at many archives and libraries. But before I acknowledge them for their courtesies I want to answer a question that many friends, students, and colleagues acquainted with my scholarly endeavors have asked over the years: I am not an Ohio native. Nevertheless, for nearly thirty years, the Buckeye State played a prominent role in my professional and personal life. I completed my graduate education at Ohio State and Miami of Ohio. I met my wife, Earline, at Wilberforce University, my first employer, and she gave birth to our three children in Ohio. Our oldest, Stephen Middleton II, would have been twenty-five years old on October 9, 2005. Stephen, a jewel of a son, departed this life when he was only sixteen years old. Stephen, Eric, and Jessica were born in Dayton. Ohio is where we lived, worked, and played until we moved to North Carolina in 1989.

If you are like me, you probably have wondered if the praises usually given to librarians, scholars, and editors were standard accolades extended to people who had an interest in the publication of a book. But I have learned that such acknowledgments are more than mere courtesies. I could not have single-handedly unearthed the data I used in this study; nor did I write this book alone. I feel so blessed to have benefited from the expertise of some of the most talented librarians in the world. The staffs at the Ohio Historical Society, the Western Reserve Historical Society, and the Cincinnati Historical Society are second to none. There are too many of these knowledgeable and helpful people for me to single out here, but I do want to give a special word of thanks to Barbara Dawson, who works at the CHS and who also was my classmate at Miami. Barbara went beyond the call of duty in answering my many queries sent by e-mail.

I benefited from the resources in other depositories and from those that funded my research. The American Antiquarian Society in Worcester,

Massachusetts, awarded me a Kate B. and Hall J. Peterson Fellowship, which allowed me to spend a month doing work in its rich collections. The National Endowment for the Humanities awarded a Travel to Collections grant. And the College of Humanities and Social Sciences (CHASS) at North Carolina State University awarded me a summer fellowship to support my research. In addition, the New York University School of Law awarded me one of its Samuel Golieb Fellowships, which gave me access to its Legal History Seminar; I profited from the feedback I got from commentators who read the chapters I presented. The law school also allowed me to enroll in the first-year curriculum to deepen my understanding of legal principles and the uses and techniques of law. I will always be grateful to Professor William E. Nelson and to the other participants in the weekly seminars at the law school.

I also benefited from the contributions of scholars who commented on the papers I read at professional meetings, including the Ohio Academy of History, the British Legal History Association, and the British American Studies Association. Many other historians and legal scholars read parts of this work at my request. Professors Kermit Hall, William Wiecek, Herman Belz, Barbara A. Terzian, Jack R. Pole, Michael Les Benedict, Thomas D. Morris, and Loren Schweninger read from one to several chapters in the manuscript and gave me helpful advice. Professor Morris, while doing research in England, met me at the University of Wales at Aberystwyth to go over his comments. Professor Schweninger also took time off from his work to read several chapters of my manuscript. I am grateful for their generosity.

Numerous friends and colleagues in the Department of History at North Carolina State University, where I teach, assisted me. I benefited from the insights of William H. Harris and John David Smith, who read this work at various stages. Linda McMurray Edwards helped me with the chronological focus and the conceptual framework of the book. Alexander De Grand read several versions of my manuscript and improved upon it at each step in the process. Other scholars and friends at N.C. State also made substantial contributions to this work. Professor Thomas Lisk, who teaches in the Department of English, gave me meaningful editorial advice. Julie Dumont Rabinowitz, formerly with the College of Humanities and Social Sciences Extension and Publications Office at N.C. State, read and made substantial contributions to two drafts of the manuscript.

I am also grateful to the professionals who work at the Ohio University Press in Athens. Gillian Berchowitz, senior editor, believed in this project from the start, and kept me on track when I felt pushed by readers. Paul Finkelman, editor of the Ohio University Press Series on Law, Society, and Politics in the Midwest, surely knows how to push my intellectual and scholarly buttons, and he challenged me to reevaluate my assumptions about various topics, including Article VI of the Northwest Ordinance of 1787. I am also appreciative for the contributions of Ricky Huard, the project editor for the press; my copy editor, Bob Furnish; and many other anonymous readers who evaluated this manuscript for the press. These friends and colleagues did their part; any weaknesses in this book can be attributed to my failure to accept all their suggestions. A mere thank you seems inadequate. As an expression of my appreciation, I am dedicating this book to one of them, Alexander De Grand.

Introduction

That no black or mulatto person or persons shall hereafter be permitted to be sworn or give evidence in any court of record, or elsewhere, in this state, in any cause depending, or matter of controversy, where either party to the same is a white person.

—5 Laws of Ohio 53, approved January 25, 1807

IN 1841, the *Colored American,* an African American newspaper, ran a story entitled "Civil Condition of the Colored People in Ohio." It reported the murder in Cincinnati of a black man by a white. The *Colored American* had frequently published articles describing how the Black Laws had subordinated and degraded African Americans. It reported this story not only because it was news that merited coverage but, more important, because it illustrated the continued injustice of the Black Laws. This article specifically exposed how the "oath law" protected unscrupulous whites by excluding "the testimony of a colored person against a white person."[1] In previous articles, the paper had reported numerous instances of whites embezzling, swindling, and even stealing property and money from blacks. The paper had already predicted that the testimony law would enable "a white to murder a colored man, in the presence of colored persons only, and under the operations of this law, or as it had been interpreted, the murderer might go unpunished."[2] The 1841 case tragically proved the accuracy of this prediction.

The episode involved Charles Scott and his brother (whose name is unknown), two free African Americans who lived in Cincinnati. White men hired the Scotts, ostensibly to help them drive cattle across the Ohio River into Kentucky. The editors of the *Colored American* suspected that whites, including local constables in Covington, had invented the scheme to kidnap the men. Once in Kentucky they immediately had the brothers arrested as fugitive slaves. Luckily, a white individual from Cincinnati immediately came forward to offer testimony of the free status of Charles's brother. Charles, however, remained in jail for six weeks, until another Cincinnati white finally vouched for him.[3]

Infuriated by his ordeal, Charles Scott immediately filed a complaint against his abductors in Hamilton County. The kidnappers demanded that he withdraw the suit, and when Charles refused, they shot him dead "in his own house, by his own fireside."[4] The Hamilton County prosecutor obtained a warrant for the arrest of the assailants. When they were brought to trial, the testimony law became the center of the controversy. Under this 1807 law, "no black or mulatto person" was "permitted to be sworn or give evidence in any court" in Ohio "where either party" was "a white person."[5] The testimony law barred Scott's wife, a witness to the murder, from offering evidence against the white defendants. The prosecution called another witness, a light-complexioned mulatto woman, whose testimony was challenged on grounds that the rules of evidence also applied to this class of persons. Forced to consider these objections, the trial judge faced a disturbing dilemma: should he strictly adhere to the law and allow the accused to go free, since there were no approved witnesses against the defendants? Or should he admit the mulatto witness under a broad interpretation of the statute? The judge chose the latter route, and the defendants were convicted for the murder of Charles Scott.[6] (The *Colored American* did not report on their sentences, nor is the official transcript of the trial available.)

Ohio did not inaugurate the practice of using legal principles to abridge the civil and natural rights of racial minorities. The thirteen original English colonies had done so for many years, relegating African Americans to the status of chattel property. By the time of the Revolution, American slavery stood out as a glaring contradiction in the new political community being forged in the New World. The philosophy of natural rights was laid down in the Declaration of Independence and was one of the core foundations of the new Confederation government. As a committee of the judiciary of the Ohio state house of representatives reported in 1837,

The right of citizenship, of ingress and egress, to and from all the States, and the privileges of trade and commerce, was secured to all free persons within its jurisdiction, irrespective of color. From the formation of the Confederacy until the adoption of the present Constitution of the United States, there were no constitutional restrictions imposed upon this race, unless they were slaves. They were entitled to the rights and privileges of any other class, and recognized as citizens, in the several States of the Confederacy. Under the Territorial government, they exercised the right of suffrage, in common with all other citizens, down to the time of the adoption of our present constitution, and formation of a State Government. They voted for delegates to attend the Convention, to form our present Constitution, in 1802.[7]

Moreover, the Constitution created in Philadelphia in 1787 embodied many of these principles. The preamble asserts that two of the aims of government are the duties to "establish justice" and "insure domestic tranquility." It also implies the equality of all people before the law. Political repression solely on account of race, color, or ancestry would seem to have been contrary to these principles written into the documentary history of the United States.

The founders of Ohio also expressed lofty ideals when they declared their reasons for establishing a state. The purpose of the state, the Ohio constitution of 1802 declared, was "to establish justice, promote the welfare and secure the blessings of liberty to ourselves and our posterity."[8] The theory of natural rights formed the underpinnings of both federal and state governments, including that of Ohio. One of the challenges facing Americans and Ohioans, therefore, would be reconciling the ideals of the republic with the history of American slavery and legalized discrimination.

From the territorial period in the mid-1780s through the early years following admission into the Union in 1803, Ohio enacted a category of legislation commonly referred to as the Black Laws. These statutes had one specific objective: to make life for African Americans in Ohio so intolerable that these men and women would not use the free state as a refuge from the oppression of slavery. The "Negro evidence law" was only one of many statutes Ohio lawmakers enacted to accomplish this purpose. Others included a registration law that required blacks entering the state to show on demand a certificate of freedom, authenticated by a court of record and filed with the clerk in the county where they resided. The residency law directed African Americans already living in the state to register with a county clerk. A labor law provided that Ohio residents could hire only those African Americans possessing a certificate. The state fugitive slave law granted slave owners a right of recapture and penalized anyone who interfered with the process. Revised in 1807, the registration law provided that, within twenty days of their entry into Ohio, African Americans were required to enter into a five-hundred-dollar bond with two property holders and that these freeholders, if called upon, would be required to apply the funds to the welfare or liability of the emigrant. Other Black Laws barred African Americans from enrolling in the militia, serving on juries, and attending public schools.[9]

Racial discrimination was obviously a glaring contradiction of the natural rights philosophy.[10] This book argues that race-specific laws could not long endure in a country that made freedom and equality the birthright of its people. It chronicles the black struggle to bring the political community and the social culture of Ohio in line with the American creed. Specifically, it tells the story of the injustice aimed at African Americans and it identifies an early civil rights movement dedicated to eliminating the Black Laws of Ohio and to limiting and abolishing slavery.

Some of the stories presented in this work have never been told before, such as the experience of Charles Scott—his death and the trial that came after. These narratives give a fuller picture of how Ohio evolved from a state that initially denied equality to black Americans to one that eventually changed these laws. By the 1840s, progressive whites in the North and blacks had become optimistic, believing that they had finally begun to change hearts and minds. There is evidence that Ohio judges began to place greater emphasis on fairness in their courtrooms and that they began to minimize the effects of the Black Laws whenever possible. If strictly interpreted and enforced in the Scott case, state law in 1841 would have protected the white defendants because neither a black nor a mulatto could have given sworn testimony against them. The murderers would have been set free.

Since at least the early 1830s, the Ohio Supreme Court consistently had ruled that only persons with over 50 percent white blood were entitled to the privileges of whites.[11] The judge in the Scott case made whiteness and blackness a variable and more subjective factor than the supreme court had established. Applying case law loosely, he concluded that various shades of persons could be at least 50 percent white. While the *Colored American* lamented the testimony law, it considered the Scott case a hopeful sign—a positive indication of a new day when "[t]he 'Black Laws' will soon give way to make room for just ones."[12] The correspondent looked to the day when common defense, safety, and justice would become the norm in Ohio "without regard to complexion."[13] The Ohio legislature abolished the Black Laws piecemeal, eliminating the registration law and the testimony law in 1849, as well as a few other provisions, such as the exclusionary public school law. The legislature finally abolished the remaining Black Laws in 1886.[14]

The murder of Charles Scott highlights the grave injustice of the Black Laws of Ohio. The subsequent trial also illustrates that Ohio judges were forced to take a stand on how these laws would be executed. However, we cannot be sure that the judge in the Scott case was defending black rights. He may have been acting to prevent violence that could go beyond the black community and threaten whites. If a white person killed anyone in the presence of a black witness he would get away with it. Thus, the trial judge modified the testimony law to give the murderers what they justly deserved—their day in court and the possibility of conviction.

The editors of the *Colored American* considered the decision an important one. They used the Scott case to argue that a growing number of progressive whites had begun to realize that the testimony law undermined the prosecution of justice:

> The Ohio people are beginning to arrive where they might necessarily expect to be carried by warring against right, as they have done in the enactment of such laws. They find it necessary now, as one might argue, to violate their *intent* (for it was intended to operate only against the colored people and cut off all colored testimony), necessary to save themselves, to keep society pure. It will not do to let the murderer loose. If the flood gate to murder is let down, he might murder some of us; therefore, though we

have but *colored testimony,* which this law intended to rule out, I will adhere strictly to the letter, and allow this colored person, being neither a "black or a mulatto," to offer testimony against the defendant, and rid society of a murderer.[15]

In an age when state and federal law by omission or commission denied blacks the equal protection of the laws, civil rights reformers looked for a silver lining wherever they could find one. They considered the verdict in the Scott case and others like it as a sign that they were making progress. The *Colored American* and progressive whites marked the decision as a victory for their cause. This book tells the story of how Ohio grew from a state that denied fundamental rights to blacks into a state that eventually provided most, if not all, of the legal protections the *Colored American* and its readers sought. In the late antebellum and Civil War era, Ohio did not immediately become a society where people were judged by the content of their character and not the color of their skin. Nevertheless, by the 1880s Ohio had become a state with black men serving in its legislature. Benjamin W. Arnett, of Greene County, Jere A. Brown, of Cuyahoga County, and George W. Williams, of Hamilton County, served in the Ohio General Assembly before 1890 and played a decisive role in abolishing the last remnants of the Black Laws in 1886.[16] From this perspective, black Ohio offers one example of the origins and evolution of the civil rights movement in America.

ONE

Ambiguous Beginnings

1787–1801

WHEN THE OHIO TERRITORY began making preparations for statehood, the region had great promise for almost four hundred African American residents and for the many more who surely would enter the new state. The Northwest Territory, from which it evolved, had outlawed slavery in 1787, and the Constitutional Convention of 1802 enforced that ban. However, any hopes African Americans might have had for equal rights with whites quickly vanished during the convention. The delegates made it clear that ending slavery did not automatically secure civil rights for African Americans. The Constitution restricted suffrage and elective office to white males. Article VI of the Northwest Ordinance of 1787 prohibited slavery, but the ordinance did not dissuade proslavery white inhabitants from launching a movement to nullify or circumvent Article VI. Ohio inherited an ambiguous interpretation of Article VI, and the state legislature opted to write laws that limited black rights. The rest of the Northwest Territory also inherited this legacy, and slaveholding persisted into the 1830s and 1840s in what became Indiana and Illinois.[1]

A great deal of activity had been under way since the end of the Revolutionary War to organize the western territory. Several men associated with the Continental Army led the way, including Rufus Putnam, Timothy Pickering, and Rufus King. Their motives varied, but generally they wanted to parcel out western lands to veterans and to sell public lands quickly to discharge the federal debt. Other men had been working on the project longer—even before the French and Indian War—and had organized the Ohio Land Company to better exploit the resources in the Ohio valley. After the defeat of the European imperial powers, there was a greater urgency among these leaders to derive some benefit from the western territory. Timothy Pickering already had developed settled beliefs about the opportunities a free territory would offer army veterans. Rufus King was excited to partner with him in this enterprise. "Your communication on the subject thus far was ingenious," King told Pickering: "Your ideas have had weight with the committee who reported this ordinance." Rufus Putnam believed that organized efforts in lobbying Congress would be more effective than the piecemeal initiatives that had come before. The three men teamed with the Ohio Company and with other leaders, such as Manasseh Cutler and Nathan Dane, to persuade Congress to act expeditiously and place the western territory under a stable political framework.[2]

Cutler, a physician and minister, was one of the Ohio Company's most prominent directors. A persuasive negotiator, Cutler spoke directly to Congress, advising that his company was poised to purchase more than 5 million acres of public land, which instantly would put badly needed funds into the federal treasury.[3] To seal the deal, he told Congress it had to establish a political framework in the western territory. Other trading companies soon formed, increasing pressure on Congress. William Duer of New York, as a former member of Congress and the Board of Treasury for the Articles of Confederation, helped organized the Scioto Company and pledged to purchase at least 3.5 million acres. As Cutler had done, Duer urged Congress to act quickly or risk losing well over a million dollars in sales, money the federal government desperately needed.[4] Congress appointed yet another committee on May 9, 1786, to deal with the crisis.

Headed by James Monroe of Virginia, the committee made its report on the western territory, but it made little headway because it had not resolved the conflicting interests of northerners and southerners. Later in the year, on September 18, Congress replaced it with a committee headed by William Johnson of Connecticut. For almost ten months, the Johnson committee wrangled futilely over an acceptable plan. The most important member of the committee turned out to be Nathan Dane, of Massachusetts, who replaced Johnson as chair on July 9, 1787. While Congress continued to debate a plan of government for the territory, the Philadelphia convention was meeting to propose revisions to the Articles of Confederation. It was apparent to many in Congress and the convention that the western territory was connected to discussions in Philadelphia.[5] "We found ourselves rather pressed," Nathan Dane told Rufus King, and "finally found it necessary to adopt the best system we could get."[6] Dane finally came up with an acceptable compromise, which resulted in the Northwest Ordinance. At the last possible moment, Dane added Article VI of the ordinance, which provided, "There shall be neither slavery nor involuntary servitude in the said territory." This wording proved acceptable, so long as it applied to the area northwest of the Ohio River.[7] To further make the plan tolerable to slave owners, Dane added a fugitive slave clause, thereby empowering slave owners to enter into the Northwest Territory and forcibly remove fugitives from labor. This was the substance of Article VI. Dane later confessed, "When I drew up the Ordinance, I had no idea the states would agree to the article prohibiting slavery."[8] He had underestimated how well the measure had spoken directly to those favoring slave labor and to those wanting to reserve the western territory for free labor. Congress approved the Northwest Ordinance on July 13, with only Abraham Yates of New York dissenting. Dane dismissed Yates as uninformed. Enthusiasm for the Ordinance of 1787 followed ratification of the Constitution, and, when the new government was inaugurated in 1789, Congress quickly affirmed the territorial law.[9]

As Dane later learned, Congress and the Philadelphia convention had kept a watchful eye on the committee he headed. Indeed, some of the delegates served double duty in Philadelphia and New York. The slavery settlement was on the minds of everyone. As James Madison much later surmised, "The distracting question of slavery was agitating and retarding the labors of both."[10] The Philadelphia convention wanted Congress to resolve the matter before slavery derailed their work. By the time the

Constitution was written, it had a fugitive slave clause, just as the ordinance did. This similarity was not by chance. A few decades later, the senator from Ohio, Salmon P. Chase, a leading advocate for federal restrictions on slavery, explained the similarity of the slavery provision in the Ordinance of 1787 and the Constitution this way: "The Congress of the Confederacy was sitting in New York, while the Constitutional Convention was sitting in Philadelphia. Several distinguished gentlemen were members at the same time of both bodies."[11] Thus well informed of the "transactions" of both bodies, Chase surmised, both assemblies took concurrent steps to restrict slavery. Missouri's first U.S. senator, Thomas Hart Benton, considered Article VI essential to successfully negotiating the federal constitution. If "the slavery question had not been settled as therein done—Territory divided and runaway slaves to be given up—there would have been no Constitution."[12] Political scientist William Lee Miller writes that resolution of the slavery issue was a "significant accomplishment, not to be taken for granted."[13] Chase interpreted the ordinance to mean that the leaders from this era believed that the nation was taking a turn in policy toward ending slavery. "No one contemplated the permanent or even very long continued existence of slavery in any state."[14] He considered their agreement to pass such a law a pledge, binding the slave states to cooperate in bringing an end to slavery as soon as it was possible and convenient to do so.

It appears, however, that southerners were primarily concerned with making slavery legal in the southwest—the present-day states of Kentucky, Tennessee, Alabama, and Mississippi. At the time, southerners believed that this region would grow much faster than the territory north of the Ohio. Congressman William Grayson, of Virginia, offered this corollary: southerners approved the Ordinance of 1787 for economic reasons. Writing to James Madison a few weeks after Congress passed the territorial law, Grayson asserted, "The clause respecting slavery was agreed to by the southern members for the purpose of preventing tobacco and indigo from being made on the Northwest side of the Ohio." Certainly, southern farmers understood their advantage in agriculture should they maintain a monopoly on cheap labor. Grayson, however, conceded that there were "several other political reasons" that might have included an interest in limiting slavery in the western territory.[15] Historian Robert G. Kennedy concludes, "[T]he Northwest Ordinance was passed with southern support as a scheme for debt reduction, and thus tax reduction, though it inhibited the spread of slavery."[16]

While Article VI was written in clear and explicit language, its supporters did not object to slavery on moral grounds. Timothy Pickering advocated a ban on slavery because of his primary interest in free men and free labor. James Madison had reservations about slavery for another reason: "Where slavery exists the republican theory becomes still more fallacious."[17] Of the federal officers who had contemplated a solution to the practice of slavery, Thomas Jefferson was probably the most pragmatic—and reticent. He was overly concerned about how his fellow slave owners would view this as a call to abolish slavery. While in Paris, Jefferson told the Marquis de Chastellux that he favored emancipation but that he did not want his views known until he could better determine how southerners would receive them.[18] Thus, instead of proposing an immediate prohibition on slavery in the western territory, Jefferson suggested only a prospective ban. Indeed, he too believed that slavery was vital to the settlement and economic development of the western territory; yet, he favored separation of whites and blacks. Article VI of the ordinance did not suggest much more; its framers probably contemplated a territory with a sparse black population. It was up to federal officers to codify it and put it into effect. When called upon to interpret Article VI, they assumed that it was not clear whether its framers had intended to divest slave owners already in the territory of their chattels. Thus, a controversy quickly arose in the Northwest Territory about the meaning of Article VI. Indeed, it is not clear whether the framers were aware of the extent of slavery in the region.

As news of Article VI circulated in the Northwest Territory, its residents interpreted it as an abolition law. As historian Theodore Calvin Pease concludes, the "literal construction [of Article VI] was apparently assumed by everyone."[19] Article VI intimidated slave owners, and many avoided going into the Northwest Territory lest they lose their chattel property. Historian Walter Havighurst quotes a transient slave owner who stated to a resident of the Northwest Territory, "Well, sir, your soil is fertile, but a man can't own Negroes here, god-durn ye."[20] R. K. Meade, an emigrant from Virginia, considered Article VI to be a positive ban on slavery and that it was respected "in southern states."[21] However, others already in the Northwest Territory, including slave-owning French settlers, did not give up so easily. They stayed in the Northwest Territory in defiance of Article VI and hired Bartholomew Tardiveau to negotiate with Congress to rescind or modify the clause. The English settlers also arranged for him to help them negotiate land purchases and, presumably, to secure their legal right to hold slaves.[22]

Tardiveau had been a slave owner in the western territory when the region was under French control, and he believed that the treaty ceding it to Britain protected the interests of French settlers, which included slaves. He agonized over the prospect that Article VI prohibited "slavery in that country."[23] He insisted to Congress that the ordinance would be disastrous for French inhabitants and that he wanted it rescinded, or at least modified. Soon after Arthur St. Clair assumed his post as governor of the territory in February 1788, Tardiveau approached him with the complaint, reporting that certain gentlemen in Congress had told him that Article VI was intended "solely to prevent the future importation of slaves into the federal territory; that it was not meant to affect the rights of ancient inhabitants."[24] He argued that he had been promised that a clause would be inserted into the article to properly characterize it as prospective legislation. He also claimed that the ban on slavery amounted to an ex post facto law, which was unconstitutional. He urged Congress to repeal the measure he considered unjust.[25]

In response to Tardiveau's petition, Congress appointed James Madison to head a committee to investigate the allegations. Joined by Hugh Williamson, of North Carolina, and Abraham Clark, of New Jersey, the committee apparently believed that Congress did not intend to abolish slavery with Article VI. Its passage had been more about closing the territory northwest of the Ohio River to slavery than about liberating slaves already there. The committee supported Tardiveau's interpretation that the ordinance did not deprive French inhabitants of their legal right to hold the slaves they possessed in the territory before July 1787. Congress, however, never voted on the committee's report. Whatever the status of the old settlers' slaves, there is little doubt that Congress in 1787 intended Article VI to prohibit anyone from taking slaves into the territory. Federal officials embarked on a course of containing slavery, and, although illegal activities occurred in the territory, they never wavered from that determination. Without congressional action to clarify the status of the old French slaves, it appeared that slavery was officially dead in that part of the territory northwest of the Ohio River, and Tardiveau remained discontented. He took his case directly to Governor St. Clair, urging him to give a definitive ruling on the matter.[26]

Armed with circumstantial evidence of the intent of Congress, Tardiveau told St. Clair that he had reliable testimony that Article VI did not end slaveholding. Nevertheless, he told the governor that slave owners, fearing a loss of their property, were abandoning their farms in droves. St. Clair was not impartial on the subject. When living in western Pennsylvania, he had purchased two slaves—Ben and Bell—from Thomas Galbreath and brought them to the territory, where he held them in bondage in violation of Article VI. St. Clair also reportedly held a slave by the name of Eve, and her child, as late as 1802. St. Clair, therefore, obviously did not share the philosophy of those who voted for Article VI. Although Frazer Ells Wilson, his biographer, claims that he later joined the antislavery movement, during the pioneer period of the Northwest Territory he clearly identified with slaveholding farmers; not surprisingly, he offered them a favorable interpretation of Article VI.[27]

St. Clair endorsed the Tardiveau theory, that applying Article VI to slaves in the area before its adoption made it a retrospective law, which he considered invalid. He believed that the laws of France and Britain had secured the property interest of slave owners who resided in the Northwest Territory before Article VI was adopted and declared that a literal reading of Article VI "would deprive a considerable number of whites of their property acquired and enjoyed long before they were under the dominion of the United States."[28] The founders of the federal republic, he assumed, did not intend to deprive a citizen of his property without just compensation. Thus, St. Clair issued an edict declaring Article VI enforceable on slaveholding immigrants only—a verdict that made it ineffective in abolishing slavery immediately. When St. Clair informed President George Washington of his decision, Washington offered no objections, thus by default endorsing Article VI as a ban on importing slaves into the Northwest Territory.[29]

Naturally, disputes involving freedom or slavery in the Northwest Territory went before the courts for judges to make a final determination on Article VI. Such a complaint was filed in 1793, when Henry Vanderburgh, a territorial judge, forcibly detained Peter McNelly and his wife, Queen, as slaves, in defiance of the prohibition. Actually, Peter and

Queen had never been his slaves; rather, they had escaped from slavery in Kentucky in the fall of 1793, and Vanderburgh captured them to hold them as slaves. He recognized that his claim to them was without merit, and, in a move to validate their detention, he coerced the couple into signing indenture contracts. McNelly escaped and filed a complaint with territorial judge George Turner, who issued a writ of habeas corpus demanding that Vanderburgh appear before his court. When Vanderburgh refused, Judge Turner had him jailed for contempt.[30] Judge John Cleves Symmes later ordered Vanderburgh's release; the controversy became moot when the McNellys apparently fled the territory. Slaveholding inhabitants in the Northwest Territory took offense at Turner's ruling, and they successfully petitioned Congress to remove him from office.[31]

Land speculators also endeavored to undermine Article VI, arguing that slave owners would not migrate to the Northwest Territory without their chattel property. John Edgar, Congressman Joshua Coit, and their associates presented a petition to Governor St. Clair on May 12, 1796, seeking to reverse Article VI. They argued that the slave codes of Virginia had effectively secured the rights of slave owners to their chattels. These efforts continued into the next century. On December 2, 1802, William Henry Harrison, the new governor of the Indiana Territory, presided over a meeting at which the delegates drafted a petition to be submitted to Congress, asking it to suspend Article VI. In February 1803, Congress assigned the petition to a committee chaired by John Randolph, of Virginia. The committee issued a resolution in February, "That it is inexpedient to suspend, for a limited time, the operation of the Sixth Article of compact between the original states and the people and states west of the river Ohio."[32]

A body of nineteenth-century case law supports Turner's interpretation of Article VI, as the state judges consistently upheld it as an immediate ban on slavery in the territory.[33] For example, a Mississippi court affirmed this construction in *Harry v. Decker and Hopkins,* decided in 1818. The plaintiff in the case sued John Decker on grounds that Decker had carried him into the Northwest Territory and held him in slavery in contradiction of the Northwest Ordinance. Decker countered that he had settled in Vincennes in 1784, before passage of Article VI. Although he remained there until 1816, he contended that, as prospective legislation, the prohibition had no effect on his slave. The court ruled that Article

VI abrogated all previous laws on its ratification, including the slave codes of Virginia that had operated in the territory. It changed the condition of all inhabitants, including enslaved blacks, "from absolute subjection to the condition of freemen."[34] Any reversal of that compact, the court concluded, required the common consent of the people in the Northwest Territory.

In the nineteenth century, Ohio abolitionists claimed that Article VI immediately had outlawed slavery in the Northwest Territory. Starting in the mid-1830s, James Birney and Salmon Chase made Article VI the basis of antislavery litigation, arguing that the founders approved the Ordinance of 1787 as a barrier against slavery. In their judgment, Article VI was an antislavery provision that set the western boundary for slavery at the Ohio River. They also argued that, by approving the ordinance, the founders had set a precedent for closing federal land to slavery. Birney and Chase thus believed that passage of Article VI was a deliberate and calculated effort to contain slavery to areas where it already existed. Under this theory, they waged a war against its extension into lands belonging to the federal government.

The framers of Article VI are responsible for differing interpretations of their language, as exemplified by the Tardiveau–St. Clair position that slaveholding could continue but that no new slaves could come into the territory and by the abolitionist position that the ordinance ended slavery immediately. The sixth article is ambiguous, and reading the rest of the ordinance does not help explain the intention of its framers. Other references to free men in the ordinance might suggest that federal officials recognized that American slaves remained in the Northwest Territory. Certainly blacks could have used Article VI to challenge their servitude in court, but such a theory was in its infancy in the late eighteenth century and perhaps was unknown on the frontier. Moreover, Article VI was not self-executing, and slave owners could not have known whether it went into effect immediately or at some future date. If the authors of the article intended it to do something immediately, they did not make that purpose clear. Congress later learned its lesson and included enforcement mechanisms when it ended slavery almost one hundred years later. It did not risk abolition's becoming misconstrued; it affirmed that Congress—through appropriate and specific legislation—was to carry out its edict. Without such explicit instructions written into the ordinance, Article VI appeared ambiguous, and slaveholding settlers already in the Northwest Territory took advantage of its vagueness.

Although his interpretation of Article VI was questionable, St. Clair understood the role of slavery in American legal culture. The North was in the process of ending slavery either by gradual emancipation laws or through judicial decrees. Except in northern New England, however, the northern states did not immediately invalidate existing claims to slaves. As Frederick Douglass declared, "The chains of slavery with us were loosened by degrees."[35] Tardiveau had based his claim of the invalidity of retrospective legislation on settled legal doctrine. However, the Northwest Territory was unique in one respect: it did not have an extensive slaveholding tradition. Emancipation, therefore, could have been effected without any significant economic harm, except to the relatively few slave owners in the Northwest Territory. From this perspective, it was reasonable to consider Article VI as an abolition law, especially given the long history of slavery in America.

Initially, Article VI may have gone beyond the comfort zone of federal officials in the nation's capital. Apparently, they believed in the ultimate extinction of slavery; thus the construction of Article VI as a prospective law satisfied them. St. Clair might have taken this into account when he rendered an interpretation of Article VI. Indeed, St. Clair did not directly challenge the authority of the federal government to regulate slavery in federal territory. Instead, he conceded that the prohibition in the ordinance automatically freed enslaved persons brought into the territory after 1787 (although he brought his own slaves into the territory after 1787). Hence, St. Clair brought the region formally in line with then current legal policies, which favored a gradual end to slavery. This compromise seems to have been a workable solution, and leaders in the federal capital left the matter to the territorial governor. Proslavery advocates applauded St. Clair, who offered them a legal basis for having violated Article VI. However, there were limits to what they could achieve. Slave owners in the Northwest Territory were a minority, without the ability to change Article VI to openly allow slaveholding.

Certainly, slave owners successfully weakened the application of Article VI in the Northwest Ordinance. The decree, "There shall be neither slavery nor involuntary servitude in the said territory," was interpreted to mean no one could legally carry slaves into the Northwest Territory after

1787. Nevertheless, Article VI was a significant achievement for the country, and it created a permanent barrier to the expansion of slavery into the west. Article VI also brought new language into the American lexicon at the time. An undertaking to prohibit slavery in such a massive territory had not been made by any American government before 1787. When one considers that slavery still existed throughout the country, the Ordinance of 1787 was a remarkable document. From its prohibition of slavery grew the antislavery fervor that struck the United States in the nineteenth century. Moreover, Article VI was the substance of the ban against slavery adopted by five new states formed from the Northwest Territory, including Ohio. The growth of slavery in the West was permanently aborted. As historian Beverly Bond puts it, "[T]he few slaves who survived from the earliest period of American control of the Northwest Territory were of negligible importance."[36]

Much to the dismay of scholars and the two thousand or so slaves in Indiana and Illinois, slavery persisted in the Northwest Territory for many years, and that accounts for their criticisms of the ordinance. Slavery survived in the Old Northwest beyond 1787, at least in part, because the federal government allowed slave owners to circumvent Article VI. Indeed, tolerance for slavery was still widespread in the 1780s, and that made it easy for federal officials to view Article VI as a prospective law. Their sentiments alone doomed the article as an abolition law, yet Article VI was remarkably effective in weakening slaveholding on public land and in producing the first free zone in American history. Moreover, abolitionists and historians have erred in their interpretation of the article.

Leading abolitionists such as James Birney and Salmon Chase rhetorically elevated Article VI to an emancipation proclamation; they used it to further their political and social agenda. Progressive historians have embraced their interpretation; however, they have overextended the original intent behind the antislavery measure. In attempting to correct what they perceive as a romantic construction of Article VI, revisionist historians have gone too far. No one says otherwise except Onuf and Finkelman, who point out that Illinois came close to legalizing slavery after statehood. Although Article VI was never intended as a civil rights measure, it was a definite bar to the extension of slavery. Under its guidance, Ohio came into the Union with a ban on slaveholding. Thus, Article VI was remarkably effective in regionalizing slavery; it was an early ring of freedom in the Ohio Country.

TWO

The Many Meanings of Freedom

1800–1803

THE FIRST MAJOR POLITICAL TEST of freedom in the Northwest Territory came between 1800 and 1802, as Ohio moved toward statehood. The Northwest Ordinance guaranteed the inhabitants of the territory the right to establish a republican government; it also prohibited slavery. Article V in the ordinance provided that any state formed from the Northwest Territory should adopt "the principles contained in these articles." Despite these provisions, the inhabitants in the Ohio Country faced resistance from the leadership in the territorial government. Determined to maintain Federalist control of the Northwest Territory, Governor Arthur St. Clair opposed early statehood, but the survival of the St. Clair government was in doubt after the election of Thomas Jefferson. Riding the coattails of the Republican Party, St. Clair's opponents put the Ohio Territory up for statehood in defiance of the governor.[1]

Article VI of the ordinance already had survived challenges by speculators and slave owners, who had endeavored to modify or rescind the antislavery clause. Article VI survived as a prospective abolition law and officially closed the Northwest Territory to slave owners entering after 1787. However, the leadership in the Ohio Territory was divided over whether Article VI was a mandate or whether they could revoke it under the theory of state sovereignty. While some leaders in both the Republican and Federalist parties believed that Article VI was a mandate for them to outlaw slavery, others believed that it was unenforceable upon a sovereign state.[2] The unusual mix of people in the Ohio Country was responsible for the controversy. Americans from various regions in the United States—New England, the South, the Mid-Atlantic states—had brought eastern and southern political leanings and cultures to the western frontier. This mixture of politics and cultural heritage influenced the debate over the character of the seventeenth state to join the Union.[3] Upon statehood, the Ohio Country was overwhelmingly white, with only a few hundred African American residents.[4] No one expected that to soon change; however, some whites did not want to leave the racial and political character of Ohio to chance.

The diverse regional backgrounds of Ohio settlers led to intense debate over slavery. Slave-owning immigrants pressed to make involuntary servitude legal, but others in Ohio wanted to establish a community of free men and free labor. Many in this latter category had abandoned the South to separate themselves from slavery. Moreover, New Englanders, who had little direct experience with slavery, usually opposed the institution. Removed from the founding of the republic by only a few years, many Ohio leaders articulated the ideals of that period: life, liberty, equality, and republicanism. The vast majority of whites in Ohio envisioned a free state, where black slave labor did not compete with wage-earning white men. The vast majority of them envisioned a community based on equality. However, they went only partway toward reaching that goal.[5] The Ohio constitution prohibited slavery, but its framers laid the cornerstone for the Black Laws by limiting voting and office holding to white males.[6] Thus, by placing restrictions on African Americans, the first constitution of Ohio offered more than one meaning to freedom in a state with no slavery.

Both the white and black population in the Ohio Country was small during most of the 1790s. American Indians had been the primary inhabitants for centuries, but, by 1800, key tribes in the area had been virtually conquered, and whites considered it safe to immigrate. The population of the Buckeye State grew exponentially over the next six decades, and, by 1850, Ohio had become the third-most-populous state in the Union.[7]

In 1788, Rufus Putnam, Manasseh Cutler, and others in the Ohio Company of Associates established the town of Marietta in the Muskingum River valley, on the northern bank of the Ohio River. Putnam and his associates recognized the potential of the valley's vast supply of raw materials and rivers that easily accommodated trade, and they immediately assigned surveyors and boat builders to exploit this treasure and transport its resources to eastern markets.[8]

That same year, New Jersey migrants led by Col. Robert Patterson founded Cincinnati on the southwestern bank of the Ohio River. By 1792, more than nine hundred whites lived in Cincinnati, where they immediately established various commercial enterprises. A visitor to Cincinnati commented, "The town is overrun with merchants and traders and overstocked with merchandise; there are already over 30 stores and warehouses here."[9] Cincinnati soon became a center of trade, linking the Ohio Valley to eastern and southern ports. With its ideal location, Cincinnati soon led the entire Northwest Territory in business, communications, and manufacturing. The fastest-growing town in Ohio, it was also becoming the pork capital of the United States, with pork generating almost $8 million in income annually. Other industries, such as iron, added another $6 million annually to the Cincinnati economy, helping make the Queen City a mecca in the West.[10]

Greater population diversity came to the Ohio Country in 1796, when Quakers and German Americans from Pennsylvania and Virginia farmers founded Steubenville, a river town in Jefferson County. Slave owners moving across the Ohio River frequently brought blacks into eastern Ohio, and from that source a free black population gradually developed in the area. In that year, Nathaniel Massie and Arthur Duncan organized the town of Chillicothe on the Scioto River in south-central Ohio. Originating as a military district, Chillicothe quickly evolved into a town of distinction with a bountiful economy. Using the fine river systems flowing south, Chillicothe and Cincinnati made early connections to markets as far away as New Orleans. Farms and mills soon dotted Chillicothe's countryside, and its appealing landscape attracted large numbers of migrants to southern Ohio. Chillicothe quickly became the most densely populated area in the Ohio Country and was selected as the capital of the Northwest Territory and the first capital of Ohio (Columbus became the capital in 1816).[11]

The diversity of politics in the Ohio Country equaled that of its peoples. While northern Ohio attracted emigrants from the North and from New England—largely members of the Federalist Party—southern Ohio attracted the Republican followers of Thomas Jefferson, drawn largely from the South. These ex-southerners made the political culture of Ohio unique. Like Jefferson, who since the 1780s had expressed confidence in the ability of the yeoman farmer as a civic leader, these new immigrants believed that every white man should have the right to vote, without any of the restraints that still existed in some of the original states.[12]

The Republican Party in Ohio quickly attracted talented and influential leaders, including Massie, a land speculator and one of the organizers of the Virginia Military District; Edward Tiffin, a medical doctor; and Thomas Worthington, a land surveyor. Massie, Tiffin, and Worthington served in the territorial assembly and later were elected to the legislative branches of the state and federal governments. These men also played prominent roles in the statehood movement and, in the process, became the nemeses of territorial governor Arthur St. Clair, who considered statehood in 1802 to be premature. Tiffin and Massie had moved to the Northwest Territory in 1796, as Jefferson and his allies were forging the coalition that united as the Republican Party. Until that year, Tiffin and Worthington had been slave owners in Virginia but undoubtedly had turned against the practice and moved to the territory where federal law prohibited slavery. However, Tiffin and Worthington were not abolitionists: they did not support any systematic movement to end slavery nor were they champions of black civil rights. The idealism of some Republicans in their organization undoubtedly raised the issue of black equality in Ohio much sooner than Tiffin or Worthington desired. The contest between republicanism in its purest form, which included black equality, and the republican idea of greater democracy for whites also would be played out in Ohio.[13]

As Ohio Republicans began the task of building the framework for a new state, they faced a challenge from former slave owners and from speculators, who were determined to reverse Article VI. Speculators considered involuntary servitude in Ohio vital to their prosperity as well as to the continuing development of the new state. They doubted that slave owners would migrate without slaves. John Edgar, joined by colleagues interested in speculation, led the movement to overturn Article VI and to open the Northwest Territory to slavery. These investors assumed that a state without slavery would not be attractive to migrating slave owners. Undeterred by the failures of Bartholomew Tardiveau, who had argued for the rescission of Article VI in the 1780s, they boldly asked Congress to repeal Article VI. Speculators like Edgar extolled the "fine qualities" of the fertile farmland in the Ohio Valley, which surely attracted slave owners. Resurrecting a Tardiveau argument, they contended that slave owners would be more likely to purchase western lands if they could keep slaves. The speculators asserted that enforcing Article VI deprived an individual of his property without just compensation. Not forgetting that the St. Clair government had applied Article VI as a prospective prohibition of slavery and had approved of French Americans holding slaves, the speculators argued that the children of any slave already in the territory should retain the status of his or her mother. Congress unequivocally rejected their petition in 1800.[14]

Gen. Thomas Posey, who represented veterans from Virginia, also supported using western lands for the benefit of veteran slave owners. Posey appealed to the Virginia legislature, imploring it to join him in convincing Congress that rescinding Article VI in the Virginia Military District in Ohio was vital to compensating veteran officers. Submitting the petition in 1799, Posey believed that it would be more effective if submitted by Virginia, because the Old Dominion had recognized slavery in the area before ceding it to the federal government. The Virginia legislature complied with his request, but modified it to add a clause providing for the manumission of slaves at age thirty-five if male and twenty-five if female. Congress rejected the proposal because it contradicted Article VI of the Ordinance of 1787.[15] General Posey then revised the proposal, seeking to disguise it under a system of indentured servitude, but the charade failed when the territorial legislature declared that Article VI outlawed any form of involuntary servitude.[16] This was a victory for the proponents of enforcing Article VI as a prohibition on slavery in the Northwest Territory; however, it did not reverse the notion held by many whites in Ohio that slavery antedating Article VI remained permissible.

Ohio whites were not alone in holding this idea. A movement to undermine Article VI arose in another area of the Northwest Territory. As described in chapter I, an 1802 convention in the Indiana Territory petitioned Congress to rescind the sixth article. William Henry Harrison, the governor of the territory and future president of the United States, supported repeal. He argued that Virginia law had protected slavery in its former territory; and, like the French settlers, he argued that the law secured their property interest in slaves.[17] Congress replied, "It is inexpedient to suspend, for a limited time, the operation of the Sixth Article of compact between the original states and the people and states west of the river Ohio."[18] Slavery undermined free labor, the legislature continued, and limited the economic choices of whites. Jacob Burnet, a New Jersey–educated lawyer who lived in the area during this time, put it more bluntly, stating that slavery made "labor less reputable and created feelings and habits" that could make whites lazy. Historian Daniel Ryan, almost a century later, observed that northern emigrants "believed that slavery would be detrimental to the progress and prosperity of the territory."[19] White emigrants had left the South to escape its slave culture, Ryan continued, and, considering slave owners an aristocratic group, "feared political domination by" them.[20] Because of such sentiments in Ohio, the pressure to open it up to slavery was ineffective. Though there were slave owners who violated the law and successfully evaded prosecution under federal officers sympathetic to them, the number of individuals forcibly detained against their will remained small.

While pioneer Ohio wrestled with the slavery issue, Republicans launched the campaign for statehood. It was inevitable that the campaign raised the question of citizenship for people of color. Some Republicans frowned on slavery, and many were genuinely against denying suffrage to any man. However, there were also many Republicans, like Jefferson himself, who favored slaveholding and vehemently opposed giving blacks political rights. Indeed, the vast majority of white emigrants in Ohio opposed equality between the races; they also wanted to exclude blacks from the political culture of the new state. Ironically, while Republicans were pursuing statehood, it was in the interest of the white majority to support the democratic rights of every man. They also dangled the franchise before blacks already in Ohio, who were allowed to vote under the Northwest Ordinance; they applied the politics of pragmatism.[21] Ultimately they opposed black rights, giving a different meaning to freedom for whites and blacks in the state of Ohio.

The statehood movement in Ohio was intimately linked to partisan politics. The Federalists recognized the growing popularity of Republicans and opposed Ohio statehood in part to stymie the growth of their rival. Most farmers and laborers who had migrated to the Ohio Valley gravitated to the Republican Party, taking literally its pledge to liberate them from the upper class.[22] Jefferson, elected president in 1800 by a slim margin, was eager to bring the yeomen of Ohio into the Union before the next election.

When the territorial legislature considered a statehood measure in 1801, the only Federalists with a vote—Ephraim Cutler and William R. Putnam—were against it. Arthur St. Clair argued that Ohio did not yet possess the resources to adequately fund a state: "My view of the country becoming a state at this time is that it would impose on some a burden they are not able to bear."[23] Obviously speaking for the prosperous residents in the territory, St. Clair pointed out that a minority paid taxes disproportionate to their numbers. As an alternative to creating such an inequitable system, he suggested that Ohio delay its application or change its boundaries to include a larger number of free inhabitants. His concern was mainly political. With the influx of Republicans, the Federalist leader feared a loss of control, and he successfully obstructed statehood until the turn of the century.

The election of Thomas Jefferson made a powerful difference in the drive for Ohio statehood. Ohio Republicans wasted no time in presenting the new president with a list of grievances against Governor St. Clair. Thomas Worthington charged him with usurping legislative powers, levying arbitrary fees, proposing to divide the Northwest Territory, and making unethical appointments, including that of his son as attorney general.[24] Under siege by the Republican majority, St. Clair's efforts to prevent statehood were futile, and he eventually lost his job as governor of the Northwest Territory.

The Chillicothe Group was the most powerful Republican faction in Ohio and was determined to benefit from the economic potential of the region. Massie and Duncan MacArthur, who were among the first surveyors in the area, had accumulated vast tracts of land and amassed a small fortune. Others joining them in the Republican movement were

Worthington and his brother-in-law, Edward Tiffin. Emboldened by Jefferson's election, they accelerated the move toward statehood. Republican leaders recognized the benefits of bringing a new state into the Union, especially one in which a significant portion of the population shared their political philosophy. This helped extend their party into the West and possibly secure the reelection of Jefferson in 1804.[25] With Republican support in Washington, a favorable vote on Ohio statehood seemed likely.

———

Even though Ohio Republicans had supported statehood since at least 1798, they continued to face many hurdles. Article V in the Ordinance of 1787 required a population of sixty thousand "free inhabitants" before a territory could apply for statehood. The population in Ohio, however, was slightly less than fifty thousand. Ohio Republicans did not consider applying for statehood to be futile because Article V had given Congress flexibility when admitting a territory. If Congress accepted the application, Ohio's elevation to statehood would be meteoric but not illegal. On April 30, 1802, anticipating the population in Ohio to soon increase, Congress authorized a constitutional convention.[26]

Ohio Republicans were determined to replace the Federalist regime of Governor St. Clair. "We certainly need a change," Tiffin told George Todd in 1802, predicting that the "Republican interest will prevail in the elections." Others declared the Republican ideology to be an American birthright. Looking back, Zabdiel Sampson, a Massachusetts congressman elected in 1817, declared, "The nature of our Union is Republican."[27] Some Ohio Republicans asserted that they favored freedom and equality, which also included an effort to secure civil rights for African Americans. It was a campaign slogan to win votes, however; few Republican candidates actually supported racial equality. The position of Ohio Republicans remained deeply ambivalent on the issue of race in this period. Abolition was not a major issue for any political party in 1800, however, and few whites could have predicted that race or slavery would become controversial in Ohio. The 1802 campaign for a referendum on Ohio statehood set the stage for divisive politics. With Republicans in the majority, Ohio Federalists stood little chance of controlling a constitutional convention and thus they tried to defeat the call for a convention.

Ohio Republicans fell into two factions, each hoping for greater economic opportunity in the burgeoning West. Each had fixed ideas about politics and culture and the type of political community they desired. However, they differed on how to achieve their goals. Many of the Republicans' Federalist rivals had migrated from the North. These emigrants had had limited contact with blacks, and most had never owned slaves. They already had witnessed the trend toward emancipation in their former states and they stood for free labor and a free Ohio. They also were willing to support modest civil rights reform. The Federalists caused alarm in Ohio by suggesting that the Republican Party would legalize slavery. Republicans, however, were not united on many issues. Some of them had grown disillusioned with slave labor as an important component in the local economy and wanted nothing to do with it in their new state. They eagerly joined northern emigrants in the opinion that slave labor competed with free labor.[28] Other Republicans held the opposite opinion, wanting to transplant the slave culture to the Ohio Country. This mixture of interests and goals made intense debate in Ohio inevitable, and the convention was forced to compromise for the sake of statehood.

Many ex-southerners in Ohio opposed slavery. Edward Dromgoole, a Virginia minister, directed many southerners to Ohio, urging men like W. P. Pelham, a fellow Virginian, to move there because Ohio was not "contaminated with slavery." Pelham arrived in Xenia in 1807 and later reported to Dromgoole that it had been a good move; he was "so well satisfied and enjoy[ed] so much peace in being free from a land of slavery."[29] Other emigrants, like Phillip Hamburg, left the South because of a rumor that one of his slaves "bore his resemblance." Hamburg needed a fresh start, and moving to a free state meant that he could free his slaves. Israel Donaldson, who was elected to the Ohio Constitutional Convention, left Kentucky and its toleration of slavery to seek his fortune in Ohio. Caleb Atwater, a pioneer historian and resident of Ohio during those years, was famous for declaring that the people of Ohio were known for "their hatred of slavery."[30]

Despite their divergent views and motivations, ex-southerners in Ohio generally had much more in common with each other than they had with northerners. John Woods, a correspondent for the *National Gazette*, asserted that Republicans from the South "retain many of the prejudices they imbibed in infancy, and still hold Negroes in the utmost contempt."[31] W. P. Pelham, the Virginia emigrant, shared this view, confessing delight at "having no blacks about me and my family."[32] Debate at the constitutional convention reflected these sentiments and resulted in shifting alliances among Republicans on slavery and civil rights.

In the campaign for statehood, Ohio Republicans intended to alarm voters by suggesting that the Federalists favored slavery and would even make slaves of whites. Republicans repudiated every form of servitude, including the enslavement of African Americans. They made support for Article VI an election issue. Frank Stubblefield, a correspondent for the *Ohio Gazette*, insisted that Article VI "is binding upon the Northwest Territory." He believed that the prohibition of slavery attracted white migration to Ohio, primarily those interested in free labor.[33]

Once the campaign for statehood started, Ohio Republicans used slavery and civil rights to intimidate lukewarm voters and Federalist opponents. Republican politicians put James Caldwell, a Federalist candidate for the convention, on the defensive by accusing him of supporting slavery and opposing civil rights. Caldwell explained that he stood for a free Ohio and a republican government. Andrew Marshall and John Thompson, both Republicans, came to his defense, informing writers for the *Scioto Gazette* that Caldwell had publicly "expressed his wishes for an alteration in our government, and was among the first in Belmont County to secure a petition with five hundred signatures to support statehood."[34]

Territorial Governor Arthur St. Clair had enforced the Federalist agenda, intending to keep power out of the hands of the Republicans. His overbearing demeanor alienated the yeomen in Ohio because he, like other Federalists, endeavored to unite the government with the wealthy. St. Clair proposed to divide the Northwest Territory into two distinct regions in order to prevent statehood, a suggestion that infuriated Republicans. In the end, his conduct turned most voters away from the Federalist Party. He alienated loyal Federalists such as Ephraim Cutler, who confessed, "It is impossible for me to approve of the conduct of the governor."[35] Republicans skillfully manipulated such distaste for the Federalists. Edward Tiffin labeled all his political enemies Federalists, knowing that most Ohioans would automatically reject them at the polls.

Republicans, however, misrepresented the Federalists. For one thing, the Federalist Party was most powerful in New England, the region most

opposed to slavery. Those Federalists who migrated to Ohio came looking for economic opportunity, not to own slaves. They actually encouraged opposition to slavery and they generally led the fight to abort the
expansion of slavery into the West. The Federalists also turned slavery
into a political weapon, asserting that the Republicans intended to legalize slavery in Ohio. St. Clair led the charge by arguing that hardly a "man
in the county of Hamilton that is not a Republican both in principle and
practice . . . except perhaps a few who wished to introduce Negro slavery among us." He also warned that anyone who enslaved Africans would
make chattels out of his neighbors.[36]

Many Federalists saw themselves as heirs to the tradition established by
the framers of the Ordinance of 1787, who had used federal power to
curtail slavery.[37] For various reasons, Federalists in some southern states
also opposed slavery. Virginia Federalists correctly blamed the three-
fifths clause in the Constitution for John Adams's defeat in 1800. They
also blamed slavery for the sad economic condition of blacks and for any
disruption in southern agriculture. "Perceiving slavery as an evil on both
human and political ground," writes Linda K. Kerber, "they increasingly expressed bitter opposition to it." Terminally wounded in the election of 1800, the Federalist Party would advocate the containment policy
until their organization finally collapsed in the 1820s.[38]

Thus, Republicans invented the myth that the Federalists favored making Ohio a slave state in order to wrest political power from them. At the
same time, many Republicans did put themselves forward as opponents
of slavery and advocates of equal rights. The Republican Corresponding
Society of Hamilton County encouraged voters to elect delegates who
opposed slavery, arguing that it "is contrary to the rights of man, and to
the true interests of the country." Cincinnati Republicans also recommended that voters elect delegates who were willing to grant suffrage to
every male inhabitant of Ohio, including blacks. John Hut, a correspondent for the *Scioto Gazette*, joined them, asserting that "human nature re-
coils at slavery, with all its horrible train of evils." Should voters elect
Republicans, he continued, "SLAVERY shall not be known on this bank
of the Ohio River."[39]

Correspondence committees launched an "interrogation" movement,
questioning candidates on their commitment to freedom and equality.
Traditional Federalists stood little chance of success at the polls in early

Ohio. To be successful, they needed to do two things: oppose slavery and push for equal suffrage in Ohio. After all, the voters surmised, the fifth article in the ordinance had guaranteed the inhabitants a government based on the consent of the people. Republicans in Ross County came up with a list of questions to put before candidates seeking election to the constitutional convention. Handbills with questions appeared everywhere, and civil rights headed the list. The committee declared its unequivocal opposition to any form of racial discrimination. "We want a Constitution that will set the natural rights of the meanest African and the most abject beggar, upon an equal footing with those citizens of the greatest wealth and equipage."[40] Both Republicans and Federalists seized on the civil rights issue in order to win votes. Some Republicans demanded that candidates for the convention disclose their views on slavery. The *Western Spy* asserted that slavery was an unprofitable moral evil and urged voters to send antislavery delegates to the convention.[41] Two candidates in Ross County admitted that they supported slavery, and both were defeated by a margin of more than five hundred votes.

The campaign, and especially the questions put to the candidates, revealed the complexity of Republican views on race and slavery. Republicans generally agreed that Ohio would be a free state, but they disagreed on whether Article VI in the ordinance amounted to an a priori prohibition on Ohio. John G. Macan, a candidate to the convention, believed the state legislature in the future could create slavery: "I should be very unwilling to have any clause inferred in the Constitution that would prohibit us from admitting slaves." Macan considered slavery to be a choice that a sovereign state could rightly decide. Every "state in the Union has it in its power either to admit or prohibit slavery. Let the will of the people be done."[42] Thus, Macan concluded that to apply Article VI as prior restraint on the legislature to admit slavery was itself a violation of the republican idea.

James Grubb, who was also a delegate to the convention, disagreed, asserting that the Northwest Ordinance had settled the slavery question in the Ohio Country. The only option available to the convention, he continued, was to enforce the ban against slavery. Such "a pernicious scheme ought to be guarded against as I conceive it a bad policy which cannot be advocated by any Republican." Grubb considered slavery itself contrary to the republican idea and urged the party to remain steadfast in opposing it. A true republican, Grubb declared, cannot justify slavery. If elected to the constitutional convention, he pledged his support for enforcing Article VI in Ohio. John Hut shared this view: "Negro slavery is the bait by which the Federalist Party means to catch Republicans."[43] These assertions notwithstanding, the question of whether a state from the Northwest Territory could adopt slavery was never tested; however, there were men in the Northwest Territory who argued that Ohio could choose to make slavery legal if it wanted to.

Prominent leaders in the early campaign for statehood, who would continue their political careers if the constitutional convention succeeded, responded to the interrogation. Edward Tiffin, the future governor of Ohio, had migrated from Virginia and had owned slaves, whom he emancipated in 1796 on entering Ohio. Had slavery been legal in the Northwest Territory, it is possible that Tiffin would have retained them. His brother-in-law, Thomas Worthington, also had owned slaves in Virginia and released them on entering the Ohio Territory. Both admitted that slavery was immoral, but were unwilling to fight for its immediate abolition. Conversely, they believed that slavery hurt economic development in Ohio and they did not demand its legalization.[44]

Slavery was not the only issue that concerned blacks and their supporters. Whites had turned to indentured servitude as a way to exact labor from their former chattels. The constitutional convention of 1802 could not dodge this issue; some of its delegates held blacks as indentured servants. Edward Tiffin used indentured servitude for personal gain, contracting for the services of four black children as early as 1801. Bill, a mulatto, was born on June 11, 1789, while one of the others, a "black boy named Charlie, was born on the 18th-day of February 1791." Another servant, "a black boy named Jeremiah, was born on the 12th-day of September 1792." The boys would serve "the said Edward Tiffin and his heirs," who agreed to take good care of them by feeding, clothing, and providing them adequate shelter until they reached the age of twenty-one. Everhard Harr and John Collett, the overseers of the poor in Scioto County, arranged the indenture with Tiffin. Thomas Worthington and William Chandler were the justices of the peace who conducted the hearing.[45] The children, under Ohio law, were not eligible for state welfare. What can be made of these indenture contracts? Did Tiffin purchase their services as an act of philanthropy? Did he exploit their labor? Tiffin was not a civil rights reformer; he voted against enfranchising blacks at the constitutional convention, and the Black Laws developed during his tenure as governor. While Tiffin did not propose the racial codes, he did not dissuade the legislature from subordinating blacks. Yet indentured servitude was a recognized institution for blacks as well as whites.

Nathaniel Massie also provided written responses to the interrogation. He once had owned slaves in Virginia and Kentucky and would have carried them to Ohio had it not been for the prohibition in Article VI. In contrast to Tiffin, he admitted the economic benefits of owning slaves, yet he too recognized how slavery might ultimately harm the economy of Ohio: "I believe the introduction of slavery would ultimately prove injurious to our country." Although slavery might temporarily contribute to our prosperity, Massie admitted, he vowed to vote against it.[46]

Michael Baldwin, a young lawyer who had migrated from Connecticut, had never owned slaves. He considered the practice repugnant to republican government, yet he embraced conservative views regarding civil rights. As speaker of the Ohio house of representatives, Baldwin presided over the adoption of the notorious Black Laws in 1804 and 1807. He did not repudiate those laws during his lifetime.[47] Clearly, Tiffin and his colleagues in the Chillicothe Group did not have the credentials of civil rights reformers. Nonetheless, each agreed to enforce the ban against slavery in Ohio.

Following the Ross County example, voters in Clermont County pledged to elect only delegates who vowed to enforce the ban against slavery in the Ordinance of 1787. Republican hopefuls Philip Gatch and James Sargent provided an unequivocal pledge to enforce Article VI. Gatch, a Methodist minister, had backed abolition in Virginia before migrating. Sargent had migrated from Maryland and, like the Chillicothe Group, had emancipated his slaves. Clermont County voters declared that they voted for both Gatch and Sargent because of their opposition to slavery.[48]

After an exhaustive campaign in 1802, Ohio voters went to the polls on Tuesday, October 12, to decide whether they wanted a constitutional convention. They simultaneously cast ballots for delegates. As the day approached, all signs pointed to a Republican landslide. African Americans shared in this excitement and, under the ordinance, they were among the electorate. When Congress authorized Ohio to form a government, it directed all "male citizens of the United States who reside within the said territory to choose representatives."[49] Governor St. Clair used similar language when he executed the order: "All male citizens of the United States, who shall have resided within the said territory for one year" and paid taxes were eligible to vote in the coming election. Moreover, free blacks were voting elsewhere in the country, including the slave states of North Carolina and Tennessee.[50] It is plausible, therefore, that blacks voted in the election for the Ohio Constitutional Convention.

A few African Americans also voted in early Ohio elections. In 1836, a correspondent for the *Philanthropist,* an antislavery newspaper, reported, "Colored people used the right of suffrage before they were deprived of it."[51] An 1837 Ohio senate report on the Black Laws also asserted that African Americans "exercised the right of suffrage, in common with all other citizens, down to the adoption of our [state] Constitution. They voted for delegates to attend the Convention."[52] In 1851, the State Convention of Colored Men argued that it was likely that blacks had voted in Ohio. William Howard Day, a member of the Colored Men, told the Ohio Constitutional Convention in 1850, "When the Constitution of the United States was framed, colored men voted in a majority of these states," and many voted long after it was adopted. The Colored Men also credited Michael Baldwin—the speaker of the Ohio house who died circa 1811—with saying that neither the constitution of Ohio nor federal law had denied black suffrage.[53] Evidence of black voters in pioneer Ohio is sparse, though it is likely that Kit Putnam, an African American, voted in the referendum on the 1802 convention.[54]

Because the federal census recorded only 337 blacks in Ohio in 1800, whites had few reasons to deny them the vote. Moreover, the vote of every Republican in Ohio was crucial in the march to statehood, and party leaders understood, in turn, that civil rights reform was also vital in harnessing the power of the electorate. Other whites understood that blacks had helped transform Ohio from a wilderness to a territory on the brink of statehood. On the eve of the constitutional convention in 1802, therefore, some whites believed that suffrage was a just reward for all men in Ohio.[55]

The constitutional convention met in Chillicothe, where thirty-five delegates began the task of establishing a political framework for Ohio. Southern Ohio had elected thirty-three of the delegates, twenty-six of

whom were Republicans. The majority of them had come from the southern states, many of them former slave owners. The Federalist Party won
only seven seats. Ohio voters also elected two self-proclaimed independ-
ents. As the point of entry for many emigrants, Hamilton County in
general—and Cincinnati in particular—easily had the most heavily populated districts and thus elected ten delegates. Ross County and Chillicothe, equally accessible for southern migration, elected five. Following this
pattern, the vast majority elected to the convention came from southern
Ohio, and most had migrated from the slave South. They were well educated and represented diverse professions, including business, medicine,
and law.[56]

The southern origins of many of the delegates did not automatically
determine how they voted on social issues. Indeed, the legal status of blacks
weighed heavily on them. Some delegates believed they had a mandate to
prohibit slavery and to secure the civil rights of all Ohio residents. The
"meager" record of the convention, however, makes it difficult to recon-
struct the debates. Only journal notes and a smattering of private letters,
memoirs, and newspaper articles are available. While sparse manuscript
sources have hindered the writing of the constitutional history of Ohio,
they show that party affiliation did not always forecast how a delegate
voted on civil rights. Republicans had cast their organization as a defender of civil rights, yet they were far from united on this question or
on enforcing Article VI in Ohio.[57]

Delegates to the constitutional convention began pouring into Chillicothe on Monday, November 1. After submitting their credentials and
taking an oath to discharge their duties faithfully, they devoted the first
few days to organizational matters, including electing a secretary, door-
keeper, and president. The convention chose Edward Tiffin as president, and he reassured them of his fairness in applying the rules they
adopted. The convention established various committees that addressed
the critical issue of civil rights. These included committees on privileges
and elections, rules, a bill of rights, and the qualifications of electors, all
of which would determine to some extent the future of race relations in
Ohio.[58] Before the convention could turn to substantive issues, territorial governor Arthur St. Clair made a futile attempt to delay delibera-
tions on the constitution. The Republican-dominated body approved his
request to address them and listened politely, though with indifference.

He defended his record, affirming his opposition to statehood on grounds that Ohio lacked adequate resources to fund a state. He unsuccessfully urged the convention to abandon its course.[59] On November 22, Jefferson finally removed St. Clair from office "for the disorganizing spirit, and tendency of every example, violating the rules of conduct enjoined by his public station, he displayed in his address to the convention."[60]

St. Clair was only a temporary distraction, and the convention quickly returned to substantial issues. The status and future of blacks became the most controversial and held the potential to derail the convention. As historian Charles Galbreath suggests, the color question aroused "intensity of feeling."[61] Historian Helen Thurston carefully labels the delegates by their positions on civil rights, with categories such as problack, ultra-problack, and antiblack. Thurston places John W. Browne, Ephraim Cutler, William Goforth, and Nathan Updegraff in the first category for consistently voting favorably for black rights. She considers Francis Dunlavy unique, placing him in the ultra-problack category because he voted in favor of extending civil rights to blacks on every question raised in the convention. Finding that Michael Baldwin, Israel Donaldson, James Grubb, and Elijah Woods consistently voted against black civil rights, she labels them antiblack.[62] As noted earlier, neither the political affiliation, county of residence, nor regional background of the delegates explains their votes. Hamilton County, in southern Ohio, elected problack delegates, while Belmont County elected antiblack delegates. Republicans accused Federalists of favoring slavery, yet Ephraim Cutler, a Federalist, voted for many civil rights proposals.

Republican delegates of northern ancestry were in the majority on the bill of rights committee. Baldwin had migrated from Connecticut, Donaldson from New Jersey, Dunlavy and Goforth from New York, and Updegraff from Pennsylvania. John W. Browne had recently emigrated from England to Kentucky, then to Ohio. Elijah Woods had migrated from Virginia. The background of James Grubb is uncertain, but it is widely believed that he also had migrated from a southern state. Though no African Americans were elected as delegates, they made their interest known as the convention got underway. Blacks in Clermont County sent a petition to Chillicothe on November 16, asking that the "privileges which are the absolute right of all men be secured to them."[63] The convention tabled the memorial without comment—possibly because many of the delegates considered blacks to be outside the political culture of Ohio. As the convention discovered, other delegates wanted to bring African Americans into that political culture.

The bill of rights committee began its work on November 10, at the home of convention chairman Edward Tiffin. It does not appear that Tiffin sought to influence the committee. Evidently, the delegates who lived in Chillicothe helped provide lodgings and meeting venues for the convention. At the suggestion of John W. Browne, the committee's chairman, they addressed slavery first. Browne had actually given the matter considerable thought. He presented for discussion the proposal that "[n]o person shall be held in slavery, if a male, after he is thirty-five years of age; or, if a female, after she is twenty-five years of age."[64] Browne believed his idea was consistent with settled laws governing slavery, which he interpreted as measures providing for the gradual emancipation of slaves. Similar plans were in place in a number of northern states. Browne also believed that slave labor would further economic development in Ohio. Should Ohio uphold Article VI, he reasoned, it would discourage large numbers of slave owners who would not migrate without slaves. As Browne put it, abolition "would operate against the interests of those who wished to immigrate from the slave states to Ohio."[65]

His thinking was that of Republicans, who believed that the diffusion of slavery was a step to ending it. It was a perspective many Republicans would embrace for several more years. Ephraim Cutler later claimed that this was the strategy of the chairman. As Cutler put it, Browne hoped "that what he had introduced was thought by the greatest men in the nation to be, if embodied in the constitution, a great step toward the emancipation of slavery."[66] Although scholars have questioned the evidence, Browne had borrowed the theory from the founder of his political party. Moreover, Browne's contemporaries believed that Thomas Jefferson had written the resolution to admit slavery in Ohio. Cutler claimed that the Browne resolution actually was written in Jefferson's handwriting. Jefferson allegedly had told Congressman Jeremiah Morrow that he regretted that Ohio had not made slavery legal.[67]

Although Republicans frequently charged the Federalists with favoring slavery, more often than not they were the ones most willing to reverse the sixth article in the ordinance. The Federalists were a minority party and lacked the votes to unilaterally win approval for slavery. Moreover, there is no evidence that the Federalists of Ohio had ever been proslavery—or had conspired to rescind Article VI. On the contrary, Ephraim Cutler, the only Federalist on the bill of rights committee, introduced an alternative resolution on slavery. Cutler proposed the clause "There shall be neither slavery nor involuntary servitude in this State." Later, reminiscing on his years of public service in Ohio, Cutler claimed authorship of the antislavery "section that stands in the Ohio Constitution."[68]

The proposal to prohibit slavery led to conflict among Republicans, their preconvention pledges of harmony notwithstanding. Some Republicans of southern origins were eager to approve slavery in order to induce slave owners to migrate to Ohio. They argued that Article VI required ratification by a state before it became binding. Thus, they believed that a state could reject Article VI. In contrast, those of northern extraction, who were committed to free labor, favored the ban against slavery. These divergent opinions on slavery created the first deadlock at the convention. Unable to agree on a slavery resolution, the convention tabled the subject until November 20, ten days after the committee first considered it. When the convention returned to the subject on November 21, a proposal to ban slavery everywhere in the Northwest Territory was presented: "Nor shall there be either slavery or involuntary servitude *ever* admitted in any State to be erected on the northwest side of the river Ohio, within the limits of the United States, except as above excepted" (emphasis in original).[69]

This proposal to decide the fate of slavery in other states taken from the Northwest Territory was an extreme measure, possibly designed to place slavery back on the agenda. Certainly, Ohio law was not enforceable in the Northwest Territory, and the convention lacked authority to ban slavery in a region under federal control. The motion failed by a vote of 2 to 31, with only John Paul and John Reily, both from Hamilton County, voting for it.[70] Apparently, they sarcastically made the point that, should Ohio wish to ban slavery, let it do so in the entire Northwest Territory. The convention returned to the slavery proposal on Wednesday, November 24. Although Ephraim Cutler had managed to win greater support for his resolution to ban slavery, he became ill and was absent when the measure came to a vote. Meanwhile, the Republican delegates who had pledged to support the prohibition had been lured to the proslavery camp in his absence. With the prohibition of slavery threatened, Rufus Putnam counseled his Federalist colleague to "get well, be in your place or you will lose your favorite measure."[71] Cutler rose from his sickbed to argue for banning slavery in Ohio, and his impassioned appeal won over John Milligan, who had reservations about legalizing slavery but was still straddling the fence.[72]

The convention ultimately approved by one vote the clause to prohibit slavery, a weak endorsement of Article VI. Supporters of slavery in Ohio next proposed indentured servitude, suggesting that male servants could be held until thirty-five years of age, and female servants until they were twenty-five years old. Ephraim Cutler feared such a clause could be used to disguise slavery. The convention decided in favor of indentured servitude, but with a lower age for terminating the contract: "Nor shall any male person arrived at the age of twenty-one years, or female person arrived at the age of eighteen years, be held to serve any person as a servant under pretense of indenture or otherwise, unless such person shall enter into such indenture, while in a state of perfect freedom, and on condition of a bona fide consideration, received or to be received for their service, except as before excepted."[73]

Hiring out servants and bondsmen had been a common practice in pioneer Ohio. Indeed, such a policy empowered an unscrupulous person to violate the rights of a servant. Supporters of the clause suggested that including it in the constitution enabled the state to regulate it. Opponents of the scheme challenged it, only to lose their motion, 12 to 21.[74] The convention approved the indentured servitude clause. Theoretically, a person of any race could become an indentured servant; however, it was more common for blacks to become servants in Ohio. Indentured servitude made it possible for whites to hold large numbers of African Americans in virtual slavery, and the scheme survived for several decades.[75] The committee on qualifications of electors proposed to restrict suffrage to adult white males who had paid or were charged with state and local taxes. Jeremiah Morrow reported the clause to the convention on Saturday, November 13. After several hours of debate, opponents of the measure made a motion to strike *white* from the proposal. The motion failed on the first ballot by a vote of 14 to 19. A revised motion to base the franchise on the tax roll also failed by 8 to 26.[76] Evidently, a problack delegate moved to offer a modest civil rights clause: "that all male Negroes and mulattos now residing in this territory shall be entitled to the right of suffrage, if they shall make a record of their citizenship."[77] The motion passed on the first ballot, 19 to 15, with Republicans voting favorably on the measure.

Passing the motion might suggest that Republicans had decided in favor of black suffrage. However, the clause was carefully crafted to extend the vote only to blacks living in Ohio at the time. The majority at the convention considered blacks in Ohio a vanishing race, with little chance of influencing the political process. African Americans would diminish in population in ensuing years, and Ohio would mature as a state without any direct influence from people of African descent. It is reasonable to assume that a few delegates in the antiblack category voted for the measure because black refugees would not be entitled to the rights of citizenship. Apparently, some Republicans interpreted the positive vote as a sign of support for black suffrage, and a zealous Republican delegate proposed an amendment to give voting rights to descendants of enfranchised African Americans. The motion, "That the male descendants of such Negroes and mulattos as shall be recorded, shall be entitled to the same privilege," failed 17 to 16.[78]

Upon the third reading of the black suffrage clause, a new motion was made: "That all male Negroes and mulattos now residing in this territory, shall, at the age of twenty-one years, be entitled to the right of suffrage if they shall within one year make a record of their citizenship with the clerk of the county in which they may reside; and, provided also, that they have paid or are charged with a state or county tax."[79] The motion ended in a tie, 17 to 17. The modification in the bill satisfied moderates, who agreed with the poll tax. Edward Tiffin, the president of the convention, had not voted on any of the previous ballots. As a Republican, he had promised to vote favorably on civil rights, but now he cast the final vote to deny black suffrage.[80] The matter was not resolved, however. Some delegates feared that the suffrage law might disenfranchise white male servants and apprentices; they thus proposed the superfluous clause that nothing in the suffrage law would "prevent white male persons above the age of twenty-one from having the right of an elector." The motion failed on a vote of 13 to 21.[81] In the end, article IV of the proposed constitution provided suffrage for white male inhabitants above the age of twenty-one who met the residency and tax requirements of the state.

Writing the racial proscription into the state's constitution emboldened antiblack delegates at the convention. They had successfully driven back an attempt to enfranchise African Americans. Thus, they proposed a constitutional provision to further regulate African American residents:

> No Negro or mulatto shall ever be eligible to any office, civil or military, or give their oath in any court of justice against a white person, be subject to do military duty, or pay a poll-tax in this State; Provided always, and it is fully understood and declared, that all Negroes and mulattos now in or who may hereafter reside in, this State, shall not be entitled to all the privileges of citizens of this State excepted by this Constitution.[82]

The motion clearly made a distinction between African Americans and white citizens by barring blacks from the military and civic life in Ohio. It deprived blacks of the ability to testify against whites in court, apparently leaving them with only such legal rights as the ability to marry, make contracts, and own property. Although the convention initially approved the proposal on a vote of 19 to 16, it struck the measure without comment on November 26.[83]

The convention, however, could not ignore some of the issues raised by the black law it rejected. The militia issue was a matter of great importance, especially given the history of black military service in America. The Northwest Territory had also enrolled blacks in the militia when conditions there warranted it. The framers of the Ordinance of 1787 were influenced by practical considerations. The Ohio Valley was still not safe for white settlement during the late 1780s, with Indian wars almost a certainty out on the frontier. Hence, the ordinance did not deny militia service to blacks. The territorial legislature affirmed this color-neutral militia policy in 1788, when it opened the militia to all able-bodied males between the ages of sixteen and fifty. Thus, for slightly more than a decade, black soldiers had toted rifles in the Ohio Valley.[84]

The national government was the first to place restrictions on the enlistment of free African Americans in the militia. Its policy had little to do with any realistic danger from blacks, yet whites had historically associated violent behavior with dark-skinned peoples. Moreover, though blacks had served in colonial wars and in the Revolution, whites still assumed that they would not make good soldiers. Equally important, southern leaders feared that armed blacks might lead a revolt against slavery. The Militia Act of 1792 limited service to "able-bodied white males." Leaders in the Northwest Territory cited the federal militia law as reason to bring the western militias in line with the policy to bar enlistment of free blacks. By the end of the eighteenth century, white settlers in the Ohio Valley had begun to feel more secure from attacks by Native Americans, especially following the stunning defeat of the Shawnee, Miami, Delaware, and other tribes at the battle of Fallen Timbers in 1794.[85] In the wake of this hard-won security, the territorial government adopted the policy of excluding African Americans from the militia in 1799 and expelled blacks already in service. In the end, the constitutional convention did not endorse the exclusionary militia policy. The convention ignored restricting the racial makeup of the state militia; thus, presumably, African Americans were free to enlist.

The opponents of racial equality suffered several other defeats in their efforts to deny basic rights to African Americans. Provisions guaranteeing that "justice [would be] administered without denial or delay," the right to a jury trial, freedom of assembly and petition, and access to public education were all set out without racial qualifications.[86]

Few delegates had actually wanted to make Ohio a color-blind society. Ultimately the results were mixed. The convention prohibited slavery but allowed a system of indentured servitude. The constitution reserved suffrage for white males. The constitution mandated the enumeration of the white population to determine representation in the state legislature and for the appropriation of funds, but excluded blacks and mulattoes. The state thus denied African Americans significant political rights.[87] At the same time, rather than specifically excluding black Ohio residents from other basic legal rights, such as militia duty or access to public education, the constitution virtually ignored African Americans. The compromises on civil rights clearly contradicted the widely articulated position of the Ohio electorate before the convention, and many Republican delegates abandoned their pledge to the secure the civil rights of all Ohioans. Neither side got exactly what it wanted. It was enough for the convention to finalize the constitution on November 29. As it closed the session, the convention violated republican ideals one more time by deciding against putting the constitution to a popular vote. The convention itself voted for ratification.

Many factors influenced the decision to avoid a referendum on the constitution. Time and money were certainly important considerations; however, the convention mostly feared that the issues which had divided them would surely put the constitution in jeopardy if put to a popular vote. The irony did not escape Ephraim Cutler, and he seized the opportunity to humiliate the Republican Party by casting the only vote against the constitution.[88] Surprisingly, the ratification process did not disturb Ohioans, who considered their new constitution a capstone of liberty. The constitution did not place qualifications on white male suffrage, and it guaranteed basic rights to the white majority. The U.S. Congress approved the document in 1803, and Ohio entered the Union without opposition.[89] Congressional approval made compromise on racial issues imperative. The convention debates proved that Republican commitment to black rights was shallow, and the commitment diminished after statehood. The failure to specifically grant African Americans civil rights left an open door for antiblack forces to immediately begin to make Ohio into a white man's republic.

THREE

"A State for White Men"

1803–1830

OPPOSITION TO SLAVERY in Ohio was not the same as wanting to ensure the civil rights of African Americans. Although Article VI of the Ordinance of 1787 had been in effect for fifteen years when the Ohio Constitutional Convention met in 1802, the convention closed Ohio to slavery by only one vote. Moreover, by both forbidding runaway slaves from becoming citizens and authorizing their removal, the sixth article stood as a significant impediment to black civil rights. The convention followed this example when it denied explicit civil rights protections for African Americans, despite the preconvention pledges of Republican delegates. Drafted in the wake of the Jeffersonian revolution, the Ohio constitution was heralded for enlarging the free republican culture. The constitution did not require property qualifications for voting and guaranteed such basic rights as habeas corpus, jury trials—and, of course, it prohibited slavery. All these features came out of the philosophies of Revolutionary America; they were not unique to Ohio. As early as 1776, states like Pennsylvania and Vermont had extolled the natural and inalienable rights of their citizens, listing among them life, liberty, and property. Vermont also provided for an end to slavery.[1]

Constitutions, however, do not always function the same in real life as they prescribe on paper, as the constitutions of several states illustrate. For example, Indiana and Illinois prohibited slavery in 1816 and 1818 respectively, yet slavery persisted in both states for several decades.[2] Both states also adopted black codes. Similarly, the prohibition against slavery in the Ohio constitution did not guarantee blacks state citizenship. Its explicit discriminatory clauses notwithstanding, Ohio's constitution, if strictly interpreted and enforced, still could have provided a basis for black advancement. Without a firm commitment from state officials and a consistent and favorable application of the laws, however, the liberal features in the constitution were deaf and dumb for blacks. Thus, except for ending slavery, the Ohio constitution proved to be only a paper victory for African Americans. The constitutional convention of 1802 reflected the discomfort most whites had with the thought of a color-blind society. The Chillicothe convention came close to codifying racial restrictions, but for practical reasons the delegates decided on a constitution that would win support from various constituencies in the state as well as Congress. The convention ended by restricting suffrage to white males, and it created a system of indentured servitude that relegated black servants to the status of de facto slaves.[3]

The expansion of civil rights in the new state was unlikely to happen immediately, given the background of the men who were elected to run the new government. Many white emigrants from the South already had direct experience with black laws. Since at least 1732, Virginia law had proscribed black testimony against a white litigant. The state legislature affirmed its testimony law in 1801, allowing black testimony only in cases that involved another African American.[4] Given this history, it is not surprising that, within a year following Ohio's admission into the Union, the legislature codified the Black Laws, thereby officially designating the state as a community for whites. Looking back from the vantage point of nearly fifty years, a delegate at the 1850 constitutional convention surmised, "Ohio was a state for white men. The Negroes were intruders."[5] And the vast majority of white emigrants in Ohio at the time had come from the South, slave country, where most African Americans were considered chattel property, not citizens.

—

Southern whites had a profound impact on the political and social character of Ohio. For many years, migrating southerners considered the Ohio

Country to be a place where they could establish their traditions and replicate their plantation economies. During the pioneer period and until the federal government barred it, many emigrants continued to buy and transport slaves to the territory, and others practiced slavery in defiance of federal law. Once it became clear that Congress would not legalize slavery in the Ohio Territory, these whites developed policies to prevent the migration and settlement of free African Americans there. All southern emigrants in Ohio did not embrace the same values, however. Some had migrated westward to get away from the slave economy of the South (see chapter 2). These emigrants considered slavery repressive and blamed it for limiting the economic prospects and quality of life for whites. While they opposed slaveholding in their adopted state, they did not support civil rights for blacks. Ohio produced many leaders with this conviction. This breed of politician entered the new state legislature and saturated it with these values. They produced the Black Laws and created a culture of exclusion, segregating and subordinating free African Americans in Ohio and endeavoring to close the state border to their migration.[6] Social relations not explicitly proscribed by statute were established by custom, resulting in racial separation in churches, hotels, and other public places.

The vast majority of whites in early Ohio were Republicans who had migrated directly from such southern states as Kentucky, Virginia, and North Carolina to settle in southern Ohio. Southern Ohio quickly became the most densely populated and racially conservative area in the state, and its elected officials dominated state lawmaking for decades. They also ensured continuity in the racial policies established in Article VI, its fugitive slave clause, and the racial proscriptions in the Ohio constitution. One of these Republicans, Edward Tiffin, was one of the most learned men in Ohio and the natural choice for governor. Although trained in medicine, he was an experienced politician, having already served in the territorial legislature and the state constitutional convention. The Ohio house elected Michael Baldwin its speaker, and the senate elected Nathaniel Massie its president. Tiffin, Baldwin, and Massie shared similar views regarding the social character of Ohio, and they helped inaugurate its racial policy. Each had affirmed the racial proscriptions with his votes at the constitutional convention, and Tiffin actually had cast the deciding vote against black male suffrage. Both

Baldwin and Massie presided over their chambers when the new legislature began to codify the Black Laws.[7] As their contemporary Jacob Burnet later explained, these laws deprived blacks of citizenship and "excluded them from the description of persons." Ohio defined blacks as "aborigines who could remain in the state" but obtain nothing beyond subsistence.[8]

Ohio was not alone in seeking to legally codify the status of free blacks in the young nation. Because slavery had become linked to African ancestry, an African American who was not property became something of an anomaly to American whites. The slave population was extensive in the South, and few whites there could imagine life without slavery or the control they as whites exercised over the slave population. While many northern whites began to believe that African peoples should not be enslaved, most simply could not conceive of living with them on terms of political and social equality. With the increase in emancipation following the Revolution, the question arose as to how these larger numbers of free blacks would fit into society. This was a troubling question that few whites wanted to address. Their avoidance meant that the answer to this question would not lead to the development of a coherent plan for racial equality or even assurances of basic civil rights for African Americans. The answers would evolve piecemeal, over decades of social confusion, and the equitable application of the law to all races of Americans was always doubtful. The uncertainty regarding the status of blacks plagued governments at all levels, creating a contradictory and confusing mishmash of statutes and judicial opinions by state and federal courts.

Whites throughout the nation already were adept at simultaneously espousing and restricting the egalitarian principles that had given birth to the federal republic. Indeed, the founders had created a glorious republic; yet the Constitution had given national, formal recognition to slavery. To determine representation in Congress, the Constitution included the slave population but counted their numbers only as three-fifths of free persons. The Constitution deprived Congress of any authority to prohibit the international slave trade for at least twenty years. The Constitution also included a fugitive slave clause, making it possible for runaway slaves to be recaptured and removed by their owners. Congress codified the fugitive slave clause in 1793, outlining a summary process for the removal of a slave. This support given to slavery by the federal government was not benign; it affected every facet of society. Federal law elevated whites to a higher level of citizenship than blacks.

The racial policy of the federal government immediately influenced its departments and officers. The 1793 Fugitive Slave Act of Congress is one example. That same year, Supreme Court Chief Justice John Jay, in a case that had nothing to do with African Americans, identified blacks as a subordinated class.[9] Under the American system of federalism, the states had authority to determine the basis for citizenship, and federal citizenship hinged on state policy. In some cases, therefore, free African Americans were believed to have federal citizenship, but in other cases they were not considered citizens. Similar confusion also existed over whether the federal government could lawfully provide for the recapture of fugitives from labor and whether the states would be obligated to enforce federal laws.

The federal government and each state had to cope with the issues of the status and rights of African Americans. The new state of Ohio joined the union just as the tide of revolutionary sentiment was waning, and strides made toward improving the status of African Americans were slowed in most states—in the North as well as in the South. As the first state to be created from the Northwest Territory, Ohio did not have a history of legalized slavery. However, its geographic location at the nexus of the North, South, and West made Ohio a cultural crossroads. The timing of its statehood was also significant, following two terrifying events from the previous decade. The 1791 insurrection of Toussaint L'Ouverture in Haiti aptly demonstrated the determination of enslaved Africans to be free.[10] As alarming as the Haitian revolt was to white Americans, news of a domestic revolt or conspiracy was even more disturbing.

At the time of Ohio's admission to the Union in 1803, the Gabriel Prosser conspiracy in Virginia was still a fresh memory. The conspirators had planned on capturing Richmond in August 1800 and establishing a black kingdom in Virginia, with Prosser as its first governor. Governor James Monroe noted that Richmond-area whites had held "fears of a Negro insurrection" for many months after Prosser's arrest. The character of the black rebels frightened Virginia whites, and many undoubtedly migrated to southern Ohio with the belief that blacks were dangerous. They did not believe that free blacks and runaway slaves could be assimilated. Concluding that a state policy was needed to control its black residents, the Ohio legislature, dominated by southern-born Jeffersonians, created the Black Laws. The influence of southern emigrants on these racial codes is evident because they approximated the slave codes of the South more so than the laws of the northern states.

The urgency felt by Ohio lawmakers in the General Assembly to develop Black Laws was influenced partly by the location of the new state. Bordering the slave states of Kentucky and Virginia, Ohio was accessible to free black migration and to runaway slaves from other southern states, most frequently North Carolina and Tennessee. The National Road and the Ohio River increased eastern traffic to the western states. Not only did runaway slaves seek refuge in Ohio, slave drivers and merchants transporting people or foodstuffs down the Ohio River regularly stopped in the state. This increased traffic, especially that of the runaway slaves, not only created a new cultural mix but also caused a plethora of interstate problems. For instance, white emigrants had established a southern-style culture in the river towns along the Ohio River and in cities bordering the National Road. Because of their southern backgrounds, these whites favored imposing racial proscriptions on blacks, such as the requirement that free blacks register when entering the state.[11]

Ohio's economic relationship with the South was another crucial factor that influenced the General Assembly in its decision to enact the Black Laws. Ohio legislators worried that a reputation as a safe haven for runaway slaves undermined the state's commercial relations with southern states. Political and business leaders in Ohio joined together, asserting that a liberal racial policy would ruin this commerce. And they urged the state government to place their economic interests ahead of any implicit rights its laws had given to blacks. Whenever Ohio leaders sensed a problem with the southern trade, they assumed that it was because of slavery. Ohio lawmakers therefore believed that a stringent racial policy restricting the status of African Americans was a sign of goodwill for their southern neighbors, as well as a sign of their determination to keep Ohio for whites.[12]

As it turned out, the Ohio General Assembly did not share the same reservations as the delegates to the 1802 constitutional convention, who first faced questions of whether and where to draw the color line. While convention delegates worried over such matters as getting the state constitution approved in Ohio and by Congress, the legislative enactments faced only judicial review. Secure in the belief that their legislation would survive judicial scrutiny, Ohio lawmakers began hammering out a racial policy soon after they convened. Ohio was practically a one-party state when it entered the Union, and Republicans easily dominated the legislature in 1803. Without any opposition, they laid the foundation for the Black Laws. Most Republican members of the early Ohio legislature opposed black migration and residency, favored the federal fugitive slave policy, and believed blacks and whites should be segregated. Not surprisingly, they wrote the Black Laws to deprive African Americans of all but a little more than residency, assuming they could prove their free status.[13]

In 1803, the Republican-led legislature enacted the state militia policy restricting military service to only "white male citizens." In 1792, Congress had barred blacks from the militia, and the legislature of the Northwest Territory had followed suit in 1799. In 1803, the state codified the federal militia policy.[14] The General Assembly thus drew the color line and devoted much of the next half-century to making it more rigid.[15] The Ohio constitution had established the basis for excluding African Americans when apportioning the population for determining representation in the General Assembly. Enumeration at the state level determined how representatives would be apportioned for the state legislature and also suggested how resources should be allocated. The Ohio constitution (article I, section 2) required the enumeration of white males above the age of twenty-one. Ohio codified that policy on March 1, 1803, when it excluded blacks from enumeration, and it affirmed the policy for many years.[16] By eliminating blacks, the legislature also sent a signal about the degree of citizenship rights to which African Americans would be entitled.

In case blacks did not understand the message, some whites sought more direct action to keep black communities under their thumb. The Ohio house of representatives organized a committee on December 15, 1803, to consider the bill of Fairfield County representative Philemon Beecher, which would restrict black migration to Ohio. The house named James Dunlap, of Jefferson County, chairman and placed Stephen Wood, of Hamilton County, and James Smith, of Belmont County, on the committee to draft the statute. The house also appointed William Gaffs, of Fairfield County, to advise the senate about this legislation. The house committee performed its duties quickly and presented the measure to the senate, where, after amendments, it passed on December 31. The General Assembly then approved the bill on January 3, 1804, as "An act to regulate black and mulatto persons."[17]

The Black Law of 1804 reconciled past difficulties by defining African American citizenship, since as free individuals blacks would automatically have some rights. The act also imposed legal barriers on black migration. Furthermore, the code made it clear that Ohio was a society for whites, not for blacks and mulattoes. The Act of 1804 imposed restrictions equally on blacks and mulattoes, although the state supreme court later concluded that mulattoes with predominately Caucasian features were exempt from the disabilities of blackness. The law further developed a rigorous residency policy, making it increasingly difficult for immigrating blacks to make Ohio their domicile. The act, for example, required black immigrants to provide proof of their freedom on demand, such as filing a certificate of manumission with the clerk in their county of residence. Recognizing that it could not expel the black residents already in Ohio, the legislature granted asylum to any free person who had entered the state before June 1, 1804. To establish Ohio as their domicile, they would also pay a registration fee of twelve and a half cents with the county. The statute allowed blacks a two-year grace period to conform to the residency requirement. However, state law would not bar any lawful claim to a fugitive from labor. Thus, all African Americans in Ohio were expected to hold a county-issued certificate to prove their free status.[18]

The Act of 1804 also supported the federal Fugitive Slave Act of 1793, which made it a misdemeanor for anyone to interfere with a lawful owner capturing and removing a runaway slave. On conviction, such a party could be fined from fifty to one thousand dollars. Although they faced this discriminatory legislation, free blacks were allowed entry into Ohio.[19] However, free blacks also needed to show proof of their status upon demand. Ohio lawmakers apparently hoped that these laws would prevent free blacks from coming into the state.[20] In addition to attempting to shut down its border to both free blacks and runaway slaves, Ohio offered favorable conditions for those who claimed an individual as a slave. Recapture was merely procedural—a claimant needed little documentation to verify a claim. The law entitled a claimant access to the state judicial and legal system to capture and remove an alleged slave. On satisfactory proof that a person was a runaway, a judicial officer could issue a warrant to a law enforcement officer to arrest and deliver an alleged slave to the person claiming him or her. Ohio made its law enforcement officers "slave catchers," and directed claimants to pay them "such compensation as they are entitled to receive in other cases for similar services."[21]

Historians have not satisfactorily explained why Ohio mandated the registration of African Americans. There are at least two theses to consider. First, that the Black Laws protected free African Americans already in Ohio. While this might initially appear too simplistic, it is possible that the legislators who were interested in protecting free blacks from seizure, allowing them to own property and charting their own way, viewed the registration law as a means to protect them. Registration bolstered the safety of free blacks by giving them and the government proof to use when dealing with slave catchers and state officials from slave country. The second and more likely alternative was that the General Assembly passed the immigration law to maintain white supremacy. As some whites claimed, "if we should equalize our laws, it would encourage [blacks] to settle in our state in greater numbers." Others further poisoned the attitudes of the white community by using language that described African Americans as "worse than drones to society," warning that a few of them would multiply "like locusts."[22] Thus, the virulent racism of Ohio whites is inescapable, and such bigotry figured prominently in the decision of the General Assembly when it enacted the Black Laws. Indeed, the number of sympathetic lawmakers elected from antislavery precincts in northern Ohio eventually would increase, but for many years their numbers paled beside those elected from southern Ohio.

———

The possibility of increased black migration continued to trouble Ohio legislators following adoption of the Act of 1804, and Philemon Beecher revisited the matter in 1806. However, he would not openly admit that the increase of black residents was the motivating factor behind the racial codes. Instead, Beecher argued that Ohio was teetering on the brink of a civil war with slave owners, pitting Ohio whites against southern whites, solely because runaway slaves frequently passed through the state to gain refuge in American Indian communities. He surmised that slave owners would not allow blacks such a sanctuary, and thus Beecher warned that war was imminent and Ohio would be caught in the crossfire. To discourage the flight of blacks to Ohio, for either domicile or passage, he proposed making the immigration law more stringent:[23]

> That sundry black and mulatto persons, supposed to be the property of citizens in the neighboring states, have made a settlement within this state, on the lands on which the Indian title is not yet extinguished, and are of course measurably under Indian protection. That it is reasonable to expect the owners of these persons will take measures to reclaim them, and by the event may involve our frontiers, and perhaps the nation, in troubles which prudent measures, in proper season, may prevent.[24]

Under the leadership of Philemon Beecher—and in the name of a state emergency—the Ohio General Assembly revised the state's black code in 1807.

There can be little doubt that the Beecher bill was drafted to force Ohio to assume greater responsibility for keeping blacks out and facilitating the recapture and removal of runaway slaves. Beecher's original bill also provided that the governor should be authorized to appropriate monies to pay slave owners who lost fugitives from labor due to their contact with Ohio. Such a proposal seemed extreme, and the majority of the assembly rejected this provision.

In addition to offering new guidelines for recapturing runaway slaves, the revised immigration law made it even more difficult for free blacks to become legal residents of Ohio. The statute required them to "enter into bond with two or more" property holders "in the penal sum of" five hundred dollars to guarantee their good behavior and welfare.[25] Ostensibly, the legislature wanted proof that a black migrant would not become a dependent of the state by requiring these immigrants to secure their welfare. The code was primarily prohibitive legislation, however, designed to deter black settlement in Ohio. As a correspondent for the *Anti-Slavery Examiner* claimed three decades later, "The legislature well knew that it would generally be impossible for a stranger, and especially a black stranger" to meet this criterion.[26] The statute also increased the base fine for interfering with recapture to one hundred dollars. Moreover, it established the infamous Negro evidence law, which provided, "No Negro or mulatto shall testify in a Court of Justice of Record, where the party in cause pending is white."[27] The change in the statute reflected the growing white fear of a larger free black population. Although census figures would not be available until 1810, whites increasingly saw more blacks in their state. Given the rise in the black population, Ohio legislators originated the bill to deter future black immigration. The Ohio senate presented the revised bill to the house on December 21, 1806. After the house reviewed it, the General Assembly enacted it on January 25, 1807.

The Act of 1804 had said nothing about the ability of blacks to present evidence in court. It is possible that courts had summarily denied them testimony against a white. The history of discriminatory legislation in the United States shows that statutes frequently follow custom. The Black Law of 1807 officially established the rule of evidence for Ohio courts. A white could offer testimony against a black; a black could do so only in a matter that involved a member of the same race. The Negro evidence law deprived blacks of the right to offer testimony for or against white defendants. The statute thus offered a dual system of evidence because the state now shielded whites from prosecution based solely on black testimony. The statute ultimately hampered prosecuting attorneys. For example, in 1838, two whites who allegedly had caused a riot at the home of Charles Burnet were acquitted because the only witness against them was an African American. A correspondent for the *Philanthropist* scoffed at the verdict, claiming that the statute had denied black Americans their fundamental rights.[28]

In the wake of this verdict, slave owners and professional slave catchers brazenly violated the sovereign laws of Ohio, eventually compelling the legislature to reenact the personal liberty law in 1819, making it a crime to remove free blacks. Any person using "violence, fraud, or deception," that statute read, to effect the removal of a free black person "shall be deemed guilty of a high misdemeanor."[29] Punishment for violations included up to ten years of hard labor in the state penitentiary. Revised in 1831, the statute again outlawed the seizure and removal of an African American by violence or fraud, or by "keep[ing] such free black or mulatto person in any kind of restraint or confinement" for that purpose. In order to legally remove a slave, the law required that the person making the claim first take the "black or mulatto person before some judge or justice of the peace." It reduced the jail time of someone violating the law to a maximum of seven years and raised the minimum penalty to three years. Ohio continued to place restrictions on slave catchers by closing its jails for the temporary detention of alleged slaves for many years.[30]

During this period, public assistance was the responsibility of the state and localities, and Ohio established its own welfare system. Most early-nineteenth-century jurisdictions made distinctions among the poor, recognizing categories such as the "virtuous poor," who became destitute from no fault of their own, as opposed to "those of a contrary character." Lawmakers considered the latter group undeserving of public relief. The Ohio legislature followed this custom to a point by creating a decentralized welfare system, in which the townships assumed responsibility for indigents. The relief law barred African Americans who had not become legal residents from obtaining public assistance.[31] Thus, by making such stipulations regarding relief, Ohio integrated welfare with its Black Laws.

The overseer of the poor comes closest to being a state agency charged with enforcing the Black Laws of Ohio, at least for indigent blacks. A defendant could be charged and convicted under the statutes, but some action on his or her part was required to trigger a prosecution, although whites concocted some of the charges against blacks. Public school officials also were expected to enforce the color line, but they were not officially charged with doing so. While black property owners "generally paid their full proportion of the school taxes, they derived no benefit whatever from the schools."[32] The state legislature also compelled employers and other whites to enforce the Black Laws, specifically the state's employment law. The statute mandated that employers legally could hire only blacks who could provide proof of their freedom. This directive effectively turned neighbors into spies, and to compound the insult the state offered a cash reward for informants. Section 2 of the Act of 1807 authorized the courts to collect a fine up to fifty dollars, with "one half thereof for the use of the informer." The revised Section 3 imposed a fine up to one hundred dollars, with "the one half to the informer." Given the response of employers to it, the employment law seems to have been mainly a nuisance for whites, who rarely bothered to enforce it.[33]

The employment law also made it possible for unscrupulous employers to abuse black workers. Strictly enforced, the employment law limited the prospects of blacks to find work. The law injured whites and blacks, an abolitionist declared—it encroached on the rights of Ohio citizens to employ whomever they chose, while at the same time it denied employment to blacks on the presumption that they were in Ohio illegally. These individuals, unable to find work, would become destitute, the abolitionists asserted. The Ohio Anti–Slavery Society made the same point about the employment law, declaring, "This enactment cuts off the last hope of refuge from southern oppression."[34] Racism further hindered black workers. Labor associations closed their guilds to African American workers or consigned black men primarily to menial jobs such as coachman, dockworker, and barber. Black women also faced discrimination, finding work primarily as housekeepers, laundresses, and waitresses.

More often than not, many naturally intelligent, industrious, eminently employable African Americans were the ones who made their way to freedom. They had the initiative to work long hours and to save their earnings to buy their freedom, and they were among the slaves who were manumitted for meritorious service. These individuals had high expectations for a new life in a free state, but Ohio fell short of their dreams. Skilled blacks who had learned trades as slaves were not able to find jobs in their craft.[35] As a slave in Virginia, John Malvin had become a skilled carpenter, yet he could not find a job in the trade in Ohio in the 1820s. Dismayed by his bad luck, Malvin wrote in his autobiography, "I thought upon coming to a free state like Ohio, that I would find every door thrown open to receive me, but from the treatment I received by the people generally, I found it little better than in Virginia. I found every door closed against the colored man in a free state, excepting the jails and penitentiaries."[36]

William Lyons, born free in Virginia, found employment as a journeyman in Columbus but was fired when white employees protested. It was also nearly impossible for a black to become a member of a trade association. When the Mechanical Association in Cincinnati took a bold step in 1830 and apprenticed a black worker, white members criticized the leadership for opening the union to a black. A few years later, an African American carpenter who was hired by a cabinetmaking company faced resistance—the whites walked off the job, threatening to stay away until he was fired. The factory owner acquiesced and fired the black carpenter.[37] "Colored mechanics," lamented a writer for the *Philanthropist,* "are restricted to the business given them by people of their own color, and a few white friends."[38]

Fearing increased migration to Ohio upon the outbreak of the Civil War, Democratic Congressman Samuel Sullivan Cox hearkened back to the method adopted by his predecessors, asserting, "keep out the blacks and prevent their competing with white labor."[39] By proscribing black entry into Ohio and subordinating black residents, the General Assembly erected a firewall between blacks and whites. To further engineer Ohio society, the General Assembly periodically enacted various other measures to subordinate blacks, including affirming its militia policy in 1829 and passing jury laws in 1816 and 1831, which officially barred blacks from jury service.[40] The new racial codes reflected white fears of the growing black population in the state, although the increase in the African American community in the 1820s was only marginal.

—

Discrimination under the Black Laws also prevailed in public education, although Ohio law never prohibited the education of blacks. The original state constitution had not explicitly addressed the role of race in public education. Early in the century, a few proprietary schools admitted both blacks and whites, while others exclusively served only one race. When the Ohio General Assembly established the public school system in 1829, it restricted schools to white youths. Nothing "contained in this Act shall be so construed as to permit black or mulatto persons to attend the schools hereby established."[41] The exclusionary rule in Ohio public education prevailed for many more years. The state legislature established a segregated school system in 1849, and in areas with too few students of either race to warrant separate schools, it allowed mixed classrooms.[42]

The effect of the public education act of 1829 in Ohio immediately provoked controversy among blacks and progressive whites. Because the school system was funded by property taxes, almost everyone realized the injustice of taxing black citizens to pay for schools they could not attend. Subsequently, the legislature ordered school boards to fund black education or rebate taxes paid by African Americans. The state, however, would not be responsible for providing that education. Although it did not immediately create a public school system for blacks, Ohio theoretically allowed assessments from black property owners to help fund black education. County officials could have legally directed fees from black property owners to finance schools exclusively for their children, but they had no mandate to do so.[43]

———

The racial codes of Ohio clearly were harsh, but they did not seem unusual to the majority of whites. Indeed, the Black Laws approximated the slave codes of the South, in that they used race to exclude blacks from state benefits or presumed that a black individual living in Ohio was a slave. Throughout the southern states, local legislation routinely deprived free people of color of many of the "common elements of education." By these acts, slave owners intended to reduce African Americans to limited individuals, uneducated or illiterate and dependent on their white owners. The lives of free blacks in the South were also circumscribed. They had to answer to any white man who questioned them, for whites lived under the presumption that blacks were slaves. If unable to prove their free status by presenting documents, they could be apprehended as runaway slaves and sold into slavery. With so many whites in the Ohio legislature who had vivid memories of race relations in the South, it was natural for them to subordinate blacks.

Various statutes in southern states illustrated that whites there operated under the presumption that all blacks were slaves or, if free, subject to the social control of the state. On this basis, South Carolina enacted the Negro Seamen Acts, which authorized the arrest of black sailors at port and had them held until their vessels disembarked, ostensibly to prevent them from inciting slave revolts. Virginia applied similar reasoning when it required manumitted blacks to leave the state within twelve months or face reenslavement. Georgia imposed a fine on free blacks entering the state and authorized the authorities to sell into slavery any African American who could not pay. Moreover, only evidence presented by whites was admissible in the courts, and without sponsors or documents an African American stood little chance of prevailing in a legal action against whites.[44] It requires little imagination to see that the Black Laws of Ohio had a great deal in common with the codes regulating free blacks in the South.

———

Of course, when laws differentiated on the basis of color, it became important to determine who belonged to a particular race. In one of its earliest opinions on civil rights, the Ohio Supreme Court evolved a definition of whiteness in law when it reviewed *State v. George* (1821). Elizabeth George, a quadroon, was indicted for murdering her own infant child. The only witness to the crime was Mary Copper, an African American. The defense objected to her testimony on the grounds that state law prevented a black from giving testimony against a white. The defense argued that the testimony law of 1807 did not consider the "different grades of people of color," such as a mixed-race individual. Asserting George was legally white, her attorneys argued that a black witness could not testify against her.[45] The supreme court, pushed to decide the meaning of whiteness, prevented the testimony of the black witness. A mixed-race individual with more than 50 percent Caucasian blood, the court concluded, was white and entitled to the privileges belonging to that race.[46]

A Hamilton County court considered this same question in 1829, in the robbery trial of Polly Gray. The prosecution's key witness, who could place Gray at the scene of the crime, was black. The state initially gave little notice to the racial background of the witness because Gray, the defendant, was an octoroon, and it considered her to be an African American. However, Daniel Van Matre, Gray's attorney, insisted she was "of a shade of color between the mulatto and white" and as a white was immune from testimony from a black. Gray was nevertheless convicted in a common pleas court, and she appealed to the state supreme court.[47] Before the supreme court, Van Matre further developed the theory that Ohio law prohibited the testimony of a black against a white. He explained that Gray was not a mulatto, as the Negro evidence law had designated. A mulatto, he said, was the offspring of pure black and pure white parents. Gray, however, had a pure white parent and a mixed parent. Gray, coming from this admixture, the defense explained, was not a mulatto and should not be subject to the disability of blackness. "She thus being on a level with whites, the same privileges ought to be extended to her."[48]

The supreme court ruled in Gray's favor, stating that the testimony law applied solely to a case "where a white person is a party." Moreover, the statute referred to "three descriptions of persons," namely white, black, and mulatto. "We believe that a man of a race nearer white than mulatto, is admissible as a witness, and should partake in the privileges of whites."[49] It would seem that the Ohio Supreme Court did not approve of the Black Laws; thus, it offered a verdict consistent with its belief that those laws were unconscionable and should be restricted whenever possible. The court was unwilling to extend the statute further than what was required by law. Its reservations had less to do with Polly Gray and her status as a mixed-race individual, than with their revulsion by such legislation. Unwilling or unable to strike down the testimony law, however, the court only restricted its reach—its application.

Although the penal code of Ohio did not explicitly provide for a dual system for handling criminal cases, the Black Laws naturally made race an element in the criminal justice system. Whipping posts, for example, were popular as the place for dispensing punishment in Ohio, and they were prominently located at the county seat in most counties. Though the Black Laws did not specifically mandate their use, the whipping post became a venue where race, crime, and punishment were inextricably linked. Steubenville officials put it in the center of town, "on the market square," where miscreants of either race could get a public flogging in public view. Any convict could get a public flogging, but the justice system more frequently sentenced black men for the humiliation of public beatings. For allegedly stealing groceries valued at $2.50 circa 1825, a Steubenville judge sentenced an African American, whom the newspapers referred to as "negro Cuff," to pay for the stolen goods, serve one day in jail, and be "whipped twenty-five times on the bare back."[50] Cuff had received a public beating in the market square on more than one occasion for other crimes he (allegedly) had committed.

Charles Johnson, a well-known storekeeper in Jefferson County, also was whipped in public. Johnson had run out of meat with a long line of customers yet to serve; thus, he allegedly broke into a smokehouse belonging to Bazaleel Wells, a white merchant, and stole several hams "under cover of darkness." As news of the crime circulated through town, one of Johnson's customers came forward to report that he had spotted Wells's stamp on ham purchased from Johnson. Although he asserted his innocence, Johnson was convicted and was sentenced to serve nine days in jail and be given nine stripes on his naked back. He was also ordered to pay damages and court costs. Both the prosecutor and the store owner apparently felt vindicated when spectators reported that Johnson broke under the lash and confessed to the crime.[51] The Black Laws of Ohio, therefore, went beyond what was codified, to consign blacks to cruel and unusual treatment from which most whites were exempt.

Ohio was the first free state to develop a black code after the Revolution. When its sister states in the Northwest Territory entered the Union, most copied Ohio's laws.[52] When Indiana entered the Union in 1816, its bill of rights affirmed freedom and equality, including the prohibition of "slavery or involuntary servitude." Yet Indiana's constitution left its African American residents without a voice in the government. Article III, section 2, excluded blacks from "enumeration," restricting the population count to "all the white male inhabitants." Indiana disenfranchised blacks and deprived them the right of testimony against whites in court. Article VII, section 2, barred black males from the militia. When it codified these principles, the General Assembly denied blacks testimony against whites. It required African Americans entering the state to prove their free status. In an 1851 referendum on the immigration law, 83 percent of Indiana whites voted in favor of keeping the statute.[53]

Illinois entered the Union in 1818, and though article VI, section 1, of the state constitution prohibited slavery, it laid the cornerstone for a discriminatory policy. Article II, section 5, apportioned representation in the General Assembly "according to the number of white inhabitants."[54] Article II, section 27, restricted suffrage to "all white male inhabitants."[55] The militia clause in the constitution excluded "Negroes, mulattoes and Indians."[56] The Illinois legislature immediately adopted black codes, including an immigration law that required blacks to prove their free status upon entering the state. It also authorized the overseer of the poor to remove indigent blacks from its towns. Illinois law also made proof of freedom a qualification for work. In a referendum on the immigration clause in the state constitution in 1848, 70 percent of the electorate voted favorably on the provision.[57]

Michigan entered the Union in 1837. Its constitution declared, "Neither slavery nor involuntary servitude shall ever be introduced into this state."[58] Assuming the posture of a progressive state, the Michigan constitution authorized the legislature to "provide for a system of [public] schools"; however, it specifically excluded blacks. The constitution restricted suffrage to "white male citizens."[59] Though a movement surfaced to open elections to all male residents, the majority of white voters rejected black suffrage in a referendum in 1850. Significantly, the state placed no restrictions on black migration.

Wisconsin had a smaller black population than its neighbors in the Northwest Territory. Taking its cue from Article VI in the Ordinance of 1787, Wisconsin also banned slavery. Although it holds distinction as the only state from the Northwest Territory that never codified black laws, its white residents shared the belief that blacks were not their equals, and the state constitution denied blacks suffrage. Although there were efforts throughout the 1840s to bring the state in line with democratic principles, white voters narrowly rejected enfranchising black males or striking the word *white* from the constitution.[60]

It was one thing for Ohio to lead the way in codifying racial codes and alleviating white fears by discouraging social integration among whites and blacks, but the true test of the Black Laws was whether the state had the power and will to enforce them. The question of whether Ohio effectively and consistently enforced its racial code is a complex one. An evaluation of its immigration clause suggests selective enforcement, although whites did not vacillate in their belief in their superiority. The immigration law required migrating blacks to record their names with county clerks, and a few surviving records show that some African Americans complied with it. The records are woefully inadequate; they provide data mostly on the physical descriptions of the registrants. These data also enable scholars to construct biographical sketches of these individuals drawn from references to their height and weight, place of origin, special skills and abilities, complexion, visible marks, and literacy. Moreover, county recorders occasionally included the testimonials of the slave owner who brought the individual to Ohio, which add variety to the biographies of these refugees.

The clerk in each county played a critical role in enforcing the immigration law. While the state constitution created the clerk's office, the court of common pleas in each county appointed the official to serve a seven-year term. Immigrating African Americans needed clearance from the clerk to obtain legal residence, and this gave him enormous power over them. The clerk was supposed to file a complete record of all civil actions, but in practice the clerks were inconsistent when registering black immigrants. Therefore, it is impossible for scholars to determine how many African American immigrants conformed to the code. The records of various county clerks provide interesting glimpses into the process and the people charged with enforcing the code.

The first entry for Greene County occurred on September 1, 1805, when Owen Davis presented Jonathan, "a Negro boy age nine years." The terse entry indicates nothing else about Jonathan. The individual making application for permanent residence in Ohio could have provided additional biographical data, but the law did not require him or her to do so. Without such data, the clerk recorded whatever he pleased. Clerk John Paul thus made the terse entry about Jonathan. Sometimes white slave owners or their agents brought blacks into Ohio and presented them as free individuals. Bennett Maxey, a white farmer from Powhatan County, Virginia, had apparently turned against slavery, even though his family held slaves. It seems that as soon as his father died, Maxey brought Looby Johnson to the office of John Paul in 1805 to free him from bondage.[61] On February 2, 1807, William Stanton brought Kinchen, Amy, and David, "three fine Negroes," before the Greene County clerk. Again, the entry adds little more about them.[62]

Frequently, blacks immigrated alone, without white sponsors. David Patterson migrated from North Carolina, where he had been a slave on a Guilford County plantation owned by John Tombleson, who emancipated him for meritorious service. Patterson had a letter signed by Tombleson and two other whites, proclaiming that "David Patterson, a freeman, hath lived in this county and is esteemed by all acquainted with him as an honest, industrious and obliging man."[63] Patterson signed the registry on September 1, 1816. The last entry for Greene County occurred in 1844, when John Perkins brought "William Thomas, a light mulatto aged about 25 years, as a free man."[64] While the 1807 statute required immigrating blacks to provide securities for a five-hundred-dollar bond, clerk John Paul did not consistently require this. John Malvin believed that the bond law in actual practice was applied to outspoken blacks, an analysis that has credence. Whenever a white or black was accused of violating Ohio law, the state or a band of white residents could, under the pretense of upholding the rule of law, demand that illegal blacks leave the state or prosecute whites for offending a state law.

While the majority of the whites who freed blacks in Ohio released their own slaves, a review of the register from Greene County suggests Bennett Maxey was unique. Maxey brought the family of Joseph and

Belinda Johnson to Ohio in 1816. Apparently, Joseph came to Ohio alone in 1815 and was followed by his wife and their six children.[65] The evidence is not conclusive on Maxey's relationship to the family. Maxey might have owned them and unilaterally freed them, or he might have helped them escape from slavery. Indeed, his name appears in the records frequently enough to make him conspicuous. Moreover, he believed that slavery limited economic opportunities for whites, and he advised whites in Virginia that by living in Ohio they could add "four fold to their property with industry and frugality."[66] Maxey also believed the future of African Americans would be brighter in Ohio.

Maxey was not alone in the opinion that Ohio offered whites greater opportunities than the slaveholding states. Edward Tiffin, Thomas Worthington, and Methodist preacher Philip Gatch all shared this philosophy, though they did not support civil rights for blacks. It was the free and fertile soil of Ohio that lured Tiffin and Worthington from Virginia in 1796. In conformity with the Ordinance of 1787, they emancipated the slaves they brought to Ohio. They all served as delegates to the Ohio Constitutional Convention in 1802. Gatch was especially critical of slaveholding, and when he wrote his family he admonished them: "Virginians were too 'accustomed' to slave labor."[67] A family working the farm in Ohio, he told them, could do the work of any gang of slaves in Virginia. Although Gatch admitted that the family would have to give up having people wait on them, he considered it a good thing. Gatch believed that whites would work up to their own potential if they did not own slaves. Success in Ohio would come only when "they had purged themselves of 'the harmful practice of trading on their fellow creatures.'"[68] Gatch was exceptional. Tiffin and Worthington did not push for immediate abolition of slavery. Nonetheless, sentiments like theirs made it unlikely that Ohio would turn to slavery.

Greene County immigration records are more extensive than those in any other jurisdiction. A few counties, such as Cuyahoga and Columbiana, were lackadaisical in enforcing the state immigration law. From 1832 to 1837, only 401 African Americans signed the county registry in Cuyahoga County. The most likely explanation for this low figure is the county's location in northeastern Ohio. No other registrations exist in the records for the years after 1837. Indeed, it is possible that such documents are lost to history. It is also likely that the county clerk did not rigidly enforce the law. Like the black immigration and registration records in other counties, these documents are equally succinct and they rarely included biographical data more extensive than that of Thornton Kinney and Jesse Burwell. Kinney, a twenty-one-year-old mulatto, was the first entry in the registry. The last entry was Burwell's, a forty-nine-year-old man with "a scar on the forehead and another above the left eye."[69]

Edward Moins, forty-seven, entered Columbiana County, in eastern Ohio, in 1807. He complied with the law to the letter by posting a five-hundred-dollar bond and securing signatures from two freeholders. His ability to raise the bond and find cosigners suggests that he was not an average nineteenth-century American of either race. Moins might have been emancipated by his owner, been hired out, or never been enslaved. Two years later, Henry Todd, fifty-two, entered the county, noting that he had saved his wages from working odd jobs as a hired-out slave and then had purchased himself and his whole family. His master allowed him to do so, he reported, because of his "conduct and industry."[70]

Slave owners frequently brought African Americans to Ohio to free them. Their explanations were clear expressions of their turning against slaveholding. Beverly Whiting represented John Lingan when he brought the slave Louis to Jefferson County in 1809. "Know all men that I Beverly Whiting by virtue of the authority of John Lingan of the county of Gloucester by power of attorney affirms that Lingan manumitted and set free from all kind of servitude whatever Negro Louis, a slave." He described Louis as being of "a black complexion," about thirty-five years of age, and about five feet seven inches tall.[71] After emancipating David in Franklinton County, Kentucky, Nathaniel Landers presented him as a freeman in Ohio. Landers posted the five-hundred-dollar bond required by state law. The clerk issued David a certificate, noting that he was "a mulatto man, formerly the property" of Landers, and from that day forward, he would "not become a charge of this county." Moreover, the entry reported that Landers and his heirs surrendered "forever" any property interest they had in David.[72]

Seff Hill brought documentation from Bourbon County, Kentucky, that proved that he had freed his slave Harry. Seff confessed that he no longer practiced the "injustice of holding in a state of slavery our fellow brethren. I do hereby emancipate and set free a black man by the name of Harry, and do for myself, my heirs," forfeit any further interest in his service.[73] The clerk of court certified the document in 1811. When James Wright of Virginia emancipated Sam, a female named Charlotte, and three other slaves—Ben, Milly, and Jane, possibly the children of Sam and Charlotte—Wright explained that he had turned against the institution of slavery and had set the slaves free, "being convinced in my own judgment that it is contrary to the principle of Christianity to hold our fellow creatures in bondage or slavery."[74] Wright also absolved his heirs of further interest in the slaves he manumitted. He insisted that the slaves were not hired-out servants in Ohio and that he expected them to work for their own benefit. The clerk in Ross County approved their residence in Ohio, effective in 1814.

Frederick Bonner also had a change of heart regarding slavery. He acted after the Virginia General Assembly had passed "An act to authorize the manumission of slaves" in 1782, authorizing slave owners to unilaterally emancipate slaves. "Whereas Almighty God hath so ordered human events that liberty has become a general topic—I Frederick Bonner of Dinwiddie County from clear conviction of the injustice of depriving my fellow creatures of their natural right, do hereby emancipate and set free from a state of slavery the following Negroes, namely Sam, Lelia and Lucy."[75] Bonner documented their free status in Greene County in 1816.

The Black Laws did not exclude unofficial documentation for residency. Blacks sometimes appeared in Ohio with questionable records. John Freeman and his wife, Nancy, faced such a dilemma in 1809, when their official papers were supposedly destroyed in a fire in Virginia. Upon relocating to Ohio, they persuaded white Virginians to write letters to attest to their free status. Said one, "This is to certify that John and Nancy Freeman have traveled from the state of Maryland to the state of Virginia. [They have] behaved themselves very well. Their paper as a certificate of freedom was burnt after falling in a fire." John and Nancy presented the statement in Ohio in 1813, and the Ross County clerk registered them as "free people."[76] John Littleton faced a similar problem when he came to Ohio armed with only a poorly spelled statement that affirmed his free status. It was enough to satisfy the clerk in Ross County, who entered Littleton's name in 1818. Certainly it was impossible to determine if the statement was authentic. Scholars can conclude only that the success of blacks in seeking freedom in Ohio was frequently dependent on the county clerk. In these matters, the clerk had the power of a judge; he held the absolute authority to declare free any person who came before his court.

The Ohio constitution included an indentured servant provision, which authorized residents to hold blacks as servants until they were twenty-one, if male, and eighteen if female. These servants could be held for longer periods, providing they "enter into such indenture while in a state of perfect freedom," and were paid for their labor. Moreover, such servants could be licensed to work outside Ohio for up to one year, and for longer periods under apprenticeships.[77] Under the indentured servitude and apprenticeship practices, whites could legally gain authority over black children for many years. Nicholas Cox and John France, overseers of the poor in Ross County, approved the application of Benjamin Harris, a white resident of Ohio, for the services of William Brown, a thirteen-year-old "Negro boy." Justice of the Peace Joseph Gardner conducted the hearing and certified the contract, basing his decision on his belief that William would be destitute without such an arrangement. Benjamin Hardyson faced the same fate in 1811, when he was bound out to Thomas McNeil. This agreement, the Ross County clerk noted, conformed to "our act entitled 'an act regulating black and mulatto persons.'"[78] Also in Ross County, Sam, "a poor boy of color" about fifteen years old, was apprenticed in a poultry factory and would be given instructions in English. At eleven years of age, Esther Smith was made the indentured servant of Richard Barrett "to be taught the occupation of common housework." At eight years of age, Amanda Ann, "a girl of color," was bound to Joel Brown for the same purpose. Three-year-old Edmond Mathes was bound to William Scott and William Murphy "to be taught the occupation of farming." James Carter, two years old, was bound to James Young. Similar arrangements were made in other parts of Ohio.[79]

The residency and indenture records in Ohio show that some African Americans and slave owners complied with the law governing black immigration to Ohio. However, few records reveal more than the foregoing sketches. Some black immigrants were skilled craftsmen; some were veterans of the Revolutionary War; some were born free or were freed by their owners. They came alone, in pairs, or as families. Sometimes they presented authentic manumission papers and entered their names before county clerks; on other occasions, slave owners or their agents presented blacks to the clerks. More than III pages in the *Emancipation of Negroes* registry for Ross, Clinton, Logan, and Highland counties show that immigrating African Americans filed their names with the clerks.[80]

As the African American population swelled during the 1830s, Ohio whites became increasingly worried about the possible social integration of blacks with whites. The Black Laws established that the races could not work, be educated, or pursue justice under the same circumstances. The Black Laws fostered segregation in Ohio, even though the state did not officially use the term. To reinforce their assumed superiority, Ohio whites also portrayed blacks in negative ways, asserting, "Evils might arise by the introduction of such a class of people so degraded and debased."[81] The vast majority of Ohio whites had come from the South, where they had eschewed social contact with blacks. As we have seen, southern-born whites in Ohio typically embraced the mores of the region they came from. With most of them living in southern Ohio, they established a southern enclave in a region that did not allow slaveholding. Former southerners virtually ran Ohio—dominating the legislature, codifying the black laws, operating many Ohio newspapers, and setting the tone for the rest of the community.[82] The *Painesville Telegraph* stated, "If the black race continues to increase among us as it has done for the past few years, there will hardly be room for us."[83] Notions such as these infected the Buckeye State with a tone that was hostile to black rights, especially in communities that bordered the slave states across the Ohio River.

Many Ohioans also criticized slave owners from other states for emancipating blacks in Ohio. They charged that slave owners had benefited from the labor of their chattels and then purposely set them free in Ohio to be at the public charge. Ohio officials charged slave owners with using the state as a "dumping-ground" for diseased and disabled blacks who were no longer productive.[84] Indeed, Ohio correctly surmised that slave owners did not want to support aged or sick slaves, but these were only a small number of the individuals who came to Ohio. Ohio stood a greater chance of receiving healthy African Americans who had been manumitted for various reasons. After 1806 Virginia sometimes compelled emancipated blacks to leave within a year or face reenslavement. Thomas Beaufort brought forty slaves to Ohio to free them because doing so in

Virginia might have again resulted in their enslavement. Samuel Gist left Virginia for the same reason; he brought nine hundred slaves with the intention of establishing a black community in Ohio with schools, churches, and farms. An ambitious effort, the enterprise failed miserably, primarily because Gist had been swindled by real estate brokers who sold him cheap but infertile land. A North Carolina Quaker freed sixty-four slaves in Ohio after turning away from the holding of human beings as property.[85] Undoubtedly, Ohio faced the prospect of a growing black population, and since many of its migrants came primarily from slaveholding states, the vast majority of Ohio whites simply did not want to live among African Americans.

Sometimes Ohio whites suggested that African Americans preferred slavery to freedom. They were quick to point to the failure of the Gist experiment as an illustration. Certainly unemployed refugees were frequently disillusioned following their emancipation and were fearful of starting a new life in Ohio. As we have seen, John Malvin, the black carpenter who could not find skilled work in Ohio, concluded that life there was comparable to Virginia. Although he had experienced a moment of unhappiness when he made the declaration, he would never voluntarily return to slavery. Moreover, after purchasing his freedom, John Parker, who was also the son of a slave owner, relocated to Cincinnati to start a new life as a freeman. Malvin, Parker, and scores of African Americans participated in the Underground Railroad, which led thousands of runaway slaves to Ohio. Those blacks that murmured of their difficulties after the Gist fiasco were not endorsing involuntary servitude, as some whites interpreted their lamentations. They were expressing their anxiety during bleak periods of adjustment in which they found themselves to be without adequate resources to tide them over until they found work. They had discovered that the free soil of Ohio beckoned to them with possibilities of liberty, but instead they faced the Black Laws. As Ohio whites discovered, neither the laws supporting racial oppression nor the ostracism of blacks or the threat of recapture of a runaway successfully deterred African Americans from crossing the border.

—

Under the fugitive slave provisions of the Black Laws of Ohio, slave owners possessed a legal right to recapture fugitives from labor in Ohio, and any person who interfered with them could be prosecuted. Despite the laws, cities in southern and central Ohio experienced consistent growth in black communities throughout the nineteenth century as a direct result of runaway slaves seeking a haven. By 1829, *Freedom's Journal,* an African American publication, reported that large numbers of American-born blacks were living productive lives in Canada.[86] Indeed, slaves courageous enough to escape were zealous and self-confident and would succeed anywhere they were given a chance. Canada was not paradise, but as one black American emigrant put it, "It is the best poor man's country that I know of."[87]

Slave owners, however, were not content to let their chattels escape without a fight, routinely tracking the fugitives or advertising for their capture. Advertisements in Ohio newspapers provide a chilling reminder of the horrors of slave life; they also offer a glimpse into the character of the African Americans who challenged their enslavement. Abolitionists chided slave owners who posted such advertisements, explaining that they found it ironic that slave owners would argue on the one hand that the slaves "couldn't take care of themselves but as soon as a slave leaves his master to take care of himself the master instantly offers from $200–$1000 to anyone who will return him. In advertising for the deluded, who are running away from their happiness, they will, of course be very exact in describing them."[88] The advertisements for runaway slaves illustrate that the "hapless slave" suddenly becomes "an intelligent fellow"—a mason, shoemaker, or "first-rate cook." When asked if slaves could care for themselves, a black man retorted that he had paid eighteen hundred dollars for his freedom; stretching out his hands, he said they had taken "care of my master in the daytime" and enabled him to earn enough money "in the night to pay for myself three times."[89]

Advertisements in Ohio papers for runaway slaves also show that a brotherhood was created among blacks in bondage that united them against an oppressive regime. Habbord Taylor placed an ad for Packolett and Joshua, who had escaped his farm, and it clearly shows that young and old black men united in their search for freedom, when ordinarily they would have been divided by age as well as different interests and responsibilities. Packolett was forty years old upon taking flight; his protégé was only nineteen.[90] Advertisements for runaway slaves also show the states from which blacks most frequently took flight. Obviously, Kentucky and Virginia, the slave states bordering Ohio, had the greatest incidence of slaves running away. But slaves escaped from further away; no slave state was immune. David Shelby of Tennessee advertised for Josh, a slave of great value to him. Josh spoke the language of at least one American Indian community. He changed his name to Jack Sweet and then assumed the identity of an interpreter for the army. Equipped with his fraudulent credentials, Josh marched across Kentucky to Ohio, unmolested by the claimant or slave catchers.[91]

Advertisements for runaway slaves during the first couple of decades after Ohio entered the Union recount many chilling stories of daring flights to freedom. Daniel had been a model slave in the nation's capital when Thomas Jones hired him out in Chillicothe. He surprised Jones when he disappeared soon after entering the state. Humphrey Jones, no known relation to Thomas, also was deluded in his belief that his slaves were content until Jerry escaped from his farm in Madison County, Kentucky. Another slave, Jacob, at twenty-two years of age, forged free papers in Virginia, then fled the plantation of Mr. A. Donnally. In 1820 an advertisement in a Cleveland newspaper for Martin and Sam indicated that they had escaped from the plantations of Edward and Jonathan Jackson in Clarksburg, Virginia. Martin was handsome and compactly built, the notice read. He had a "light black complexion," chewed tobacco, and maintained an erect posture. Sam was "very black" and had large white eyes. While Martin was quiet, Sam was talkative; Sam also had a hearty laugh. The average runaway slave carried only a two-hundred-dollar reward, but Martin and Sam, whose ages were twenty and thirty respectively, each carried a five-hundred-dollar reward when delivered to the claimant in Clarksburg, but only three hundred dollars if turned over to Ohio officials.[92]

Similar advertisements frequently popped up in Cincinnati, which borders the Kentucky cities of Covington and Newport along the Ohio River. Sandy, Ned, and Kitty fled the farm of Peter G. Voorhies of Frankfort. Apparently, Ned, a violinist and "excellent craftsman," forged the papers required in Ohio to prove their free status.[93] Thousands of others braved incredible odds in pursuit of their freedom. Mingo, Anna, Jack, Frank, Charles, Ben, John, Susan, Mary, Margaret—young and old, male and female, and mothers with infants whom they had not weaned—vanished in Ohio. By 1850 the Canadian Antislavery Society reported that more than thirty thousand American slaves had used Ohio as a springboard to Canada. Historian Betty Culpepper estimates that more than forty thousand runaway slaves traveled the "highways" of Ohio to freedom before 1860.[94] Naturally, these figures cannot be confirmed; yet they are reliable enough to determine that running away from slavery was not a rarity for many blacks and that Ohio was a popular stopover—if not final destination—on the road to freedom.

Obviously, all fugitives from labor who reached Ohio did not merely pass through. Despite the Black Laws, the black population grew consistently following statehood. The 1800 census found only 337 blacks in Ohio. By 1810 this population had grown to 1,899. The African American population had grown to 4,723 by 1820, 9,568 by 1830, and more than 25,000 by 1850.[95] Many of these new immigrants to Ohio faced poverty and illiteracy. Cincinnati herded blacks into wards such as Bucktown, East End, and Little Africa; similar ghettos could be found in other Ohio cities, such as Columbus and Dayton.[96] Whites locked African Americans out of the mainstream of society and then expertly used their impoverishment to justify their oppression and discourage further black settlement.

The Black Laws made blacks uneasy and empowered whites to randomly enforce those laws. In some ways, selective enforcement was more difficult to deal with than consistent application of the law. The Ohio General Assembly obviously viewed the Black Laws as a deterrent to African American settlement.[97] The racial codes also empowered hostile whites to use the law to drive away African American residents. When forcing African Americans out of the state, hostile whites frequently claimed that they were in the state illegally. With so many African Americans coming into the state without free papers, there were always suspects they could charge with violating the immigration law.

In 1829 a violent white mob stormed into an African American neighborhood in Cincinnati and ordered them out. Competition with black workers for jobs was an underlying factor in this specific attack on the black community. So too was white Cincinnati's ties with slave owners across the river in Kentucky. Ohio was increasingly under pressure from slave states to do more to protect slavery. Many whites feared that the state's reputation as a haven for runaway slaves would ruin their trade with the southern states.[98] Citing the state residency law, William Mills, other Cincinnati trustees, and overseers of the poor issued a proclamation on June 29 that blacks and mulattoes living in Ohio illegally would be expelled in thirty days. Moreover, the proclamation put employers on notice that the state would prosecute violators of the law. "The cooperation of the public," they said, "is expected in carrying these into full effect."[99]

Cincinnati blacks preparing to leave the city gave great thought and careful planning to their undertaking. Should they merely relocate to another city, they might face the same fate as they had in Cincinnati. Thus, black leaders organized a committee to decide a course of action. James C. Brown, James King, and Henry Archer were elected, and they petitioned Cincinnati for a brief respite from the proclamation until they could find a free jurisdiction to take them. The committee assigned Israel Lewis and Thomas Crissup to negotiate with the legislature for funds to indemnify black homeowners for their losses, which the legislature refused. After assuring the city of their intention to leave Ohio, they traveled to Canada, asking that it open its border to black American refugees, marking waves of free blacks entering Canada, which had adopted a gradual emancipation act in 1793, freeing all slaves upon reaching age twenty-five.[100] John Colborne, lieutenant governor of Upper Canada, granted American blacks a sanctuary. Disdainful of American independence, he asked the Cincinnati committee to "Tell the republicans on your side of the line, that we loyalists do not know men by their color. Should you come to us, you will be entitled to all the privileges of the rest of his majesty's subjects."[101] More than twelve hundred African Americans abandoned their homes in Cincinnati to take refuge in Canada. Back home, African Americans who did not emigrate faced angry mobs of local whites, whom abolitionists described as thugs, who stormed into their communities and ransacked their homes and businesses.[102]

Other Ohio communities also induced blacks to flee their homes in hopes of finding a foreign state that would take them in as refugees. Portsmouth was a quaint little town in Scioto County, located not far from Charleston, Virginia. Blacks there too faced the prospect of expulsion in 1830, when the overseer of the poor threatened them. On January 21, the official told whites that they were breaking the law when they hired blacks who did not hold bona fide papers. The official then ordered blacks out of Portsmouth, giving them no time to pack or determine a place of refuge. Approximately eighty African Americans left the city under duress, leaving behind their homes and personal belongings.[103] These expulsions were popular actions that enforced the immigration and residency laws of Ohio.

Blacks would be forced to leave Cincinnati and other communities on several other occasions. The justification for ousting them was usually that they lived there illegally. Another such catalyst for an expulsion from Cincinnati occurred in 1836, as reported a few decades later by Wendell Phillips Dabney, a black newspaper publisher in Cincinnati. A "colored boy had a row with a white boy, and the colored boy won the fight," Dabney wrote. Unsettled by the arrogance of a black lad who belted a white one, Cincinnati used the immigration law to drive away another group of African Americans.[104] Three years later, African Americans living in Huron County, in northern Ohio, faced the same fate. Acting solely on a rumor that a black had raped a white woman, a mob gathered to drive black residents from the state. And blacks were driven from Starke County, Ross County, and elsewhere in Ohio where they "have been frequently threatened."[105] Although many blacks left Cincinnati—possibly to join their predecessors in flight in Canada—in taking this action, the Queen City on the Ohio River merely made room for large numbers of refugees fleeing bondage in the South.

—

The state of Ohio itself would never officially enforce the immigration law by expelling illegal blacks. Yet, by their silence, state officials clearly approved the self-help measures used by whites and the acts of local officials. Government officials at the state and local levels, as well as white mobs, shared a general understanding that the Black Laws were designed to subordinate African Americans. Moreover, the evidence suggests that an array of methods were used to enforce the Black Laws and exercise the control of the state over African Americans. As Ohio resident C. H. Knight pointed out, blacks "have neither voice nor fellowship among whites in the state, and are but partially under protection of the law."[106] He reminded whites that the employment law had made it a crime for anyone to hire a black individual who did not possess a certificate of freedom. Knight even questioned whether Ohio blacks were actually free. He attributed black oppression to the natural diversity that existed between the races. Knight lamented "[s]o great an antipathy from the Americans to the free blacks as to keep the latter in a state of hopeless" existence.[107]

By 1830 there could be little doubt that Ohio was a "white man's re-public." The legislature had successfully imposed barriers on migrating blacks, barred them from militia service, required them to prove their free status on demand, and imposed a host of other measures on them. Moreover, other states replicated Ohio's policies throughout the Old Northwest.

However, there were many reasons for African Americans to hope for a better future for themselves and their families in Ohio. Although it is a paradox, the political and legal culture that created the Black Laws also created a constitutional system under which the principles for a movement against them would sprout. Ohio outlawed slavery and the legislature criminalized kidnapping, one of the most pernicious crimes carried out against blacks in the state. The vast majority of Ohio whites considered "man stealing" unconscionable and immoral. Ohio whites consistently condemned the crime, labeling it as a "trampling" on the sovereignty of the state. They were adamant in the belief that kidnapping eroded some of the core principles of an autonomous government, and they would never waver from that belief.[108]

The state would not deny all constitutional rights that blacks could rightfully claim. Ohio never questioned the legitimacy of the black press nor prohibited black education. It placed restrictions on blacks giving testimony against whites, but it opened the courts to judicial controversies involving blacks and whites. Therefore, in spite of the ghastly Black Laws, Ohio secured some citizenship rights for African Americans. It is not surprising that whites sympathetic to blacks mounted a movement to repeal the Black Laws. The attitude of Ohio whites would gradually shift from giving scant attention to the racial codes to outright revulsion for them.[109] A repeal movement would be launched against the Black Laws that would ultimately transform Ohio and topple many of the detestable provisions of those laws.

FOUR

The Battle over the Color Line

1830–1839

FOR ALMOST THREE DECADES, the Ohio General Assembly had woven a virtually seamless web of discriminatory legislation they labeled the Black Laws. By drafting these statutes, the legislature had acted on the notion that African Americans were primarily inhabitants of the state—quasi citizens with limited rights. The Ohio legislature pursued its agenda with great enthusiasm, as the racial codes illustrate. Specifically, the state subordinated African Americans and erected a legal barrier to limit immigration by requiring that migrating blacks obtain a $500 surety bond from at least two property holders within twenty days of entering the state. Furthermore, the General Assembly barred African Americans from the militia, deprived them of jury service, refused their testimony against a white litigant, excluded their children from white public schools, and withheld state welfare. Overall, the Ohio General Assembly planned a community that made life for its African American residents not only uncomfortable but also without the protection of the state.[1]

When the Ohio General Assembly enacted the Black Codes, few whites considered them incompatible with the written legacy of natural rights in America or the bill of rights in the state constitution. Whites apparently believed that discriminatory legislative acts were appropriate restrictions on a race they deemed inferior.[2] The state legislature—and whites in general—later advocated colonizing free blacks and slaves outside the United States. The General Assembly had many reasons to believe that its racial codes would be effective. However, it did not anticipate the social and political transformation that would come to Ohio in the 1830s and set the stage for a virtual civil rights revolution.

The civil rights metamorphosis of the 1830s, which ultimately led to the repeal of the Black Laws, stemmed from the rise of the abolition movement. A vociferous white minority and a new class of black leaders, some educated in Ohio, launched a petitioning drive that made it difficult for the General Assembly to ignore them. Strict enforcement of the Black Laws was unlikely in that environment, and during the 1830s the Ohio legislature began to conduct formal hearings on its racial codes. Pressed by these determined social activists, the General Assembly began to reconsider its regulation of race.[3]

In the chain of events leading to a full-fledged repeal movement against the Black Laws, the birth of the abolitionist movement in Ohio is an essential link. Without such a commitment to doing away with slavery, it is unlikely that a campaign against the Black Laws would have developed. As a few Ohio whites struggled with the contradiction between slavery and their society's free institutions, a new age was born—the first "liberal" movement to hit the United States since the American Revolution. This new social consciousness brought with it a tenderness of spirit and a desire for reform. Americans at large, and Ohioans in particular, began to look inward, focusing on personal freedoms.

An antislavery consciousness had already begun to grow in the Buckeye State before the national movement came on the scene in the 1830s. In 1815, for example, Charles Hammond, editor of the *Cincinnati Gazette,* and Benjamin Lundy, publisher of the *Genius of Universal Emancipation,* founded the Union Humane Society in Ohio. In addition to establishing the first antislavery society in Ohio, they also edited the first antislavery newspaper in the state. That same year, Charles Osborn, a Quaker abolitionist, opened an office in Mt. Pleasant, Ohio, where he began publishing the original *Philanthropist,* a newspaper dedicated to antislavery causes. Dyer Burgess soon followed and established an antislavery society in West Union. By 1817, John Rankin was using his home in Ripley, on the Ohio River, as a conduit for runaway slaves seeking freedom. In many ways, Rankin was the first true abolitionist in Ohio, and he is credited with opening the state's first station on the Underground Railroad. In 1826, sympathetic whites in Monroe County established the Aiding Abolition Society.[4]

Despite their commitment to ending slavery, however, Hammond and Osborn were not abolitionists in the tradition of those who would follow after 1830. At best, they called for increased dialogue with slave owners, collected data on slavery, and submitted grievances and memorials to the Ohio General Assembly and to Congress. They assumed that by moral persuasion they could change hearts and minds among whites. However, the two were unimaginative and unassertive, and their reticence in speaking out against slavery made them ineffective. Unable to fight slavery, they were also reluctant to attack the Black Laws.

The spiritual revival sweeping America during the 1820s ultimately transformed the budding antislavery movement.[5] By the 1820s, it was apparent to many antislavery Christians that America had drifted away from the faith. Evangelists were determined to use their faith to civilize the nation and purge it of its secular ways. The Second Great Awakening brought a revival aimed at rescuing lost souls from eternal damnation. It also shed light on other social maladies, such as alcohol abuse. Temperance societies emerged, expressing concern for impoverished families abandoned by wayward husbands. On moral grounds, many began to question slavery. In this age of reform, some Ohio whites could no longer ignore the plight of African Americans in Ohio or those enslaved in the South.

In 1833, abolitionists coordinated the energy against slavery by establishing the American Anti-Slavery Society (AASS) in Philadelphia.[6] Under the leadership of white abolitionists, including William Lloyd Garrison and Arthur and Lewis Tappan, and black reformers such as James Forten and Robert Purvis, the American Anti-Slavery Society began to demand an immediate end to slavery. The society undoubtedly benefited from the reform impulse that had been developing for almost two decades, and by the end of the 1830s it boasted a membership exceeding two hundred fifty thousand. The dawning of the new age left an impression on more than a few Ohio whites. David McBride, a newspaper editor, told Zebina Eastman, himself an editor, that he had not heard the word *abolition* in Ohio before 1830.[7] The Great Awakening immediately gave a lift to antislavery agitation, and inevitably antislavery turned many Ohio whites against the Black Laws.

The national abolition movement also gave Ohio reformers confidence in their ability—and their duty—to demand the end of slavery without delay. In 1832, James C. Ludlow established the Cincinnati "Hall of Free Discussion" to encourage unencumbered dialogue on slavery.[8] After 1833, the AASS set up state organizations throughout the North. As the goals of the Ohio Anti-Slavery Society (OAS) crystallized, it discovered new ways to talk with the state legislature and the public. Abolitionists drafted resolutions calling on the General Assembly to pressure the South into adopting gradual emancipation policies.[9] They sent orators on statewide tours to spread the news of their opposition to slavery. For example, Marius Robinson, born in Dalton, Massachusetts, had seen slavery up close while at a seminary in Maryville, Tennessee. He immediately loathed it and detested the haughtiness of the seminarians who practiced it. The young minister became an abolitionist, convinced that it was a part of God's plan for his life. As an agent of the OAS, Robinson was moved by the positive responses to his message in the North, writing his wife enthusiastically, "There are men in Greene County who will work thoroughly and efficiently themselves more on a principle and love for truth than for their own race."[10] In 1834, Thomas E. Thomas and three other students at Miami University organized a chapter of the OAS in Oxford, Ohio. Nancy Hopkins and other women formed the Canton Ladies Antislavery Society, declaring unequivocally, "We are persuaded that slavery is wrong and that it ought to be immediately abolished."[11] As 1837 began, the OAS could boast of having approximately one hundred local chapters and ten thousand members.[12]

The American Anti-Slavery Society not only quickened the pace of abolitionism, but it also galvanized its opponents. Some supporters of slavery had earlier offered colonization as a solution to the race problem in America. The roots of the colonization movement dated back to the eighteenth century, when many whites considered resolving the race question by removing blacks from the country or at least containing slavery in the South by closing federal territory to it. Thomas Jefferson was one of the first individuals seriously to consider colonization. In *Notes on the State of Virginia*, Jefferson advocated separating blacks and whites.[13] Since whites and blacks would never live in harmony, he argued, the only practical solution was to remove blacks from the country or again to close the western territory to slavery. His proposal to ban slavery in the western territory was made with racial segregation in mind, though he would have approved slavery there temporarily. The American Colonization Society, established in 1817, promoted relocating free blacks to Africa as an alternative to emancipation and permanent residence in the United States.

By the 1830s, colonization had begun to attract northern whites who wanted to end slavery yet were unwilling to consider blacks as their equals. Thinking that colonization might be the silver bullet to do "away with slavery in the United States by gradually removing all the blacks to Africa," many abolitionists started their antislavery careers as agents of the society.[14] As they eventually would learn, colonization, as conceived by slave owners, was as racist an ideology as the enslavement of human beings. Slave owners were mainly interested in removing refractory slaves or free blacks and leaving intact the existing system of slavery. For fifteen years following its inception, the American Colonization Society removed only about three thousand African Americans from the United States— out of a black population estimated at 3.5 million. Although the society established the colony of Liberia in 1822, only about thirteen thousand free blacks had made it there by 1867.[15] Simple mathematics demonstrates the impracticality of the colonization enterprise, and at no time did the society possess the ships or funds necessary to expatriate black Americans in numbers of any consequence.

Some white supporters of colonization had a genuine interest in human rights. They advocated colonization because they believed that separating the races was a means for achieving liberty and fraternity for blacks. Ohio congressman Benjamin F. Wade was among them, and he defended colonization until the Civil War. James G. Birney, one of the first abolitionists in Ohio, was an agent in the organization until he discovered that he could "no longer give to the enterprise that support and favor justly expected from all connected with it."[16] Birney decided that the colonization society was designed to remove free blacks when their "enslaved brethren" needed them most. Theodore D. Weld was also an early proponent of colonization, as was Salmon P. Chase, whom slave owners later mocked as the "Attorney General for Runaway Negroes" (though his friends considered the title a badge of honor).[17]

As popular support for colonization expanded, both the humanitarian and nonhumanitarian advocates in Ohio petitioned state and federal officials to appropriate funds to carry it out. Warren County senator Thomas Van Horn submitted one such petition to the Ohio General Assembly, encouraging legislators to put pressure on slave owners to emancipate and colonize enslaved blacks. The legislature acted on such petitions, and, starting in 1818 and for several decades thereafter, it passed a series of resolutions supporting colonization as an alternative to slavery. Governor Allen Trimble also sent one of the resolutions to the governors of Kentucky and North Carolina, urging them to consider the viability of expatriating enslaved blacks. "Persons now held in slavery," the resolve stated, "would be freed upon reaching the age of twenty-one, provided they agreed to be colonized."[18]

Even though the Black Laws circumscribed the lives of African Americans in Ohio, only a few blacks backed colonization. More often than not, those who did so hoped that racial justice lay beyond the shores of America. At various moments in the first three decades of the nineteenth century, a few Ohio blacks would assert that colonization was the only viable solution to racial persecution. The Cincinnati riot of 1829, for example, pushed many of them to wonder whether voluntary exile was not preferable to living in America under threat of random acts of violence.[19] Time and again, their doubts and despair were replaced by the conviction that they would sacrifice their lives for the cause of freedom here in America.

The vast majority of African American leaders rejected colonization because they saw it as an ill-fated scheme concocted by slave owners. All over the North during the nineteenth century, black leaders sponsored national conventions on the status of their race. In 1817, Philadelphia blacks hosted such a meeting, where they agreed that they were the descendants of American-born parents. They felt "entitled to participate in the blessings" of the "luxuriant soil" of America, which the "blood and sweat" of their ancestors had helped make prosperous. These black Americans resolved never to separate "voluntarily from the slave population in this country"; they considered enslaved blacks to be "brethren by the ties of consanguinity and of sufferings."[20] Because the majority of blacks wanted to remain in the United States, the policy of colonization faded from the national debate over slavery and what to do with free African Americans.

The emergence of the second party system in the mid-1830s led to intense political competition in Ohio. Most Democrats supported slavery in national politics and opposed black rights at the state and local level. This reflected the southern domination of the party and the slaveholding status of most Democratic presidents, such as Jefferson, Jackson, and Polk. A few Ohio Democrats—most notably Salmon P. Chase—were antislavery and favored black rights. Nationally, the Whig Party was not as aggressively proslavery as the Democrats, but it was never antislavery. However, throughout the North politicians who were moderately—or even aggressively—antislavery, such as William H. Seward in New York, Abraham Lincoln in Illinois, and Joshua Giddings in Ohio, gravitated to the Whig Party. They ended up supporting slaveholding moderates like Henry Clay and General Zachary Taylor.[21]

Ohio Whigs were divided on the issues of slavery and race but were generally more accommodating than the Democrats. However, in the 1830s and 1840s, Whig opponents of slavery and the Black Laws were a minority within their own party. Most Whigs in Ohio shared the philosophy of those who had initially codified the Black Laws, and they were hostile to any efforts to reverse them. For example, Ohio governor Duncan McArthur, a conservative Whig, advised the legislature to strengthen the state's immigration policy in 1831, following Nat Turner's bloody insurrection in Southampton, Virginia.[22] McArthur predicted that the Old Dominion would take a hard line against African Americans and would "drive many free people of color" to friendlier states. "I suggest the propriety of adopting such measures as may guard us from black immigration," he asserted.[23] The Ohio General Assembly complied by affirming the immigration policy, requiring that blacks present a bona fide certificate of freedom upon entry. The legislature also affirmed the exclusion of black children from its public schools and upheld the policies depriving black adults of the right to jury service and denying runaway slaves a jury trial.[24]

Whig supporters of equality would remain a minority in Ohio, yet their efforts to do away with slavery troubled slave owners in the southern states—especially those in Kentucky. More troubling still to them were the growing number of Ohio abolitionists. Kentucky slave owners, in response to the "Ohio problem," frequently followed runaway slaves into Ohio and placed advertisements in local newspapers for their capture. A typical advertisement posted a bounty. One slave owner offered five hundred dollars for runaway slave James C. Ludlow, if he was delivered to him in Kentucky. In 1836, Kentucky slave owners also hired thugs to sabotage the press office of the *Philanthropist* newspaper, endeavoring to silence its antislavery message. Kentucky men also targeted James G. Birney, easily the most celebrated Ohio abolitionist of the 1830s. Ironically, Birney had been one of the Kentuckians' own, having grown up in Danville. He had also been a slave owner until 1833, when he came to the realization that slavery was wrong. Birney freed the slaves in Ohio and then returned to Danville, hoping to convert others. His slaveholding neighbors drove him away, and Birney, for the sake of his family, moved to Cincinnati with his newspaper.[25]

However, Birney did not begin his career as an abolitionist. Initially, the editor had called for increased dialogue on slavery, inviting writers of every persuasion to submit articles to be published in the *Philanthropist*, both for and against slavery. Dogged by the opponents of abolitionism, he immersed himself in abolitionist culture. Ultimately, Birney helped develop in Ohio a legal strategy that would undermine support for slavery in the state. Arguing that local law had permitted slavery, Birney insisted that blacks brought into Ohio were now automatically freed by its local prohibition of slavery. Birney used the legal arguments developed in *Somerset v. Stuart* (1772) in Britain, *Commonwealth v. Aves* (1836) in Massachusetts, and *Jackson v. Bulloch* (1837) in Connecticut to refute the idea that an individual could forcibly detain a person brought into Ohio as a slave.[26] Birney would become a nationally prominent opponent of slavery, and would make a bid for the presidency on the ticket of the Liberty Party in 1840 and 1844.

Evangelist Charles G. Finney was another key figure in the development of antislavery in Ohio. Early on, Finney converted to abolitionism and through his thunderous sermons persuaded many other whites that ending slavery without delay was a Christian obligation. As Finney stated in his memoirs, "I had made up my mind on the question of slavery, and was exceedingly anxious to arouse public attention to the subject. In my prayers and preaching, I so often alluded to slavery, and denounced it, that a considerable excitement came to exist among the people."[27] Applying the concept of "higher law" against slavery, Finney argued that the practice both contradicted natural law and was contrary to the principles of the American republic.

As individuals like Finney joined the abolitionist movement, they drew other men and women of conscience to them. Mesmerized by Finney's sermons while in college in New York, Theodore D. Weld joined the cause of black liberation. He also played a leading role in the student revolt at Lane Seminary in 1834. Founded in 1829, Lane Seminary opened as a traditional theological institution in Cincinnati. Influenced by the social activism of Lyman Beecher, father of the famous author of *Uncle Tom's Cabin,* the seminary was decidedly against slavery but uncomfortable with the militancy of such immediatists as William Lloyd Garrison, the editor of the *Liberator.* Many Lane students were moved by the social consciousness associated with abolition, and they rejected tradition to join the abolition movement. Led by Theodore Weld, they left Cincinnati to establish a seminary in Oberlin, where they would freely pursue social reform including abolition and temperance.[28]

Through Weld, Finney was able to influence the abolition movement in Ohio. Weld helped shape the abolitionist philosophy of Oberlin College, and in 1834 he was a key figure in organizing the Ohio Anti-Slavery Society, which quickly established chapters throughout the state. In addition to Weld, Finney also made an impression on James Gillespie Birney. Finney, for example, helped Birney understand that natural law took precedence over the civil law that provided for slavery. Birney soon attracted like-minded professionals, especially lawyers, who could help him transform Ohio both morally and politically. John Jolliffe, a "constitutional attorney," came on board and would later have a number of famous clients, including Margaret Garner—the protagonist in a chilling fugitive slave case decided in 1856. Ephraim Brown, one of the pioneer settlers of Trumbull County, in northeastern Ohio, intuitively recognized that slavery was morally wrong, though he took no immediate action against it. On hearing Birney lecture on slavery, Brown immediately concluded, "not even the least plausible excuse . . . can be offered in favor of slavery."[29] Salmon Portland Chase was probably the most influential individual to become associated with Birney. From the first fugitive slave case he argued in 1837, Chase likely defended more runaway slaves and abolitionists than any lawyer in Ohio. Braced by talented leaders of great conviction, Birney confidently confronted slavery and called for ending it without delay. He and his associates also forced white Ohioans to consider the negative effects of the Black Laws on African Americans. As larger numbers of Ohio whites joined the cause of freedom and reform, they formed an alliance with civic-minded African Americans, many of whom were college trained.

The participation of African Americans in the reform movement in Ohio allowed them to demonstrate that it was oppression that limited the choices of others of their race. When, in 1835, Oberlin College admitted James Bradley as its first black student, he was able to interact with his white peers and sharpen their perceptions of the black experience. Following Bradley at Oberlin were George B. Vashon, William Howard Day, and John Mercer Langston, each earning a degree before 1850.[30] The faculty and students at Oberlin also formed a chapter of the state antislavery society, which helped transform the college into an antislavery and anticolonization community. Professor William Gay Ballantine lectured on this metamorphosis: "[T]here was a general consent in the institution that slavery was somehow wrong and to be got rid of."[31] This "activist culture" developing in Ohio during the decade inevitably helped launch the movement to repeal the Black Laws.

As successful as Oberlin was in training socially conscious graduates, it was not the lone Ohio institution dedicated to this cause. Ohio University, located in Athens, played a vital role in providing educational opportunity for blacks in southeast Ohio. In 1828, the university reportedly conferred a degree on only the fourth African American graduate in the country. That graduate, John Newton Templeton, was born into slavery in Alabama in 1805 and at age eight was freed upon the death of his owner. William Williamson, a Presbyterian minister and the son of the deceased slave owner, took Templeton to Ohio, where he received a classical education. Templeton enrolled at Ohio University in 1824, with the generous support of Robert Wilson, the president of the college and an abolitionist. After graduating, Templeton committed himself to black liberation as a teacher. Another student, Edward James Roye, commenced his education at Ohio University around 1832 and then transferred to Oberlin College. He later became the president of Liberia.[32]

Their contributions to the black struggle took place largely outside the state, yet these college-educated men helped demonstrate that racism and discrimination—not the lack of ability or desire—limited the potential of blacks in Ohio.

———

Schools such as Oberlin admitted a diverse group of students from various walks of life and backgrounds. Their activism played a direct role in challenging the oppressive Black Laws. James Bradley, an Oberlin student, had been a slave in Arkansas and had "bought his freedom with a great sum, which his own hands had earned." A crucible for abolitionist thought, the seminary brought theory and practice together. White students admitted to growing up in slaveholding families and then turning against slavery. In February 1834, the students officially issued a resolution "that slaves long for freedom."[33] As the students questioned slavery, they also concluded that Ohio's racial codes were inconsistent with the founding principles of the new American republic. It was inevitable, therefore, that these reformers educated in Ohio would organize a repeal movement to challenge the Black Laws.

Ohio law barred black youths from attending the same public schools as whites, but the counties were free to establish educational institutions for blacks. Moreover, private schools at every level, whether started by whites or blacks, could admit black students. By the 1830s, many Ohio blacks had access to some formal education, while Oberlin, Ohio University, and later Antioch and Wilberforce provided higher education for some blacks.[34] When the Ohio General Assembly initially had codified the Black Laws, there were approximately three hundred illiterate African American residents in Ohio. The legislature surely did not envisage an articulate African American community that would fight for equal rights. Moreover, it had appeared that most whites shared the view that Ohio was a white state; neither abolitionism nor opposition to the racial policy was on the radar in the white community. A constellation of black and white leaders did what was unimaginable—they came together in Ohio to transform the state.

The institutions in Ohio that had opened up to black students did a great deal to energize the nascent civil rights crusade. Black schools and the white colleges that admitted their graduates produced an educated leadership class that could attack the system of oppression in the state and give aid to runaway slaves and free blacks upon their reaching Ohio. Blacks like William O'Hara, Peter Clark, and John Woodson led the Ohio civil rights movement. In addition to protesting the Black Laws and showing that blacks had the capacity for higher learning, such individuals were also positioned to raise funds to resist kidnappers and slave catchers who violated state law when removing an alleged slave.

Documenting the work of O'Hara, Clark, Woodson, and other black reformers in the civil rights movement in Ohio is difficult. Those involved in the movement did not intuitively recognize their own importance to history, and they rarely kept journals or preserved their correspondences. They were ordinary men doing extraordinary things. The available evidence, though scant, does enable historians to sketch an outline of black involvement in the civil rights movement in Ohio. For example, William O'Hara financed the defense of Frank, an alleged runaway slave who needed legal counsel in 1835. Other leaders left more of a trail. Molliston Madison Clark, who was educated at Jefferson College in Delaware and at Oberlin College, wrote the *Tract on American Slavery* (1847).[35] Titus Bosfield was educated at New Athens College and had a reputation as an electrifying speaker. Charles H. Langston, a schoolteacher, was likely the first African American elected to public office in Ohio. His famous brother, John Mercer Langston, graduated from Oberlin College to become one of the first African American lawyers in the country. William Howard Day, also college educated, was the first black man to address the Ohio General Assembly. A tireless organizer, Day helped schedule state and national civil rights conventions. Journalist and publisher Peter H. Clark was a founder of the Cincinnati Colored Orphan Asylum, which provided apprenticeships and scholarships for black students into the twentieth century.[36]

These men and others like them played a vital role in creating civic and religious organizations dedicated to black causes and in raising awareness among African Americans as well as developing the infrastructure to allow them to pool their capital. They organized black farmers, barbers, maids, and many others to raise funds to establish schools.[37] Once these training centers for blacks had been established, the professional class became self-replicating. John Malvin established a school for blacks in 1831 and urged others to consider the possibility of organizing similar institutions across the state. At a state convention in Columbus in 1835,

Malvin urged the delegates to establish a statewide private school system for black youths. The convention immediately created the School Fund Society and named Molliston Madison Clark its chief fund-raiser. Soon, the society established schools in Cincinnati, Columbus, Cleveland, and Springfield. At its highest point, it could boast of funding forty private schools simultaneously. Black educators offered vocational training and apprenticeship programs. White philanthropists supported their efforts, and others, like Augustus Wattles, founded schools for black youths.[38]

After black and white social activists turned against the status quo in Ohio, the society created under the Black Laws was doomed. An important irony is that by depriving blacks of integrated education with whites, the Ohio General Assembly apparently assumed that without access to the white educational structure black residents had little chance of acquiring the tools to transform the state politically and legally. However, by making blacks responsible for finding ways to educate themselves, the legislature made them equally responsible for charting their own course and managing their own institutions.

In addition to improving the quality of black life, the growing professional class of blacks united with whites in the cause for reform in Ohio. A repeal movement aimed at toppling the Black Laws surfaced as a crusade as systematic and organized as any other campaign for social change. Its mission was to challenge the assumption of Ohio legislators that the state's racial codes were universally accepted. The School Fund Society immediately but unsuccessfully challenged the state law barring black children from state-funded schools. Through this challenge, African Americans made the important discovery that some whites in state government were ready to present arguments in the state legislature on behalf of black civil rights. State Senator Leicester King was poised to fight for equality in 1837, when the senate first considered a school bill. King made a futile effort to strike the word *white* from the bill.[39]

Even as the General Assembly held fast to the law that excluded black and mulatto children from state schools, the surprising question arose as to what constituted a white individual. Unexpectedly, the Ohio Supreme Court began to chip away the foundation of the Black Laws, though it would not void any of the statutes. The court found its first opportunity to address the question of who could legally be barred from a public school in *Williams v. Directors of School District* in 1834. In a prior case, the court had ruled that anyone "above the grade of mulatto was white," but it had not applied the opinion to public education. Ohio law had explicitly separated white and black youths, and it would be important to whites if this rule remained without modification.[40]

The *Williams* case originated in Xenia, where light-skinned children had been denied access to Greene County schools. The father, an octoroon, had married a white woman, and their children had prominent Caucasian features. Because they were visibly white, only those people in their hometown acquainted with their parentage could question their heritage. The Williams family was socially white and had freely moved in white circles.[41] They paid taxes, attended church, and assumed their children would be allowed to attend public school. But when Williams presented the children to be enrolled, the superintendent of schools, as well as others in Greene County, blocked their enrollment under the state law barring blacks and mulattoes. Williams sued, but the trial court held that the Williams children were not white and could not attend the common school in the county.[42]

Williams promptly appealed to the state supreme court. He claimed to have been accepted as white in virtually every other quarter in the county. His family lived and socialized among whites, and their tax dollars went to finance white schools. The supreme court discovered that the legislature had not made provisions for residents who looked white. Justice Ebenezer Lane wrote the opinion criticizing Greene County officials for taxing Williams yet barring his children from the public schools. They had "the shabby meanness to ask from him his contribution of tax, and exclude his children from the benefit of the common schools he helped to support."[43] To protect Williams, the supreme court defined a white person as anyone with a preponderance of Caucasian blood, making the percentage of blood, not complexion, the standard. A strict construction of the law would have barred too many residents of mixed heritage from enjoying the privileges of being white, the court said.[44]

The supreme court did not strike down the public education law, which had banned blacks from the common schools. It explained that the common schools of Ohio were open to white children only. The court addressed only the question of race, concluding that if visibly white, the Williams children were "entitled to the privileges of whites." Justice Lane was obviously concerned about defining "whiteness," and he rejected that anyone with a hint of African ancestry was black. He believed such criteria "might exclude many children not intended to be excluded by the legislature." He offered a legal definition of "white," ruling that any individual with overwhelmingly white features was white in the eyes of the law.[45]

One might question whether the admittance of mixed-race children to white schools in Ohio was a step toward integration. However, it was certain that whiteness granted privileges, while blackness conferred a disability before the law. The decision highlighted the assumption of the legislature that "black inferiority" justified the Black Laws. Black life in Ohio had begun to undermine this view. If the Williams children—with some black blood—were worthy of the benefits of citizenship rights, was it not reasonable to extend the argument that other children in the same family, but of darker hue, should also not be excluded? It was a question the Ohio court would not answer immediately, but the prospect of mixed schools turned the black inferiority argument upside down. Civil rights reformers quickly attacked the very assumption of black inferiority, and they combed the state for new evidence to support their arguments against the Black Laws.

By the 1830s, Ohio reformers had begun to dispute the assertion that African Americans were inferior, and they produced evidence that blacks were making stunning progress in spite of the racial codes that restrained them. African American populations flourished in Ohio's urban centers, especially in Columbus and Cincinnati. The construction of the National Road, canals along Lake Erie, and other improvements in transportation had made these cities more accessible to free blacks and runaway slaves. In Cleveland, the black population grew gradually, from 106 in 1820 to 224 by 1850. In the next decade blacks poured into the city and the population increased to approximately 800. Columbus witnessed a more rapid growth in the population of blacks, increasing from only 63 individuals in 1820 to approximately 1,300 by 1850. Cincinnati, on the Ohio River, had the greatest number of African Americans in Ohio, boasting a black population of 1,090 in 1830, and 3,172 in 1850.[46]

Not only did African Americans become more visible in Ohio, but they began to transform its cities. Blacks in trades such as barbering, carpentry, and masonry were able to use their income in cooperative business ventures. Black investors funded the Iron Chest Company and various steamboat companies, and they owned the Dumas House Hotel in Cincinnati.[47] These free and prosperous blacks were positioned to help runaway slaves in various ways: finding them work, lodging, or a temporary hiding place. They shielded runaway slaves when slave catchers were in hot pursuit—pointing them to Underground Railroad stations, helping them cover their tracks and change their names, and coaching them on how to conduct themselves as free persons. Moreover, urban blacks and whites forged alliances for the cause of freedom and civil rights reform. James Poindexter, who had escaped from Kentucky in 1828, joined such white individuals as James E. Coulter and Samuel H. Smith to direct runaway slaves to safety and improve the quality of life for free blacks.[48]

By the 1830s, many white abolitionists were ready to conclude that only the racial codes of Ohio would limit the progress of African Americans. Given an opportunity, they believed that blacks would become as productive as any other citizen, as many had already done. While on a speaking tour through Ohio, Marius Robinson exhorted whites to remain open to the idea of allowing blacks to enter the mainstream of society. "This is the only way the colored man can [succeed]—we must give him a chance."[49] Ever since its organization in Ohio, the state antislavery society had doubled as a political action committee, calling for abolishing the Black Laws as well as for ending slavery. The society formally launched a campaign to present evidence of black achievement to government leaders, hoping that this information would persuade the legislature to repeal the Black Laws.

In the 1830s, the OAS began sending out investigators to interview blacks in order to collect data on their economic and social progress. It issued a report in 1838 extolling black achievements in a number of Ohio cities. Blacks did not burden the state—as some whites had feared— the OAS reported. On the contrary, blacks had entered various trades and professions. The state antislavery society documented sixteen artisans in Columbus alone, working in such trades as masonry, painting, and shoemaking. It offered statistics on successful black farmers. It documented at least twenty-three black farmers in the capital city who owned, in the aggregate, land valued at more than fourteen thousand dollars. These residents had used their resources well, the society reported, and financed a variety of social and religious causes. They had established at least one church and operated a school that provided training for more than seventy students. Furthermore, they had formed civic organizations such as the Young Men's Union Society, founded in 1839. Blacks continued to establish self-help organizations for decades to come, including local chapters of the Odd Fellows in 1842 and the Masons in 1855, and the Ohio Militia Company in 1858. To better talk to the community, blacks started newspapers, including Cleveland's *Aliened American*.[50]

The society investigators who had been sent to Columbiana County found a sparsely populated community of blacks, primarily because of the county's location in eastern Ohio. Founded mostly by Quakers in 1806, Salem, the county seat, had quickly become an abolitionist community. It was the headquarters of the Western Anti-Slavery Society, which published the *Anti-Slavery Bugle*. Its population, approximately one thousand by 1839, included some three hundred African Americans, and Salem was also a vital link on the Underground Railroad. Salem hosted prominent abolitionist speakers, including Frederick Douglass, William Lloyd Garrison, and Wendell Phillips.[51]

The black community in Salem had started as a colony of former slaves. By 1830, the community had grown to nearly thirty families. African Americans made a stake in the city by establishing businesses and purchasing land. Black farmers held more than two thousand total acres, with an estimated value of more than thirty thousand dollars. Black farmers also owned livestock valued at approximately five thousand dollars. They used their resources wisely and established a school, a church, and a temperance society. The society's report identified their leaders, citing such individuals as Jacob Heaten, Benjamin B. Stanton, and Samuel C. Prescott as an "intelligent group" of civic and professional men.[52]

African Americans enjoyed similar successes in Guernsey County. Among the black mechanics and farmers living there was Charles McFeeters, a blacksmith. Ezekiel Lewis, a farmer, owned approximately 200 acres of land. Another, Thornton Alexander, had 520 acres. James Clemens owned 790 acres. Alexander, a slave until he was thirty years old, came to Ohio with only five dollars to his name. Isaac Holland fled slavery in Virginia with only a knapsack, yet he built up an impressive farm and saved enough money to purchase his entire family.[53] African Americans in Pickaway County were also growing in numbers, from slightly more than one hundred in 1820 to more than four hundred by 1839.[54] Neither the immigration law nor the state and federal fugitive slave laws had been successful in keeping blacks out of even some more remote areas of Ohio.

In addition to presenting documentation on the progress of black communities, the society also singled out a few blacks in such cities as Cincinnati and Cleveland to use as role models. The OAS reported that George Peak had received a patent for inventing a "new type of hand mill that facilitated the production of meal from grain." Alfred Greenbrier bred horses; Madison Tilly built up an excavation business and employed an integrated work force. Robert Boyd Leach, a graduate of the Western Reserve Homeopathic College, was a physician in Cleveland. His private residence, wrote historian Lenwood Davis, contained "all the pleasant surroundings which well directed industry and economy usually bring with competence when directed by good taste." Robert Brown owned a successful coal business. Henry Boyd started his career in Cincinnati as a carpenter, and, after saving approximately nine thousand dollars, opened a plant manufacturing bedsteads. By 1839, he owned a patent for his design and was producing roughly a thousand bedsteads a year. Samuel T. Wilcox operated a grocery store in Cincinnati and reputedly had made a small fortune in real estate. In later years, Robert Gordon, a former slave, owned a company in Cincinnati with a net worth of nearly fifteen thousand dollars, acquired mainly from selling coal. Thomas Ball and J. Pressley ran a successful photography studio in Cincinnati. Among others listed in the report were horse traders, pickle makers, and tailors.[55] Abolitionists considered the evidence overwhelming that African Americans in Ohio had acquitted themselves very well, in spite of significant odds against their success.

The society also solicited testimony from whites, especially those in close contact with blacks. David Powell, William Robertson, and Joseph Brooks reported that their black neighbors were friendly and industrious people. Brooks condemned the Black Laws, declaring, "There is no necessity for laws distinguishing between blacks and whites."[56] John H. Dunn told Hiram Wilson that he considered blacks to be loyal and honest people.[57] From his contact with blacks, it did not appear that they tended to commit more crimes than whites. This is the conclusion the society hoped to impress on many other whites: only the Black Laws separated the races. In a free society, the OAS anticipated that many blacks would follow the examples of those in its report. The society intended to show that blacks had become responsible citizens and to counter the white assumption that African Americans would become dependent on the state. Though the society was not naive, it also hoped that its findings would remove "false impressions from the minds of our legislators."

———

While the civil rights movement, including the cooperative efforts of blacks and whites against the Black Laws, was gaining momentum in Ohio, the fugitive slave debate rose to prominence there as well. Indeed, the fugitive slave question had bedeviled the United States ever since it had adopted the Northwest Ordinance of 1787, with its clause providing for the removal of runaway slaves. The federal Constitution also included a fugitive slave clause indicating that a slave owner had the right to remove an individual who had escaped from labor. The young republic had also affirmed the right of recapture in a 1793 law, providing that runaway slaves were subject to removal upon a claim by their lawful owner.[58] Therefore, when Ohio entered the Union in 1803, federal law had already established several guidelines covering the removal of fugitives from labor. Essentially, an owner needed to verify his claim with a judge, magistrate, or justice of the peace, who would then grant a license for removing the slave; any person who interfered with the process was subject to a fine or imprisonment. The right of slave owners to recapture runaways was settled law, and Ohio leaders initially intended to enforce those laws to the letter.

The Ohio General Assembly considered the fugitive slave matter in 1804, when it passed the act to regulate black and mulatto persons. There was no immediate catalyst for the legislation other than the belief of many Ohio legislators that problems would surface without state laws to govern the process. The statute regulating blacks and mulattoes thus made it a crime for anyone to harbor a fugitive or hinder an owner from recapturing a fugitive from labor.[59]

Before the 1830s, there had been little controversy in Ohio regarding recapture. Most early applications to remove fugitives from labor in Ohio were successful; free African Americans were often at risk. The state policy underwent a transformation during the 1830s, sparked by several factors. Abolitionists objected to recapture, arguing that state sovereignty did not require the enforcement of federal fugitive slave legislation. Those advocating the repeal of the Black Laws also argued that recapture violated the civil rights of all blacks because of the possibility of any person of color falling victim to kidnapping. Moreover, unscrupulous slave catchers raised the ire of most whites when they targeted mixed-race individuals whose light complexions brought higher profits. These "man stealers" did not respect the rule of law, some whites asserted, and their conduct increasingly made kidnapping an important topic of discussion.[60] In response to the illegal abduction of whites, the Ohio legislature passed an act to prescribe penalties for anyone who removed "any white person or persons" from the state. Upon conviction, a defendant would be liable for court costs, as well as imprisonment in the state penitentiary for three to five years.[61] The idea of white slavery, though a minor occurrence, troubled many residents.

White slavery, no matter how rare, was a consequence the Ohio General Assembly did not anticipate when it enacted its first comprehensive racial code in 1804. The legislature obviously assumed that only bona fide slave owners would lay claim to actual slaves who had escaped to Ohio. Theoretically, someone who had removed a person contrary to law would have been punished under existing state law. However, most of the courts that considered the civil rights of its black residents were bent on securing the property interests of slave owners. State officials never imagined that the policy would have a negative impact on whites. By the 1830s, however, newspapers reported that white children were being removed as slaves. State officials now realized that hardly anyone, especially a female, with a hint of African blood was safe. As the *Philanthropist* reported, "the whiter the slave, especially if a female, the more extravagant the price and the more desirable the victim." Another correspondent stated, "If slavery endures, poor white children, as well as the colored, will soon become the victims of its hopeless horrors."[62] This was a chilling thought for most people whom the law considered white, especially those of a darker hue.

Ohio residents with African features were especially vulnerable, regardless of their free status. Riverside cities and towns scattered along the Ohio increased the likelihood of wrongful seizure. Men from Virginia and Kentucky preyed on blacks in border towns. Ohio abolitionists were gravely concerned about this geographic factor, claiming that these men made their state a hunting ground for human prey. The state employment law also exposed blacks to danger. The employment law required whites to hire only blacks who provided proof of their freedom. This law's impact on blacks could be devastating. Unable to find work, impoverished blacks frequently became the targets of traps set by kidnappers who advertised jobs. These so-called professionals would enter a city pretending to be in need of help transporting goods to, or near, Kentucky or Virginia. They would lure their unsuspecting targets away from the city where the black person was known, then, after subduing them, the kidnappers would carry their prey across the Ohio River to be sold as a slave. Other kidnappers, pretending to be in Ohio on a holiday, as a correspondent for the *Philanthropist* described, would "hire a colored boy or man to assist him in bringing horses to Cincinnati" only to abduct him.[63]

Because of these outrages, many whites began to realize that the state and federal fugitive slave policies were flawed. The Ohio legislature thus began to modify its laws, presumably to shield mixed-race individuals from kidnapping. In addition, state legislators began to understand kidnapping as a violation of the sovereign laws of Ohio. Some whites who had been on the fringe of abolition turned toward securing Ohio from kidnappers. They also accused slave catchers of trampling on Ohio laws, contending that state and federal policy required that a slave owner obtain prior approval before removing someone as a slave. While they recognized that federal and state law approved the recapture of slaves, they deplored such tactics as trickery and fraud. Abolitionist James Birney told federal Judge Joshua Leavitt that the wrongful removal of alleged slaves had become epidemic throughout Ohio: "Scores of unsuspecting colored people, born free, are annually spirited away from Ohio and sold into slavery in the South."[64] Ohio residents disapproved of the use of such chicanery in accomplishing recapture.

A series of kidnapping episodes during the 1830s aptly illustrate that free blacks were at risk in Ohio and that both kidnappers and unscrupulous slave catchers had become enormously skilled at this cat-and-mouse game. The best sources that document kidnappings are newspapers and abolitionist writings. An abolitionist tract tells the story of Thomas Mitchell, who came to Dayton during the late 1820s and for several years lived there as a freeman. He worked on the Miami Canal project and probably lived in "Africa," a black settlement on the city's east side. He was highly regarded as an industrious individual, and whites took an interest in his arrest as a fugitive in 1832. J. W. Deinkard identified Thomas Mitchell as Benjamin, a fugitive from labor. Deinkard initially observed state procedures for removing a runaway slave, but he did so only for convenience. He assumed he could dupe the state into approving his removal request. His plan, however, backfired.

The official reviewing the case initially considered the evidence against Mitchell insufficient and ordered his release. However, on presenting new evidence, Deinkard obtained the certificate he sought. Sympathetic whites joined in support of Mitchell and raised money to purchase his freedom, which Deinkard refused to grant. Mitchell was escorted to Kentucky under armed guard. For reasons unknown, Deinkard brazenly stopped in Cincinnati and took up lodging in the Main Street Hotel before crossing the river into Kentucky. Now desperate, Mitchell took matters into his own hands, leaping from a fourth-floor window to his death.[65]

Mitchell's sad tale is just one example of the many runaway slaves who never made it safely to permanent freedom. Another incident that outraged many Ohio residents occurred in 1836, when kidnappers conspired to remove any free black they came upon. They made a pact with a Kentucky jailer, who agreed to open the jail as a holding cell. They seized a mulatto boy and removed him without detection. Returning to Cincinnati, they searched for other prey whom they could easily control. Meanwhile, the jailer turned against them and alerted Kentucky officials to the conspiracy.[66] Why this jailer took an interest in the case is unknown. He might have suddenly had a crisis of conscience. It is also possible that he sympathized with the mulatto prisoner, whose complexion was close to his own. What is known is that the jailer aborted the seizure. Kentucky officials, taking the high ground, immediately ordered the release of the victim. Newspaper accounts also indicate that the men faced prosecution, but there is no record of such a trial. Apparently, whatever public indignation was associated with the case disappeared once the victim was freed.

Young black males were especially vulnerable to being abducted—possibly because it was natural for a teenager to be reckless, believing that such a thing could not happen to him. Samuel Devall, age seventeen, was apparently a typical teenager in some ways, and he evidently felt invincible. In other ways he was not representative of the majority of young black men growing up in America. He was born free in Brownsville, Pennsylvania, in a family many whites regarded as respectable. They raised Devall to be industrious and independent, and, as a young man without impediments or entanglements, he left home to make his mark on the world. His parents had undoubtedly warned him of the dangers facing black people.

In 1836, Devall boarded the *London,* a passenger ship originating near Pittsburgh and traveling south on the Ohio River to Cincinnati. Due to low water on the Cincinnati side of the river, the captain piloted the vessel to Newport, on the Kentucky side. Devall had made a series of errors. Among them, he did not have his free papers and had taken no precautions to secure his liberty on landing in Kentucky. Once the vessel docked at the harbor, he went onto the landing, where a gang of white men promptly seized him as a runaway and removed him from the city. The crew took notice of the abduction but reported it too late to save him.[67] Samuel Devall never reached Ohio, and neither angry abolitionists nor government officers had a chance to rescue him. They were better positioned to intervene on behalf of Eliza Jane Johnson, a free woman living in Cincinnati. Her abduction was an unsettling reminder of the crimes kidnappers perpetrated against free blacks. Johnson was victim to a conspiracy concocted by Arthur Fox, of Kentucky, who instructed his son to seize a servant for the family. Fox the younger considered Johnson easy prey and potentially useful in their home. He subdued her without difficulty and immediately shunted her out of town without detection. On discovering that Johnson was likely taken away as a slave, her family advised abolitionists, who complained to Ohio officials.

The incident infuriated Governor Joseph Vance, who reported the abduction to the General Assembly in 1837. A Kentucky resident, Vance told them, had removed a free woman "under the pretense that she was a fugitive from labor."[68] After Vance put Kentucky on notice of its error, its officials took the high ground, boasting that their citizens would not commit such a crime. They assumed that Johnson was a slave under state law and confidently opened an investigation to prove it. Certain of their opinion, they assured Ohio abolitionists that they would return Johnson upon finding proof that she was illegally abducted.

Meanwhile, they incarcerated Johnson pending the review. Surprisingly, Arthur Fox broke under pressure and admitted that he did not own Johnson. As they had pledged, Kentucky officials ordered her release. Abolitionists had fought the state of Kentucky and won, and they had done so with the aid of Ohio officials. Emboldened by their success, they began to see that the fight against kidnapping and the civil rights movement—the crusade against the Black Laws—were inextricably linked. Earlier in the movement, abolitionists had primarily been concerned with ending slavery—they had been learning over the years that the struggle for abolition of slavery or the monitoring of the process of removing fugitives from labor intersected with the fight for civil rights and racial justice in Ohio.

Not only were local abolitionists offended by Ohio's cordial relationship with slaveholding states, but at various times nationally known abolitionists also condemned Ohio. Frederick Douglass accused Ohio of allowing slave states to "spread blight and mildew over her legislation." Furthermore, he continued, Ohio law provided "impunity to every white ruffian who may desire to insult or plunder, who may desire to rob, or commit other outrages on her colored population—Ohio has been corrupted by slavery."[69] William Lloyd Garrison confessed that he did not care for racially conservative Cincinnati, asserting that it was soiled with "Negrophobia." The new fugitive slave law accelerated the civil rights reform movement in Ohio, and its advocates called on the legislature to repudiate the act as well as abolish its racial codes. Ohio abolitionists had finally recognized that should they desire the moral authority to denounce slavery it was imperative for them to condemn the Black Laws. Therefore, a full-fledged repeal movement was under way in Ohio.

In many ways, the Black Laws had retarded the abolitionist movement in Ohio. Working in a state steeped in its own conservative racial culture, abolitionists were naturally tentative in their denunciations of states with slave codes. Support for the Black Laws grew weaker throughout the 1830s as the repeal movement mounted a protracted attack against them. Ohio social reformers also discovered new weapons to use in the fight for civil rights reform. They learned that filing petitions with the General Assembly was an effective way to generate discussions with legislators about the pernicious racial codes of the state.[70] While petitioning had been a strategy of radical groups in America since colonial times, it had been limited among social reformers in the early nineteenth century. Indeed, it had been used against slavery, but the abolitionists evidently caught the Ohio General Assembly by surprise. As the *Philanthropist* reported, "Petitioning is one of our surest and most efficient modes of agitation."[71] And petitioning quickly became one of their most useful weapons.

Indeed, the civil rights movement in Ohio overlapped with and benefited from the efforts of other social groups that were calling for various reforms, such as temperance and the Second Great Awakening. The Second Great Awakening was very much in the forefront of these pleas for social change. Charles G. Finney, Theodore Weld, and many others called upon people to embrace faith. In their evangelistic appeals they also exhorted Christians to take a stand for social change, and not merely religious revival. As one of the fastest-growing states in the Union, Ohio attracted various religious organizations and faiths that became dedicated to social reform. Indeed, it had a higher proportion of religious orders than any other state at this time. Various Christian denominations could be found there. Presbyterians and Methodists were the largest, followed by Episcopalians, Lutherans, and Catholics. Large numbers of Quakers were in Ohio, and they led the way in carrying the message of equality to the Ohio legislature.

While some members of the Society of Friends had once been slave owners, the Quakers had turned against involuntary servitude, and many had left the South precisely because of its slaveholding culture. Having rejected slavery, Quakers turned to philanthropy, including funding educational programs for blacks. The society also formed strong links in the emerging Underground Railroad. And Quakers were among the first religious order to send petitions to the legislature, urging them to repeal the Black Laws.[72] The first known petition sent to the Ohio General Assembly was submitted in 1829, when Ohio Quakers condemned the Black Laws as "pre-eminently cruel, impious and disgraceful."[73] The Society of Friends urged the legislature to abolish the laws because they operated "oppressively on our colored population."[74] They would continue their opposition until the General Assembly repealed the Black Laws. The Ohio Anti-Slavery Society formally launched its petition drive in the early 1830s, challenging the state legislature to repeal the Black Laws.

With the Black Laws in place, the OAS argued, "the unprotected condition of our colored inhabitants" left them vulnerable to whites who would abuse them. The society argued that color was not a crime, that blacks were human beings, and that the Black Laws generally degraded Ohio society as a whole. In addition to its contentions that the Black Laws were unjust, the society asked "that all those statutes which discriminate between men, on account of color, be immediately repealed." The Ohio house responded to the petition in 1835, in a report given by the committee on the judiciary. After a lengthy review of state history and the motivation of the lawmakers who had drafted the Black Laws, the committee took a stand against repeal, stating that it "is inexpedient . . . to take any legislative action on the subject."[75] The committee feared that a reversal of the Black Laws would entice even more free blacks and runaway slaves to immigrate to Ohio; it also decided that the majority of whites would not accept blacks on terms of equality.

Not surprisingly, black Ohioans took a keen interest in the petitioning strategy. African Americans had sent their first known petition to the Ohio Constitutional Convention of 1802, only to have it ignored. The delegates considered blacks to be noncitizens and to exist outside the political spectrum, and thus they gave little thought to their concerns. Also in the 1830s, the African Methodist Episcopal (AME) Church in Cincinnati began using the petitioning strategy to address civil rights with the legislature. However, the discussion divided not only the church and the city but also whites and blacks. Some African Americans worried that the quest for civil rights might backfire. Conservative whites advised that African Americans should avoid such a radical course. Undeterred, the leadership of the AME Church went on record to insist on repealing the Black Laws. However, the Methodist Episcopal Church (the church from which Richard Allen broke away when he established the AME Church) in Cincinnati, another black congregation, feared a white backlash and thus sent a conciliatory resolution to the legislature, assuring them that their congregation was not a part "of that indefinite number that are asking a change in the laws of Ohio."[76] They wanted to live in peace, they assured city leaders, and were content with enjoying the kindness whites willingly gave them.

Certainly there were representatives who believed that blacks did not have a right to petition the General Assembly. But, as the AME Church would discover, there were also lawmakers who would enthusiastically deliver petitions on their behalf. Some of the most prominent lawmakers to submit repeal petitions for blacks included future governor Thomas Corwin, U.S. senator Benjamin F. Wade, and lesser lights such as Leverett Johnson and Joseph Kyle, both abolitionist lawmakers. In addition, Representative Jonathan W. Andrews read a petition from blacks in Franklin County in 1832 demanding the repeal of all laws that made distinctions based on color. Abraham Hegler presented a similar petition from Chillicothe blacks. Elihu Johnson joined them and presented a petition specifically asking legislators to repeal the testimony law. The statute made blacks vulnerable to violence, he told the General Assembly, and made it unlikely that a black plaintiff would get justice in a judicial action involving a white. The legislature, however, was not in the mood to act favorably on these petitions. As early as 1828, antiblack representatives were taking steps to strengthen the Black Laws, urging the General Assembly to adopt measures to prevent black migration to Ohio.[77]

African American involvement in petitioning gained an important boost in 1839, when Whig leader Thomas Corwin submitted a repeal petition on behalf of disenfranchised blacks in his district. His involvement alarmed the conservative majority in the legislature, who now argued that by reading such petitions Corwin was actually endorsing the idea that blacks had citizenship rights. Representatives James Hughes and Jonathan M. Jenkins, both Democrats, argued that reviewing petitions submitted by blacks was a gross waste of time. Democratic representative George H. Flood, of Licking County, agreed, urging the house to postpone Corwin's petition indefinitely. He also offered resolutions against further discussions on the repeal issue and abolitionism, asserting that Ohio law did not give blacks a right of petition. Instead, Flood and Jenkins proposed a bill to reject every petition submitted by an African American or by others on their behalf. Ultimately, Representatives Flood and Jenkins won the day, when the legislature concluded that it was inappropriate to entertain the petitions of black residents because it might imply that the legislature recognized black citizenship.[78]

This victory secured, Flood offered a resolution that would deny any rights to blacks implied by the legislative review of the petitions blacks had submitted previously. Flood's resolution asserted that black and mulatto residents of Ohio had no constitutional right to present petitions to the General Assembly for any purpose whatsoever. Moreover, the declaration suggested that any review of such petitions by the General Assembly was an act of privilege and not a duty imposed on the legislature by any expressed or implied power of the constitution. Affirming the Black Laws, he stated that it "is unwise, impolitic and inexpedient to repeal any law now in force, imposing disabilities upon black and mulatto persons."[79] He defined blacks as residents, rather than citizens, of the state of Ohio. He argued that blacks did not possess any of the constitutional rights that whites were granted or that the law recognized. Flood's colleagues apparently agreed with him in principle, but they did not codify his proposal in terms more explicit than those already in the Black Laws.[80] Legislators could have merely seen the resolution as an unnecessary redundancy, or they might have considered the Flood resolution too draconian for a free state to publish. It soon became obvious that, by turning away black petitioners, the legislature had unwittingly given white reformers greater motivation to push for civil rights for blacks.

The Ohio Anti-Slavery Society and other informal associations pressed for the repeal of the Black Laws. Although founded to oppose slavery, the state's antislavery society could not ignore civil rights issues, which had become inextricably linked to slavery and its consequences. As a policy matter, the society could not in good conscience fight against slavery without carrying on the fight against the Black Laws. The OAS thus argued that the Black Laws were inconsistent with the free laws of Ohio. The society disputed assertions that the racial codes were designed to deter black immigration to Ohio, arguing that they had a deleterious effect on the life of all black people in the state. In a report written in 1835, the society explained that the Black Laws "prevented or restricted the education of the people of color" and that they were "pre-eminently cruel, impious and disgraceful." Remaining true to abolition, the society declared that, by elevating black life in Ohio, it would simultaneously be taking a positive step toward eliminating slavery in the United States. Theodore Weld, one of the society's important leaders, exclaimed that repealing the Black Laws would help "effect the destruction of slavery."[81]

As antislavery voters elected more Whig politicians to state office, the call for social reform in Ohio grew louder. Of course, the Whig Party itself was not united on this issue. But by the mid-1830s, a number of

Whigs had determined that ending slavery and doing away with the Black Laws were at the top of their agenda. John A. Foot, a Whig politician from Cuyahoga County, owed much of his political success to abolitionist voters in the Western Reserve. He was genuinely committed to abolitionist ideals and did not support reform merely for political expediency. In 1833, Foot had helped organize the Cleveland chapter of the OAS. Indeed, his commitment to social change served him well, and upon his election to the Ohio house, he served as the floor leader for civil rights causes. Presenting repeal petitions was one task he accepted with great enthusiasm, and in 1838 he submitted one such petition signed by almost four thousand voters. The petitioners asserted that for some reason the founders of Ohio had not written extensive provisions in the constitution to oppress blacks. In fact, they argued, the state constitution had initially protected the rights of all its citizens. They pointed out that the bill of rights, Article VII of the state constitution, secured equality for all men, black and white. All men are "born equally free and independent," it declared, "and have certain natural, inherent and unalienable rights." The General Assembly, they surmised, was wrong when it adopted the Black Laws. In doing so, it had restricted the natural rights of its African American residents without constitutional sanction.[82] The petition, like many of the others, thrust the General Assembly into debate but fell short of a revision of the racial codes of Ohio.

Legislative measures as well as petitions submitted by private citizens continued to reach the Ohio General Assembly. Benjamin Wade, a leading antislavery advocate in Ohio, introduced a bill calling "for the immediate repeal of all laws in the State which make any distinctions among its inhabitants on account of color."[83] Wade asked specifically that the legislature secure the right of blacks to be tried by a jury of their peers. Another petition, submitted by Samuel Hopper and eighty-five residents in Jefferson and Belmont counties, joined Wade in urging the legislature to repeal the Black Laws and to protect African American citizenship. Following these initiatives, Mary Wildman and Samaria T. Robinson collected more than a hundred signatures from Ohio women who demanded the unconditional repeal of the Black Laws. They simultaneously urged Ohio lawmakers to send a resolution to Congress urging it to outlaw slavery in the nation's capital and to bar its extension into federal territories.[84]

The majority of members of the Ohio General Assembly, of either party, did not immediately take the repeal movement seriously. Conversely, they could not easily dismiss it. In time, the petitioners would prevail—to a certain extent—as the legislature gradually came to see the act of petitioning as a federal right, one that it could not reasonably deny its citizens. Civil rights reformers kept up the pressure, and the General Assembly actually confessed that it was receiving "numerous petitions asking for the repeal of certain laws imposing restrictions and disabilities upon persons of color." Unable to disregard these petitions any longer, the state house of representatives established special committees to review them. Their reports represent the first legislative analysis of the Black Laws, and they offer the only official explanation for their passage and survival.

The state senate also appointed a committee in 1837, charging it with reviewing the recent petitions on the Black Laws. The committee promised a thorough investigation, and pledged to set aside an "array of vindictive feelings" from supporters and opponents of the Black Laws. The committee would "proceed calmly and dispassionately," it vowed, and its members would "firmly and conscientiously discharge the duties assigned to them, under a deep sense of all their responsibilities to their fellow beings, to their country and its constitutional authority, to the immutable principles of justice and equity, and to that Supreme Being, from whom all power is derived, and to whom all moral agents are amenable."[85] The committee began its work by reviewing the brief history of petitioning, ostensibly to find the core arguments of those who submitted them. The petitioners considered the Black Laws inconsistent with the state constitution and contrary to republican government. Each petition had regarded the denial of such civil rights as trial by jury and offering testimony as a violation of the state and federal constitution. The petitioners believed the Black Laws stemmed from racial prejudice and doubted the assumption that Ohio would be in danger of promoting an explosive black population without the immigration law.[86] The committee based its report on these themes.

Following its preliminary declarations, the select committee turned to American history. It observed that every American was a rightful heir of the country's credo of life, liberty, and property. These had been among the natural rights whose defense had made the American Revolution necessary. The natural rights doctrines of the United States were not a vague "political theory" or speculative philosophy, the committee asserted. "They were inculcated as practical maxims, applicable to the condition of man, suited to the state of human society." Ohio embraced these national principles without reservation, and the new state adopted the ban against slavery in the Ordinance of 1787. The committee surmised that the ordinance had immediately abolished slavery in the territory. The committee asserted that many of the founders of the republic, northerners and southerners alike, had reservations about the survival of slavery and the continuation of racial oppression. The committee quoted James Iredell, of North Carolina, appointed to the first U.S. Supreme Court: "When the entire abolition of slavery takes place, it will be an event which must be pleasing to every generous mind and every friend of human nature." They cited representative William Pinkney's declaration to the Maryland legislature that "by the eternal principles of natural justice, no master has a right to hold his slave in bondage for a single hour."[87]

Moreover, the committee found that the United States—as well as the state of Ohio—had established policies that contemplated the inclusion of diverse peoples in the nation. It regarded the United States as an experiment, whereby it took in peoples who were different from the Anglo-Saxon founders. The committee also rejected arguments put forth by racial conservatives in Ohio, who believed that the state was not obligated to provide refuge to runaway slaves. Ohio, in the committee's opinion, was not "exempted from its responsibilities, nor absolved from the moral obligation of extending shelter and protection" to blacks. Furthermore, the committee criticized the state policies that led to the expulsion of blacks, finding that it was immoral and unethical for anyone to argue that the state "may drive blacks from our borders by acts of outlawry or subject them to a state of perpetual degradation and suffering."[88] The committee concluded that the Black Laws violated the core principles of republicanism.

As the committee examined specific provisions of the Black Laws, it also called attention to the provisions it considered most revolting. The committee singled out the laws preventing black jury service, prohibiting black testimony against whites, and limiting immigration as "repugnant to the constitution of this state, and to the principles of free institutions;

they are also in direct contravention of the Constitution of the United States." In examining the legal policies of other states, the committee found that some of them had actually extended civil rights to black Americans. "In every light in which your committee has viewed this branch of the subject referred to them, they have been impelled to the belief that these provisions in our laws should be repealed."[89] The state senate however, took no immediate action against the Black Laws. As civil rights reformers in the General Assembly later concluded, the house and senate did not take them seriously. The General Assembly had permitted the study only to placate the liberal Whigs and their reform-minded constituents. In their opinion, the majority of the assembly had assigned the committee what amounted to busywork. The study itself was the only action the senate would take on the subject.

Nevertheless, as 1837 came to an end, civil rights reformers saw petitioning as a powerful tool to put their objections to the Black Laws into the legislature's records. They urged continuation of the campaign, and their supporters responded with thousands more signatures. Finally, the reformers scored a victory when the house also agreed to examine that "branch of laws which abridges the competency of black and mulatto persons to be sworn and give evidence in courts of justice or elsewhere." The house committee began with a question: Does the testimony law "infringe either natural or constitutional rights?" The committee, composed mostly of liberal Whigs, obviously thought so, explaining that the state constitution had not explicitly denied civil rights to blacks. Certainly it had denied them suffrage and elective office, but the constitution left it up to the legislature to decide on other measures or even to reverse the constitution. With this opening, the committee surmised that before 1804 blacks had certain rights, which included giving testimony against whites. "Colored persons were then competent witnesses; were able to obtain witnesses in their favor; and the white man and the colored could go before the court and substantiate his innocence by the testimony of the black or mulatto person."[90] Moreover, the committee reasoned that only after a full year did the legislature deny the right of blacks to offer evidence against whites. The Negro evidence law had actually reversed the civil rights initially conferred on all Ohio residents, including blacks. The testimony law of 1807, without a constitutional mandate, effectively sealed the mouth of a black witness in cases involving a white.

The law covered guilt and concealed innocence; it denied a white defendant and deprived the state of the opportunity to call on a black person to confirm the guilt or innocence of an accused. This ghastly rule "would send the murderer out of court" acquitted; it would send innocence to the gallows.[91]

In accordance with these considerations, the committee concluded that the testimony law should be rescinded because it was contrary to the state constitution and was a violation of natural rights.[92] The report, however, swayed no one. The representatives who argued for revising the Black Laws could be heartened only by the knowledge that when the repeal movement began, the General Assembly had given little consideration to any petition that had come before it. Almost a decade after those initial inquiries, Ohio reformers had at least accomplished legislative review of the Black Laws. Although they had not achieved the goal of repeal, they nonetheless considered it a victory to have had their ideas entered into the legislative record. They regarded the petitioning movement to have been a success, and they urged their supporters to continue the protest.

—

Frequently in United States history, judges have been more willing than legislators to take action when dealing with controversial issues. Perhaps it is easier for a single person, or even a judicial panel, to make a decision than it is for a legislature, whether state or federal. Ohio courts, therefore, were more prone than the legislature to support civil rights and equality. While the judiciary did not void any of the Black Laws, it did not always validate racial discrimination. An equity dispute involving a black plaintiff and a white defendant provides a case in point.

In 1833, in one of the first equity cases to come before the Ohio bench, an obscure black worker known as Lawson sued his employer for allegedly defrauding him. Although the documentary evidence is scant, it seems that Lawson was a steward aboard a passenger vessel on the Ohio River. At some point, Lawson discovered that the captain of the boat had paid him wages lower than the pay generally earned by white stewards. Lawson sued, and a jury of whites heard the evidence. Justice John C. Wright instructed the jury that the race of the plaintiff was immaterial and that they should not be prejudiced by it in any way. "You have nothing to do with the color of the plaintiff." As directed, the all-white jury made its decision on the evidence, concluding that Lawson was entitled to common wages paid to stewards, and the court ordered the defendant to pay the sum.[93]

The state supreme court apparently remained objective when assessing conflicting evidence offered by litigants of different races, as *Woods v. Green* (1834) illustrates. Green, a black woman, claimed a horse that Woods, a white man, said had actually belonged him. Unable to prove his case in local courts, Woods carried the dispute to the state supreme court. The facts in the case were difficult to decipher. First, both parties had witnesses who could testify regarding their alleged ownership of the animal, and each party had in fact owned at least one horse. Further, the "two horses were nearly alike," and each party could rightly claim that his or her horse had visible scars. Evidently, only one horse was still around; the other had either been stolen or had escaped. The testimony of the witnesses neutralized each other and was insufficient to determine ownership of the animal.[94]

The defendant explained that the horse "had a habit of leering with his ears, and would obey her call." Obviously intrigued, the trial court engineered a test to determine if it would actually recognize the defendant. Moving outdoors, the court ordered the defendant to "whistle for the horse, which immediately came to her from a distance." After repeating the test several times without failure, the court considered it a positive indication of ownership. The court next ordered a voice recognition test, asking the defendant to call to the horse by the name she used when talking to him. The court found the exhibition incontrovertible and gave specific instructions to the jurors deciding the case, admonishing them that racial preferences had no place in a court of law. They were instructed to decide the question of ownership based solely on the testimony they had heard and the field test they had observed. The jury returned promptly with a verdict favoring Green. She had thus prevailed in a property dispute that involved a white litigant.[95]

An 1838 case involving an African American woman named Phoebe and a white man named Johnson also illustrates how a sympathetic magistrate could make a significant difference in a case where the testimony of the parties involved was the deciding factor in a dispute between black and white litigants. Johnson attempted to swindle fifty dollars from Phoebe, who had come to him to make change. He took the note, informing Phoebe that he had change at home and advised her to stay where they had met. Unwilling to take his word, she followed him to his house and demanded her money. Johnson denied the transaction, obviously confident that Phoebe could not testify against him. Initially, Judge Richard Ayres denied her a warrant on grounds that her testimony would not be admissible. Later, Phoebe found a white man who could testify to relevant facts, which Judge Ayres used to justify the warrant. At the hearing, Johnson's only defense was that state law barred the testimony of a black witness. Ayres believed the woman and decided to pursue a strategy to deceive Johnson into confessing. The judge interrupted Johnson: "Don't be too fast—a white girl was standing not far off, and saw the whole affair; she'll swear against you."[96] Johnson, staggered by the disclosure, asked, "Suppose I give up the money now, will that stop" the proceedings? Satisfied that the hoax had worked, Ayres agreed that Johnson would not be charged, since he had agreed to return the money.

Despite these favorable court decisions, civil rights reformers in Ohio continued to face opposition when seeking to topple the Black Laws. Some whites were unwilling to recognize any black rights. These opponents frequently used extralegal means, including terrorism, to enforce the Black Laws. Mob violence had become a potent weapon of white supremacists throughout the country. Such incidents escalated into full-fledged race riots in Ohio, especially in such cities as Toledo, Cleveland, and Cincinnati.[97]

African Americans in Cincinnati were embroiled in a race riot in 1836, when they observed an Independence Day celebration. Black Cincinnatians had long commemorated the holiday without any hostility against them. However, some whites now considered their program menacing because white bigots believed that the African Americans were fomenting social integration. Black organizers of the observance had invited prominent whites to the program, including abolitionist James Birney, whose notoriety further prejudiced the event. Conservative whites claimed that Birney would use the platform to call for equal rights for blacks, to which they objected. To exacerbate matters, slave owners across the river in Covington, Kentucky, wanted to silence abolitionists, whom they regarded as "wicked and misguided."[98] Though they stalked Birney and threatened to tar and feather him, they neither deterred him nor frightened blacks into calling off the observance.

Consequently, during the summer of 1836, an angry mob organized to punish black residents and shut down the *Philanthropist*.[99] The attack on the office of the antislavery publication was intended as a warning to the OAS to cease printing the newspaper. Moreover, the mob hoped to persuade Achilles Pugh, a local publisher, to terminate his contract with the organization. The assault on the property was premeditated. Between July 12 and 14, an array of "respectable and wealthy gentlemen" in Cincinnati led the mob in attacks against the press office, shredding newspapers, breaking the press into pieces, and dragging its damaged parts through the streets.[100] The riot produced one desired effect—it disturbed the publisher, who lost an estimated fifteen hundred dollars in damages. Pugh announced that henceforth he would have "nothing to do with printing that paper."[101] To convince him to continue publication, "the Executive Committee of the Ohio Anti-Slavery Society had to guarantee his property to the amount of $2,000."[102] The mob, however, did not intimidate Birney, although he sent his wife and young children away for safety. Birney and his eldest son, William, brazenly stayed put at the Franklin Boarding House in Cincinnati. William Johnson, the proprietor, remained steadfast in providing lodging for them, though some patrons feared for their own safety and canceled their reservations.[103]

The Cincinnati mob underestimated how the crisis would influence other whites. Until 1836, many important individuals had been on the fringe of the debate over civil rights, unwilling to support antislavery causes. The riot brought them into the fray, and Salmon P. Chase was the most notable convert. On July 23, Chase, a young lawyer, and other parties interested maintaining law and order convened a public meeting to explore ways to end the conflict peacefully. Cincinnati mayor Samuel Davies, an opponent of abolitionism, presided. It was a lopsided affair, and the two factions never achieved common ground. The anti-abolitionists demanded that Birney and the society cease publication of the *Philanthropist*. Chase found their demand untenable: "Freedom of the press and constitutional liberty must live or perish together." In a quiet moment, Chase reiterated these sentiments to an abolitionist companion, who made a mental note of his declaration. And when abolitionists needed a lawyer who had not been branded as a fanatic, they called on Chase. Yet Chase did not approve of their sweeping denunciations of slavery, considering the practice a legal right in the states that allowed it.[104] Nonetheless, his subsequent participation in the abolition movement as a lawyer launched his political career and eventually carried him to the U.S. Senate, the governor's mansion, Lincoln's cabinet, and the U.S. Supreme Court.

Although the rioting in Cincinnati had initially been directed toward abolitionists, the mob also turned on blacks. Angry whites marched into a black neighborhood on West Sixth Street nicknamed the Swamp. They set the neighborhood on fire and burned down several houses. The mob moved on to Church Alley, where armed blacks fought back but were ultimately overrun as the mob destroyed their property. Several days passed before the city restored order. Interested parties collected donations for black victims, but neither city nor state officials made any arrests. Mobs acted with impunity to attack both blacks and white abolitionists.[105] The mobs came to believe that such acts would be exempted from prosecution.

The Black Laws had undoubtedly fostered a tolerance for violence and lawlessness in Ohio. It was a society where people of color not only did not enjoy the same civil rights as whites, but also lived under constant threat of violence and of the destruction of their homes and shops. Conditions did not improve for Ohio abolitionists or for their antislavery press. An antiabolition mob gathered again in 1837 to make another run on the press office of the OAS. Birney, editor of the *Philanthropist,* was away in Hillsboro, Ohio, organizing a branch of the society. When he returned home on the morning of July 30, his friends intercepted him on the outskirts of town, assuming that he "would have been seized and lynched."[106] Birney remained in hiding for three days. The mob again broke into the press office, shattered the type, and shredded newspapers. It then hauled the parts into the street to burn them, but was warned that such a fire might incinerate nearby buildings. They ended the episode by dumping the press and newspapers into the Ohio River.[107]

Salmon Chase again rose to lead during the crisis, expressing his abhorrence for both mob rule and its obvious indifference to freedom of speech. Yet he held abolitionists equally culpable for the crisis. Joined by Charles Hammond, William D. Gallagher, and other "friends of law and order," Chase called another public meeting, hoping to convince abolitionists "to give up their publication." He also urged Ohio whites "to give up the ultimate design to employ violent means if necessary to effect the object."[108] Judge Jacob Burnet presided as a parade of speakers arose to condemn mob violence. They also adopted resolutions pledging to preserve the peace and reproached abolitionists for inciting public feelings. They denounced abolition, recommending the strategy approved "by the colonization society as the only method of getting clear of slavery."[109]

Although Chase disagreed with the abolitionists' strategy and denounced any effort to label him as one of them, he held strong feelings against slavery. Chase and his law partner Harvey Hall emerged as counsel for the abolitionists in the action against the leaders of the mob who had engineered the destruction of property. Apparently Chase relished the opportunity because he faced the formidable counsel for the defendants, including Judge Nathaniel C. Read, of Ohio, and U.S. Supreme Court justice John McLean. Achilles Pugh and the OAS filed the complaints, seeking damages for the Pugh Publishing Company and its publication, the *Philanthropist*. The trial began on February 27, 1838.[110]

The plaintiffs in the case were among the most prominent residents in Cincinnati. So were the defendants—Joseph Graham and Joseph S. Bates. All the men were well known to the jury. Witnesses for the plaintiffs testified that they heard Graham and Bates instruct the mob to "destroy the press of the *Philanthropist*." Unable to contradict them, the defense turned the trial into an indictment of abolitionism itself. A writer for the *Philanthropist* reported that the defense "exaggerated, distorted, and made false representations of doctrines, measures and designs of abolitionists." In the end, neither side could claim unconditional victory. The jury convicted Graham and Bates of riot, and then they awarded the OAS a measly hundred and fifty dollars in damages. The society had estimated its losses at more than a thousand dollars in subscriptions alone.[111]

The attorneys tried the case of Achilles Pugh separately. The defense could not easily attack his character, for the public highly regarded him. Pugh had a strong case, and the guilt of the party responsible was incontrovertible. A correspondent for the *Philanthropist* noted that in this trial, "Nobody pretends to doubt their guilt." Yet the court awarded Pugh only fifteen hundred dollars. Abolitionists bemoaned the amount, believing it was inadequate for the damage done to the company.[112] Ohio state representative John A. Foot shared their belief that the verdict was friendly to the defendants and initiated legislation in the General Assembly that would make the city liable for whatever property a mob might destroy during a riot. The bill, however, did not pass. Ohio, particularly Cincinnati, remained divided. The antiabolitionists had demonstrated that they would do harm to person and property. Many in Cincinnati were now cautious about associating with either side. In 1836, for example, the First Presbyterian Church in Cincinnati turned down the OAS when the society asked to use church facilities for meetings.[113] This strategy—intimidation—would be used against individual abolitionists under the cover of law across Ohio and the nation as well.

The Black Laws of Ohio had also made it possible for prosecutors to punish whites suspected of supporting civil rights, because the law required anyone hiring an African American to verify that the employee was free. Most whites, however, could safely ignore this requirement of the employment law, but abolitionist "trouble-makers" were always in danger of prosecution. James Birney faced such a fate in 1837, when Hamilton County prosecutors charged him with violating the statute.[114]

James Birney and his wife had hired Matilda Lawrence in the spring of 1836, initially without knowing that she had escaped from slavery. Larkin Lawrence, a Missouri slave owner, was also her father, and she had accompanied him on a trip north. Matilda had prominent Caucasian features and easily passed as white, and Lawrence apparently found it amusing that northerners did not know her legal status was that of a slave. Matilda obviously had enjoyed her experience while in the North, even if she was only feigning freedom. Her brief trip aroused in her a greater desire to live free, and she pleaded with Lawrence to emancipate her. When he refused, she escaped in Cincinnati, finding a safe haven with a black barber in Church Alley. Once her new friends learned that Larkin Lawrence had left for Missouri, they directed her to families who could use her services. Mrs. Birney, recovering from a difficult pregnancy, hired Matilda without hesitation, but no doubt suspected that her new nurse had escaped from slavery.[115]

Matilda easily merged into both the Birney home and the Cincinnati community. According to William, the eldest of the Birney children, almost everyone assumed that she was white, and this made life simpler for her. By the spring of 1837, Matilda began to take greater risks by venturing into the city, unaware that Lawrence had set a trap for her. The slave owner had hired James M. Riley, a professional slave catcher, to continue searching for her. Riley apprehended Matilda in the spring of 1837, and prosecutors in Hamilton County seized the opportunity to punish Birney for violating the state employment law.[116]

The prosecution began in the common pleas court of Judge David K. Estes. He was on record as being sympathetic to the Black Laws but also had enforced federal and state fugitive slave legislation without hesitation. The prosecution correctly expected a sympathetic hearing, and confidently argued that Birney had violated the employment law as well as the federal fugitive slave law. The employment law required an employer to certify the status of an African American worker. Furthermore, the prosecution contended that hiring a black worker in violation of the law automatically amounted to harboring a runaway slave. Birney retained Salmon P. Chase as counsel, and Chase countered that only a federal official could enforce the Fugitive Slave Act of 1793. He also suggested that the federal statute was unconstitutional. His arguments did not sway the judge, however.

Although they did not help Birney or Matilda Lawrence, those arguments would gain some support five years later, when the federal Supreme Court decided the case of *Prigg v. Pennsylvania,* holding that state officials could not be required to enforce federal legislation. On the other hand, the Supreme Court would never recognize Birney's assertion that the federal fugitive slave law was invalid. Thus, Birney was convicted and ordered to pay the maximum $50 fine. Outraged abolitionists criticized the ruling, contending that to enforce the employment law in this case was "a perversion of an established principle of law."[117] They considered the trial to be a sham, and Birney subsequently appealed the verdict. The Ohio Supreme Court reversed the conviction because the prosecution did not show that Birney had known that Matilda was a runaway slave when he hired her. His knowledge, the court held, was "necessary to constitute his guilt."[118]

The Ohio Supreme Court had taken important steps to secure the civil rights of individuals who had at least some African heritage. It had also taken important steps to protect black litigants whose race might have rendered their judicial complaint invalid in a controversy involving a white. As in the case against Birney, the court had also protected abolitionists who had been unfairly prosecuted for their political views. However, the court recognized the Black Laws and enforced without reservations the federal fugitive slave policy. The reform movement could have counted important judicial victories at the end of the 1830s, but they had many challenges ahead.

There can be little doubt that the 1830s were critical years for civil rights reformers in Ohio. The General Assembly further codified the Black Laws, intending to make Ohio a white state. What legislators did not predict was that, partially as a result of their actions, a cadre of white and black leaders would launch a civil rights movement against the Black Laws. This battle over the color line had begun in an era when whites overwhelmingly favored laws that circumscribed black life. By 1839, after many years of persistent struggle, there was evidence of greater sympathy and tolerance for African Americans. Large numbers of Ohio whites joined blacks to urge the legislature to rescind or revise its Black Laws. The ability of civil rights reformers to talk with elected officials improved during the decade, in part due to a transformation in the state fueled by the abolitionist movement. Liberal Whigs sympathetic to the civil rights movement began to be elected to state office. The protest against slavery had inevitably turned Ohio liberals against the Black Laws as an obvious extension of the evils of slavery and inequality.

Moreover, African Americans, despite both the periodic episodes of violence against them and the colonization movement, also pressed the General Assembly to protect their civil rights. The legislature listened, but did not act to modify or abolish the racial codes. Civil rights reformers in Ohio accelerated the repeal movement in the next decade, and their work made it difficult for political parties to ignore them. Ultimately, the Black Laws were struck down because those opposing them landed in the right political position to demand their repeal. That battle actually started in 1830, and culminated with the legislature forming special committees to discuss the racial codes. No one predicted such an occurrence when Ohio was founded. This movement had been brought forth from the ideals of the American creed, the new creed that had announced to the world in 1776 that all men are created equal and endowed by their Creator with inalienable rights. Had America—its federal or state governments—continued to approve laws of oppression it could not have survived as the land of the free. The seeds of racial equality had taken root in states such as Ohio, where citizens launched a civil rights movement to abolish the Black Laws and bring African Americans into the mainstream of society.

FIVE

The Struggle to Abolish the Color Line

1840–1849

The decade-long struggle against slavery and the Black Laws had tempered antiblack sentiments in Ohio. Race continued to matter in Ohio, and the Black Laws still limited the choices of African Americans. Nonetheless, civil rights reformers had made some important achievements. Their numbers had grown significantly. Progressive Whigs elected antislavery and pro–civil rights leaders to the General Assembly, and these representatives were positioned to fight for the repeal of the Black Laws.[1] Repeal petitions were being submitted to the legislature in greater regularity, and progressive lawmakers pressed the General Assembly to consider them. A shift in the racial outlook of some white Ohioans was obvious, and the house and senate appointed committees to review complaints about the harmful effects of the Black Laws and to hear arguments for their repeal.[2] As it turned out, the legislature did this solely as a courtesy to its progressive Whig members. The majority in both parties was not committed to abolishing the Black Laws.[3]

Before the 1840s, antislavery advocates assumed the task of seeking the repeal of such laws. Many of these supporters of equality were members of the Whig Party. As the repeal movement gained momentum in Ohio, it became evident that the Whig organization had two wings, progressive and conservative. Only progressive Whigs pushed for civil rights reform. Ohio Democrats were more united than Whigs, but they also opposed changing the racial policy of the state. Conservative Whigs and Democrats were ever conscious of the views of their fellow party members in the slaveholding states. Hence, despite the efforts of Ohio reformers, they had not achieved any immediate modifications in the Black Laws.[4]

Nevertheless, Ohio activists had woven a fabric for reform, and during the 1840s they could boast of many victories. Their ranks had increased exponentially, and, as a result of the petitioning strategy, they were able to speak directly to state lawmakers about the importance of repealing the racial codes. Times had never looked brighter for reformers. Before the decade ended, they had established two political parties dedicated to abolition and repeal. Little did they know in 1840 that nine years later they would be parties to a compromise resulting in substantial modifications of the Black Laws and the creation of a state-funded public school system for black children. In the meantime, radical and conservative Whigs engaged in a protracted struggle for the conscience and agenda of their party.

—

Naturally, Ohio abolitionists faced resistance from whites who chided the crusaders for interfering with a legal institution that lay outside the state border. One significant factor that turned Ohio politicians and merchants against abolitionists and civil rights reformers was the state's strong economic ties with the South. Connected to southern markets by the Ohio River, goods manufactured in the Buckeye State flowed as far as New Orleans. Ohio merchants obviously benefited from this trade, and many of them believed that state policies favorable to blacks would put this lucrative commerce in jeopardy.[5] To protect it, Ohio merchants and politicians regularly admonished politically active whites to avoid topics that might harm the already tense relations with the South. Elected in 1829, Governor Duncan McArthur, the last Federalist to hold that office, told whites that abolitionism threatened relations with their southern friends and would hurt the Ohio economy.[6]

Not only did conservative politicians and merchants in Ohio worry about abolitionism, they also agonized over the ongoing movement to elevate the quality of black life in the state. Should Ohio repeal the Black Laws, they feared large numbers of southern blacks would migrate to Ohio, presuming that the state was a haven for them.

Conservative Whigs and northern Democrats were prepared to contain slavery where it existed, just as federal leaders had done when they passed the Northwest Ordinance in 1787. These politicians assumed that the peculiar institution would ultimately become extinct on its own. Progressive Whigs, however, never questioned the merits or necessity of immediate abolition, or even banning slavery in federal territory, yet their support for these measures did not exclude their commitment to do away with the Black Laws. Thus, halfway measures such as gradual emancipation would not close the chasm in the Whig organization. The conservative Whig majority did everything but advocate for greater freedom and equality. Furthermore, they also backed the ideology of colonization as a solution to the race problem. The Whig Party had an impossible mix of members: there were Whigs willing to extend civil rights to blacks, while others wanted to enforce the Black Laws; still other Whigs favored slavery anywhere it was legal, and others wanted it abolished without delay. Party unity was increasingly difficult for Ohio Whigs.

One outcome of the civil rights movement in Ohio was the growing disillusionment within the Whig Party. The Whig Party had quickly become powerful in Ohio politics from its inception in 1834. Its rapid growth can be attributed to many factors, but the most significant was its humanitarian philosophy, which attracted many factions in Ohio. Civil rights reformers readily turned to the Whig organization, though the party would disappoint them time and again by not pushing to rescind the Black Laws or for the immediate abolition of slavery. Ultimately, it became clear to antislavery activists that the party could not survive with half its members committed to reform and the other half devoted to the status quo.

Instead of joining abolitionists to advance the perception that their party favored social reform, conservative Whigs turned against the radical element in the party. As civil rights reformers demanded repeal of the Black Laws, they were attacked by antiblack mobs. Ironically, conservative Whigs blamed reformers for any disturbance that occurred, and it did not matter that the abolitionists themselves had not initiated the confrontation. The majority in the Whig Party shared this negative view of social reformers, regarding them as culpable for any hostilities directed toward them. As a correspondent for the *Cincinnati Whig* put it, "We deem abolitionism an insult to our slaveholding neighbors." He took exception to their "attempt to brow-beat the public in this question."[7] When mobs resorted to extralegal tactics to put civil rights reformers in their place, conservative whites blamed it on abolitionist agitation. A succession of antiblack and antiabolition riots erupted in Ohio in the 1840s. As conservatives continually sided with terrorists, it eroded the confidence of progressive leaders and thereby further divided the party. The Whig organization would never overcome this abyss.

———

Another concern of progressive Whigs was that their party did not provide them with adequate representation in the General Assembly. The majority in the party of Ohio considered themselves conservatives, and they elected officials who shared their views. Geography exacerbated this problem. Located along the northern bank of the Ohio River, the Buckeye State shared borders with Virginia and Kentucky; the area was accessible to migrating whites, and they made southern Ohio the most densely populated region in the state. In contrast, former New Englanders settled in northern Ohio. Residents of Cleveland and other cities in Ohio's Western Reserve had been far removed from the obligatory interaction between blacks and whites in the racialist culture of the South and apparently were not as bigoted as white emigrants from the South. Antislavery activity and civil rights reform, therefore, flourished in the environs of the Western Reserve. Southern Ohio shaped the character of the Buckeye State in another way—it was the point of entry for migrating free blacks and runaway slaves. In sharp contrast to the Western Reserve, southern Ohio had a denser African American population, the majority doubtlessly fugitives from labor.[8] By the 1840s, whites in all these regions were mostly Whigs, but southern Ohio representatives controlled the legislature, infusing it with a pro-South and antiblack philosophy.

Before any political party could chip away at the Black Laws, therefore, it had to transform or outvote this extension of southern culture in Ohio. Ironically, these emigrants had once belonged to the Jeffersonian Republican Party and were heirs to its common-man philosophy. The Democratic Party claimed Jefferson's legacy, and the party had strong roots in southern Ohio. Many Whigs, however, also had Jeffersonian roots. The main political organizations in Ohio, therefore, had a great deal in common. Whether controlled by Whigs or Democrats, the majority of the Ohio legislature was determined to maintain the Black Laws.

During the 1840s, the fight to secure civil rights for blacks underwent another important transformation. In addition to fighting to end slavery, abolitionists turned to a new legal strategy aimed at limiting the ability of slave owners to control enslaved blacks in Ohio. The doctrine of state sovereignty united conservatives and progressives. Abolitionists believed that if state sovereignty made it possible for whites to keep slaves, as it did in the southern states, it also secured a state's right to outlaw it and to enforce that choice by law.[9] Antislavery lawyers successfully applied these arguments in the courtroom. In 1841, Ohio judges ruled that slaves were automatically freed upon entering the state with the knowledge and consent of the owner.[10] This principle became an impetus in the transformation of Ohio from a state that tolerated various forms of slavery and racial oppression to a state that challenged the efficacy of maintaining discriminatory laws and slavery.

The reform movement in Ohio took another step forward when progressive Whigs adopted the tactic of interrogating candidates for elected office. Before progressive Whigs began using this tactic, the party appeared to be a monolithic, conservative bloc. As civil rights reformers charted a political course that differed from the conservative agenda, they sought a way to counter, if not neutralize, the party platform. James Birney suggested that they use a strategy of interrogating political candidates, advising Whigs to elect only pro–civil rights men.[11] Birney's suggestion became a rallying cry for progressive Whigs. Ultimately, however, interrogation was ineffective as a strategy because, once elected, officials tended to vote according to their predilections and interests. Progressive Whigs and the third parties they later established could only play the role of spoilers in state elections, and they never gained control of the state government.

Despite the failure of social reformers to shape the agenda of the Whig Party, the progressives succeeded in electing lawmakers sympathetic to abolition, especially in areas like the Western Reserve. For example, Leicester King was a guiding light behind the construction of the Pennsylvania and Ohio Canal and had played a significant part in advancing waterborne commerce in Ohio. A successful attorney and judge, he was also a prominent abolitionist and president of the Ohio Anti-Slavery Society until 1838. Confident in his position in the community, King successfully ran for the state senate with support from voters who shared his antislavery views. King quickly emerged as the floor leader for anti-slavery causes. Benjamin F. Wade was one of the most notable politicians in Ashtabula County. Born in Springfield, Massachusetts, he relocated to Ohio in 1832. He was the law partner of outspoken abolitionist Joshua R. Giddings and was elected to the Ohio senate in 1837 and 1841. Wade was a judge and served in the U.S. Senate, where he was a local and national spokesman for civil rights reform for several decades. Invariably a champion of antislavery causes, Wade launched a campaign against the Black Laws.[12]

Cuyahoga County also elected progressive representatives to the Ohio house. John A. Foot, a Connecticut Yankee who moved to Cleveland, the county seat, in 1833, was elected to the Ohio legislature in 1837. Foot, a Whig, dutifully read petitions and resolutions favorable to civil right reforms. Trumbull County, in northeastern Ohio, elected Jediah Fitch. Delaware County, in central Ohio, elected Elijah Carney. Voters in Clermont County, on the Ohio River in the southwestern part of the state, elected Thomas Morris to the state senate for several terms, and in 1832 the state legislature elected him to the U.S. Senate, making Morris the first abolitionist in that chamber. In later years, the Ohio legislature would elect the antislavery crusaders Wade and Chase to the U.S. Senate. Just as progressive Whigs pressured the Ohio legislature to repeal the Black Laws, the congressional delegation advanced antislavery causes by urging Congress to prohibit slavery in the capital, close federal territory to slavery, and end the domestic slave trade. They also discouraged the forced colonization of free blacks.[13]

As progressive Whigs entered state and national offices, they invariably made the halls of government friendlier to the plight of the downtrodden. In this context, social reformers began to extend the gains made in the previous decade. From their experience, they knew that a direct attack on the Black Laws would be futile. Instead, they expanded the antislavery strategy of transforming hearts and minds, assuming that the party might follow public opinion. As a correspondent for the *Cleveland Herald* aptly stated, "The Whig Party has always kept pace with public opinion in giving Blacks their rights and that is as fast as any party can go with good effect."[14] Meanwhile, the Ohio Anti-Slavery Society led the campaign to change white attitudes by educating them in the theory of social engineering and the impractical society the Black Laws had intended to bring about.

The Ohio Anti-Slavery Society explained that the Black Laws had harmed African Americans. Indeed, it was a simple message, but until the OAS articulated it, many whites assumed that the laws were benign and had served only to close the state border to runaway slaves. This was not so, the whites learned. Only people of color were barred from exercising the right to testify in a dispute with a person not of his or her race. A white litigant could injure an African American and, without a white witness, leave the aggrieved party with no legal recourse. As a correspondent for the *Rochester North Star* put it, "this exclusion of colored testimony, alike repulsive and humiliating to manhood and a proper sense of justice, is virtually refusing to take cognizance of injuries, that colored citizens may suffer at the hands of the white."[15] Simply put, the testimony law empowered whites to persecute blacks with impunity. Moreover, the society contended that the Black Laws as a whole fostered a segregated world in which whites and blacks worked in different capacities, often lived in segregated neighborhoods, and frequented taverns and hotels that admitted only one race.[16] The leadership of the society declared that their Christian faith compelled them to reject laws that led to such results.

The civil rights movement in Ohio immediately met organized opposition. The Anti-Abolition Society was established with the explicit purpose of resisting any revision of the Black Laws. Referring specifically to the immigration law, antiabolitionists drafted a resolution asserting that it had always "been the policy of this state to exclude Negroes and mulattos from her territory."[17] As the anti-abolition party read the state constitution, no black could become a citizen. While antiabolitionists conceded that the Black Laws had not been effective as a deterrent to African Americans entering Ohio, they believed that this failure indicated instead that the policy should be strengthened. To further deprive blacks of any hope of a free life in Ohio, the antiabolitionists urged the General Assembly to adopt statutes that would prevent a black from holding property.[18]

The Anti-Abolition Society also argued that it was inappropriate for Ohio, a state that had no slaves, to advocate abolition or civil rights for blacks. Ralph R. Gurley, an agent in the American Colonization Society, believed it was impractical for Ohio to be identified with abolition or civil rights reform because it bordered slave states. Gurley agreed that the removal of blacks from Ohio as well as the rest of the United States was a way to end the controversies over slavery and the repeal of racial codes. Jonathan Blanchard, pastor of a Presbyterian church in Cincinnati, shared Gurley's opinion of colonization. Blanchard feared that abolitionist activity would damage Ohio's economic ties with the South.[19] A few others demonstrated their antipathy for reform by leaving the state. George Smith made scathing comments about Daniel J. Smith, his abolitionist nephew, then abandoned his political career in Ohio, sold the family business, and moved to the slave state of Missouri.[20]

Generally speaking, the chief executives of Ohio had been indifferent to civil rights reform since the territory entered the Union in 1803. Edward Tiffin, the first governor of Ohio, remained silent when the legislature initially codified the Black Laws. Over the years, the chief executives of the state were frequently drawn into discussions about the Black Laws. Joseph Vance, for example, had resided in Ohio since he was nineteen. He started his political career as a commissioner in Champaign County, in eastern Ohio, and was elected to both state and federal office. In 1835, Ohio voters made Vance the first Whig governor of the state. His tenure coincided with a period of heated debates about eliminating the Black Laws and abolishing slavery. While governor, his most controversial issue involved Kentucky abolitionist John B. Mahan, who had fled to Ohio after being accused of assisting runaway slaves. Kentucky governor James T. Morehead requested his extradition, to which Governor Vance complied, a decision that later proved costly. Antislavery Whigs held the Mahan affair against Vance, and he subsequently lost his reelection bid to Democrat Wilson Shannon, the first Ohio governor to be born in the state.[21]

The Whig Party lost far more than the executive office in that election. Democrats also won the General Assembly. As a *Philanthropist* correspondent boasted, antislavery Whigs punished Vance by not voting for him, hoping to use their vote to sway conservative Whigs to support their causes or risk defeat at the polls.[22] The election demonstrated that the Whig

Party would continue to lose ground if it remained divided, but this recognition did not favor progressive Whigs. Instead of uniting the party, abolitionists increasingly became disillusioned with its temporizing on the Black Laws and slavery. The election of a Democratic governor further crippled the already divided Whig Party. As progressive Whigs shifted from more moderate causes to what some Ohioans considered radical politics, such as abolitionism and "repealism," the party's downward spiral accelerated. To make matters worse, the antiabolitionists and slave owners on the other side of the political spectrum targeted abolitionists and African Americans for persecution.

Racial riots had been boiling up in the United States for some time and had spread to the West by the early 1830s. Invariably in these tragic events the abolitionists and African Americans suffered the brunt of vicious attacks. Amos Dresser, a Lane Seminary student caught distributing abolitionist pamphlets in Kentucky, was one of many unfortunate victims. An angry mob stripped and lashed Dresser, then warned him that he would be lynched should he return to Kentucky. In 1836, abolitionists meeting at Pennsylvania Hall in Philadelphia also faced furious opponents who were determined to silence them. Some well-known abolitionists, including William L. Garrison, were in the building when the mob assembled. However, Angelina Grimke, a white abolitionist from South Carolina, became the star of the night. Garrison explained that she confidently rose to the podium, urged the assembly to stand fast, and reminded them that the slaves in the South were getting worse treatment. One year later, antislavery editor Elijah Lovejoy died in Alton, Illinois, at the age of thirty-four defending his printing press against a proslavery mob. Mob assaults against social reformers reached as far north as Portland, Maine, where John Murray Spear was beaten. Mobs also opposed abolitionists and civil rights reformers in Ohio. In 1837, they savagely beat abolitionist Marius Robinson while he was on a speaking tour through Ohio.

Despite these attacks, Ohio abolitionists and social reformers were among the most energetic in the nation. Their commitment to their cause was further demonstrated by the extent of the Underground Railroad in the state. This abolitionist network directed thousands of runaway slaves traveling in Ohio.[23] Mobs frequently targeted abolitionists in

Ohio, with such weapons as verbal threats, tarring and feathering, and throwing rotten eggs, seeking to punish them for being friendly to runaway slaves.[24] Senator Thomas Morris was one of the most radical and articulate critics of conservative Whigs, and his harsh attacks of their policies made him a target of mob violence. In early 1836, Morris escaped an angry mob in Dayton by sneaking out of town. Two years later, Morris declared

I have opposed and voted against the further extension of slavery in every case in which I was permitted to do so by the Constitution. The Whig convention most undoubtedly had viewed slavery with a very favorable eye and felt willing for its extension into every state in the Union. I have opposed the slave trade between the different States and with the Republic of Texas. The Whig convention probably thought this trade an honest mode of turning a penny. I have contended that all men were born equally free and independent, and have an indisputable right to life, liberty and the pursuit of happiness. In this particular I have no doubt I am entirely antipode to the Whig convention.[25]

The high emotion surrounding the issue of slavery became even clearer when antiabolitionists and anti–civil rights groups made Dayton a scene of violence again in 1841. Thomas Morris had returned on January 24 to deliver a speech there, only to find that a throng of angry whites had gathered against him. The *Dayton Transcript* reported, "There appears to be a settled determination in the minds of the citizens to prevent a discussion of that question among them." Morris again fled the city, apparently shaken by the "insolent language" he had heard.[26] Unable to satisfy its lust for violence on Morris, the angry mob lashed out at a local physician who had provided lodging for him.[27]

As they often were in antebellum Ohio and elsewhere in the nation, race relations were the underlying cause for mob violence against abolitionists. After the departure of Senator Morris, the mob turned on an African American neighborhood in Montgomery County, where it destroyed property and intimidated residents. Although local constables arrived on the scene to restore order, they stood by and watched as the mob burned down a house belonging to a black family, hoping "that the fury of the mob would be appeased." The mob, still seething and determined to vent its rage on other blacks, "entered the dwelling of a respectable colored man, drove the family from their beds, naked and barefoot." As the family stood outdoors on "frozen ground, the mob set fire to the house and burnt it and all its contents to ashes."[28] Before they could set fire to another house, its owner pleaded to be spared. The mob delayed burning the house, then advised her to leave town. Although the authorities knew the identities of the assailants, they made no arrests.

Because of these events, antislavery leaders in Ohio increasingly doubted the Whig Party and its commitment to black rights or abolition. Antislavery Whigs were convinced that the party had done nothing to ameliorate the social and political problems facing African Americans. Whether they were in control of the state legislature or in the minority, the conservative Whigs consistently voted to maintain the status quo in race relations. Dr. Gamaliel Bailey explained that the Whig legislature had taken no action against the Black Laws "because the Whigs in the southern counties of this state are too much under the writhing cause of slavery to vote for equal justice to the colored man."[29] The Whig leadership, unwilling to fight for social reform, left the party in continual turmoil. Meanwhile, African Americans also accelerated their demands for social reform. The State Convention of Colored Men, under the leadership of African Americans—including Oberlin-educated William H. Day, Cleveland barber and bathhouse owner John L. Watson, and their colleague R. R. Chancellor, of Chillicothe—pressed the legislature to repeal the Black Laws.[30] Whig lawmakers apparently listened politely, but they did not take any action or make any commitments to Day and those he represented.

Although progressive Whigs remained dedicated to the repeal of the Black Laws and to the abolition of slavery, many of them still clung tenaciously to the hope that an amicable way to resolve party differences would be found. Many believed that they could not reach their political goals without the support of a major party. The editors of the *Philanthropist* also opposed third-party politics on grounds that it would weaken the movement for social change. Now under the editorial direction of Bailey, who had relieved Birney as editor, the *Philanthropist* actually took a more conservative tone, and Bailey was willing to court Democrats. Unlike other abolitionists, Bailey condemned progressive Whigs in the Western Reserve. He contended that it was their single-minded commitment to black rights and abolition that had blinded them and made it difficult for them to compromise. Thus, Bailey initially blamed Whigs for fragmenting their own party, and he called on moderates to unite. Bailey and the *Philanthropist* had no confidence in third-party politics.

Desperate to hold the fragile Whig organization together, Bailey frequently reminded party members of its past successes. Bailey had a penchant for reminiscing, and frequently pointed to the congressional election of 1836, in which James Alexander, an antislavery Whig, had defeated a Democrat. From the distance of his New York office, James Birney actually agreed with Bailey: "Votes should be given to the most worthy candidate without partisan distinction."[31] However, Birney insisted that Ohio voters hold all state officers responsible for repealing the Black Laws. Benjamin Wade, Leicester King, and Joshua Giddings initially hoped for unity among Whigs. Giddings believed that the Whig Party needed to take the lead in securing equal rights and abolishing slavery. Moreover, the American Anti-Slavery Society was also tentative about establishing a rival political party. At its national convention in Cleveland in 1839, it rejected a resolution that called for establishing a new party. Its Ohio branch, however, viewed the need for a new party differently: "We can see no other course for abolitionists to pursue."[32] Many of their abolitionist colleagues, including Joshua Leavitt and Elizur Wright, viewed the positions of Bailey and Birney with skepticism, suspecting that party division would ultimately doom the Whig organization.

Although civil rights reformers had attempted to sway the hearts and minds of Ohio whites, conservatives held the day during the first quarter of the 1840s. The abyss within the Whig organization grew wider as conservatives in the party reacted violently to abolitionism. Instead of attracting more voters to their positions, the Whig majority drove many whites to social reform. Antislavery Whigs began to doubt their political future within the party. They took an important step in shaping a new political identity in 1840, when they formally organized the Liberty Party. However, launching the new party did not dampen the enthusiasm of moderates like Giddings for Whig unity. Unable to abort the birth of the Liberty Party, Giddings next attempted to unite the two parties—Whig and Liberty. If the Whig Party embraced social reform, Giddings surmised, "then the great body of the Liberty party will be with us."[33] Giddings was not naive in holding tenaciously to this hope; he had earlier predicted that abolitionists would desert the party if it did not back reform. Moreover, he had long recognized that the Whig majority had merely tolerated civil rights reform and that this stance contributed to the anguish of progressive members who supported social change. Something had to be done to hold the fragile organization together, and Giddings continually looked for ways to cement it.

Joshua Giddings's career and experience as a Whig illustrate the dilemma that faced the party throughout the 1840s. He began his political career in the Ohio house, first elected as a representative from Cuyahoga County in 1838; he went on to serve eleven consecutive terms in Congress. He supported various social causes, including temperance and the rights of American Indians. His most controversial cause was the abolition of slavery; in Ohio, he remained committed to the elimination of the Black Laws. With the support of like-minded politicians, Giddings had helped bring the Whig Party to Ohio. His maiden congressional campaign platform included opposition to the gag rule on slavery, abolishing slavery in the District of Columbia, and repealing the Black Laws—an agenda that endeared him to voters in the liberal Western Reserve. Although his issues were popular in his district, they were anathema to most whites elsewhere in Ohio and the nation. Moreover, Giddings faced threats because of his beliefs wherever he traveled, even on Capitol Hill itself. John Bennett Dawson, a Democratic representative from Louisiana, threatened Giddings with a knife in 1843. Two years later, Georgia representative Edward Black, a Democrat, charged at Giddings with a cane. Obviously, an antislavery and pro–civil rights agenda brought out the wrath of conservatives in either party. As Giddings and other antislavery politicians were besieged in Ohio and around the nation, conservative Whigs refused to defend them. Indeed, conservatives blamed abolitionists for inciting mob violence and stood on the sidelines while progressives in the party were attacked. Abolitionists then defected to the Liberty Party in increasing numbers.[34]

The Liberty Party of Ohio had an auspicious beginning, stating squarely that it stood for both abolishing the Black Laws and doing away with slavery. Prominent Ohio men were among its founding members, including Salmon Chase and James Birney. Ohio newspapers, including the *Cleveland Herald* and the *Ohio State Journal,* immediately supported it.[35] Yet the Liberty Party stumbled locally and nationally for many years, and it barely existed anywhere after 1844. Although the party managed to place Birney on the presidential ballot with Thomas Earle of Pennsylvania for vice president in 1840, it never captured enough federal or state offices to become a force in the political life of the nation. Nevertheless, the mere existence of the party provided an alternative for moderates disenchanted with the policies of the Whig and Democratic parties. Whigs did not take the challenge lightly and forged ahead by making a futile attempt to close the chasm between the radical and conservative wings of the party. Indeed, the Liberty Party never attracted Whigs, primarily because Liberty men were uncompromising on civil rights reform.[36]

There was one crowning achievement of Liberty men during the 1840s: they succeeded in getting the Ohio legislature to review the volatile issue of the Black Laws. Some Liberty members initially assumed there was finally a changing of the guard. From 1843 to 1848, the General Assembly was solidly in the hands of Whigs. If the Whig Party had any chance of fulfilling its humanitarian mission, it was during these sessions. The house authorized a committee to examine the testimony law. On the other hand, the committee assumed that African Americans were habitual criminals, and it expected them to face the judicial system more frequently than whites. Presuming that blacks envied whites and harbored hostility against them, the committee doubted that blacks would be impartial. Thus, the committee concluded that it was "inexpedient" to reverse the testimony law. The state senate in 1845 approved a bill to repeal the testimony law on a vote of 17 to 16, only to have Whigs and Democrats in the house unite to defeat it.[37]

As Liberty men would discover, the General Assembly held similar reservations about changing the immigration law. As the majority of conservative lawmakers in the assembly understood, their predecessors had enacted the immigration law to keep blacks out of Ohio. These legislators, Whigs and Democrats alike, agreed that the state would be better off if the races were entirely separated. However, they conceded that colonizing blacks was an impractical goal, although the assembly had considered the matter. The forced colonization of blacks was unlikely to occur or to be successful, and the assembly surmised that African Americans had at least a "right of existence" in Ohio. Any law depriving them of this limited right would be going too far, it reported. However, it was not "prepared to say that some amendment" reversing the immigration law should be made. The legislature refused to go further because it believed that this was "not a proper time for any legislative action upon any branch of the subject."[38] It decided that neither the legislature nor the white community was ready for any alteration of the Black Laws. Furthermore, the committee concluded that the legislature had permitted reviews of the Black Laws only as a concession to progressives. The reviews had achieved nothing, and the committee asked to be relieved of further responsibility on the race question.[39]

Nevertheless, antislavery Whigs and Liberty men put a positive spin on legislative review of the Black Laws. The willingness of the General Assembly to assign committees to this question was a direct result of the petitioning strategy, they said. These reformers did not dwell on the obvious—that the repeal movement had not achieved any modifications of the Black Laws. However, resistance to the civil rights movement had not dampened their enthusiasm, and they urged social activists at the grassroots level to continue to use petitioning as a way to talk with Ohio lawmakers about repealing the codes. Antislavery senators and representatives continued to submit repeal petitions to the state legislature, no matter what the opposition to them. Alfred Phelps and H. S. Carter made one such futile effort when they proposed a bill in 1843 "for the repeal of all laws making distinction on account of color."[40] The repeal bill faced the same fate as earlier attempts. Unable to strike the racial codes, progressive members of the legislature altered their approach and sought modest revisions instead of wholesale repeal. The senate reviewed such a bill in 1844, which proposed that the legislature modify the testimony law to allow a black witness with a white sponsor to offer testimony against a white defendant. The senate defeated the bill, 30 to 23. In the following year, Governor Mordecai Bartley, a Whig, asked the General Assembly to abolish the Black Laws, a request Ohio lawmakers ignored.[41]

The Liberty Party made its last significant push in Ohio in 1846, when it nominated Samuel Lewis, of Hamilton County, an abolitionist who defected from the Whig organization, for governor. Lewis had migrated from his native state of Massachusetts. He had a reputation as an eloquent constitutional lawyer and was considered a valuable find for Liberty. Although Lewis won nearly 11,000 votes, William Bebb, the Whig candidate, won almost 121,000 votes, and David Tod, the Democratic candidate, received almost 116,500. Whigs also elected a majority in the Ohio house and tied Democrats in the state senate. Liberty had tried its best but was clearly a failure, even as a minor party in Ohio.[42]

Conservative lawmakers in Ohio had successfully weathered the storm of protest for more than a decade, having defeated each repeal bill that came before them. Emboldened by their success, they proposed making the Black Laws more stringent. Representative George H. Flood wrote a bill to reject without review all civil rights petitions that came to the legislature. The bill passed the house on a vote of 37 to 22. In addition to the conservative lawmakers supporting the measure, other public figures, including Dr. John Watkins from the state board of education, declared that "it would be impolitic" to modify or repeal the Black Laws.[43] The *Colored American,* an African American publication, blasted the Ohio legislature for its failure to modify the Black Laws. The legislature, the newspaper reported, "having been together four months, and passed 33 general laws, 237 local laws, and 46 joint resolves," left "all the disgraceful black laws" on the statute books. Instead of initiating reform, the Ohio legislature forestalled any modifications in the Black Laws. "The Palladium of Liberty thinks the most important act of the session was the decision to adjourn."[44]

—

In contrast to the Ohio General Assembly, justices on the state's supreme court continued to use whatever opportunities it got to secure greater civil rights for blacks. In 1842 the court reviewed the suffrage clause in the Ohio constitution that enfranchised white males. Parker Jeffries had resided in Greene County as white, at least socially. He was one-fourth Indian, but his predominately Caucasian features had opened many doors for him until a new registrar, John Ankeny, refused his ballot in an election solely because of his race. As Ankeny saw it, Jeffries's predominance of white blood was inconsequential under a strict construction of state law. The constitution, he told Jeffries, prohibited him from enfranchising any person of color. Although the constitution did not specifically mention American Indians, he continued, it did not exempt them from the prohibition.[45] Parker Jeffries sued the registrar for abridging his right to vote.

The supreme court now had a new opportunity to chip away at the authority of the Black Laws. It had ruled in *Gray v. Ohio* (1831) that anyone who looked white was legally white.[46] Justice Ebenezer Lane considered these precedents when he asserted in *Jeffries v. Ankeny* that many productive people in Ohio were of mixed racial ancestry. Turning to his colleagues and to clerks in the courtroom, he implied that many of them had traces of nonwhite blood—Indian as well as African. Yet they were productive citizens and participated fully in the affairs of the state and nation. Lane explained that the court had stated its views on whiteness in earlier cases. It considered a white person as anyone who is "nearer white than black and they were entitled to every political and social privilege of the white citizens." Justice Nathaniel Read believed that the law defined *white* as a person who did not have any trace of racial admixture.[47]

The problem of whiteness in the judicial proceedings of Ohio would not go away quickly. A registrar in Gallia County denied Edwill Thacker a ballot because he was of mixed racial heritage, relying solely on anecdotal and circumstantial evidence. Thacker was visibly white and had lived as such in the town of Gallia for many years, where only a few individuals knew his true ancestry and no one would have automatically assumed that he was anything but white. The registrar knew it and refused Thacker a ballot. The common pleas judge sided with the registrar, charging the jury that if Thacker had any black blood he should be denied the vote. The case reached the Ohio Supreme Court as *Thacker v. Hawk* (1842). Writing for the court, Justice Lane pointed out that the common pleas judge had erred in his instruction to the jury.[48] Although Justice Read again dissented, the majority on the court had evidently grown tired of the question. The court considered it settled law that anyone with a visible admixture of "white blood" was entitled to the privileges associated with being white. The only valid test for whiteness recognized by the court was sight, not blood.

Although the court had been consistent in its rulings on "whiteness," the administration of the Black Laws of Ohio naturally produced judicial controversies. The testimony law was called into question again in *Jordan v. Smith* (1846), and the court once again used this opportunity to criticize the Black Laws. Jordan, who was white, did not object to entering into an agreement with Smith, who was black; nor did Jordan earlier refuse to use Mary Shoemaker, another black, as a witness to the contract.

He received a promissory note from Smith for a purchase, on which Smith reneged, disputing that she had ever signed the document. When Jordan called Shoemaker, the defense objected, explaining to the court that Ohio law barred a black person from offering testimony in a case involving a white. The supreme court began tentatively, allowing Shoemaker to offer testimony only to establish the facts in the case.[49] While it had upheld the testimony clause and various parts of the Black Laws in previous cases, the court had reservations about the appropriateness of the racial codes in a free society. It used the *Jordan* case to set additional limits on the operation of the Black Laws.

The irony of the case did not escape the supreme court. Many whites had come before it demanding that the testimony law be invoked to bar a black witness. Now, in a turn of the tables, the white plaintiff called on the court to accept a black witness. Justice Peter Hitchcock ridiculed the statute: "The truth shall not be received from a black man to settle a controversy where a white man is a party. Let a man be Christian or infidel; let him be Turk, Jew, or Muslim; let him be of good character or bad; even let him be sunk to the lowest depths of degradation; he may be witness in our courts if he is not black." The statute does not look at character, he said sarcastically; it looks at color only. Furthermore, under the pretext of law, "The white man may now plunder the Negro of his property; he may abuse his person; he may take his life: He may do this in open daylight, in the presence of multitudes who witness the transaction." But the white man would get off scot-free if only black people were witnesses to the crime. He considered this a horrifying by-product of the Black Laws. We "are not disposed to extend it by construction," Hitchcock continued, "It is a law which requires strict construction."[50]

The court's opinion in the *Jordan* case is an illustration of this strict, or narrow, construction. By curtailing the testimony clause, the court allowed the witness because the statute did not prevent a black person from swearing "to the truth of his plea" in a contracts case. Thus, the court concluded that blacks had at least access to a courtroom in disputes with whites. Any other interpretation of the testimony law, Hitchcock stated, would give whites even greater power over blacks. Hitchcock offered various examples of how whites could defraud blacks in contract cases if the statute barred the testimony of a black witness. A white individual could forge a document and then sue a black, knowing that the latter could not contradict him in court. The courts of Ohio, Hitchcock said sadly, could be used to further oppress "colored" people. The majority of the court rejected the notion that a person, merely because of her color, should not be allowed to swear to her plea.

The court considered a similar controversy in 1848, when creditors of John Woodward, a mulatto, alleged that the executor of his estate had failed to discharge the obligations of the decedent. The executor, represented by Salmon P. Chase's firm, called two individuals, a Mr. Bond and a Mr. Phillips, as witnesses. The plaintiff objected to their testimony because they were black and thus barred from giving evidence against a white. The trial court agreed with the plaintiff and barred the evidence. On appeal, the supreme court reversed the decision, pointing to a state statute that allowed an action against an administrator for dereliction of duty. Chase urged the court to strike the testimony law, asking, "What remedy can a man have, if the witness to establish his case be excluded?" The court did not think it was relevant that a white party was involved in the dispute.[51]

However, the Ohio Supreme Court, in making this decision, walked a judicial tightrope. Mary Shoemaker sat in the witness box to swear to her written testimony only; the court denied her the ability to testify about the promissory note in question. It was sympathetic in offering people of mixed race the right to offer testimony against whites. The white plaintiff apparently had a good case but could not prove it because the Negro evidence law had barred blacks. This was a natural by-product of prejudicial legislation, Hitchcock lamented: "[it] has been used to prevent justice, both public and private."[52] While the court was progressive in this instance, it continued to uphold the Black Laws. *Chalmers v. Stewart* aptly illustrates this tendency.

The Ohio Supreme Court heard the *Chalmers* case in 1842, when the plaintiff appealed the decision of the Greene County trial court. The plaintiff, James Chalmers, had enrolled his child in a public school directed by Hugh Stewart and agreed to subsidize the instruction by making direct payments to the tutor. Upon his discovery that the tutor had also enrolled black children, the plaintiff withdrew his child and refused to pay the remaining fees. The trial court sustained the defendant's objection to evidence that he was paid from the common school fund. By doing so, the trial judge deprived the plaintiff of the opportunity to prove that the defendant operated a state school. Without that evidence, the jury ruled in favor of the defendant, and the court ordered the plaintiff to pay past-due fees. The plaintiff appealed, and the supreme court reviewed the question whether the trial court had erred in rejecting the evidence. The court concluded that the school was public and was therefore governed by state law. By admitting black students to a common school contrary to law, the instructor had violated the statute and forfeited the privilege "to keep a legal school."[53] The court affirmed the principle that a public school education was a privilege offered only to white children.

The political culture of Ohio continued to influence the rulings of the court and actions of the legislature. The Whig Party, supposedly committed to reform, degenerated into bickering among its conservative and radical factions. Conditions would grow worse for the civil rights movement in Ohio before they would improve.

—

Southern Ohio continued to be adamant in its opposition to civil rights reform. The majority white population there had not accepted the radical philosophy of the Western Reserve, and southern Ohio, because it had more people than northern Ohio, continued to dominate the state. Indeed, southern Ohio lawmakers had written the Black Laws, and those officials had perpetually presented the most vociferous arguments against repealing them. Whites there had also opposed the humanitarian impulses of an abolitionist minority in the region, who had frequently accused conservative whites of conspiring with the South to transfer slaves to federal lands. Progressive Whigs asserted that the conservative majority of their party had aligned with southern Democrats to advocate "perpetual slavery." With these arguments, Ohio abolitionists turned the issues surrounding slavery into a political weapon that they wielded against conservative Whigs and their southern allies. "It is the determination of southern men to press" for the extension of slavery until they succeeded. Abolitionists expected "true Whigs" to reject any state or national candidate "who panders to slavery."[54] They criticized Whigs who were soft on slavery, and they made the annexation of Texas as a free state a test of Whig commitment to antislavery reform. In doing so, abolitionist Whigs believed they would simultaneously further reform in Ohio itself.

The Liberty Party was attracting more abolitionists, and the Whig Party was mired in continual bickering, leaving the Democratic Party in

Ohio in a position to dominate state politics. The Democratic Party, however, had also taken a hard line against abolitionism and social reform in Ohio, and this limited its effectiveness. To exacerbate matters, Ohio Democrats attacked nationally known Whigs, including Henry Clay and Daniel Webster, inaccurately classifying them as abolitionist fanatics. "They make war upon slavery in the District of Columbia and in all the states in the Union," the Democrats alleged.[55] Democrats also argued that the policies of progressive Whigs would lure runaway slaves into Ohio, suggesting that such a development would be a threat to state sovereignty. Using the theory that a state could regulate its own domestic institutions, northern Democrats argued that only slaveholding states could legally do away with slavery. Using that same theory, they argued that the Ohio legislature could rightfully enforce the immigration law and other provisions of the Black Laws.[56] Thus, just as antislavery Whigs used the concept of sovereignty against the Black Laws and slavery, Ohio Democrats used sovereignty as an argument to strengthen the Black Laws and undermine abolitionism. They expected the conservative Whig majority in Ohio to bolster their agenda.

In 1840, the Ohio Democratic Convention took a definite stand on slavery. The Democracy unequivocally condemned abolitionism, and advised Congress to take no action against slavery in the District of Columbia without the approval of Virginia. Those attending the convention considered any move against slavery in the capital reminiscent of the irresponsive British government that had precipitated the American Revolution. Democrats also accused the abolitionists of seeking to overthrow democracy, a vague assertion they made without offering any evidence. Indeed, northern Democrats had generally put the Whig Party on the defensive, especially because of its association with antislavery causes. The *Philanthropist* ran an article taken from a conservative Indiana newspaper that accused the Whig Party of officially having an abolitionist branch operating in the state.[57] Of course this was nonsense, but it was also characteristic of the partisan political culture that had developed in the country.

One may question whether or not Ohio Democrats had properly read the political scene in the mid-1840s. Henry Clay, for one, believed they had made a mistake, conceding only that such Whigs as Joshua Giddings, Benjamin Wade, Joseph Vance, and Thomas Morris constituted an antislavery "clique at Washington." At various times while serving in Congress, Giddings and his colleagues had supported a ban on slavery in the capital. They had also opposed the internal slave trade and the expansion of slavery into federal territory. Furthermore, they had opposed the expatriation of free blacks. Although Giddings and his colleagues were enormously influential in Ohio, Clay charged that they were out of step with the Whig majority back home. The Whigs of Ohio were not a radical party, Clay argued, and he believed conservative Whigs in Ohio were actually "embarrassed with antislavery feeling."[58] Sentiments such as these had a negative effect on the already troubled Whig Party in Ohio, and progressive members in the party continued to drift away from it, as abolitionist leaders had anticipated.

The congressional election in Ohio in 1844 was a test between the conservative majority and radical minority in the Whig Party. Giddings, who had been optimistic about keeping the party together, now believed that the only way for it to survive was to advance the protection of the "constitutional rights" of all Ohio residents. They needed to support a candidate "who will step forth boldly and declare his intention and desire to maintain and support all the rights of the free people of the free states."[59] Such a policy, Giddings surmised, would also draw Liberty men to the Whigs. His optimism notwithstanding, Whigs finally came to the inevitable conclusion that civil rights and slavery reform had terribly divided their party. As a result, the Democratic Party profited at the polls, not because of its agenda, but because both Liberty men and Whigs had diluted their own political power. As an antislavery correspondent lamented, "We, the Whigs of Ohio are beaten, and that most essentially."[60]

Nevertheless, antislavery Whigs benefited from the resignation of Democratic governor Wilson Shannon in the spring of 1844, when he accepted an appointment as ambassador to Mexico. Upon his resignation and until the end of his term in December 1844, Thomas W. Bartley, the Democratic speaker of the state senate, became acting governor. In the 1844 election, Mordecai Bartley, Thomas's father, was elected governor as a Whig. Mordecai Bartley, a successful farmer, had begun his political career in the state legislature. Significantly, he had a reputation for supporting civil rights causes, including personal liberty laws to shield free blacks from kidnappers. As governor, Bartley used state officers to prosecute kidnappers, and Ohio had played a vital role in seeking the release of Jeremiah Phinney, who had been removed as a runaway slave in 1846. Bartley opposed the Black Laws, explaining that they imposed "useless and unjust restrictions and disabilities on the colored population of this state."[61] Black immigration had continued to flourish in spite of the Black Laws, he insisted. Furthermore, Bartley believed that the time had come for white Ohio to treat African Americans with respect and justice. Without legislative support, however, he accomplished little toward the goal of repeal, and the Black Laws remained intact during his tenure.

For much of the 1840s, national events impinged on Ohio more than state-level politics. The election of James K. Polk to the presidency in 1844, for instance, damaged the cause of social change in Ohio. Polk, a Tennessee Democrat, had supported western expansion and favored war against Mexico with the aim of obtaining its territory. Polk also made Ohio Democrats uncomfortable, for they did not favor sending troops to Mexico. His desire to gain new territory brought the slavery issue squarely into the national limelight, fueling the tempers of all Ohio politicians. Joshua Giddings and other antislavery reformers urged Americans to take a firm stand against the extension of slavery and the annexation of Texas. He also advised Whig lawmakers to abolish the Black Laws. As Giddings explained to Oran Follett, a Sandusky abolitionist, indecision "may prove fatal to the Union. It appears to me that only one hope is left to our Whigs, and that is to meet promptly all attempts to encroach upon the rights of the free states by annexing Texas or otherwise. I hope our Whigs will meet their responsibility in our legislature as becomes them. Let them give us banks (restore the bank of the United States) at once, and pass strong resolutions against Texas, as well as repeal our odious Black Laws." The Mexican-American War crystallized Whig opposition to the Black Laws by linking the racial codes to the extension of slavery.[62]

Not only did the explosive issue of Texas annexation divide Ohio Whigs, it also split Democrats. The Democratic Party could imagine a free Texas, where they envisioned greater opportunities for migrating whites. However, when John C. Calhoun proposed adding slavery to the equation in 1844, northern Democrats, and particularly those in Ohio, opposed the idea.[63] The Democratic *Ohio Statesman* called annexation "a southern, slaveholder's plot." Its "real object," the correspondent added, "was the perpetuation and extension of slavery, and the political power of the slave States!"[64] The national Democratic Party divided over the presidential candidacy of Martin Van Buren in 1844. Many Ohio Democrats loyal to Van Buren took offense when pro-Texas members at the national convention invoked the two-thirds rule for the nomination. After seven fruitless ballots, the convention chose Polk. Ohio Democrats remembered the event as the "crime of '44."[65] Van Buren ran for president on the Free-Soil ticket in 1848 but he never again captured a national office. Thus, slavery extension splintered the Democrats as well as the Whigs.

In February 1845, progressive Whigs in the state senate continued their efforts to eliminate the Black Laws. Under the leadership of Representative William Perkins of Ashtabula County, the Whigs managed to push a repeal bill through the senate that would have modified the testimony law to admit a black male as a witness if a white male could vouch for him. Having only a slight majority in the session, progressive Whigs barely pushed the measure through the chamber, 17 to 16. The senate bill caused a great deal of excitement in both major parties. Both Whigs and Democrats invariably asserted that this was a step toward Ohio's becoming inundated with African Americans. The editors of a Dayton newspaper made the problem plain for whites: "Are you ready for this state of things? We appeal to the laboring portion of our fellow countrymen. Are you ready to be placed on a level with the 'niggers' in the political rights for which your fathers contended? Are you ready to share with them your hearth and your house? Are you ready to compete with them in your daily vocations?"[66] White fears notwithstanding, a coalition of Whigs and Democrats in the Ohio house killed the bill, again by a vote of 30 to 23. Progressives remained undeterred in their efforts to build a coalition of their own, courting Democratic defectors in the gubernatorial election in 1846.

Though the alliance between progressive and conservative Whigs was tenuous at best, it was effective enough to elect William Bebb governor of Ohio. Born to parents who had emigrated from Wales, Bebb enjoyed a wonderful reputation in his home state. He was the proprietor of the Sycamore Grove School, a successful boarding school that graduated many future political leaders, including William Dennison, who became governor of Ohio. Bebb was also drawn to the law, and, after passing the bar in 1831, he closed the school and started his practice. In due course he became an active Whig politician and won the nomination for governor in 1846. The campaign against his Democratic rival, David Tod, had caused Bebb a great deal of anguish and embarrassment. Tod had sensed the rising tide against his candidacy and tried to salvage it by raising some controversial issues, such as the Black Laws. Bebb was initially silent on the volatile issue, but, as he gained experience on the campaign trail, he learned to attack certain provisions in the Black Laws, tailoring his remarks to his audience. In some places, he merely condemned the testimony law, while in other areas, such as the Western Reserve, he called for the wholesale repeal of the Black Laws.[67]

The Democrats accused Bebb of favoring social equality among the races. Tod's comments, however, backfired. He had gone on record supporting repeal of the Black Laws during an abolitionist interrogation in 1838, when he was a candidate for the state senate in Trumbull County, and again in the 1844 campaign for governor. Antislavery editors chided him, asking whether Ohio whites would join David Tod in admitting blacks to the public schools attended by whites. Such a position clearly went beyond what progressive Whigs and Liberty men had proposed. When Democrats queried him on the subject, Tod categorically denied any interest in "Negro equality," explaining that he opposed blacks serving as jurors and rejected enfranchising blacks or admitting black youths to Ohio common schools. Although his position ingratiated him to conservative Democrats, his reversal nonetheless harmed his credibility, and Bebb won the election by slightly more than two thousand votes to keep the office under Whig control.[68]

Partisan newspapers throughout Ohio cast aspersions on both candidates, each faction seeking to gain an advantage in the campaign. A Democratic newspaper asserted, "Bebb will at once recommend and advocate passage of such laws as will place the negroes on the same footing with white men." Another tract for the Democracy claimed Bebb would give blacks the same privileges as white youths in the public schools. Still another paper asserted that Bebb was the first gubernatorial candidate in Ohio to run on the principle of "Equal Rights to the Negro." Moreover, Bebb was sharply criticized by newspapers controlled by fellow Whigs. While some editors wrote that repeal would encourage black immigration to Ohio, others asserted that such a controversial position would threaten Whig success at the polls.[69] The charge that William Bebb was straddling the fence on controversial issues such as civil rights reform was essentially correct—the politically astute leader sometimes supported but at other times opposed the Black Laws. An Ohio journalist humorously pointed out that Bebb first decided which region he was in before making public his views on the racial codes.[70] But Bebb became more decisive on the subject after his election. "I cannot forget that the Black Laws still disgrace our statute books. All I can do is to earnestly reiterate the recommendation for their unqualified repeal."[71]

That encouragement notwithstanding, Bebb did not have any immediate influence on the Ohio legislature. Though the General Assembly was solidly in the hands of the Whigs in 1846, 65 to 43, they blocked the initiatives of progressive members to abolish the Black Laws. As conservative Whigs and Democrats saw it, legislative support for repeal meant political suicide in most districts in Ohio. The radical press was unforgiving. The *Salem Anti-Slavery Bugle,* for example, said

> Every body who put faith in the promises of Whig leaders, anticipated the speedy repeal of the odious Black code. Action was however put off from day to day, there were so many more important things to be attended to—there were dogs to be taxed and grave-yards to be protected, Insurance companies to be chartered and Banking corporations to be defended, License laws to be re-modeled and gambling laws to be enacted, new counties to be erected and old quarrels to be revived, party squabbles to be attended to and speeches made for Buncombe.[72]

In this regard, Bebb led the legislature closer than it had ever come to abolishing the Black Laws. In the 1846 gubernatorial campaign, Bebb called for a modification in the Black Laws, an idea that surely alienated conservative Whigs. As it turned out, Bebb called for reversing the testimony clause in the Black Laws to attract voters in the Western Reserve. Later in the campaign, while in conservative Mercer County, he insisted that he opposed enfranchising blacks, admitting them as jurors, or enabling black children to attend schools with white youths.[73]

His speeches in Mercer County resonated with conservative whites, who generally opposed the immigration of African Americans to Ohio. After Virginia slave owner John Randolph emancipated slaves in Mercer

County, a number of whites organized to expel them. During the political campaign, Bebb played on the racism against blacks. As a writer for the *National Era* put it, "a few demagogues attempted to turn the thing [expulsion] to political account, and make it work out a balance in favor of 'the Democracy.'" Although some editors of Democratic newspapers apologized for the outrage, they stood in favor of "the vigorous enforcement of the Black Laws."[74] Conservatives in the Whig Party did little better. On the one hand, when it was expedient to do so, they were conciliatory to the antislavery interest. They were careful, however, not to alienate proslavery voters. Both parties exhibited "contempt for the claims of the colored population."[75]

Nevertheless, progressives in the state legislature pushed for civil rights reform, as Bebb had suggested. Representative Brewster Randall of Ashtabula told the 1846 house that the Black Laws were impractical and unjust. He doubted that by merely repealing them a "flood of colored persons" would enter Ohio.[76] Two years later, Representative Samuel Russell of Harrison County made a motion to the house that it should form a special committee to consider repealing the Black Laws. The fight to repeal the Black Laws finally began to show signs of progress when Governor Mordecai Bartley expressed a desire to see the codes repealed. His successor, William Bebb, advised the same. The house formed a five-man committee on January 11, 1848, to study the question. Next, Harrison G. Blake, of Medina County, proposed a repeal bill, which the committee approved. However, the bill failed by a 41 to 25 vote on February 1. Russell immediately proposed a personal liberty law to discourage kidnapping. The measure would have prohibited Ohio officials from using the instruments of the state, such as its jails, for the reclamation of runaway slaves. The Russell Bill also failed on a vote of 24 to 36.[77] Alfred Phelps, of Geauga County, appealed to white paternalism: "How does the Negro deserve this treatment—does he come upon you from his wild fastnesses to bring midnight conflagration and death? No! He comes a poor, humble, and servile being, content to be your hewer of wood and drawer of water."[78] Phelps obviously believed that the Black Laws were unjust, yet he did not contend for admitting blacks into the mainstream of Ohio's political or social culture. The Phelps appeal was conservative, and he joined Ohio's chief executives, who called for the repeal of the Black Laws while they denounced any interest in achieving an integrated society. As conservative as these appeals were, they still turned the Ohio legislature into a battlefield over civil rights reform.

The Mexican-American War also dragged Ohio into the slavery extension debate and further exacerbated discussions over repeal of the Black Laws. Many Ohio lawmakers believed the war illustrated the dangers associated with race mixing, and a senate committee recommended maintaining the Black Laws. Governor William Bebb was also thrust into the controversy. Bebb opposed the war, but he responded favorably when President Polk called on him to contribute Ohio troops to the cause. However, behind the scenes Bebb convinced Polk to adopt resolutions against the war and condemned the president for leading the country into it.[79]

For social reformers who were unable to pass anything through the Ohio General Assembly, tying civil rights to antislavery reform was still the best strategy. It is not surprising, therefore, that the slavery question continued to bedevil Ohio and the rest of the nation late in the 1840s. Antislavery Whigs were dismayed by the presidential prospects of Zachary Taylor, a Louisiana slave owner. But his views were not well known, and the Whig leadership believed that his military record (he was a general in the war with Mexico) and his popularity among his fellow slave owners would be enough to capture the presidency. For the most part, Ohio Whigs saw the war with Mexico as a conspiracy to extend slavery. As a Xenia newspaper put it, "They fight for their country, their altar and their homes! We, for power, for plunder, and extended rule! They are fighting for liberty—we, to extend the area of slavery. They are in the right, we are in the wrong."[80]

Concerned about the political future of the nation and state, antislavery Whigs encouraged John McLean to run for public office, but, as he told John Teesdale, he would not accept a nomination as a Whig because of interparty bickering. Although the Whigs had properly assessed troubles in the party, they had misjudged Taylor on the issue of slavery extension. As it turned out, Taylor was against the extension of slavery. He supported the admission of California into the Union as a free state and the organizing of New Mexico, Nevada, Arizona, and Utah as free territories, and he could count on northern Whigs in Congress to side with him.[81]

The Mexican Cession would dramatically affect both national parties as well as the party faithful in Ohio. Pennsylvania representative David Wilmot, a Democrat, proposed a plan in 1846 to outlaw slavery in any territory acquired by the United States after the war with Mexico. The Wilmot Proviso immediately reverberated through Ohio, where Whigs had yet to take a stand on the status of slavery in the new territory. As Salmon P. Chase surveyed the political landscape, he told a colleague, "Whig Conservatism is a formidable antagonist to the progress of liberal views."[82] President Taylor could not muster enough votes in Congress to get California admitted to the Union. Moreover, the subject became moot in the short term when Taylor died suddenly. He had been in office fewer than five hundred days. The future status of slavery in California would remain uncertain until Congress struck a compromise ultimately put together by Senator Stephen A. Douglas, a Democrat from Illinois. In the fall of 1850, Douglas pushed through Congress a series of laws that formed the Compromise of 1850.[83]

The continual uncertainty in the Whig organization over its philosophy did not benefit the Liberty Party in any appreciable way. While such men as Chase and Giddings were committed to abolition, both remained attached to other parties—Giddings to the Whig organization and Chase to the Democracy. Indeed, both men loathed slavery, but Giddings believed unity among Whigs and Liberty men could still be achieved if they could reach agreement on containing slavery where it existed. In 1847, Salmon Chase confided to New York representative Preston King, a Democrat, "I sympathize strongly with the Democratic party in almost everything except its submission to slaveholding leadership and dictation."[84] Had Democrats been willing to restrict slavery to the southeast, Chase would have supported them without reservation.[85]

Although Liberty men had labored diligently, they never managed to elect a slate of abolitionist candidates to both state and national office. To the dismay of party leaders, it had also failed to secure enough votes to repeal the Black Laws of Ohio. Amid growing dissatisfaction in its ranks, Liberty itself began to splinter. On the one hand, Liberty men such as Birney, Chase, and Giddings were willing to draw a line against slavery and press for repeal of the Black Laws. They interpreted an "antislavery republic" to mean that the founders sought only to restrict slavery, though in the long term they envisioned a free America. Such a program, they believed, would draw more voters to the organization. On the other hand, less pragmatic Liberty men advocated immediate abolition, thus setting the stage for a party showdown. The Liberty Party did not survive past 1847, and the new Free-Soil Party arose to fill the political vacuum.[86]

In Ohio, the tensions between slave and free were a microcosm of the national debate and led national leaders from all parties to focus their attention on the racial divide as it existed there. Positioned between slave and free states and with its connection to Article VI, the slavery prohibition in the Ordinance of 1787, Ohio was destined to provide national leadership in the quest to reach a settlement on the slavery issue.

By 1848, Chase and those of his colleagues who were dedicated to a pragmatic party agenda turned toward establishing an organization dedicated primarily to opposing slavery extension. In June 1848, they organized the Free-Soil Party, a new coalition of progressive Whigs, Liberty men, and Democratic defectors. They announced in the new party's antiexpansion platform: "We wage no war against the slave states. We do not ask that Slavery be abolished by congressional enactment in any State. But we do demand that slavery shall not lay its foul hands upon us. We do demand that slavery shall cease to control the action of the national Government. We do demand that slavery shall be excluded from national Territory."[87] At the Free-Soil convention in Buffalo that August, former president Martin Van Buren was nominated for president.

Although opposition to slavery extension was one of its national goals, the Free-Soil Party also embraced the cause of its Ohio branch, focusing on the abolition of the Black Laws. Benjamin Bofinger, a founding member, asserted that the organization would have a clear racial policy dedicated to "the repeal of the disgraceful Black Laws of Ohio." As the party officially declared, "all men are free and equal" and entitled to equal protection under the law.[88] Obviously, they meant black men as well as white men, and Ohio activists relished a showdown at the polls. Senator Thomas Corwin, a Whig who had not defected, stated plaintively that Free-Soil would "break down the Whig."[89]

Although African Americans were separated from the mainstream by race and denied the vote almost everywhere in the country, they were still politically savvy—in Ohio and elsewhere in the nation. Since the 1830s, a black convention movement had risen in the North in response to slavery and northern laws of discrimination. By the 1840s, both state and national conventions turned to political activism in an effort to achieve greater civil rights for blacks. The National Convention of Colored Men established state chapters throughout the North and met annually to explore ways to improve the quality of life for blacks. Furthermore, its members published newspapers in several northern states, called for temperance, and established schools for a classical education as well as vocational training. Black activists in Massachusetts vowed to participate in the convention movement "as a means to operate and cooperate with our white friends, against TWO of the greatest evils ever inflicted upon an innocent and inoffensive people—slavery and prejudice."[90] Civil rights reformers in Ohio shared their sentiments and organized the State Convention of Colored Men.

Forced to choose between Whigs and Democrats on the national level, black voters and civic activists in the North usually gravitated to the Whig organization. Although Democrats and conservative Whigs shared many interests, the former had a reputation for supporting white supremacy far more stridently than did the Whigs. Southern Whigs were drawn more to the party's states rights philosophy than to social reform. Northern Whigs often held the reigns of power, and in the states where African Americans were allowed to vote, they cast ballots for the Whig ticket. Thousands of African Americans voted in New York and most of New England.[91]

In 1838, the State Convention of Colored Men, led by John Mercer Langston, the first black attorney and first black elected official in Ohio, advocated enfranchising black males, arguing that it was "unjust, antidemocratic, impolitic and ungenerous to withhold from us the right of suffrage."[92] The state legislature would not consider expunging the designation "white males" from its constitution until 1850, a move that was soundly rejected. Whereas progressive Whigs in Ohio were willing to join the states that enfranchised blacks, conservative Whigs and most Democrats were against it. Thus, Ohio blacks observed the political scene in 1848 from the distance created by the color bar, declaring at the National Convention of Colored Freemen in Cleveland that repealing the Black Laws was its top priority.[93] The delegates resolved, "Let us be diligent, doing all we have the ability to do; so that if we must be made longer to bleed beneath the heathenish proscription, we must at least have this consolation—That we have exerted ourselves to the utmost to escape the bloody scourge."[94] As the Whig Party disintegrated, African Americans gravitated to the Free-Soil Party, which declared, "We go for the repeal of all laws in this state that make any distinction among men, on account of color, or anything else."[95] Free-Soil blacks and whites parted ways on slavery, however; blacks called for its abolition without delay and whites officially opposed its extension.

African American leaders also continued to pressure the Ohio legislature to rescind the Black Laws. These spokesmen included Columbus minister James P. Poindexter, Cleveland barber John L. Watson, William H. Day, and attorney John Mercer Langston. Under their leadership, the State Convention of Colored Men succeeded in attracting Democrats in the Ohio house. Lobbying the Democrats was critical to any reform that might take place. Franklin L. Backus considered the arguments for repeal compelling and agreed to use his influence among his colleagues.[96] William H. Seward, Abraham Lincoln's future secretary of state, made a speech in 1848 urging Ohio Democrats, "Reform your Codes, extend a cordial welcome to the fugitive who lays his weary limbs at your door, and defend him as you would your paternal gods; correct your errors that slavery has any Constitutional guarantee which may not be released and ought to be relinquished."[97] Their appeals were apparently sincere, but the Democracy, like the Whigs, would not voluntarily strike the racial codes of Ohio.

The National Convention of Colored Men also pressured the Ohio congressional delegation to use its national platform to further civil rights reform. The Colored Men considered Joshua Giddings a spokesman for their causes. Giddings, in addition to advocating repeal of the Black Laws, insisted that African Americans had as much a natural right to pursue happiness as any American. In 1849, the Colored Men praised Giddings for "advocating our claims in the United States Congress."[98] They also declared "[t]hat the constitution of the State of Ohio, which limits the elective franchise to 'all white male inhabitants,' is inconsistent with the fundamental principle which asserts, that 'all men are equally free and independent.'"[99] The Colored Men also spoke directly to blacks, committing their resources to purchasing copies of the *David Walker Appeal* for distribution. Introduced in 1829, the *Appeal* was among the most militant political newspapers written by an African American; it urged enslaved blacks to overthrow the yoke of oppression.[100]

Indeed, there remained powerful opponents to civil rights reform in Ohio. A writer for the *National Era*, for example, accused state senator Thomas Ewing of introducing a bill that would have "enslaved a portion of the people of Ohio." In sum, the bill proposed the "registration of each particular black, mulatto, and quadroon" in townships throughout Ohio. Ewing reasoned that local whites and township officials could keep better tabs on blacks who were legal residents of Ohio. The bill also called "for the expulsion of any colored visitor from another township, and from any other State." Ewing went on to advise the state to authorize the sale "of any colored person who, after having been removed from the township or the State," returned in defiance of Ohio law. The sale, however, would not be in perpetuity; it would have amounted to temporary servitude, "six months for the first offense and twelve months for the second."[101] Equally exasperating to the editors of the *National Era*, Senator Ewing was from Cincinnati, easily one of the most racist cities in the Midwest. It is with little irony that the state legislature elected Ewing as U.S. senator in 1830, and in 1850 Governor Reuben Wood appointed him to serve the remainder of the term of Thomas Corwin, who had resigned from the Senate.

Though they were frequently rebuffed, African Americans and their allies in Ohio faced the future with optimism. During a period of heightened anxiety for free blacks following the revised and more stringent federal Fugitive Slave Act of 1850, the Colored Men carried their grievances directly to Ohio lawmakers. In 1850, the State Convention of Colored Men and the state constitutional convention were meeting in Columbus. The Colored Men petitioned for the opportunity to speak to the assembly, and Oberlin-educated William H. Day and John M. Watson of Cleveland delivered their messages. In his address to the state convention, Day appealed to the assembly to strike from the constitution the word *white*, which had restricted suffrage to white males. Day explained, "Law finds its home and its definition nowhere but in the bonds of universal brotherhood, the claims of equality or equity, the demands of inherent and inalienable rights, identical with the principles of democracy and the genius of the Christian religion."[102] The *National Era* reported, "The speeches of both gentlemen exhibited much thought and patriotic devotion to their country and race." Ohio lawmakers listened with great interest and in good behavior, which the editors of the newspaper interpreted to suggest "a most cheering state of progress in the public mind."[103]

To support the African American argument for civil rights, Day explained that Ohio stood out as an exception in the North in denying black suffrage. He pointed to Pennsylvania and New York and the New England states that had granted black suffrage. He also explained that some southern states had also enfranchised free blacks. "We have been taught by you," Day continued, "to believe that the Constitution of the United States is the supreme law of the land. The Constitution of the United States makes no distinction of color." To dispute the notion that blacks required state subsidy for their survival, Day offered as evidence that the approximately twenty-five thousand African Americans living in Ohio had already accumulated property valued in excess of three million dollars. Despite state policy that initially deprived them of state-funded schools, they now operated twenty-four schools, and, where the state allowed it, black and white children attended mixed schools.[104]

William Howard Day and other college educated men clearly illustrated what the founders of Ohio and its early general assemblies had suspected: educating African Americans meant ending white privilege. College-trained leaders had established the State Convention of Colored Men, and they were the ones who pressed for full inclusion of African Americans into the mainstream of Ohio society. The AME Church founded Wilberforce University in 1856 precisely to train ministers and provide a classical education for blacks. Wilberforce, the first black institution of higher learning in the country, quickly became a mecca in black education. African Americans and their white allies expected educated blacks, the "Talented Tenth," to grow larger once the state eliminated the Black Laws. Their allies included the Society of Friends, which, at its annual meeting in 1848, called on the Ohio legislature to "repeal all laws which make civil distinctions between the white and colored citizens of this State."[105]

As everyone knew, black as well as white, defeating the Black Laws would come only by legislative enactment. The Free-Soil Party offered their best chance of success. However, as a minor political party, Free-Soil needed to form a coalition with Democrats or Whigs. And this was the quandary facing the party. Its leaders, Chase, Giddings, and Bailey, had hoped to achieve a reversal of the racial codes, but opposition from the majority parties was not easy to overcome. Indeed, they recognized that civil rights reform was anathema to the hardliners in either party. Yet, Chase and his colleagues were well aware that racial codes were inconsistent with the principles of equality embedded in the legal systems of the state and federal governments. They recognized that the Black Laws were badges of injustice. But Chase and his colleagues were also realistic. Although the Free-Soil Party favored social change, the organization had officially resolved, "We desire a homogenous population for our state and believe that we shall have it whenever slavery shall cease to force the victims of its tyranny into the uncongenial North."[106] Free-Soil was not seeking to enlarge the black population in Ohio; it had determined only that the racial codes of the state had no place in a free society. Hence, repealing the ghastly laws remained a priority of the Free-Soil Party in Ohio. But integrating blacks into the mainstream was not yet on the radar of most progressive whites.

By its opposition to slavery extension, the Free-Soil Party immediately attracted Ohio voters who had spurned the agenda of liberal-minded Whigs, who favored immediate abolition. Perhaps sooner than expected, the Free-Soil Party was embroiled in a bitter election struggle in Ohio in 1848. The Whig and Democratic parties had been oscillating in their control of Ohio for some time. Free-Soil advocates recognized that they could not immediately seize the reins of power, but, with the major parties closely positioned, they would likely win seats in favorable districts. The new party approached 1848 with this in mind, especially in counties with a strong Free-Soil constituency, such as Hamilton. Democrats solidly controlled some of the most conservative districts in the state, including Hamilton County, where they could count on winning at least seven seats in the election of 1848. The Whigs, now in control of the legislature, conspired to weaken the Democratic Party by gerrymandering Hamilton County and other parts of Ohio. The Whigs in the legislature pushed an apportionment law through the assembly; little did they know that the scheme would ultimately spell their doom as a political force in the country.[107]

Historically, the Whig Party had a poor record on civil rights reform in Ohio. The Whigs in Ohio "claim to be the true friends of our race," the *Rochester North Star* reported, "yet will not repeal the odious Black Laws." Conservative Whig lawmakers in the house had consistently aborted attempts to pass a repeal bill, and reformers in the assembly had little hope that such a bill would pass. Some Whig members of the house threatened to leave Ohio should the legislature repeal the Black Laws. Whigs in the senate also opposed repeal, defeating in 1848 a bill to modify the testimony law (19 to 14), and passing a bill postponing the repeal question indefinitely. Only one Democrat voted against the repeal bill and three Whigs voted for it; it appears that members of both parties defeated the bill.[108] Unable to count on its platform to win southern Ohio in a state election, Whig politicians invented a scheme for victory.

The Whig legislature divided Hamilton County into two districts, city and county; assuming that they would have a majority in the city, the party would pick up two new representatives. Just two additional Whigs would enable them to maintain their tenuous hold on the legislature. Democrats had a majority in county precincts, and redistricting would hurt them at the polls. In a "secret" meeting at Columbus, Whig lawmakers reapportioned several Ohio counties while Democrats were unavailable to vote. Disturbed by the deception, Democratic lawmakers immediately argued that the apportionment law was unconstitutional. Chase, who considered himself a Democrat, also thought the action was unconstitutional: "The legislature possesses no power to divide a county."[109]

Statewide, the Whigs mustered enough votes to elect Seabury Ford governor. A Connecticut Yankee, Ford had come to Ohio in 1807 with his parents. Ford was educated in the common schools of Ohio, and, after graduating from Yale in 1825, he returned to Ohio to study law in the offices of his uncle, Judge Peter Hitchcock, and Samuel W. Phelps. Ford started his political career as a Whig in 1835, winning elective office as a representative from Geauga County. Ford's election as governor came at the right time for African Americans and other civil rights reformers. Ford advocated repeal of the Black Laws. As he read Ohio history, the legislature had enacted the Black Laws primarily to restrict the immigration of African Americans to Ohio. It had failed miserably. Instead of preserving Ohio for whites, Ford argued, the state's testimony law had actually injured black residents by denying them the ability to offer evidence in court. Ford also objected to the law that denied black youths access to public schools. As an alternative to the state's policies of exclusion, he urged the legislature to develop a segregated school system for the education of black youths. He could not enact those policies himself, but his support made it easier for the assembly to act. His election would be the last Whig victory in Ohio.[110]

The celebration of the election of a Whig governor was immediately dampened by the outcomes of various legislative contests in Ohio. Charges of all sorts by both parties filled the air. Democrats accused Whigs of electing ineligible candidates under state law. Alanson Jones, the Whig candidate for sheriff in Clinton County, for example, had sought a house seat in clear violation of Ohio law, which barred an elected official from seeking another public office. Jehu Trimble, the Democratic candidate, had come in second. In Portage County, Whig George Sheldon and Democrat David L. Rockwell also squared off for house seats. Democratic candidates, having lost both these elections, naturally cried foul.[111]

The most serious election challenge occurred in Hamilton County. George W. Runyan and Oliver M. Spencer, both Whigs, assumed that they had won the election in the two newly formed districts. Justices of the peace Mark P. Taylor and E. V. Brooks quickly certified the results, but court of common pleas clerk E. C. Roll protested, alleging that the apportionment law that had divided Hamilton County was invalid. Roll submitted the names of George E. Pugh and A. N. Pierce, both Democrats, who took their seats as the duly elected representatives. The Whig candidates arrived in Columbus too late to assume seats in the house chamber. Undeterred, they formed their own chamber in another part of the legislative building.[112] Such an arrangement could never work, and cool-headed officials searched for a compromise. The solution to this dilemma came from two representatives elected on the Free-Soil ticket.[113]

As it turned out, the big winner in the election of 1848 was the fledgling Free-Soil Party. The stakes were high in this election because the Ohio house of representatives would choose its speaker, elect a U.S. senator, and appoint the chief justice and an associate justice of the state supreme court, plus common pleas judges. The legislature would also help award state contracts. Both parties had an agenda, especially in their choice for senator. William Allen was the preferred candidate of Democrats, and the Whigs leaned toward Thomas Ewing. Dr. Norton S. Townshend and Col. John F. Morse, elected to the General Assembly on the Free-Soil ticket, instantly became powerful men, holding key votes that

ultimately decided the immediate future of the legislature.[114] When both
ad hoc legislatures—the assembly of Whigs and the assembly of Democrats—sought to resolve the dispute, the Free-Soil representatives came
to broker a deal. A Cincinnati physician, Townshend's position on slavery and civil rights had been clear since at least 1837, when he joined the
antislavery cause. Colonel Morse was elected from Ashtabula County in
the Western Reserve, a staunchly abolitionist area. He made the offer to
the Whigs, pledging the Free-Soil vote if they elected Joshua Giddings
to the U.S. Senate and rescinded the Black Laws. Conservative Whigs
considered Giddings, a former Whig, too radical in his opposition to
slavery and refused the offer. Townshend made a similar offer to the
Democrats, but instead of Giddings, suggested Chase as the candidate
for the Senate seat.[115]

Chase had long agreed with the Democratic ideology in principle, objecting only to its stance on slavery. An erudite and flexible politician,
Chase also argued that Democrats had been wrongly labeled as the party
of slave owners. He once accused Ohio abolitionists of driving away
Democrats by their radical politics, and had hoped to unite Democrats
and Whigs. By 1848, Chase still hoped to unite antislavery Democrats and
Whigs, and he shared his views with fellow moderates, including August
Belmont. Belmont, a successful banker and future diplomat, opposed
slavery. Yet he had reservations about any abolitionist activity he branded
as militant. Instead he shared the philosophy of Stephen Douglas, who
would debate Abraham Lincoln in the 1858 Senate race, calling for each
territory to decide on slavery. Chase, who agreed with some of these
principles, told Belmont that he hoped to "bring about a union of all
democrats on the ground of the limitation of slavery to the States in which
it then existed and non-intervention in those States by Congress."[116]
Thus, Democrats found him acceptable and cooperated with the Free-
Soil delegation. According to Salmon Chase, the compromise divided
the Ohio house of representatives among twenty-eight Whigs, thirty-
four Democrats, seven Free-Soilers, two fringe Whigs, and one who was
a questionable Democrat. Voting with the Democrats, Free-Soil struck
down the apportionment law that had been adopted by the Whig Party in
1848.[117]

As the new year began, African Americans in Ohio waited with great
anticipation for the day the legislature would abolish the Black Laws.

Although a compromise had been reached between the Democrats and Free-Soilers, blacks did not assume that the legislature would follow through. Meeting at a Methodist Episcopal church in Columbus on January 10, 1849, the State Convention of Colored Men pressed the legislature to repeal the racial codes. The Colored Men recognized that in Ohio they did not possess political power; nonetheless, they claimed to have "moral power" and would use it to pull "down the strongholds of oppression and wrong."[118] Similar gatherings were held in Oberlin and elsewhere in the state, where blacks vowed to work diligently to secure equal rights. Their activism doubtless contributed to the long-awaited abolition of many provisions of the Black Laws.

The Democratic legislature moved swiftly to carry out the agreement it had made with the Free-Soil Party. Trumbull County representative John F. Beaver submitted the bill on December 13, 1848, calling for the repeal of the immigration and testimony laws and establishing a black school system. These measures passed the house on January 30, 1849, on a vote of 52 to 10. The senate passed the bill on February 6, on a vote of 23 to 11.[119] The General Assembly elected Chase to the U.S. Senate as a Free-Soil candidate, a post he accepted enthusiastically, though he denied that it was a result of a political deal. Rather, he implied that the existence of a pact between Free-Soilers and Democrats that made his election possible was ludicrous because the legislature had elected him without any agreement that he should surrender his principles on slavery. The Democrats who had chosen him were fully aware that he would oppose slavery extension. He assumed that they had finally come to embrace his interpretation of its democratic heritage. "I have gone straight on where Democratic principles required me to go, turning neither to the right hand nor to the left hand, no matter who was pleased or was displeased."[120] The editors of the *National Era* supported his position, concluding that Chase did not compromise his moral principles or religious commitments for the election to the Senate. Moreover, in a letter to the editor, Samuel Lewis, a member of the Free-Soil Party and gubernatorial candidate in Ohio in 1853, insisted that Chase "was the very best man to accomplish the ends" of the Free-Soil Party. "Corruption," Lewis naively concluded, "could not have placed such a man in the United States Senate."[121]

African Americans in Ohio hailed the repeal bill as a significant achievement in the struggle for civil rights reform. They organized a series of mass meetings to praise the state legislature as well as affirm their commitment to further reform. At a "Mass Meeting of the colored people of Columbiana County," they adopted several resolves, extolling the virtues of temperance and dedicating themselves to "the liberation of their brethren in bondage." They considered intoxicating drinks harmful to health, destructive to the mind, and corrosive to human nature. They declared that no one who failed to act in behalf of enslaved blacks was worthy of the title of reformer. The Columbiana County meeting also condemned colonization as a vicious scheme, which they repudiated. They praised the legislature for partially repealing the Black Laws, "and look[ed] upon it as the omen of a better day."[122]

In central Ohio, African Americans assembled at the Second Baptist Church in Columbus to address their continued grievances with the state. Organized by L. L. Taylor, the convention reviewed many of the "inconveniences" suffered by African Americans under the Black Laws, and highlighted "some of the benefits resulting from their partial repeal." They resolved that they were pleased with the partial repeal of the racial codes and declared "[t]hat the repeal is not an act of grace, but of justice, and right, and evinces a return to the principles of '76, and to the Bill of Rights of this State." They pledged they would never rest until all Americans equally enjoyed the privileges of citizenship. The repeal, though partial, strengthened and inspired African Americans.[123] It was a great day in Ohio, and black leaders paused to express their gratitude to civil rights reformers and the state legislature. African Americans also assembled at mass meetings in southern Ohio. Delegates at a mass meeting at the Union Baptist Church in Cincinnati both celebrated the partial repeal of the Black Laws and praised representatives Townshend, Morse, and others for making the reforms possible.[124]

Almost every friend of the civil rights movement in Ohio considered the new law a significant modification in the Black Laws. A writer for the *Rochester North Star* observed that it secured "the right to admit the testimony of colored and white persons in all matters of law upon the same footing."[125] The new law abolished the registration law and the requirement that immigrating blacks enter into bond and surety with a freeholder, removed the testimony restriction, and struck the employment provision in the Black Laws. As great as these changes were, some provisions in the black codes remained on the statute books of Ohio, "branding the colored man with inferiority, and sinking him below the level of a common equality." The legislature made at least three exceptions in the repeal bill: it left in force the election law, the jury law, and the relief law. Moreover, in 1859, the legislature enacted a law barring anyone with a "visible admixture" of African blood from voting and provided penalties for any official who allowed such persons to vote.[126] Therefore, Ohio continued to deny black residents essential civil rights. Faced with losing control of the state to the Whigs, Democrats had agreed only to revise the Black Laws. They did not claim to have a genuine commitment to civil rights reform. Nevertheless, these reforms were significant, although final abolition of the Black Laws was still almost forty years away. Many Ohio activists celebrated because the state immigration law no longer graced the statute books. This achievement laid the foundation for greater civil rights reform after the Civil War and during the national civil rights revolution in the twentieth century.

The school law of 1849 was also a partial victory. It replaced the exclusion of African Americans from state schools with a basically—but not wholly—segregated public school system. Only in rare cases (in districts where there were only a few students of either race), and with the consent of whites, would black and white children sit in mixed state-supported classrooms. As with previous legislation, funding for black education came from black taxpayers. The state mandated that "an accurate list of all colored taxpayers" be maintained to benefit black education. But "no property of any white person in any regular district shall be charged with any tax for the benefit of the schools" established for black youths. The legislature authorized schools to be established in "every township, city, town or village."[127] The schools offered a year-long program, with periodic interruptions for the harvest season. A board of examiners certified teachers and placed a principal and an assistant in each school.

The Democratic General Assembly made another modification in the school law in 1853. The 1849 act had authorized school districts to use only funds from black property owners to fund schools for African Americans. The policy was not implemented without controversy, however. William Disney, the treasurer of Cincinnati in 1850, attempted to defraud the black school board of funds that had duly been collected from black taxpayers. The aggrieved taxpayers sued, seeking a writ of mandamus from the supreme court to compel the city to appropriate the funds as prescribed by state law. The defendant offered various arguments, including that a black had been elected school director and that "colored voters" had chosen him. The court affirmed the school law separating black and white students and held "that this school fund should be divided to them in proportion to their numbers."[128] In response to the scheme to defraud black taxpayers, the assembly revised the school law in 1853, regarding education as a right that should be afforded to all children, black and white. Although limited, these reforms were the most that could have been expected at that time, given the legacy of racial prejudice in Ohio and elsewhere in America.

—

The Ohio Compromise of 1849 was the culmination of almost twenty years of protest against the Black Laws. Since the 1830s, civil rights reformers had labored to topple them, and their successes came in small increments. First, through the tactic of petitioning they were able to place their grievances on the legislative agenda as a way to talk with Ohio lawmakers. Blacks had also organized to improve their quality of life and resist the Black Laws. The State Convention of Colored Men, established in 1835, launched a petitioning campaign against the Black Laws. Civil rights reformers managed to galvanize residents equally exasperated over such explicit racial codes in a free state. Social reformers, those committed to abolition and civil rights, also succeeded in electing antislavery lawmakers to the General Assembly. As stunning as these achievements were, they alone did not topple the Black Laws. Their demise must be credited to third-party politics, an unlikely scenario in a state ruled by Whigs and Democrats. While conservative and moderate whites quickly labeled Liberty as an extreme single-issue party, the Free-Soil Party, organized in 1848, seemed a party of pragmatism. Indeed, the Free-Soilers considered the Black Laws heinous, but they limited their complaints to opposing the extension of slavery into federal territory. The unlikely election of 1848 gave Free-Soil, a fledgling political organization, enough leverage so that it could negotiate repeal. As a result of this agreement, the Ohio General Assembly struck key provisions in the Black Laws. Whether the racial codes were partially rescinded or not, or rescinded by contract, their repudiation began with the state election of 1848.

SIX

Enforcing the Fugitive Slave Act

1803–1850

THE BLACK LAWS were not the only limitations on the lives of Ohio's African American residents. The U.S. Constitution and the Fugitive Slave Acts of 1793 and 1850 also affected the lives of blacks in Ohio. In the four decades immediately following statehood, the Ohio legislature and courts voluntarily cooperated with the federal fugitive slave policy, establishing that runaway slaves were subject to capture and removal from Ohio. In light of these legislative and judicial initiatives, civil rights reformers who challenged the Black Laws continued their fight against the federal fugitive slave policy.

Civil rights reformers raised several arguments against federal fugitive slave legislation. Some contended that the federal government had no constitutional authority to pass legislation supporting and extending slavery. Others conceded that Congress had such authority to legislate on slavery but argued that Ohio was not bound to enforce that policy. They conceded that a state had the authority to mandate the return of runaway slaves but disputed the notion that it was *required* to do so. A sovereign state, abolitionists argued, could rightly presume that anyone within its jurisdiction was free. By 1810, the drama ensuing from abolitionist protests against federal and state fugitive slave legislation had taken center stage in Ohio.

———

Article VI of the Northwest Ordinance prohibited slavery, but it also inaugurated the right of recapture by declaring: "That any person escaping into the same, from whom labor or service is lawfully claimed in any one of the original states, such fugitive may be lawfully reclaimed, and conveyed to the person claiming his or her labor or service as aforesaid." The U.S. Constitution also guaranteed that fugitive slaves could be recovered (Article IV, Section 2). Although it seemed satisfactory at the time, as such compromises often seem to be, the constitutional provision did not set up procedures for recapture, thereby leading to confusion and conflict. Thus, on February 12, 1793, Congress passed the Fugitive Slave Act to extend the authority of slave owners to accomplish the recapture of slaves.[1]

The founders, in carefully crafted constitutional language, recognized slavery as a legal right where local law had established it. The Constitution also denied other jurisdictions the authority to automatically free a slave who had fled into their territory. The Fugitive Slave Act of 1793 ostensibly nationalized recapture by establishing a statutory enforcement mechanism for the constitutional provision. The Constitution also denied other jurisdictions the authority to automatically free a slave who had fled into their territory. Federal law now made it easier for slave owners to apprehend runaways anywhere in the United States. In so doing, the act gave slave owners enormous power, authorizing them to seize runaways and requiring only that they offer oral testimony that the person sought was indeed their property. The act authorized "any magistrate of a county, city or town" to conduct a hearing and rule on the question. Furthermore, it imposed a maximum fine of five hundred dollars or imprisonment of any individual who violated the law by providing assistance to a fugitive slave. The fugitive slave clause of the Constitution extended the authority of slaveholding states by preventing a free state from exercising its sovereign power to recognize the freedom of every individual under its jurisdiction. Thus, federal law commanded the states to grant slave owners the legal authority to remove a runaway slave.[2]

Although it was not compelled to do so, Ohio enacted its own fugitive slave law in 1804 as part of its Black Laws. The state statute assumed that runaway slaves were subject to recapture, while federal law forbade any state—slave or free—from emancipating such individuals. However, in practice the fugitive slave policy of Ohio proved to be ineffective.

The Ohio "act to regulate black and mulatto persons" adopted in 1804 had put into place an immigration law governing African American entry into Ohio. In that same statute, Ohio made recapture state policy. Because only those blacks possessing a bona fide certificate could be considered legal residents, all others in Ohio were presumed to be runaway slaves. Moreover, state law required employers to verify the free status of black workers. Anyone who harbored or secreted "the property of any person whatever, or shall in anywise hinder or prevent the lawful owner from retaking and possessing his or her" servant could be fined up to fifty dollars. To claim a fugitive from labor, the statute required "satisfactory proof that such black or mulatto person" was chattel property. Revised in 1807, that policy was stiffened by formalizing the intent that only free people could live in the state. This euphemism, of course, meant that Ohio was for whites only, for it assumed by default that African American immigrants were runaway slaves. To that end, the state imposed heavy fines on those whites employing illegal residents or shielding runaway slaves from recapture. In practice, however, the fugitive slave policy proved ineffective—it neither secured the rights of slave owners nor preserved Ohio for whites.[3]

Seeking to sabotage the operation of federal and state fugitive slave laws, abolitionists seized the opportunity to confront them. Before 1850, Ohio abolitionists managed to transform the state from one that enforced southern slavery to one that recognized that free soil made free men. Ultimately, Ohio courts applied a strict construction of federal and state fugitive slave legislation and granted removal only of slaves who escaped into Ohio, not those who had been brought under their jurisdiction with the consent of the owner and subsequently escaped. By doing so, the courts limited the reach of such laws though avoided a direct challenge to their constitutionality. Such a strategy had been effective in Britain and New England, where slaves were automatically freed upon being brought into a free state.

Ohio courts did not reach this favorable interpretation of federal or state fugitive slave law quickly or without encouragement. The antislavery movement, as well as the repeal movement, did a great deal to transform Ohio courts. The antislavery movement made it difficult for people of conscience to ignore the plight of black refugees. Furthermore, slavery was rapidly becoming extinct north of the Mason-Dixon Line, and, by 1837, the courts in Massachusetts and Connecticut had followed the English precedent that freed visiting slaves and slaves in transit. In Ohio, James Gillespie Birney, Salmon Portland Chase, and others presented this new legal strategy in the courts. Sympathetic judges ruled that anyone who brought a slave, or even allowed one to enter Ohio, automatically lost control over that individual.[4] This strategy had great implications for a state at the crossroads of slavery and freedom. Whereas the New England states were relatively isolated from the direct traffic of most slaves, Ohio, centrally located at the intersection of the East and West and sharing borders with Virginia and Kentucky, was directly accessible to fleeing slaves and travelers. Only seven years after statehood, its proximity to the institution of slavery dragged it into a controversy with Virginia. In Ohio's first fracas over runaway slaves, it became clear that the issue of recapture constituted the most divisive element of the new American political and social landscape to be seen up to that period.

The dispute began simply enough, involving a woman named Jane, the slave of Joseph Tomlinson in Virginia. Apparently, Jane had been a model slave, and Tomlinson rewarded her obedience and most likely allowed her to take on part-time jobs. Evidently, the arrangement worked successfully until the summer of 1808. Although Jane was not a militant, she obviously recognized that slavery deprived her of freedom and property. Unable to escape bondage, she took her role as a hired-out slave seriously, expecting to be paid for services rendered. George Hartford, an unethical storekeeper, refused to pay her. For reasons unknown, Jane did not complain to her owner, who might have interceded because he had a stake in the contract with the merchant. Instead, she stole assorted goods as payment, which the merchant later valued at approximately four dollars. Hartford viewed Jane's actions differently and filed a complaint against her, alleging that she had stolen property from his store. The authorities speedily convicted Jane. Many whites in Charleston agreed that she should be punished, but, when the court sentenced her to death, a large number of them thought it had gone too far. The evidence was circumstantial, the whites argued, and Jane was to receive punishment worse than that given to "a hardened offender." Convinced that the sentence was extreme, sympathetic whites took matters into their own hands.[5]

Meanwhile, Jane languished in a Charleston jail cell, waiting to be executed. As the state made preparations to hang her, sympathetic whites, believing that her conviction was reached by "improper means," appealed to Governor John Tyler to grant Jane a pardon.[6] Although it was commonly known that Tyler was against the death penalty, some of the white sympathizers, not wanting to risk Jane's life on the possibility of her not being pardoned, embarked on a plan to rescue her. Tomlinson, her owner, also questioned the severity of the penalty and participated in engineering the rescue. The whites paid a jailer to unlock the cell holding Jane and to leave it unattended. On November 9, 1808, Jane walked out of jail and began her odyssey as a free woman. Doubting that the people who had released her would later threaten her freedom, Jane made her new life in Marietta, Ohio, close to the Virginia border. She soon found employment as a domestic in the home of Abner Lord and began to enjoy the comforts of freedom. Jane met her husband, a free black in Marietta, and started a family. Life for Jane, apparently, was as good as possible for a person of color living in Ohio during this period.[7]

In 1810, Jacob Beeson, a professional slave catcher, came to Ohio hunting for a runaway slave with no connection to Jane. Beeson, however, was always on the lookout for runaways, and he became suspicious of Jane because she was a black person living in a community of mostly whites. After making inquiries in Charleston, Beeson put the pieces of the puzzle together, identifying Jane as a runaway slave. Especially important to Beeson, Jane's new circumstances made her more valuable as a slave than she had been when she escaped. She had since given birth to a child, and, under Virginia law, an offspring followed the status of the mother. Back in Virginia, Beeson alerted Governor Tyler to Jane's whereabouts. Moreover, Tyler had not approved of the manner whereby Jane had left the state; he criticized Tomlinson for his role in the rescue. Under state law, Tomlinson had been due payment for the slave condemned to death, and he had accepted money from Virginia upon Jane's death sentence. However, Tomlinson had then participated in the rescue without refunding the state. His actions infuriated Tyler, who asserted that Tomlinson had relinquished "any right he might have claimed on the said slave." Beeson, therefore, offered Tyler an opportunity to secure

Jane's capture so that she might be punished as prescribed by law. The governor issued a warrant for her arrest and Beeson served the papers to Abner Lord, her employer, in February. Lord and his antislavery neighbors, including Rufus Putnam, one of the founders of Ohio, blocked the rendition.[8]

A disgruntled Beeson complained to Ohio governor Samuel Huntington that the citizens of his state had harbored a fugitive from labor, contrary to federal and state law. Prominent residents of Marietta sent a memorial to Governor Huntington, urging him to provide Jane with sanctuary in Ohio. Beeson's "avarice alone," wrote the petitioners, "has prompted him to attempt to recapture" Jane. Huntington agreed and offered Beeson the excuse that neither federal nor state law mandated his participation in the return of an alleged runaway slave. Beeson returned to Virginia, reporting to Governor Tyler that Ohio had spurned him. Unwilling to engage in a debate over the meaning of the federal Fugitive Slave Act, Tyler, in response, pursued a different tack and identified Jane as a fugitive from justice. Beeson thus returned to Ohio with a requisition for the extradition of Jane, and Huntington reluctantly advised his constituents in Marietta of his duty to honor it. He directed the police to deliver Jane to Jacob Beeson. Once safely in Virginia, Beeson obtained permission from Governor Tyler to sell Jane and the child.[9] Historical evidence does not indicate the ultimate fate of Jane and her child, but it is reasonable to assume that they lived out their lives in bondage.

The severe penalty imposed on Jane for a relatively petty theft was typical of Virginia, where merely the fear of recalcitrant slaves led to stringent laws and harsh penalties. She had, in fact, committed the infraction during a period of heightened sensitivity. In 1808, Virginian James Ward had alarmed fellow whites when he warned of an impending slave revolt. Ward wrote Governor Tyler, "[W]e are led to believe that a general massacre is contemplated."[10] Every agency used to enforce slavery was put on alert, including the slave patrol that conducted random searches looking for armed slaves.[11] In this atmosphere, many slaves who had committed only minor infractions suffered grave punishments.

As Ohio and Virginia officials negotiated the removal of Jane, signs of future conflicts loomed on the horizon. Often bold and sometimes violent, slave catchers brazenly crossed state lines exercising their legal right to recapture suspected runaways, creating problems for Ohio settlers of all races. For example, George W. Smith, a resident of New Lancaster, Ohio, reported a gunfight involving slave catchers and alleged runaway slaves who had escaped from Virginia. "We had another serious time on Friday night last," Smith wrote, "[T]here were some runaway Negroes in town from Virginia, and some slave catchers made an attempt to capture them when some black residents" tried to stop them. The town of New Lancaster had become embroiled in "a civil war with the Negroes."[12]

The reclamation of Jane illustrates the widespread confusion that prevailed regarding the enforcement of the federal Fugitive Slave Act. Although Congress had designed the statute to avoid such misunderstandings, it had become apparent that state officials read the law differently than its authors intended. Governor Huntington of Ohio initially objected to the authority of the federal government to mandate that a state official return an alleged slave. From his perspective, it was up to the federal government to enforce its own fugitive slave legislation. Huntington was thirty-two years ahead of his time. In *Prigg v. Pennsylvania*, decided in 1842, the Supreme Court ruled that federal law mandated only that a state could not obstruct the process of recapture.[13] In *Prigg*, the Supreme Court declared that the states should enforce the Fugitive Slave Act, but that they could not be required to do so. However, in the early 1800s, the majority of Ohio whites still assumed that under interstate comity the framers of the Constitution had made the states responsible for returning runaways.[14] In Jane's case, Tyler, not wanting to get into a debate with Huntington over the Fugitive Slave Act, turned to the fugitive from justice law, rightly concluding that the latter was not as controversial. Ultimately, it was effective in winning Jane's return to Virginia as a fugitive from justice, which, in fact, she was.

The aborted enforcement of federal and state fugitive slave legislation in Jane's case foreshadowed the impending fugitive slave crisis in Ohio. The General Assembly, aware of the potential for conflict, periodically affirmed its commitment to return fugitives from labor on demand. In doing so, the Ohio legislature tried to please two masters. On the one hand, neighboring slave states expected Ohio's cooperation with recapture, and state leaders in Kentucky and Virginia frequently threatened to cut off trade with Ohio in retaliation. On the other hand, Ohio lawmakers faced the implied obligation of protecting its free citizens, both black and white. Ohio's fugitive slave legislation always supported the recapture of slaves who lawfully owed service. But, at the same time, Ohio could not easily ignore its commitment to its free African American residents. The 1804 statute had, by default, made the state a sanctuary for black residents who had registered with the clerk in the county wherein they resided. Moreover, by defining the procedures by which recapture and removal could be executed—requiring a claimant to present proof to an Ohio official, who would then issue a certificate authorizing the removal of a slave—the statute made taking a free black person from the state a violation of Ohio law.[15] This tension inherent in the law would be the means by which the reformers would make large gains in securing civil rights for Ohio blacks.

The fugitive slave issue strained relations between Ohio and its neighbors for several decades. State officials in such slaveholding states as Kentucky and even as far away as North Carolina distrusted Ohio officials, accusing them of disturbing the harmony with the slaveholding states.[16] Kentucky officials frequently demanded that their northern neighbor enforce its antiblack policies. In 1822, the General Assembly of Kentucky invited the Ohio legislature to join it in sponsoring a conference to discuss the problem of runaway slaves with delegates from Illinois and Indiana. The Ohio legislature adopted a resolution on January 27, 1823, urging the governor to appoint two commissioners to consult on the matter, to which request the Ohio executive acceded.[17] However, nothing substantial came from these talks; sixteen more years elapsed before Ohio enacted a comprehensive fugitive slave law.

In addition to Kentucky, North Carolina also made the unsubstantiated charge that Ohio provided refuge for runaway slaves. Indeed, the Ohio Black Laws were anything but encouraging to African Americans, free or slaves. Despite these laws, however, the flight of many enslaved blacks to Ohio made the state appear friendly to people of color. Abolitionist efforts in Ohio also made it seem that the state itself was involved in shielding runaway slaves. Hutchins G. Burton, the governor of North Carolina, sent Ohio governor Jeremiah Morrow a sarcastic memorandum, demanding that it practice the Eleventh Commandment: "Let everyone attend to his own concerns."[18] Comments such as this worried Ohio leaders. In 1832, Democratic governor Robert Lucas advised the

General Assembly that runaway slaves had put Ohio at risk of losing its trading privileges in the South. "Commerce," Lucas declared, must "pass through her territory or touch her borders."[19] Although Lucas wanted to protect the sovereign rights of Ohio, he did not want to jeopardize its business connections with the South. Joseph Vance, the first Whig to be elected governor of Ohio in 1836, shared Lucas's anxiety. Like his predecessor, Vance believed that the federal fugitive slave law compelled Ohio to enforce slaveholding by securing "to our fellow citizens in the slaveholding states" their slaves. But unlike Lucas, Vance believed that Ohio had honored its relationship with the South, and he was willing to entertain proposals to better protect free blacks.[20]

In the 1830s, the Ohio legislature played both sides of the issue. It insisted that its laws regulating blacks and mulattos offered residency to free people of color possessing a certificate of freedom. But the state also assured slave owners that the recapture of runaway slaves was possible. The Ohio statute passed in 1834 affirmed both goals. Blacks who conformed to state law, the legislature said, were legal residents of the state; however, nothing in the statute would "bar the lawful claim" of anyone who had escaped from labor.[21] This lukewarm posture of Ohio's officials created a dangerous precedent, for slave owners believed that the state's weakness facilitated the flight of runaway slaves. Officials in Kentucky and Virginia as well as those in other slaveholding states asserted that Ohio roads had become highways to Canada for thousands of runaway slaves.[22] Canadian courts and government officials did not recognize American claims for extradition. As early as 1819, Attorney General John Beverly Robinson of Canada refused claims requisitioning refugees from American slavery, declaring that they were entitled to protection from removal. In 1829, a Montreal judge also refused a claim to a runaway slave, holding, "the state of slavery is not recognized by the laws of Canada, nor does the law admit that any man can be the proprietor of another."[23] In response, one Kentucky representative lamented, "[I]t is impossible for their masters to regain possession of them."[24] Kentucky officials blamed Ohio for allowing slaves to travel its roads to freedom. The Kentucky legislature directed Governor James Clark to open a dialogue with Ohio on fugitive slaves. The legislature accused Ohio of giving runaway slaves "refuge within the borders of [the] state." They illogically held Ohio responsible, as if the state's existence was the deciding factor in a slave's decision to escape, rather than the oppressive institution of slavery itself.[25] Ohio would never live down its reputation as a state friendly to runaways.

—

Ohio's relationship with Kentucky was further complicated by the circumstances under which a black person entered Ohio. Even in those cases in which a black resident of Ohio was clearly a runaway slave, objections to his or her removal were made. When the evidence was questionable, Ohio raised vehement objections to an alleged slave's recapture. For example, in an 1835 case, a freeman named Frank had lived in Cincinnati since his youth and, according to his testimony, had never been a slave. Although a slave owner had claimed him before he reached Ohio, Frank had always considered his detention illegal, obviously thinking that slavery itself was simply unjust. His argument had credence in the law as well. Although his mother was a slave under Maryland law, she had been traveling through Pennsylvania when Frank was born. Thus, because he had been born on free soil, he was arguably a freeman. The counter-argument—that the laws of Maryland applied—was, of course, equally credible.[26] At any rate, once Frank arrived in Kentucky, his mother passed away, leaving him an orphan. For reasons that are unknown, he was later sold and the new owner hired him out in Cincinnati in 1827.

Cincinnati's black population was still sparse in the late 1830s, and abolitionists were aware of any newcomer to the city. They also were intrigued by the circumstances of Frank's birth and his entry into Ohio. Operating under the assumption that anyone who brought a slave into the state had freed the person by that act, abolitionists advised Frank that he was free under Ohio law. Frank asserted his free status and remained in Cincinnati, unmolested by the person who claimed him for the next eight years. After the death of the Kentucky man who had allegedly taken Frank to Ohio, some of his heirs captured Frank. Pressing that claim was H. T. Harris, a Kentucky farmer, who apprehended Frank as Ohio law prescribed and took him for process before justice of the peace William Doty.[27] Abolitionists organized to mount a defense against the removal of this alleged slave from Ohio.

Few attorneys anywhere in the country had become experts in the field of antislavery law by 1835, and legal strategy was in its infancy in Massachusetts and Connecticut. Antislavery lawyers based their argument on the British case of *Somerset v. Stuart,* which held that a slave brought into England was automatically free.[28] Ohio abolitionists, without a trusted legal advisor, hired Edward Woodruff to represent Frank. Their choice was not a good one, for Woodruff lacked both the experience and the motivation to vigorously try the case. Woodruff wisely made a motion for postponement, which the court denied, and the case was virtually lost. Once procedural matters had been completed, the court ruled for Harris, who locked Frank in a box and transported him to Kentucky. Subsequently, Harris sold Frank to a Louisiana slave owner, whose claim to Frank was short-lived. Louisiana courts had adopted the *Somerset* doctrine of automatic emancipation, which said that a slave was immediately freed upon reaching free soil. Louisiana whites friendly to Frank took the case to the Louisiana Supreme Court, which then freed Frank under the residency rule because he had lived in a free jurisdiction.[29]

The Louisiana opinion was not an aberration in the South during this period. The courts of slave states recognized that freedom was inalienable and that, once free, a person could not be forcibly returned to slavery. The Kentucky Supreme Court had reached this opinion in 1820, declaring a young woman to be free because of her residency in Indiana. These courts looked only to whether an owner had taken a slave to a free state, intending to make it his or her domicile. From this perspective, these courts did not recognize the theory of emancipation upon voluntary entry or residence, which was evolving in northern states. The South exempted slaves traveling with their masters, or those on holiday, from its doctrine that an owner and slave living in a free state would make the slave free. Southern judges based their opinion solely on whether a slave owner and his chattel had become permanent residents of a free state. Nonetheless, it is still remarkable that Louisiana, a slaveholding state, emancipated a slave under the theory of domicile before any northern state would do so.[30]

Ohio courts would not immediately adopt this interpretation. Slave owners could be comforted in their understanding that Ohio courts enforced the federal fugitive slave policy. And Ohio confirmed their optimism in 1837, when a Hamilton County court reviewed a sensational case involving a young woman name Matilda Lawrence (see chapter 4). It is important to review this case again in light of the legal arguments used as they related to the fugitive slave law. Matilda had entered Cincinnati in the spring of 1836, with her white father and owner, Larkin Lawrence. Lawrence had taken Matilda to other states that did not allow slavery, and on their journey back to St. Louis in 1836, she begged him to set her free; when Lawrence refused to do so, she escaped in Cincinnati and there found refuge among black residents. By the fall of 1836, her new friends had secured employment for her in the home of abolitionist James Birney. Matilda stayed close to home until the spring of 1837. Because of her prominent Caucasian features, most strangers considered her white. James M. Riley apprehended Matilda that spring and used the legal system to process her removal.[31]

As Birney and his colleagues prepared to challenge rendition of Matilda, they realized that they needed a lawyer whose reputation would not prejudice the case. Based on a number of speeches in which Salmon Chase had criticized the persecution of abolitionists, Birney and his colleagues hired him. At this time, Chase was against slavery but had not yet earned a reputation as an abolitionist. While justice of the peace William Doty scheduled the hearing, Chase obtained an injunction from common pleas judge David K. Estes. He expected the judge to conduct a substantial review of the new theory of automatic emancipation. Judge Estes took the case but rejected the argument on the grounds that comity made interstate slave transit a legal right. He remanded the case to Doty for its final disposition. Doty ruled in favor of the slave catcher, and Riley quickly removed Matilda from Cincinnati.[32]

The goal of antislavery lawyers was to bring their arguments to the Ohio Supreme Court. Using the power of judicial review, they wanted to create new law governing the recapture of fugitive slaves—specifically that the interpretation of the federal fugitive slave law, under a strict construction, did not apply to slaves taken into or allowed to enter the state. Until this point, without a precedent to follow, Ohio trial courts could rule in whatever way they wanted—if sympathetic to abolition the court could rule in favor of emancipation or, if not, it could remand the alleged slave to the claimant.

In 1837, Judge Estes had another opportunity to decide the reach of federal and state fugitive slave legislation over blacks living in Ohio. Robert Hereford came to Hamilton County tracking Jesse Cash, who had been a slave in Virginia until the early 1830s. Although he was not compelled to do so, Estes accepted testimony from Cash about the circumstances that brought him to Ohio. Apparently, Cash and his owner had reached an agreement allowing him to work in Ohio to "earn the means to pay for his ultimate freedom." Cash kept his part of the bargain and paid Hereford as agreed. Cash then moved to Cincinnati to start his life as a freeman. Hereford had no intention of letting Cash go, however, and asserted the claim that Cash was a runaway slave. Hereford secured a certificate from a justice of the peace to remove Cash, but abolitionists obtained a writ of habeas corpus from Judge Estes. Remarkably, Estes ruled that Cash was freed upon entering Ohio with the consent of the claimant.[33] Although the decision in this case was a positive ruling for the cause of antislavery, it served only as guidance to other trial courts. Ohio attorneys committed to the cause of freedom would continue to attempt to place this question before the state supreme court.

—

Interstate relations and the difficulty of enforcing the federal Fugitive Slave Act deeply concerned the governors of Ohio. On January 19, 1838, Democratic governor Wilson Shannon reported an atrocious act of seizure to the General Assembly. Families in Fayette County advised him that slave catchers had come into Ohio and removed a black man without due process. "This case as presented is one of cruelty and injustice," Shannon told the legislature.[34] He doubted that Congress had intended for slave catchers to carry out the vicious act of removing an alleged slave without process and asked the General Assembly to write a law punishing such crimes. The legislature, however, did not immediately enact a statute against kidnapping, and the crime continued to be a major problem in Ohio throughout the 1840s.

When David S. Burnett captured George McLane in Ohio in 1838, the question of his status turned only on whether he had escaped from slavery. Burnett produced circumstantial or questionable evidence that McLane was his slave, including an advertisement that he placed in local newspapers offering a reward for his capture. The legal argument that free soil automatically emancipated McLane was still not persuasive in 1838, and the trial judge ruled against him. Burnett swiftly returned McLane to a life of slavery in Kentucky.[35]

Soon thereafter, Ohio abolitionists challenged another recovery attempt of an alleged slave. An agent with the surname Mitchell arrived in

Cleveland in 1838, holding a black man named Nash in shackles. Abolitionists in the militant Western Reserve automatically assumed that Nash had been kidnapped, and they became more skeptical upon questioning Mitchell. The Mississippi slave catcher told an incredible tale of how he had tracked Nash to Buffalo, New York, where he then had apprehended him. Mitchell then entered Ohio by way of the Erie Canal, heading to the Ohio River en route to Natchez. From their friends in Buffalo, Ohio abolitionists learned that Mitchell had actually hired Nash to help him carry goods he had purchased in New York to Cleveland. Mitchell apparently devised this scheme to get Nash out of Buffalo, where Nash had many friends who knew of his free status. Abolitionists in Cleveland obtained a writ of habeas corpus from Judge Frederick Whittlesey and made plans to argue on Nash's behalf. Sensing that the abolitionists had foiled his scheme, Mitchell offered to sell Nash to them for seven hundred dollars, an offer they refused. On the day of the trial, abolitionists crowded the courtroom to demonstrate their sympathy for Nash. As Mitchell had anticipated, there was insufficient evidence to support his claim that Nash was a runaway slave, and thus the court ordered his release.[36]

Mass actions by abolitionists, such as those in support of Nash, paid off in a number of other cases litigated in Ohio. In Marion County, in central Ohio, a man named Bill lived as a freeman, unmolested by anyone until 1839. Whites knew him to be an industrious and honest freeman. A Virginia slave owner threatened Bill's safety when he claimed Bill as a runaway slave. The Marion police arrested Bill, and the claimant scheduled a hearing before Judge Ozias Brown. On the day of the hearing, whites friendly to Bill packed the courtroom. The claimant rested his case on the second day of the trial. Because the evidence of Bill's prior status as a slave did not convince Judge Brown, he refused to remand Bill. Angered by the decision, the slave catcher and his associates kidnapped Bill. Abolitionists who had sat through the hearing attempted a rescue, but the claimant and his associates held them back with pistols. The kidnappers then dragged Bill into the street as he stiffened his body to resist. They then threatened to kill him if he did not acquiesce. They found shelter in the office of a justice of the peace. The riot grew more intense, and abolitionists, armed with knives and sticks, surrounded the office. An abolitionist then screamed, "To the arsenal!" The frenzied mob turned in unison, marched to the armory, broke down the door and armed themselves with guns. While the kidnappers were distracted by the mob, Judge Thomas J. Anderson sneaked into the office where they held Bill. Holding the door ajar, Anderson beckoned to Bill, who then slipped out the back door. Before the kidnappers could react, the crowd overtook them. After the rescue Bill left Marion, presumably settling in Canada. Convinced that the Virginia slave owner had violated the free laws of Ohio, the police arrested him, but there is no evidence that he faced prosecution.[37]

Occasionally the abolitionists took the law into their own hands to prevent kidnapping. By 1839, Alexander Johnson and his family had been living safely in Portsmouth, Ohio, for eight years. Johnson's good fortune faded when he agreed to work for Thomas Barnes, who was actually an overseer posing as a traveler. Later, abolitionists discovered that he was a notoriously unscrupulous slave driver. Barnes used the common scheme of offering Johnson a job helping to transport goods to Cincinnati, where he had already set a trap. Once in Cincinnati, Barnes told whites that Johnson was a runaway; however, Barnes ignored the legal process Ohio law required for removing a slave from the state. His failure to follow Ohio law aroused the suspicion of abolitionists, who asserted that, if the claim were legitimate, Barnes would have followed state law. Convinced that a kidnapping was in progress, abolitionists rescued Johnson.[38]

Ohio abolitionists and its trial courts were operating without guidance from the highest tribunal in the state with regard to the removal of alleged slaves. Judges were thus free to go their own way, and slave owners were always uncertain as to the outcome of a case. Moreover, abolitionists considered it their obligation to intercede to help a victim of kidnapping or an alleged slave's removal without process. Such was the weakness of the federal and state fugitive slave policy. Thus, when a Missouri slave catcher tracked an alleged runaway slave named Ralph to Ohio in 1839, confusion in state policy prevailed. After identifying Ralph as the person he sought, the slave catcher brought him before Judge Samson Mason to obtain a certificate for removal. To the surprise of the claimant, the court accepted testimony from Ralph, who explained that he and his owner had an agreement that dated to 1835. The owner, Ralph explained, knew his whereabouts. He had come to Ohio as a hired-out slave to earn enough money to purchase his freedom. However, Ralph reneged on the agreement, asserting that Ohio soil had made him free. Judge Mason agreed. He rejected the idea that the contract between Ralph and the claimant secured the slave owner's property interest. "Such a construction," Mason continued, "would introduce almost unqualified slavery into all the free states."[39] The agreement could not have been construed to mean that Ralph was a runaway slave. By allowing Ralph to come to Ohio, Mason asserted, the owner had freed him under state law.

Although it rarely happened, American whites as far away as the Bahamas became kidnappers when they abducted individuals of African descent. Once the United States had banned the international slave trade in 1808, the illegal traffic of slaves increased. More significantly, the kidnapping of blacks occurred with dramatic frequency. The federal government did little to enforce the ban on the international traffic in human beings. Slave owners and traders considered the West Indies fertile ground for kidnapping and enslaving blacks. In 1839, a traveler named M. R. Frisbie, of New York, seized the opportunity to benefit from this traffic in human beings. While on vacation, Frisbie and his wife piloted their vessel, the *Mary Ann,* to Montego Bay, where they met Margaret Scarlett, a forty-five-year-old mother of five. Margaret and her family ran a business catering to vacationers. Newspaper correspondents in the United States described her as a beautiful mulatto woman; she did realize that her light complexion made her a target for abduction as a slave.[40]

From his conversations with Margaret, Frisbie learned that she desired to see the United States. Recognizing that he could sell Margaret for a goodly sum, Frisbie concocted a scheme to abduct her. He asked his wife to feign illness so that he could appeal to Margaret for her assistance in getting his wife home, because he could not both pilot the vessel and care for her. After discussing the matter with her family and friends, Margaret agreed to accompany them on the condition that Frisbie sign a contract verifying her free status. Margaret obtained other documents confirming her identity: one from Samuel Anderson, the American consul in Jamaica, and one from a Jewish merchant in Montego Bay. For greater security, she kept these letters private. She had hoped for a vacation in America and safe passage back home, but her worst nightmare was realized when, after arriving in America, Frisbie subdued her and boarded another vessel on the Ohio River, heading south toward New

Orleans. By the time they reached Ohio, Margaret's sullen demeanor had drawn the attention of the captain on the passenger vessel, and he inquired of her welfare. The captain found the tale too extraordinary to be fabricated and reported Frisbie to the authorities in Cincinnati. Although Frisbie left Cincinnati before abolitionists could secure a writ of habeas corpus, they alerted colleagues in New Orleans of the possible kidnapping, and Frisbie was politely escorted back to Ohio. Ultimately, the trial judge reviewing the case did not need to evaluate a free state's authority to emancipate a person brought under its jurisdiction as a slave. Margaret was freed because she had documentation of her free status.[41]

Two competing factions urged Ohio officials to adopt their positions. Antislavery lawyers contended that slaves brought into Ohio were free, and when a judge remanded such a person, abolitionists accused him of capitulating to slave owners. The state faced countercharges from conservative whites and slave owners from Kentucky and Virginia, who complained that Ohio had a friendly policy toward fugitive slaves. Both slave states pressured Ohio officials to develop policies that would secure the interest of the border states in slavery. Kentucky officials also complained that Ohio served as a conduit for slaves seeking refuge in Canada.[42] To the disappointment of Ohio abolitionists, slave owners received support from national leaders, including Democratic president Martin Van Buren, who believed that the federal government should negotiate for the recapture of runaways in Canada. Neither Congress nor the president took any action in this regard, however, and slaveholding states continued to pressure free states such as Ohio to strengthen its laws favoring removal of runaways.[43] To secure greater cooperation from Ohio, the Kentucky General Assembly in 1839 formed a commission intended to persuade the Ohio legislature to strengthen its laws governing the recapture of fugitives from labor.

The Kentucky commission called on Ohio in 1839. Charles S. Morehead, future governor of Kentucky, headed the delegation. John Speed Smith, a prominent Democrat and Kentucky lawmaker, joined him. The delegation hoped to awaken Ohio to the grievances of Kentucky slave owners. Observing that runaway slaves had become a chronic problem, Morehead asserted that "losses are felt to an alarming extent."[44] He hoped negotiations with Ohio officials would make them understand that their laws were "inadequate in the protection it affords to the interests of the slaveholding states." As Senator Norton S. Townshend later reflected on the summit, Kentucky wanted to make "freedom in Ohio worse if possible than slavery on the other side of the river."[45] The commission found Ohio lawmakers cordial and cooperative. It was forthright in making its request, asking Ohio "to provide all needful enactment to prevent evil disposed persons who may shelter themselves within the jurisdiction or limits of Ohio, and others from enticing away the slaves of Kentucky."[46] Ohio swiftly gave the committee such legislative assurances, but it could not predict the effectiveness of these policies.

The Ohio General Assembly passed the fugitive slave law of 1839, the most comprehensive state law on recapture it would ever produce. Modeled on the federal Fugitive Slave Act of 1793, the statute outlined the process for removing runaways. It authorized Ohio judicial officials to issue a warrant for the arrest of anyone claimed as a fugitive from labor. The statute authorized sheriffs and other constables to serve warrants by arresting and holding alleged slaves until brought "before some judge or court of record." The review was only a summary process, in which the testimony of the claimant was deemed sufficient "proof" of ownership. The statute, Ohio abolitionists asserted, flung open the jails of the state, armed slave owners with warrants, and placed the police in the service of slave catchers.[47] The law also made it a crime for anyone to interfere with recapture, placing special restrictions on the gathering of three or more individuals who might cause a disturbance or riot.

The Ohio act infuriated abolitionists, many charging that Ohio would become a virtual "hunting-field for slaves."[48] Others complained that the legislature, by capitulating to slave owners, had made Ohio "the paradise of kidnappers."[49] Whereas the 1839 statute pleased slave owners in other states, it polarized Ohio and eroded the confidence of abolitionists, especially those who had been straddling the fence. Here again, these individuals also came to recognize that the Black Laws had created a state culture that undermined its own republican ideals and heritage of freedom. Although Ohio had not created slavery, its racial codes had transformed the state into an extension of slaveholding territory. As such, Ohio had made kidnapping a frequent occurrence. By passing the 1839 act, Ohio had also created an environment in which unscrupulous individuals could carry out outrages against free blacks, including kidnapping.[50] White and black abolitionists called on men in Ohio to rise up in the defense of African Americans—slave and free.

—

While abolitionists praised the trial courts for limiting slavery on Ohio soil, they accused the state of capitulating to slave owners. Until Ohio adopted the fugitive slave law of 1839, abolitionists and trial courts had greater leeway in deciding when to approve a removal and when to challenge it. Now, the legislature apparently agreed that its laws were "wholly inadequate to the protection pledged" to slave owners in the federal Constitution. As the Ohio legislature now read the Constitution, Article IV, Section 2, required that runaways be "delivered up on claim of the party to whom such service or labor is due." Ohio's new "act relating to fugitives from labor or service from other states," therefore, was an attempt to enforce the federal policy. The Ohio law also outlined procedural terms for removing runaway slaves. It authorized a judge, justice of the peace, or mayor to review the application of such persons seeking a runaway slave and, upon satisfactory proof that the said fugitive had escaped, issue a warrant for the arrest of such individuals. The law authorized the sheriff or constable armed with a description of the person named in the warrant to "seize and arrest the said fugitive." An owner or agent could petition for postponement of the hearing for up to sixty days, during which period the accused, if unable to post a thousand-dollar bond, would remain in custody. Contradicting the expressed convictions of many of its residents, the legislature made it a crime for anyone to entice or aid a fugitive from labor or interfere with the process of removal. As the legislature conceived it, the state fugitive slave law would bind "all courts and police officers of Ohio and abolitionists with legal chains."[51]

The state fugitive slave law of 1839 did not produce its desired effect. It remained in force for only four years. Blacks and whites, engaged in a struggle to abolish the Black Laws, viewed the Ohio fugitive slave law as merely another racial code and advocated its repeal. They contended that the law inevitably led to the kidnapping of free African Americans. During the four years the fugitive slave law was in effect, several episodes of kidnapping illustrated the frightening vulnerability of Ohio blacks. In 1841, in Newark, Ohio, a man named John was apprehended as a fugitive slave. The kidnappers quickly carried him before a Licking County judge. Abolitionist attorney Samuel White successfully arranged for a change of venue, preferring to argue the case before progressive judge Samuel Bancroft in Granville. White argued that the claimant had not presented any evidence that John had escaped from a slave state into Ohio, a fact that was necessary for his capture and removal under state and federal law. Bancroft found this evidence persuasive and ordered John's release. The delighted attorney declared, "Knock off those shackles. No fetters here. John, you are a freeman. Run, John, run for your life and liberty."[52] John, with tears dripping down his face, thanked his attorney and scurried out of the courtroom. He left the United States for good to take up residence in Canada.

In search of runaways, slave catchers frequently, and logically, targeted those urban centers that had a reputation for supporting the Underground Railroad. Cleveland, located on Lake Erie, was easily accessible to travelers on the Erie Canal. The city had a growing black community by 1840, supported by abolitionists. Many others, however, believed the black population fostered competition in the workplace, thereby hurting white workers. Slave catchers frequently took advantage of this type of antiblack bias. In 1841, slave catchers brought three blacks to Cleveland while they were en route to a port on the Ohio River to board a ship traveling south. When questioned by abolitionists, the slave catchers explained that the slaves had escaped from New Orleans and had been captured in Cleveland. Abolitionists could not verify their account, and upon further research discovered that the individuals had actually been kidnapped in Buffalo, New York. Thomas Bolton, a Cleveland attorney, took the case and obtained a writ of habeas corpus for a hearing. Bolton, who was not an abolitionist, won the case, arguing that the individuals had been kidnapped in New York. Even if the individuals had been slaves, he continued, Ohio law did not empower slave catchers to bring them into the state. The court agreed they were not fugitive slaves and ordered their release.[53]

On the international front, proslavery officials in the U.S. government pursued formal channels to win the extradition of fugitive slaves in Canada. Indeed, efforts had been made since the 1820s to arrange for the expatriation of runaway slaves who had taken up refuge in that country.[54] In the 1840s, slave owners used ongoing negotiations between the American secretary of state, Daniel Webster, and the British foreign minister, Lord Ashburton, to raise the issue. The abolitionist movement had already become an international crusade, and slave owners would not obtain exactly what they wanted. (The treaty would also repeal article I in the Treaty of Ghent, 1814, wherein Britain pledged to restore private property, including slaves, to their rightful owners.)[55] The preamble to the Webster–Ashburton Treaty of 1842 declared that "the Traffic in Slaves is irreconcilable with the principles of humanity and justice."[56] There would be no agreement for the return of fugitive slaves, although the treaty provided for the extradition of fugitives from justice. Missouri senator Thomas Hart Benton readily pointed out the weaknesses in the treaty, from the perspective of slave owners, and he accused Britain of fostering abolition sentiments in its provinces. Referring specifically to article X in the treaty, British abolitionists complained that the pledge for the extradition of criminals was a subterfuge for removing black Canadians as slaves.[57]

Stateside, the Ohio Supreme Court could not so easily massage the question. Although the court would not rule on the question of automatic emancipation before 1850, its circuit judges, Ebenezer Lane and Peter Hitchcock, each of whom would later become chief justice of the Ohio Supreme Court, took a decisive step in 1841, when they reviewed the celebrated case of State v. Farr.[58] Touted as one of the grandest rescue cases in Ohio history, the Farr case is unique because it did not involve kidnapping. The slave owners were merely traveling through the state. No Ohio court had ever given a definitive ruling on the right of masters to pass through the state with their slaves. Ohio was centrally located, and traveling slave owners frequently used its roads en route to another destination. Moreover, the fugitive slave law of 1839 had made it a crime only to rescue fugitive slaves passing through the state. The law did not affect slaves in transit.[59] Ohio abolitionists wanted to test this issue, having learned a great deal about antislavery law following the Matilda case of 1837. As a correspondent for the Philanthropist confessed, "[W]e have been seeking an opportunity to bring up this point before our [C]ourts."[60] In 1841, Virginia slave owner Bennett Rains gave them that opportunity.

Rains and a gang of slaves entered Ohio on their way to Missouri. Rains and his party made it safely through Hamilton County, but trouble started when they reached Lebanon, in Warren County. Abraham Brooke, a longtime abolitionist, assembled his own party to rescue the slaves. According to newspaper accounts, the abolitionists urged enslaved blacks to take flight, informing them that Ohio law had made them free. Rains immediately brought charges against the abolitionists, confident that they had broken federal and state fugitive slave laws. The trial judge advised the jury to ignore the argument that Ohio law freed the slaves automatically upon entry with the knowledge or consent of the owner. Moreover, he advised that any rescue operation was illegal under the state fugitive slave law of 1839. With these specific instructions, the jury decided in favor of the plaintiff.[61]

On appeal to the circuit court, the jury instructions proved to be the Achilles' heel of the case. Justices Hitchcock and Lane were sympathetic to the abolitionist argument that free soil made free men under certain circumstances. The trial judge had erred by telling the jury to dismiss the defense's arguments. The circuit court thus ruled, "[B]ringing slaves into this state even with the view of passing through it to settle in another state made such persons free."[62] Hitchcock and Lane rejected the notion that comity secured a slave owner's interest solely because the owner and slave were in transit. They also concluded that the removal of an African American in an "attempt to carry him into a slave state" violated Ohio laws. Justices Hitchcock and Lane held that a "citizen had a right to rescue slaves from such illegal custody."[63] Soon after the opinion, correspondents from various newspapers hailed the decision as a landmark case. Nile's National Register reported that a slave becomes free the "moment he or she touches the soil of Ohio."[64] The Philanthropist reported, "Ohio is redeemed from the contamination of slavery."[65] Slave owners and their supporters blasted the opinion, but Ohio courts considered it an important precedent.

A few months later, Thomas Gaither, a Kentucky slave owner, appealed to Cincinnati justice of the peace R. A. Madison to issue a warrant for the arrest of an alleged slave named Rose, who was now known as Mary Towns. Armed with the warrant, Gaither successfully apprehended the woman but faced opposition when he sought a certificate of removal. Judge Richard Ayres denied the certificate on grounds that Gaither did not produce sufficient evidence that Towns was actually a runaway slave. Nonetheless, the court granted him a continuance and committed Towns until trial. Abolitionists hired Salmon P. Chase and Flamen Ball, law partners, who immediately deposed their client. Towns claimed that

John W. Woodson had permitted her to come to Ohio in 1831 as a hired-out slave. She found work in the home of J. C. Tunis, where she stayed for almost seven years. During this period she met her husband, Watson Towns, a Cincinnati resident, and they started a family.[66]

When Gaither returned to court, he faced Nathaniel Read, the new common pleas judge. Read found Gaither's affidavit faulty because it did not state that Mary Towns had escaped from Kentucky. Possibly, the judge went on, Towns might have been allowed to enter Ohio prior to taking flight. In the latter instance, she would not have been a runaway slave under federal law. Judge Read insisted that "liberty was the fundamental law" of Ohio. An affidavit for a runaway slave "should state distinctly that said person escaped from a state where she owed service into the state of Ohio." The affidavit of Gaither lacked such details, leading the judge to wonder, how "could anyone swear that such a slave had escaped from another state into Ohio?"[67] Judge Read, therefore, dismissed the case.

The circuit court opinion in the *Farr* case proved to be persuasive enough for Judge Read and other state courts. Until the state supreme court said otherwise, or a federal court offered a broad construction of its fugitive slave law, the rule of law in Ohio favored automatic emancipation whenever a slave owner brought or allowed a slave to enter the state. In an obscure case decided in 1843, an Ohio judge rejected the claim of a slave catcher who asserted that he had mistakenly brought a runaway slave into Ohio. When pressed to produce documents to verify his claim, he had none. The judge freed the woman because the claimant did not prove that she was a fugitive from labor. However, the judge ruled favorably on federal fugitive slave legislation, adding that had the woman "escaped from a slave state and had been arrested in Ohio, a contrary decision would have been the result."[68] Ohio courts, apparently, shared this view, careful to make the point that the act of bringing a slave into the state or allowing the person to enter violated the state law.

In light of these developments, the Ohio legislature reassessed its fugitive slave policy. In its first comprehensive report on fugitive slaves on January 18, 1841, the house announced that it had received a "large number of petitions, praying for the repeal" of the 1839 act. Moreover, it reported that they had also received "sundry petitions that the right of trial by jury may be extended to every human being" in Ohio.[69] The house committee made its report, conceding that questions involving personal rights were complex. It admitted also that Ohio was obligated to respect the customs of the slave states, given federal recognition of slavery. The committee agreed that the fugitive slave clause in the federal Constitution was "binding on the states." Notwithstanding public sentiments to the contrary, it continued, "a state cannot constitute a person, escaping from service or labor from another state, a FREE MAN, while in the state from which he or she escapes, he or she would be a slave" (emphasis in original).[70] Thus, the committee acknowledged that federal protection of slavery superseded Ohio law.

Furthermore, the committee considered that the object of the state's fugitive slave policy was to "fulfill the obligation" of Ohio to the federal government and the slaveholding states. The Ohio law was intended merely to carry out the federal constitutional provision by providing procedures for delivering up fugitive slaves. By setting up such procedures, the state intended to require a claimant to prove his interest in the individual claimed as a slave as well as to protect the rights of that same claimed individual. The question the committee raised was whether the 1839 act had successfully carried out these objectives. The house committee decided that the state law did not create a new obligation, nor would repealing it absolve Ohio of its responsibility to remand runaway slaves when claimed. Pointing to the federal Fugitive Slave Act of 1793, the committee concluded that the legislation was binding on Ohio. However, the act approved recapture only and did not include safeguards against kidnapping. Federal law, for example, did not require a claimant to present an affidavit or a description of the person claimed or to obtain a warrant for the individual's arrest. The state fugitive slave law did these things—its procedural requirements secured individual rights.[71]

Recognition of the authority of the federal fugitive slave policy did not mean that the committee did not critically appraise that policy. The committee concluded that the Constitution and the Fugitive Slave Act of 1793 did not "confer power upon state magistrates." It found that doing so was "entirely beyond the power of Congress." Asserting the sovereignty of Ohio, the committee concluded that each state is separate from other states; they are "wholly foreign and alien to every other state."[72] The federal Constitution, therefore, brought the states together, yet its powers could not be conferred on the states. Hence, the courts of Ohio were not obligated to act in the capacity of the federal judiciary. More-

over, the committee applied this reasoning to the power of the state legislature, concluding that federal law supersedes state law in matters relating to the Constitution. The federal Fugitive Slave Act was paramount in
matters respecting runaway slaves; the state's fugitive slave law was thus
superfluous.[73]

The committee did not have the authority to confirm what the Ohio
trial courts had held, namely that black individuals, without proof that
they had escaped from slavery, could not legally be removed from Ohio.
However, the committee affirmed that "in all cases the presumption of
the law is in favor of freedom." Every person in Ohio was free; the provision in the federal Constitution made it possible for an individual to
be removed only if that individual was a fugitive from labor. The obligation of Ohio, the committee concluded, was to refrain from passing laws
that obstructed the process of recapture and removal. Ohio's other duty
was to protect individuals who were wrongly apprehended as slaves. The
committee found that the 1839 law was ineffectual in this regard, and it
called for new legislation to shield blacks from kidnappers by giving
blacks the right to be tried by a jury.[74] Unable to deny that free African
Americans were in danger because of the state fugitive slave law, the Ohio
General Assembly rescinded the statute on January 19, 1843. To more
effectively protect African Americans from abduction, the Ohio legislature also "revived" its 1831 kidnapping law.[75]

Not all African Americans succeeded in securing their freedom in
court, and abolitionist writers produced several reports of free blacks
subdued in Ohio as slaves and taken from the state. They reported that,
in 1841, a free black man was violently subdued while standing at the
dock in Cincinnati and rushed across the Ohio River to Covington,
Kentucky. His abductors later claimed that the individual had escaped
from slavery in New Orleans. Abolitionists demanded that the mayor of
Covington secure his release, but Kentucky officials made only a half-
hearted effort to do so.[76] Another report described the family of John
Wilkinson, whose home in Georgetown, Ohio, was invaded by a gang
of kidnappers. After severely beating Wilkinson, they abducted his
fourteen-year-old son and carried him to Virginia. Wilkinson and his
friends pursued the abductors but were unable to catch them.[77]

A similar event took place in Huron County, approximately fifty
miles southwest of Cleveland. Formed in 1809, Huron County was an

important stop on the Underground Railroad and a hiding place for runaway slaves seeking to cross the Canadian border. Judge Jabez Wright, a noted abolitionist, is said to have "[n]ever failed to lend a helping hand to the fugitive slaves, feeding them when they were hungry, clothing and employing them."[78] Slave catchers attempted to execute a removal in this fervently antislavery community in 1842. Abolitionists learned that a gang of armed men had captured twelve free African Americans in the town of Fitchville early one Sunday morning while most people were asleep. After restraining their captives, the abductors quickly returned to Kentucky without any resistance. When abolitionists discovered the abduction, they formed a committee that condemned the seizure and vowed to win the release of the victims. The abolitionists also made an offer to purchase the individuals but had no success.[79] Under state law, slave catching was legal in Ohio, so long as the claimant proved that the individual recovered was a fugitive from labor. To bolster their claim, slave catchers also cited federal law, which also made recapture legal.

Free states such as Ohio continued to assert their sovereignty in order to limit their contact with slavery. Legislatures in the North recognized that they could not do away with slavery where local law approved it, but many northern lawmakers also argued that federal law did not compel them to enforce a claim to any slaves. The trial courts of Ohio applied a strict construction of federal law, returning only those slaves who had escaped. In other cases, many judges emancipated individuals whom slave owners had brought into their state. As a committee of the Ohio legislature concluded in 1841, "Slavery is not instituted in this State, and therefore its laws always presume every man free."[80]

—

With all the controversy surrounding federal fugitive slave legislation, the issue was bound to reach the U.S. Supreme Court. During much of John Marshall's tenure as chief justice, the Court continually affirmed federal power in all cases that arose under the Constitution or federal laws. The commerce clause had evolved into a powerful constitutional provision in such federal cases as *Gibbons v. Ogden*.[81] The nation's fugitive slave policy was rich in conflicts requiring federal review; however, under Marshall, the high court never heard any cases that might have brought slavery within its purview. Marshall intuitively recognized the difficulty of reconciling southern interests with those of northerners. As historian R. Kent Newmyer wrote, the two regions would not "tolerate commerce interpretations that encroached on their prerogatives—the former because of slavery and the latter because of an interest in reform legislation (including anti-slavery laws)."[82] Thus, when the Court reviewed cases with implications for slavery, it steered clear of issues it believed would require it to follow the slippery slope of slavery. In *New York v. Miln* (1837), the Court applied a fragile construction of the commerce clause, careful to placate both North and South.[83]

A New York law required ship captains to report the names of immigrants whom they were bringing into the state. The statute required captains to post a bond that no passenger would become dependent on state welfare. The state argued that this statute was authorized under its police powers, but challengers contended that it was an inappropriate regulation of interstate commerce and a violation of federal power. Chief Justice Roger B. Taney assigned Philip Barbour to write the Supreme Court's opinion. The Court held that New York had acted within its sovereign powers to protect its internal affairs when it drafted the statute. Barbour, however, sidestepped the question of whether Congress had an exclusive power to regulate interstate commerce.[84]

The Court applied this restricted interpretation of the commerce clause and slavery in *Groves v. Slaughter* (1841), in which it reviewed an interstate dispute between slave dealers and purchasers in Louisiana and Mississippi.[85] The case did not directly involve the status of any one African American. A slave dealer had sold slaves in Mississippi, ostensibly in violation of that state's new constitution. The Mississippi purchaser had signed a promissory note to the dealer but later refused to honor it on grounds that the sale was illegal. The plaintiff argued that the promissory note was a contract and also that any state ban on the sale of slaves infringed on the commerce clause, which secured federal power to regulate interstate commerce. The Court skirted the central issue by holding that the Mississippi legislature had not enacted the ban in the state constitution.[86] Hence, without a state statute the commerce clause was not applicable to the case under review. With this narrow ruling the Supreme Court maintained its distance from the growing controversy over slavery.

In 1826, New Jersey passed the North's first personal liberty law.[87] The law authorized an owner or agent to request a warrant for the arrest of an alleged fugitive slave. A successful petition required an affidavit from the owner under the signature of a judicial officer in the state of origin. Most significantly, the statute required the claimant to appear before a judge in order to obtain a certificate for removal from the state. Pennsylvania passed a similar law that year.[88] By 1892, nine northern states had adopted personal liberty laws.[89] All were designed to shield free blacks from removal.

By requiring documentation of ownership in order to remove an individual from the state as a slave, Ohio in 1839 joined other jurisdictions in imposing conditions on recapture. Ohio judges operated under the presumption that within state borders all individuals were free until a claimant provided proof to the contrary. Southern slave owners opposed these policies, and the U.S. Supreme Court finally ruled on their constitutionality in *Prigg v. Pennsylvania* (1842).[90]

Whereas the Marshall Court had been cautious, the Taney Court moved closer to a full review of the slavery question. Roger B. Taney was the son of a wealthy slaveholding family in Maryland. Appointed to the bench by Andrew Jackson, Taney never forgot his roots and ultimately used *Dred Scott v. Sandford* (1857) to give complete judicial support to slavery.[91] The case of *Prigg v. Pennsylvania* (1842) was a major step in that direction.

The controversy arose when Edward Prigg removed Margaret Morgan from Pennsylvania in violation of the state's personal liberty law of 1826. Prigg contended that the federal Fugitive Slave Act of 1793 applied and trumped the state statute. Both sides considered the dispute an opportunity to test the policies of the state and federal government in the Supreme Court. The Court ruled that the federal Fugitive Slave Act was constitutional—but that no state was compelled to enforce it. The decision of a state to execute the federal fugitive slave policy was a courtesy only. However, the court also voided all state fugitive slave laws, as well as the personal liberty laws, making enforcement of the Fugitive Slave Act solely a federal responsibility.[92] Thus, slave owners could legally remove fugitives from labor from a free state without judicial review by that state. This ruling vindicated those Ohio judges who had maintained that federal power to compel a state to enforce its fugitive slave mandate was "entirely beyond the power of Congress." The federal fugitive slave law, Ohio lawmakers would conclude, imposed only one obligation on the states: "not to pass any law releasing slaves from service."[93]

Although the *Prigg* case specifically released a state from any presumed obligation to enforce the federal fugitive slave law, it did not settle the question of the automatic emancipation of slaves who were allowed to enter a free state. In Ohio, only a circuit court had endorsed this theory. These cases left a great deal of legal ground on which to challenge the authority of slave owners. For example, when Henry Hoppess entered Ohio in the winter of 1845, the state of the law was far from settled, and this case would change the nature of the legal battles over slaves traveling with their owners on the Ohio River.

Over many years, Ohio's reputation of being intolerant of slaveholding struck fear into traveling slave owners and their agents, such as Henry Hoppess, who was merely a passenger on a boat traveling the Ohio River. Hoppess had spent most of his life in Wythe County, Virginia, and occasionally took on the job of transporting slaves. In 1844, he traveled to Arkansas on behalf of a client to bring back Samuel Watson, a slave who had been left behind when his owner relocated to Virginia. The slave owner died before being able to bring Watson to his new home, and his heir, a Mr. Floyd, hired Hoppess to escort Watson to Virginia.

Hoppess and Watson boarded the *Ohio Belle* in 1845, traveling the Mississippi and Ohio rivers heading toward Virginia. On January 21, the vessel made a routine stop in Cincinnati, and Watson, tired from the journey, walked onto the wharf when the ship landed. While there is no evidence that Watson was attempting to escape, Hoppess panicked, fearing a rescue by zealous abolitionists. Relying on the federal Fugitive Slave Act, he asked the sheriff to arrest Watson and hold him in the "Watch House" until he could arrange a hearing with Mark P. Taylor, the local justice of the peace, for a certificate to remove him. In doing so, Hoppess drew attention to himself, and once abolitionists learned that he was in town with a slave, they appealed to state supreme court justice Nathaniel Read for a writ of habeas corpus. The abolitionists obtained counsel from Salmon Chase, while Hoppess employed Nathaniel McLean. The case excited the public, and black and white spectators crowded into a "large hall" where the court met. During the trial, Hoppess admitted that he had brought Watson into Ohio but that he was acting under federal fugitive slave law. Chase argued that his client was automatically freed upon entering Ohio, echoing a decision circuit court judges Ebenezer Lane and Peter Hitchcock had reached in 1841. Citing this case and the holdings of other trial judges in Ohio, Chase argued that a slave became free the moment an owner brought or allowed him to enter Ohio. Although the question whether Hoppess had actually entered Ohio seemed clear, the court undertook a substantial analysis of the issue.[94]

Of course, certain facts in the case were incontrovertible. Hoppess and Watson had indeed been passengers on the *Ohio Belle,* which had docked in Cincinnati. There was no evidence that Watson had escaped, however; he was merely standing on the dock. Justice Read raised the central question whether someone in transit with a slave on the Ohio River was subject to the jurisdiction of any state. As a common pleas judge, Nathaniel Read had supported the emancipation of slaves brought into or allowed to enter Ohio by the owner. Now that he had been elevated to the state supreme court, he claimed that his position had not changed. "Slavery," he stated, "is a wrong inflicted by force and supported alone by the municipal power of the state or territory in which it exists. It is opposed to the principles of natural justice and right, and is the mere creature of positive law."[95] He cited the *Farr* case and concluded, "If a slave comes ashore anywhere in Ohio, by the consent of the master, he becomes free."[96] Removing any doubt about the state of Ohio law on this issue in 1845, Read continued, "The constitution of the United States only recognizes the right of recapture of a fugitive held to service in one state escaping into another."[97]

However, Justice Read ruled in favor of Henry Hoppess, demonstrating the complexities of race and law in nineteenth-century America. He reached his decision by assessing American culture and interpreting the importance of neutral waters for trade and commerce. Justice Read did not believe that blacks would ever live in America on an integrated basis. He considered blackness to be a larger barrier for African Americans than their condition of servitude. Had Watson been white, Read confessed, there would have been little difficulty freeing him from bondage. It was not so with a black, who continually faced discrimination long after the shackles had fallen. As he saw it, the Black Laws of Ohio demonstrated that social integration was not possible in the state in 1845. Thus, Read concluded that should Watson be emancipated he would live in a society that offered him limited opportunities. Read declared the Ohio River to be neutral waters, and chattel property in transport was safe from the reach of courts in bordering states.[98]

—

State v. Hoppess made it clear that Ohio had not found a legal path to meet the needs of either enslaved blacks or slave owners. Inevitably, the morass of law, politics, and morals triggered many cases in which black freedom turned on the predilection of a judge. With many "stations" on the Underground Railroad, Ohio was poised for conflicts between slave owners, abolitionists, and African Americans. Slave owners from riverside farms, such as those in Parkersburg, Virginia, were especially vulnerable to the flight of enslaved blacks and their disappearance into Ohio. In 1845, the infamous *Parkersburg* case (*Commonwealth v. Garner*) involved another sensational controversy of slavery and freedom.[99]

Virginia slave owners alleged that Ohio abolitionists had enticed slaves to escape. A party of slave catchers, including Francis Lewis, tracked the alleged fugitive slaves to Ohio, but before they could apprehend the escapees, Peter M. Garner and his abolitionist associates interceded on behalf of the alleged slaves to shield them from removal. The slave catchers, however, overpowered the abolitionists and the alleged slaves and forcibly took them to Virginia. As the news spread, the abolitionists demanded an investigation, charging that slave catchers had abducted free blacks and whites from Ohio. Virginia authorities filed a complaint against the slave catchers, charging them with violating the federal Fugitive Slave Act, and a county court swiftly convicted them. Ohio-appointed attorneys filed an appeal and arranged bail for the defendants.[100]

Meanwhile, abolitionists held a series of public meetings around the state. On July 24, in Cleveland, state representative John A. Foot chaired a mass meeting to condemn the abduction of Ohio whites. Marietta abolitionists also convened a public meeting to inform Ohio residents of the incident. Both groups adopted resolutions, declaring that they would "defend the free soil of Ohio, and the freedom and personal safety of the citizens treading it."[101] They vowed to protect Ohio's citizens from such outrages. Caleb Emerson, a noted abolitionist, wrote Salmon Chase, asking him to lead the legal team, but Chase was away from the office and could not respond. Unable to wait for Chase, the abolitionists hired ex-congressman Samuel M. Vinton as lead counsel. During this time, abolitionists persuaded Ohio officials to convene a grand jury to charge the

Virginia men with kidnapping. After his return to Cincinnati in August, Chase suggested a legal strategy for the defendants, although he would not participate in the formal arguments himself. Chase contended that questions involving the federal Fugitive Slave Act would only complicate matters. He considered the question of the status of the African Americans involved too controversial for a speedy disposition and would only complicate the case. Chase argued that by separating the fate of the white abolitionists from that of the alleged slaves, the defense might secure the release of the whites involved.[102] Vinton and other abolitionists did not accept his advice.

Abolitionists also appealed to Whig governor Mordecai Bartley, seeking an extradition order for the return of the alleged kidnappers. They argued that the controversy, if not quickly resolved, would disrupt the harmony that existed between the states. Bartley complied with their request, but Virginia governor James McDowell refused to hand over the alleged kidnappers. He supported his decision by noting that the men were on trial in Virginia for violating the federal Fugitive Slave Act.[103] Moreover, McDowell explained, the alleged kidnappers Bartley had requested were witnesses in the pending case against the Ohio men charged with violating the federal law, and "in consequence thereof reserved from surrender by a provision of law of this state until they are fully discharged from the process by which they are held."[104] To further subvert the strategy of the Ohio attorneys, McDowell issued a requisition for other Ohio citizens suspected of violating the federal Fugitive Slave Act.

The circuit court of Virginia heard the *Parkersburg* appeal in the fall of 1845. John J. Jackson argued for the state, claiming that the abolitionists had entered Virginia with the purpose of luring away slaves. The state attempted to strengthen its case by offering Mordecai Thomas, who was illiterate and in poor health, leniency in exchange for his testimony against his associates, but Thomas refused. Vinton and William A. Harrison, a local lawyer, argued that their clients had never been in Virginia. They conceded that the defendants had helped the African Americans but had provided only such assistance as taking their bags or tying their canoe on the bank of the Ohio River—after they had entered the state. Moreover, Vinton contended that slave catchers from Virginia had positioned themselves in Ohio before the alleged slaves crossed the state border. By doing so, they had threatened to kidnap free citizens, whose liberty his clients could voluntarily protect. Virginia countered that it had plenary control of its border along the Ohio River and that as long as the slaves were in the waters it could not be said that they had left Virginia. To the surprise of no one, the Virginia circuit court sustained the conviction, and the defense appealed the case to the Virginia Court of Appeals, the state's highest court. The defendants faced the prospect of languishing in jail into the new year, because the court had concluded its summer term. Unwilling to leave their clients in custody, the defense won an appeal for a special session of the court in December.[105]

Attorney John M. Patton represented Virginia, arguing specifically that Peter M. Garner and his associates in Ohio had kidnapped slaves from the commonwealth in violation of the federal fugitive slave law. Patton extolled the virtues of slavery and condemned Ohio abolitionists who had interfered with a local institution. When Vinton presented the defense, he explained that his object was neither to defend abolitionism nor to condemn slavery; rather, his duty was to argue sovereignty and free soil, which was the basis of the requisition submitted by the governor of Ohio. Virginia, Vinton asserted, could not dictate to Ohio how it should handle its internal policy. Vinton also argued that the central question in the case was whether the defendants encouraged the slaves to leave one state for another, which was essential for the conviction of the defendants.[106]

A great deal was at stake, and the Virginia court knew it. A military confrontation was unlikely to result from *Parkersburg,* yet the case held special meaning to slaveholding states. Though it was not directly involved, Kentucky kept a close eye on the proceedings, and its legislature adopted a fugitive slave law in 1846 in direct response to the *Parkersburg* case. Whenever a person harbors or hides a fugitive slave, the statute read, two witnesses should establish his or her guilt. Upon conviction, the person could serve up to five years in the state penitentiary.[107] This statute only magnified the tensions involving slavery, including disagreements in Kentucky, where some newspaper editors agreed that the Virginia men had violated Ohio sovereignty.

The Virginia court concluded that Peter Garner and his associates had never been to Virginia and so were not subject to Virginia law. This was a fragile victory for Ohio, however, because the defendants prevailed by only one vote.[108] The decision did not resolve the controversy over the recapture of blacks whose status as runaway slaves was questionable. Following the *Parkersburg* case, Ohio's interstate relations with Virginia deteriorated, as did its relations with Kentucky, which experienced its own fugitive slave controversy with Ohio in 1846.

There can be little doubt that, by 1846, the crime of kidnapping had horrified many Ohio whites. Although many whites considered blacks inferior, they viewed kidnapping as an infringement of the moral and political concept of personal liberty as well as an assault on state sovereignty. The removal of Jeremiah Phinney in the spring of 1846 not only illustrated this position but also demonstrated how liberal-minded whites took direct action to win Phinney's release. A series of events dating back to 1830 triggered this episode. Kentucky residents Thomas Long Sr. and his wife, Sara, owned Jeremiah Phinney and his mother Rose and held them on a small farm in Frankfort. Thomas died some time before that year, and Sara chose to lease Phinney for extra money. A Kentucky gambler known only as Allagier successfully negotiated a contract for him. Long agreed but stipulated in the agreement that Phinney should not be taken into Ohio.[109]

Allagier agreed to the terms of the contract but did not abide by them, choosing instead to visit Cincinnati soon after he signed the lease. The deception alarmed Long, and she demanded Phinney's return to Kentucky. The gambler ignored her messages until she threatened to sue for breach of contract. Unwilling to risk litigation, Allagier reluctantly returned to Kentucky and restored Phinney to his owner. African Americans who lived in Cincinnati were aware of the city's strategic significance for neighboring and traveling slaves, and they frequently visited with enslaved blacks, explaining what Ohio offered as a free state. In this case, although Allagier had kept a close watch to prevent an escape or a rescue, just as Long had feared, Phinney's brief encounter with free blacks in Ohio had broadened his horizons. After he returned to Kentucky, Phinney devised a plan of escape by pretending that he wanted to fetch some personal items he had left in Cincinnati. His request did not worry Sara Long because she assumed that he and Rose were content. But once Phinney had crossed the Ohio River alone, he went into hiding in Cincinnati and later traveled to Columbus, where he merged into the free black population.[110]

Sara Long advertised for his capture in Ohio newspapers, offering a $150 reward to anyone who returned Phinney to Kentucky. Thus, Phinney became a wanted man. Although he found employment and started a family, he remained conscious of the possibility of his recapture, and his fears made him constantly anxious. In 1845, fourteen years after his flight from bondage, Phinney initiated the process to secure his freedom legally. Knowing that Ohio law slowly had evolved to regard a slave as free if he entered the state with the knowledge and consent of a slave owner, Phinney sought legal counsel, and with his attorney, concocted a plan to acquire evidence that Sara Long knew of his whereabouts and took no action. In a forum as friendly as Ohio, the attorney believed that his client would prevail should his freedom be challenged.[111]

According to Kentucky newspapers, Phinney launched a letter-writing campaign to the Long family in 1845. He acted on bad advice. Sara Long had already passed away, and Thomas Jr. was terminally ill. The rest of the Long children had left Frankfort; only Bathsheba Long, a daughter-in-law, had stayed behind. A correspondent for the *Frankfort Commonwealth* speculated that it was unlikely that Bathsheba, heavily in debt, would advertise for a slave long forgotten. By writing, Phinney tilted the odds in her favor. "But for these letters," the correspondent continued, "it is probable that no further attempts to recapture him would have been made."[112] Alexander Forbes, a neighbor, offered to track Phinney while he hunted for his own fugitive slaves across the river. Bathsheba Long signed the appropriate documents, and Phinney became hunted. Forbes, however, considered capturing Phinney a secondary goal. Runaway slaves disappeared in Ohio and often traveled on to Canada, so he needed information in order to track his own slaves. Phinney had been in Columbus for a long time, and he moved about freely. Forbes went to the black community offering reward money for information. Jeremiah Phinney, in turn, came up with a scheme to defraud Forbes.[113]

Phinney provided faulty information, and, once Forbes figured it out, he devised a hoax to remove Phinney as a fugitive slave. Forbes recognized the difficulties of removing a man widely regarded as free from a community of vigilant abolitionists. He decided that he would follow state guidelines to the letter and bring his warrant to Judge Joseph R. Swan, who initially agreed to help—for a fee, which he secretly hoped would discourage Forbes. When Forbes agreed to the terms, the judge admitted that he did not want to become involved in the matter. Forbes concluded that he needed to lure Phinney out of Columbus, and he hired a white resident named Jacob Armitage to assist in the conspiracy. Armitage posed as a bridegroom who needed help carrying the luggage belonging to his bride, who was supposedly waiting at the office of magistrate William Henderson. Forbes and Henderson waited until Armitage and his party arrived, then they subdued Phinney the moment he entered the office. Henderson, aware of the strong feelings against kidnapping and realizing that federal law did not require his cooperation, hesitated to grant his approval to the recapture, but, on the advice of attorney F. T. Matthews, he ultimately granted the certificate for removal. Sheriff Henry D. Henderson and a Columbus resident named David A. Potter witnessed the hearing. Forbes and Armitage hurried Phinney out of town under cover of night. Once the news broke, the abduction of Jerry Phinney brought out the wrath of whites and blacks, and they quickly assembled a group of abolitionists to rescue him.[114]

Although many whites considered the federal fugitive slave law valid and operative in Ohio, they still denounced the manner in which Forbes had used it. The *Dayton Journal and Advertiser* reported, "The great mass of people of Ohio are not disposed to interfere with the laws of Kentucky, but they are not willing to see the majesty of their own laws insulted, and the rights of men in their midst trampled in the dust."[115] They considered Forbes's conduct reprehensible, concluding that he had resorted to trickery because Phinney was actually a freeman. Columbus exploded with mass meetings wrongly denouncing the incident as a kidnapping. (In fact, Phinney had escaped and thus was a fugitive slave.) "The excitement that has prevailed in this city since the kidnapping of the colored man Jerry Phinney has been such as we have never before witnessed," reported the *Ohio Press.* The media condemned the hearing in Franklinton as "a sort of sham trial."[116] The incident exacerbated an ongoing dispute between Ohio and Kentucky on the issue of fugitive slaves.

Abolitionists struck out in pursuit, following Forbes to Xenia, where they learned that he had boarded a stagecoach bound for Cincinnati. Undaunted, the posse mounted fresh horses and quickly resumed the pursuit, hoping to catch Phinney and his abductors before they reached Kentucky. Meanwhile, Columbus abolitionists organized a series of public meetings denouncing the outrage. They gathered at the Methodist

Episcopal Church on Town Street, and elected an ad hoc committee chaired by the Reverend D. Eldridge, charging them with designing a course of action. The committee vowed to avenge the Phinney family for the "heaven-daring outrage that threatened to reduce them to a hopeless condition worse than widowhood and orphanage."[117] They blamed Forbes and Henderson for putting the family in jeopardy and set in motion the process to prosecute them.

Not surprisingly, whites on the other side of the river scoffed at the "excitement" in Ohio, dismissing it as a manifestation of the sentiments of misguided abolitionists. They cited the protest in Columbus as an illustration of the "disobedience of Ohio to the Constitution of the United States, which required free states to deliver fugitive slaves." Kentucky whites were also defensive and denied that they participated in any kidnappings. If Forbes had kidnapped Jerry Phinney, a correspondent for the Frankfort *Commonwealth* surmised, the majority of Kentuckians "would have defended his rights as efficiently as any zealots of Ohio." However, they seemed confident that Phinney was a slave who had escaped from a Kentucky master and thus considered him subject to capture and removal under federal law.[118] Charges and countercharges were freely flung across the Ohio River until the states involved finally resolved the matter in 1847.

Ohio's governor Bartley filed a requisition with Kentucky governor William Owsley for the return of Forbes and Armitage under the fugitive from justice law. Bartley accused them of seizing, violently restraining, and removing Jerry Phinney from Ohio. Owsley chose instead to try the case in Kentucky. To prevent Forbes and Armitage from fleeing, he had them arrested. Judge Mason Brown, who presided in the Frankfort County Circuit Court, convened the trial in April 1846 to review "the kidnapping of Jerry Phinney."[119] Bartley authorized Attorney General William Johnston to represent Ohio at the trial. In a futile effort to change the venue, Johnston argued that the Kentucky statute of 1820, which made extradition conditional in cases involving slavery, violated the federal Constitution and the Fugitive Slave Act of 1793. He insisted that the earlier 1815 state statute applied and that such a trial should take place in Ohio. Unable to persuade Kentucky officials to transfer the parties, he argued that Ohio presumed everyone to be free until proven otherwise. He contended that slavery could only exist by state law. Hence,

Phinney thus could not have been a slave while in Ohio. He also argued that even if Phinney had been a slave, he became free when Sara Long consented to his return to Ohio. Such freedom, Johnston continued, was "inalienable."[120]

Johnston faced a formidable opponent in Charles S. Morehead, future governor of Kentucky. Morehead raised two fundamental questions in the case: Was Phinney a slave? If so, did the defendants have authority to capture him as a fugitive from labor? After noting that the federal Constitution had sanctioned slavery, Morehead rejected the northern theory of automatic emancipation and reminded the court that Kentucky approved slavery. Morehead produced witnesses who confirmed that Phinney was the slave of Bathsheba D. Long, as well as the affidavit authorizing Forbes to capture and return him to her custody.[121]

Judge Brown decided the *Phinney* case by answering two questions, which were subtly different from those raised by the defense: Was Phinney the fugitive slave of Bathsheba Long? Had she given Forbes authority to capture Phinney as a fugitive slave? Having no doubts about the law, Judge Brown released the defendants and ordered the authorities to deliver Phinney to Bathsheba Long. Although the decision disappointed William Johnston, he reported that Kentucky had cooperated fully in the investigation. Ohio abolitionists regarded the decision "as one that cannot be sustained" and filed a complaint against Forbes and Armitage in absentia.[122] The Ohio Supreme Court had not yet ruled on the theory of automatic emancipation nor would it ever subvert the federal fugitive slave law. It confirmed the Frankfort court's opinion that Jeremiah Phinney was a runaway slave properly recaptured under federal law.[123]

Unable to testify to tell his side of the story, Phinney had little chance of prevailing in any court. In the following year, Henry Williams found himself in the same predicament. Williams was born free in Pittsburgh and had made a good life in Cincinnati, regarded as a "worthy and industrious man." In 1848, a gang of white men seized Williams near his home in Cincinnati, "carried him across the river into Kentucky, and placed him in a Covington jail as a runaway slave." His wife and family, the *Rochester North Star* reported, "are deeply afflicted at the brutal outrage that deprives them of a husband and father."[124] And slave catchers could readily point to the federal fugitive slave law for authority to remove an alleged slave. Without effective personal liberty laws, African Americans had little protection from kidnappers.

—

Near the end of the 1840s, antislavery lawyers in Ohio shifted their challenges to federal courts, seeking test cases or defending suits and prosecutions that might void or at least undermine the federal fugitive slave policy. Writing in 1894, James H. Fairchild suggested, "In such centers as Cincinnati . . . there were young lawyers who made these principles their study, and rendered much unpaid service in the defense of those claimed as slaves." Fairchild also surmised that abolitionist committees in the cities "carefully looked up" cases wherein they could challenge the validity of the fugitive slave law.[125] A team of Ohio lawyers and abolitionists led the way, including James G. Birney, Salmon P. Chase, Seth M. Gates, and Joshua Leavitt. Indeed, according to Leavitt, Chase had promised to "see if he could find a slave in the District of Columbia who would consent to sue for his freedom in earnest, and thus bring the matter before the Supreme Court in a way that it shall not be in the power of the court to dodge the question."[126] The U.S. Supreme Court had already legitimized a state's right to refuse enforcement of the federal fugitive slave law, and abolitionists thought a direct attack on the law was possible. Some of these cases did not directly involve African Americans, but rather the abolitionists who helped them. For example, abolitionist John Van Zandt was sued by slave owner Wharton Jones in 1843 for helping nine of his slaves after they had escaped from Kentucky. Abolitionists used the occasion to raise the constitutionality of the 1793 law. Van Zandt had gained notoriety in Kentucky for helping slaves, and this automatically made him a suspect in such cases. Jones found his slaves in Cincinnati, as expected, in the company of Van Zandt. It "was a Christian act," the latter boasted, "to take slaves and set them at liberty." Jones managed to recapture all but one of the slaves, and he brought charges against the abolitionist for damages for the slave who had eluded him and for the cost of recapture.[127]

Both parties considered the question of the validity of the fugitive slave law important and therefore hired well-known attorneys. Thomas Morris and John Jolliffe represented Van Zandt, while Fontaine T. Fox and Richard Southgate represented Jones. Federal district judge Humphrey Howe Leavitt and U.S. Supreme Court justice John McLean heard the case. The attorneys agreed on the facts: Van Zandt had transported to Cincinnati, in a covered wagon, nine black men who were later discovered to be the slaves of Wharton Jones. They also agreed that Van Zandt did not entice them to run away, but had given them a ride. They diverged on the meaning of freedom and the federal fugitive slave law. The defense argued that the state constitution "regards all men as persons" and that Van Zandt had no evidence that the black men he transported were fugitive slaves. They contended that federal law secured only the "right of redelivery of an escaping servant" from one jurisdiction into another. And they asserted that the federal fugitive slave law did not apply. Not surprisingly, antislavery newspapers supported their contentions. The *Philanthropist* claimed, "The slaves escaped from Kentucky without Van Zandt's aid," and thus he could not have violated the federal fugitive slave law. The plaintiffs affirmed the validity of that law and argued that Van Zandt had met the conditions for harboring slaves, especially since, by transporting the individuals in a covered wagon, the defendant obviously understood that he was conveying runaway slaves.[128]

Before the court turned the question over to the jury, Justice McLean reminded jurors, "Slavery is local in its character, and that it depended upon the municipal law of the state where it is established. And if a person held in slavery goes beyond the jurisdiction where he is so held and into a sovereignty where slavery is not tolerated, he becomes free." After the jury received the case, it nonetheless considered the plaintiff's argument that Van Zandt had violated the federal Fugitive Slave Act. The jury found him liable, and the court fined him twelve hundred dollars. Represented by Salmon P. Chase and William Henry Seward, Van Zandt appealed the case to the U.S. Supreme Court without success. U.S. senator from Kentucky James T. Morehead appeared for Jones. In its response, the Court only clarified its position on the crime of harboring a slave, explaining that a written notice of an escape was perfunctory; an oral notice was sufficient. Furthermore, the court stipulated that any person who learned from the individuals themselves that they were fugitive slaves had been sufficiently informed.[129]

Despite this decision, abolitionists continued their assaults on the validity of the federal act, often by violating the law in order to test it. Francis D. Parish, a Cincinnati abolitionist and lawyer, presented antislavery lawyers with such an opportunity. When Jane Garrison showed up at his home seeking work, Parish employed her without knowing that she had escaped from slavery. Garrison had fled the plantation of Peter Driskill, a Kentucky slave owner, who had sent his son Andrew and an agent, Colonel Mitchell, to find her. Parish boldly allowed Andrew and Mitchell to visit with Jane, and she obviously recognized the son of her former owner. Garrison would have returned with them, Andrew later told his father, but Parish interceded and demanded "judicial authority" to certify the removal.

Supreme Court justice John McLean heard the case on circuit. Henry Stanberry and J. H. Thompson, attorneys for the plaintiffs, produced witnesses who testified that Francis Parish had prevented removal of Garrison. Sarah Gustin, a white employed by Parish, confirmed that the defendant told Mitchell "he could not take the woman, without lawful authority."[130] Salmon Chase and John W. Andrews defended Parish, contending that the Constitution recognized African Americans as persons. They also applied Justice McLean's theory, namely that the framers of the federal Constitution had erred when they endorsed the idea of "property in men." Nonetheless, McLean instructed the jury to find for the plaintiff, should they accept evidence that Parish had harbored fugitives from labor. After the jury verdict against Parish, the court ordered him to pay a five-hundred-dollar fine.[131]

Revisions in the Black Laws of Ohio in January 1849 immediately gave African Americans greater security in the state. The repeal law had specifically struck the act that barred a black from giving testimony in a court of law against a white. In the fall of that year, a black woman named Mary Elizabeth Monroe was put on the witness stand to testify against a Tennessee claimant named Cogzell. As the story was told in Clermont County, Cogzell had come from Memphis, holding a bill of sale for a woman matching Monroe's description. He claimed that he had purchased Monroe for $350 dollars. Abolitionists did not dispute his claim but informed Monroe that Ohio law had freed her when Cogzell allowed her to enter the state as the nurse of a Mrs. Philpot. Monroe left her and obtained employment in the home of James Sloane. Cogzell seized Monroe and put "her in restraint and confinement, intending to transport her out of the State of Ohio." Before he made it out of town, abolitionists, armed with a warrant from Esquire Long, a magistrate, challenged his claim, alleging that Cogzell had unlawfully confined Monroe. The state court considered Monroe's testimony convincing—"calm, clear, and deliberate—without confusion or hesitation, and duly corroborated by the testimony of others."[132] Monroe, in addition to winning her freedom, was the first African American known to have testified in Ohio since the repeal of the Black Laws.

Ohio abolitionists would have only one more chance to attack the Fugitive Slave Act of 1793 before Congress revised it with a more stringent law in 1850. That chance came with an escape that took place in 1849, although the trial did not occur until 1853. George Washington McQuerry, a twenty-eight-year-old mulatto, escaped from a Kentucky farmer named Henry Miller. McQuerry also led four other men to freedom. Miller immediately formed a posse and posted a four-hundred-dollar reward for their capture. To throw their pursuers off the trail, McQuerry and his party split up as soon as they left Louisville. Two of them presumably made it to Canada. One was captured before he crossed the Ohio River. McQuerry crossed into Ohio, but brazenly settled in Troy, a community approximately one hundred miles from the Kentucky border, a decision that ultimately cost him his freedom.[133]

As abolitionists described him, McQuerry was a personable individual who made friends quickly. Renowned Ohio abolitionist Levi Coffin portrayed him as "industrious and upright; a man that was well respected in the neighborhood." He had little difficulty securing a job or a wife. What he did not know was that the reward Miller had offered for his capture had not been lifted and that anyone could turn him in for profit. John Russell, a Troy resident, turned McQuerry in for the hundred-dollar reward. Once he received news of his former slave's whereabouts, Henry Miller sent his son Jacob to apprehend McQuerry. Unwilling to undertake this task alone, Jacob delivered a warrant to Marshal James A. Trader in Dayton under the federal Fugitive Slave Act of 1850. Russell led them to McQuerry's home. Marshal Trader placed McQuerry under guard to discourage a rescue and escorted him south to Kentucky.[134]

Marshal Trader and his posse made it safely to Cincinnati, but before they crossed the river, African Americans and abolitionists challenged the removal in court. Peter H. Clark, a black educator, obtained a writ of habeas corpus from Supreme Court justice John McLean, on circuit in Ohio. Clark wanted him to examine the requisition under the more generous terms of the 1793 act. Marshal Trader thought that the Fugitive Slave Act of 1850 should apply and so he called on federal commissioner Samuel S. Carpenter to review the case, but the commissioner yielded to McLean.

On the day of the trial, spectators crowded the courtroom. Abolitionists had asked John Jolliffe and James Birney to argue the case. Henry Miller presented evidence to confirm his claim. McLean, himself an Ohioan, agreed with the abolitionists but was compelled to rule for the claimant because the evidence clearly showed that McQuerry was a runaway slave. Jolliffe and Birney unsuccessfully appealed to the Supreme Court for a writ of certiorari. In a move that surprised almost everyone, Miller offered to sell McQuerry for fifteen hundred dollars. His decision, no doubt, stemmed from the belief that McQuerry had become damaged goods and had to be sold. African Americans in Cincinnati could not come up with the money, however, and abolitionists did not pursue the matter. Armed with a certificate for removal, Miller carried George McQuerry to Kentucky, where contemporaries believed he was sold farther south.[135]

John Jolliffe had succeeded Chase as the "attorney general for fugitive slaves" upon Chase's election to the U.S. Senate. Jolliffe was a talented lawyer who, like Birney and Chase, risked loss of reputation and clients to help runaways. Levi Coffin noted that Jolliffe's talents as a constitutional lawyer could have made him wealthy had he not volunteered to support such an "unpopular cause." For more than a decade, Jolliffe lent his expertise to the defense of runaway slaves. The *McQuerry* case was one he could not win—George Washington McQuerry had been a fugitive from labor, and Miller had the law on his side. In the decade to come, John Jolliffe would be vilified among southern whites just as his mentors had been, but he would, however, be admired by blacks and the friends of freedom.

By 1850, Ohio trial courts had clarified their interpretation of the federal Fugitive Slave Act. No longer could slave owners boast, as Virginia's Jacob Joseph had in the *Wheeling Times* in 1839, "Happily, the laws of Ohio provide for reclamation by the owner" of any runaway slave that entered its jurisdiction.[136] Circumstances surrounding the rights of escaped slaves, if not all blacks, had changed by midcentury, and, although slaves who escaped into Ohio were returnable, those brought into or allowed to enter the state were free under local law. The state supreme court had not immediately affirmed this reasoning, however, and critics charged that such decisions as *State v. Farr* had offered only dicta on the question. Ohio courts strategically avoided a direct challenge of the validity of the federal Fugitive Slave Act of 1793. Under these circumstances, therefore, the fight for freedom in Ohio would continue on into the 1850s. And discord would continue to spread in the Union, especially as the slaveholding states bordering the Ohio River demanded strict enforcement of the federal Fugitive Slave Act and insisted on recognition of the legal right of slave owners to hold an individual in slavery while in Ohio for a limited period of time.

SEVEN

The Fugitive Slave Crisis in the 1850s

UPON PASSAGE OF the Compromise of 1850, the fugitive slave controversy in Ohio took on new meaning. Congress revised the Fugitive Slave Act as a concession to slaveholding states. It provided stringent guidelines for the recapture and return of runaway slaves, obviously aimed at circumventing the *Prigg* decision of 1842.[1] It also minimized the role of northern courts in enforcing the federal fugitive slave law. Northern states, such as Ohio, had become increasingly unhelpful in returning fugitive slaves. The 1850 act made it easier to recapture runaway slaves, because the United States government would administer the process.

While the 1850 law made it easier for slave owners to recapture and remove slaves who escaped into a free state, the act not only failed to quell dissent but it actually generated a wave of protest throughout the North and especially in Ohio.[2] Meanwhile, in 1855, the Ohio Supreme Court ruled that state sovereignty entitled it to recognize the free status of anyone who occupied Ohio soil, no matter how ephemeral the contact. The court recognized only one exception: runaway slaves who fled from a slaveholding jurisdiction into Ohio. National leaders seeking to resolve the slavery controversy watched helplessly as relations between the two major regions slipped ever more deeply into an abyss of confusion and despair.

With the debate growing more difficult to moderate and tensions between the states increasing markedly, it is no wonder that U.S. senator Salmon Chase exclaimed that "slavery was the great question of the day."[3] Neither federal law nor state courts successfully resolved the debate; the Civil War ultimately did. The state of Ohio, in the middle of this issue both geographically and politically, further fueled this controversy when its courts took the position that the state was free soil, presuming that African Americans once under its jurisdiction were free unless they were fugitive slaves who had escaped from a slave state.

The Fugitive Slave Act mandated the return of runaway slaves and criminalized any assistance given to them. To circumvent the Supreme Court decision in the *Prigg* case, Congress made enforcement of the statute a federal responsibility.[4] The new act authorized federal district court judges to appoint commissioners who would have limited judicial power, including the right to hear cases involving runaway slaves and to grant certificates for their removal. Congress established the compensation for which commissioners would be paid: ten dollars for each slave they returned but only five dollars for each they released. Abolitionists charged that the pay scale was an incentive to render decisions favorable to claimants. Moreover, the statute empowered federal marshals to execute warrants for the arrest of fugitive slaves and made the marshals liable for any slave who escaped from their custody. A marshal could also call on citizens to assist him, forming a *posse comitatus,* if necessary, to enforce the federal law. The statute directed the claimant to pay federal marshals the fee common for services rendered. Federal marshals were thereby made into de facto slave catchers, strategically stationed across the North to act on behalf of slave owners in hunting down runaways.[5]

The Fugitive Slave Act conferred enormous rights on the individuals seeking a fugitive slave but deprived local residents and free blacks of even minimal constitutional rights. The process followed by a claimant or an agent seeking to remove a slave was flexible, and the burden of proof minimal. Depositions and affidavits from whites could be sufficient proof for a court to grant the removal of a slave, but the act deprived an alleged slave of the opportunity to give testimony in his or her defense. The law prohibited a jury trial, and the disposition of the case was solely in the hands of the magistrate or commissioner hearing it. Finally, the statute imposed a thousand-dollar fine or imprisonment for up to six months for anyone who interfered with recapture and removal of a fugitive from labor.[6]

President Millard Fillmore, a moderate northern Whig, initially hesitated when asked to sign the bill into law, obviously troubled by its fugitive slave features that seemed to violate the Constitution. He doubted whether Congress could lawfully revoke the writ of habeas corpus in cases in which none of the constitutional conditions for its cancellation existed.[7] The federal Constitution provides that the privilege may be suspended only in cases when the safety of the public is threatened.[8]

Before he signed the fugitive slave bill, President Fillmore turned to his attorney general, John J. Crittenden, for advice on its validity. It "is precisely the same as that of all other prisoners under the laws of the U.S.," Crittenden said, and due process would not be violated by it.[9] He explained further that a federal officer would hold hearings on petitions for removing a slave, so it was unlikely that a free person would be remanded illegally. He also assumed that Americans would obey the Fugitive Slave Act: "The moral sense of the community is on the side of law and order, and we rejoice in the consciousness that the great mass of our people are disposed to seek peaceful remedies for either real or imaginary grievances."[10] (Secretary of State Daniel Webster also advised the president that the act was constitutional.) Fillmore reluctantly signed the bill, and, amid a storm of northern protest against it, the measure became the law of the land on September 18, 1850. Opponents of slavery never forgave Fillmore, and the Whig Party collapsed in 1854.[11]

In expecting northern whites to obey "the rule of law," Crittenden overestimated their willingness to subordinate their consciences to the will of a federal authority. Other northerners expected the new law to quickly become a dead letter. Fillmore shattered their doubts when he ordered the enforcement of the law. As a correspondent for the *Cincinnati Enquirer* put it, the president "intends to have the law enforced, and if necessary, the aid of the marshals to enable them to carry it out."[12] As other Americans reached this conclusion, protest erupted all over the North, and abolitionists vigorously questioned the validity of the statute on constitutional and moral grounds. Ohio abolitionists argued that the law was inconsistent with the founding principles of the republic and contrary to natural law.

Prominent religious leaders and intellectuals called the Fugitive Slave Act wicked and unjust. Unitarian minister Theodore Parker urged his Boston congregation to prepare themselves to rescue alleged slaves, an act he pledged to do at whatever personal or professional cost to himself. "The fugitive slave Law contradicts the acknowledged precepts of the Christian religion," he declared in 1851. "It violates the noblest instincts of humanity; it asks us to trample on the law of God."[13] William Cullen Bryant, the poet and newspaper editor, considered the nation's fugitive slave policy something every American should resist.[14] Ralph Waldo Emerson turned his pen and oratory against the statute, exhorting Americans to resist its enforcement.[15]

Unitarian minister and abolitionist Amory Dwight Mayo, addressing the New York legislature, stated, "[N]o colored person is safe in the State of New York." He anticipated that free blacks and runaway slaves under duress would resist kidnappers and slave catchers, including federal marshals. Mayo observed that the individuals he had encountered had "a different theory about recapture, and they insist on defending themselves with all the means Providence affords them."[16] In Massachusetts, state representative Robert Rantoul seized whatever opportunity available to direct the General Assembly to recognize the unconstitutionality of the federal Fugitive Slave Act. In a discussion on state policy on commerce, he turned the legislature to the subject he found most troubling: "I pass on to a subject of as much or more consequence than the tariff, as liberty is more important than property." Rantoul resisted his colleagues who discouraged such "agitation," asserting that nothing in the Constitution gave Congress the power "to legislate for the rendition of fugitives from labor."[17] Resistance to such a heinous law was the democratic way, Rantoul said, and he anticipated continued slave flight as well as resistance to the act.

To help organize their response, abolitionists in various cities held public meetings to condemn the new Fugitive Slave Act and to call on Congress to rescind it. In Pennsylvania, Frederick Douglass explained the negative effects of the law on free African Americans. Thousands of abolitionists across the North, including many in Cincinnati, attended meetings to register their objections to the statute. A correspondent for the *New York Tribune* noted that the people considered the Fugitive Slave Act lacking in constitutional and moral legitimacy. At the American Anti-Slavery Society in Rochester, William Lloyd Garrison introduced resolutions mocking the fugitive slave law. Other notable abolitionists, including Garrett Smith, Stephen S. Foster, and Abby Kelly, met in Syracuse, where they denounced all supporters of the fugitive slave law, including proslavery Christians. The three pledged to raise funds to aid African Americans wrongly captured as runaway slaves.[18]

Surprisingly, Samuel Sullivan Cox, a conservative Ohio Democratic congressman and owner-editor of the *Ohio Statesman,* stated, "Humane people revolted at the injustice of laws which called upon them to hunt down their poor neighbors who had committed no crime and which required them to aid in sending fellow beings into perpetual bondage."[19] More predictably, Whig representative Joshua R. Giddings warned that Ohio would not submit to the law. In an 1850 congressional speech, Giddings declared that Ohio residents would never obey a law that required public participation in the capture and removal of slaves and he urged Congress to repeal it. Giddings proclaimed that his constituents would never "stoop to such degradation." Moreover, he said, "Let no man tell me there is no higher law than this fugitive slave bill."[20]

Initially, the majority of his southern colleagues considered the fugitive slave law to be an effective answer to the problem of runaway slaves. During its first year of operation, it appeared that the law would be remarkably successful. As one historian described the situation, "It is said that more slaves were seized and returned to slavery during the first year of its existence than . . . the preceding half century."[21] Nevertheless, Giddings continued to pronounce that his constituents would never comply: "We shall protect ourselves against such indignity; we shall proclaim our abhorrence of such a law."[22] Should the federal government insist on enforcing the law, he predicted that the North and South would become embroiled in a civil war.

Others in the Ohio congressional delegation followed suit. Representative Lewis Davis Campbell, a Whig, wrote a letter to his constituents in Clinton County who gathered at a mass meeting in southwestern Ohio. "I will condemn and denounce the fugitive slave law on all occasions. It is the greatest outrage ever perpetuated upon liberty."[23] Senator Salmon P. Chase was probably the politician most steadfastly opposed to the fugitive slave bill and then to the act once it went into effect. He had argued that Congress lacked the constitutional authority to legislate for the extradition of fugitive slaves; furthermore, he believed Congress could not require the public to participate in the enforcement of the law. Chase had put up a valiant but futile fight against the bill, having proposed several amendments to weaken it, including a clause to guarantee alleged slaves a jury trial. "It will not do for any man to go into a state where every legal presumption is in favor of freedom and seize a person whom he claims as a fugitive slave."[24] Chase had also argued that Congress erred when it made California a part of the Compromise of 1850 instead of admitting it solely as a free state, independent of the provisions in the Omnibus Bill. While the bill was being considered, abolitionists in Ohio had transmitted several petitions to their representatives, urging Congress to end the federal practice of enforcing slavery. Senators Chase and William H. Seward of New York read their petitions calling for abolishing slavery on federal land, as well as making abolition a criterion for admitting new states to the Union. They wanted to outlaw slavery in the nation's capital. They also wanted the right of a trial by jury for alleged fugitive slaves arrested in any state. Representatives Joseph Cable and James Madison Gaylord told Congress that many of their constituents wanted the Fugitive Slave Act repealed.[25]

Moreover, Ohio abolitionists condemned the 1850 Fugitive Slave Act as a breach of the contract the founders had made with the American people in 1787. As Chase explained it,

> The expectation prevalent at the time of the adoption of the Constitution and the Ordinance, that slavery would gradually and at no remote period wholly disappear, has not been realized. Instead of slavery restriction we have slavery extension; instead of diminution of slave population we have a vast increase; instead of reduction in the number of slave states, it has been doubled. Thus a permanence and extent of operation, not dreamed of at the time has been given to the fugitive slave clause incorporated into the Constitution.[26]

Obviously, Chase's view was based on the notion that leaders of the federal republic believed slavery would become extinct. That interpretation, although disputed by both scholars and abolitionists such as William Lloyd Garrison, was widely accepted among the national leaders who believed in gradual emancipation. These leaders included Abraham Lincoln, who initially sought to stop the spread of slavery and not its immediate abolition.

Like their counterparts in Congress, many members of the Ohio General Assembly disapproved of the new federal Fugitive Slave Act. Whig representative John A. Foot urged "all good citizens to denounce, oppose and resist by all proper means the execution of the said law" at a mass meeting in Cleveland, a city with many antislavery voters from the Western Reserve.[27] However, when Trumbull County representative Wells A. Hutchins, a member of the Free-Soil Party, introduced a bill that would have made it a crime for anyone to enforce the law in Ohio, the conservative Ohio house swiftly voted it down. Another measure officially condemning the law also failed in the house on a vote of 38 to 33. Thus, as the fugitive slave bill was making its way through Congress in 1850, Ohio lawmakers hotly debated the subject, but the legislative term ended without a clear majority for or against it.[28] In March 1851, the legislature finally reached common ground. The senate, for example, passed a resolution stating that Congress was powerless under the Constitution to legislate on slavery. The federal government is one of limited powers, it said; "that of legislating upon the subject of fugitives from service is not to be found." The senate resolved that the fugitive slave law was unconstitutional; that each state in the union was required to allow to all persons the benefit of habeas corpus; and that Congress was required to protect the civil liberty of anyone charged with a crime.[29] "If said law cannot be so amended, we then recommend its repeal."[30] Furthermore, in 1856, in a joint resolution of the house and senate, the assembly voted 24 to 61 urging the congressional delegation to "use their best exertions to procure the repeal of said act at the earliest practicable time."[31]

Other Ohio public officials also expressed their antipathy to the 1850 law. Circuit judge Benjamin Franklin Wade, a Whig, was certain of his opposition to it and made a speech at a mass meeting pledging that his court would "grant to a fugitive slave the writ of *habeas corpus* and give him his liberty under it."[32] Though Wade cautioned against violence, he considered the American response to British policies during the decades before the American Revolution as a fitting model for dissent.

Seabury Ford, the outgoing Whig governor of Ohio, considered the statute contrary to the principles of a republican society. He expected rebellion against it but he also discouraged the use of violence, advising that persuasion was a more effective weapon. Ford believed that Congress would have the ultimate say on the law, and he urged the legislators to amend or repeal it without delay.[33] Reuben Wood, his Democratic successor, gave his inaugural address as the new governor on December 12, three months after the law was enacted. Wood was cautious; he expressed revulsion for slaveholding but acknowledged that the law was consistent with the federal Constitution. Wood thought Congress had authority to enact the statute, and he advised the people of Ohio to be prudent in their opposition to it. Nonetheless, Wood joined Ford in observing that public sentiment in Ohio was against it, and he anticipated that public sentiments would ultimately triumph.[34]

The fugitive slave law actually had one positive effect on Ohio. Its abolitionists and members of the colonization societies, who had earlier disagreed on many issues, closed ranks behind rescinding the law, vowing to put aside differences to speak in "one voice from every county and every village."[35] Since the 1830s, James G. Birney had consistently taken on what abolitionists called the Slave Power, the states seeking to protect slavery. Birney lamented the passage of the fugitive slave law and berated Henry Clay for "trying to again compromise the matter." Compromising with slavery, Birney continued, was futile because no "one can permanently compromise a moral question." Clay and his supporters "will find that the dislike of slavery is as great as it ever was, and perhaps somewhat greater." Birney also argued that the statute violated both the Constitution and the Northwest Ordinance of 1787, which offered the privilege of habeas corpus to any defendant under its jurisdiction.[36] In contrast, the revised statute denied judicial review to runaway slaves, and Birney considered the clause invalid.

Furthermore, Birney, an attorney, raised constitutional arguments against the legitimacy of the newly appointed commissioners. Congress had empowered circuit judges to appoint the commissioners and authorized the commissioners to serve warrants for the arrest of slaves. Birney believed that only Congress had the constitutional authority to appoint judicial officers and that such authority could not be ceded to the judicial department. His colleague Salmon P. Chase shared these sentiments.[37] Chase put a positive spin on the creation of the office of commissioner, noting that Congress had recognized that it could not compel state courts to conduct hearings on recapture. While acknowledging that additional federal judges were needed, he assailed Congress for assigning this role to individuals who were not officially judges. He argued that the Constitution gave only the president the power to appoint federal judges and magistrates. Therefore, the commissioners, by acting as judges with enforcement powers, were in violation of the federal Constitution. "The country is filled with swarms of federal officers acting upon the most delicate questions of personal liberty and State Sovereignty, in manifest violation of the plain sense of the Constitution," said Chase.[38] Conceding that, although a judge could appoint such an inferior officer, he could never equip such a person with authority equivalent to that of a judge, he continued. From this perspective Chase condemned the fugitive slave law as "offensive, unjust and unrighteous." James Monroe, "Oberlin's Christian Statesman and Reformer," shared this belief, arguing that Congress had gone beyond its constitutional authority when it enacted the revised fugitive slave law.[39]

Ohio abolitionists considered the fugitive slave law too stringent and the use of federal power to capture runaway slaves too sweeping, charging that the latter jeopardized the precarious "bond of Union." They expressed contempt for the law at mass meetings held throughout the state, and Whig newspapers published their resolves. The *Ohio Statesman* reported, "They all denounced in the strongest terms the Fugitive Slave Law and all who were either politically or officially under service to it."[40] At a Cleveland mass meeting, abolitionists adopted several resolutions stating that "some portions of the Fugitive Slave Law were unconstitutional and the whole of it oppressive, unjust and unrighteous."[41] They called on all citizens to oppose the law until its repeal. Opponents of the law did the same in Toledo, declaring that it infringed on the principles on which "our government is founded and which should be maintained by a free people."[42] After a series of speeches in Ashtabula County, in northeastern Ohio, Judge Alexander Brownlee offered a resolution that the assembly passed unanimously: "That come life or imprisonment, come fine or come death—we will neither aid nor assist in the return of any fugitive slave, but, on the contrary we will *harbor* and *secrete* and by all just means protect and defend him, and thus give him a practical god-speed to liberty."[43]

Defiance of the fugitive slave law immediately erupted in northeastern Ohio. In Huron County, abolitionists determined to rescue any person captured as a slave in Ohio. In Chagrin Falls, in Cuyahoga County, they vowed to resist the law using any means necessary. In Youngstown, they pledged their hearts and their lives if necessary to aid helpless fugitive slaves, promising to resist the law until it was voided. Trumbull County abolitionists pledged to speak as men and "Sound the tocsin of repeal!"[44] The *Ashtabula Sentinel* advised, "Do not hesitate. Slay the miscreant. If he comes to re-enslave you furnish him with a speedy and hospitable grave."[45] Farther south, abolitionists meeting in Washington County called on their neighbors to live up to the commands of God and to disobey the fugitive slave law. Abolitionists in Clinton County, in southwestern Ohio, denounced as traitors all congressmen who voted for the Fugitive Slave Act. Asserting that aiding fugitive slaves was a badge of honor, they prayed for "damnation" on all others who did not participate in their struggle.[46]

Abolitionist newspaper publishers and editors were equally adamant in denouncing the revised fugitive slave law. According to the Whig-run *Cincinnati Gazette*, published in Hamilton County, the fugitive slave law provoked "a good deal of comment and produced much excitement in some quarters."[47] The *Dayton Evening Empire* put it this way: "There seems to be a determination in certain quarters to resist the operation of the law."[48] These newspapers ran stories attacking the clause that assigned federal marshals to catch slaves: "We know of no instance of legal liability like this in the common law, or in any statute." The clauses that authorized the appointment of commissioners had more disturbing elements and thus drew sharper complaints from abolitionist editors. One correspondent concluded that the act's compensation clause "cannot be designed to induce a decision for one party against the other because that would be contrary to the first principle of justice; the provision holds out a direct pecuniary reward for a decision in favor of the claimant and against personal liberty."[49] The *Cincinnati Gazette* reported, "We have met but few apologists for the law. Let slave owners and their agents hunt down runaways, but do not employ federal officers."[50] Ohio's first African American lawyer, John Mercer Langston, declared the statute "unworthy of the name of law."[51] The *Clermont Courier* set the protest in perspective, asserting that passage of the law "to settle the slavery question is a joke." It predicted that blacks by the thousands would flee from slavery and that the law would never achieve the recapture of "one-tenth" of them.[52] Many more Ohio newspapers printed such lamentations as, "our own state begins to be convulsed by" the statute and that it would "soon be ablaze with agitation." Pressure would be placed on newly elected officials to rescind the law, others predicted. Should that tactic fail, any attempt to enforce it would "obviously be met by concerted evasion if not by overt resistance."[53]

Political action organizations also put heat on antislavery leaders to resist the new law. At its fourteenth annual meeting in 1856, members of the Western Anti-Slavery Society concluded, "There probably was never a time when the antislavery cause required of its friends a more stern and faithful advocacy, than the present." They urged "every friend of human rights" to withdraw any support for American slavery. They criticized the "infamous" fugitive slave law, and they adopted the motto "No Union with slaveholders."[54] The society believed the movement against slavery had gained momentum. In support of that claim, they noted that northern newspapers ran fewer advertisements for runaway slaves. In one instance, when the editors of the *Evansville (Ind.) Weekly Journal* violated that code, the editors faced severe criticism from Ohio abolitionists and other antislavery advocates.[55]

Although it is true that many Ohio whites objected to the fugitive slave law because of its impact on their own rights, they also considered its effects on blacks, both free and slave. They anticipated that free blacks might fall victim to kidnappers and slave catchers and they warned that kidnappers and slave catchers would enter Ohio at their peril. Many whites also considered the act contrary to the founding principles of the republic and chided the country's leaders for calling it the freest country in the world. They strenuously discouraged other whites from accepting appointments as commissioners and vowed to condemn anyone taking the job. Instead of enforcing the odious law, abolitionists chose to aid runaways, advising them to go to Canada so that they would be free.

Their advice did not suggest that African Americans were unwanted in Ohio; rather, abolitionists understood that Canada was beyond the reach of the fugitive slave law.[56] They also advised blacks to arm themselves and to use whatever weapons they had to resist anyone who threatened their freedom.

Meanwhile, supporters of the fugitive slave law held rallies throughout Ohio in defense of the revised law. Antiabolitionists assembled in Hamilton County to defend the Fugitive Slave Act as a valid exercise of federal power. Moreover, they asserted that obedience to the act was a patriotic duty. They condemned an abolitionist mass meeting in Senecaville, Guernsey County, in southeastern Ohio, as "fanatical." A writer for the *Ohio State Journal* ridiculed the abolitionist gathering: "We did not suppose that such crazy people as those who met at Senecaville existed in any other part of southern Ohio. [They are] just as crazy as the lunatics in the Western Reserve."[57]

Calling themselves the friends of law and order, the antiabolitionists convened a public rally in Dayton on October 26, 1850, to urge residents to obey the fugitive slave policy of the United States. The antiabolitionists turned to one of that city's distinguished citizens, Judge Joseph Halsey Crane, whom they expected to back them up. Crane had served in the Ohio legislature and the U.S. House of Representatives. In an open letter to Judge Crane, the antiabolitionists expressed their support for "the recent efforts of the Executive and the Congress to compromise and adjust the vexed questions which for so long have agitated the country and endangered the stability of the Union and the peace and harmony of its different sections."[58] They admitted a desire to preserve a fraternal spirit with their southern neighbors. Judge Crane, though he concurred with their goals, declined to become involved in their activities, citing poor health as an excuse. He died on November 13, 1851, less than a month after the Montgomery County rally.

Clement L. Vallandigham, a successful lawyer and newspaper editor in Ohio, was one of the most prominent defenders of the Fugitive Slave Act in the state. Vallandigham was elected to the state house of representatives as a Democrat in 1845 and, in 1856, to Congress. Vigorously defending southern interests, he admonished Ohio whites to obey the fugitive slave law. His opposition to Northern policies in the Civil War landed him in jail in 1863 and led to his banishment to the Confederacy.[59]

Responding to Vallandigham and others, the antiabolitionists staged mass meetings to articulate their support of the fugitive slave law. More than twenty-five hundred people gathered in Cincinnati to hear Thomas Corwin and William Dennison debate the new legislation and its meaning for Ohio. Corwin, a former Whig governor of Ohio and secretary of the treasury in the Fillmore administration, had never owned slaves. Yet he was not a militant abolitionist, believing as he did that the "the Constitution recognized slavery" and made recapture a legal right. The intent of the fugitive law, he said, was to affirm the right of a slave owner to capture and remove the person he owned under the laws of his state without interference. In forming this position, Corwin reviewed colonial history and cited statutes from as early as 1648 that had recognized slavery and authorized recapture. Corwin referred to a statute from a New England colony that provided that no one "should offer obstruction to a master coming after a slave and taking him home." His proslavery audience roared with approval when he described the fugitive slave law as "the bond" of Union, to which Ohio should "adhere."[60] However, Corwin also held reservations about the new statute, objecting to it because he feared increased kidnapping would be a likely by-product. He considered the use of federal marshals as professional slave catchers and of the *posse comitatus* to be repulsive.

His colleague, William Dennison, a Republican, was the twenty-fourth governor of Ohio and the first to be elected during the Civil War. He was a vocal abolitionist as a state senator and a congressman. In Ohio, Senator Dennison had fought hard to repeal the Black Laws. As a congressman, he argued against the slave trade in the District of Columbia and the extension of slavery to federal lands. Dennison also joined fellow opponents of slavery in calling for civil disobedience to the revised fugitive slave law. Although the new law repeated principles from the 1793 act, it added harsher penalties for disobedience to it and mandated that the public assist in its enforcement, regardless of their objections as a matter of conscience. Dennison called for increased resistance to the law but stopped short of encouraging violence.[61]

As troublesome as the fugitive slave law was to whites, it sent shock waves through the African American community. Blacks could only assume that law would multiply seizures and make the lives of all blacks more perilous. The fugitive slave law thus forced them to become more militant in their denunciation of federal and state laws of oppression. Frederick Douglass also anticipated increased incidents of kidnapping, and he warned free blacks to brace themselves. Douglass, contemplating a worst-case scenario, announced that "the colored population would die rather than return to bondage."[62] He called on all Americans to reduce the fugitive slave law "to a dead letter by making half a dozen or more kidnappers" dead. This, he reasoned, was the only way to constrain unscrupulous men who resorted to kidnapping. Douglass criticized those blacks who remained silent when their neighbors were remanded without resistance. He considered Margaret Garner, herself a runaway slave, a hero for plunging "a knife into the bosom of her infant to save it from the hell of slavery."[63]

William C. Nell, another black abolitionist, also envisioned the proliferation of kidnapping, and he witnessed firsthand how gangs of whites terrorized African Americans in Ohio. If free, blacks feared kidnapping; if runaway slaves, they feared recapture. Many African Americans, therefore, left Ohio for Canada, "giving neither rest to their feet nor slumber to their eyelids," Nell reported. Those remaining in the state organized mass meetings to condemn the law and asserted their determination to resist kidnapping and any encroachment on their liberties. They vowed to be vigilant and to "rescue a brother from human bloodhounds."[64] The Second Baptist Church of Columbus hosted a meeting on October 7, 1850, and adopted a series of resolutions on the fugitive slave policy of the federal government. They charged that it would deny blacks due process, supplant the right of trial by jury, and violate federal protection against unreasonable search and seizures. Thus, they resolved that the act was patently unconstitutional and should be voided. "We advise all colored people to go continually prepared that they may be ready at any moment to offer defense in behalf of their liberty." They also pledged to give assistance to any runaway slave who came among them. And they vowed "to permit no fugitive from labor or any person claimed as such, to be taken from their midst."[65]

Enslaved African Americans did not relent either, and the numbers of them who escaped from bondage after 1850 was unparalleled. Increasingly, slave owners posted notices throughout Ohio, offering rewards totaling thousands of dollars for the return of runaways. They identified among others an individual name George, "a shrewd, smart fellow" who played the violin.[66] Rachel Myers, a resident of Salem, Ohio, told her sister, Julia A. Myers (about 1850), "there are several runaway slaves here and their masters have come here after them but they will not get them."[67] She boasted that the town was planning an "antislavery fair," and she wanted Julia to bring guests to the party. The constant slave flights to the North and into Ohio made it inevitable that southerners would blame free states for undermining their way of life.

Although one can assume that Congress did not consider this consequence, the Fugitive Slave Act undoubtedly intimidated large numbers of blacks around the country, many of whom left homes and businesses in search of a haven from kidnappers and slave catchers. Ohio newspapers chronicled their flight, indicating that black migration rose exponentially during the 1850s. The *Dayton Evening Empire* reported that more than a thousand black residents left the city for a new life in Montreal in one month.[68] For the same period, the *Cincinnati Gazette* estimated that more than two thousand blacks migrated from the Queen City to Malden, Sandwich, and Windsor in Ontario. In the settlement of Dawn (Dresden), Ontario, Josiah Henson, a runaway slave from Maryland, and other Canadians established the British-American Institute, a school organized to train blacks as craftsmen. Canadian abolitionists in Elgin also started as a joint-stock company, purchased land, and then resold it to black refugees from America. And the Refugee Home Society, a Detroit-based association founded by abolitionists in 1851, supported these enterprises with money, clothing, and food. In Canada, the Fugitive Union Society provided similar support for the town of Sandwich.[69]

The number of enslaved blacks who took flight will always remain speculative, for no reliable statistical data was collected or maintained. In the 1850s alone, historian Fred Landon estimates that approximately twenty thousand runaway slaves passed through Ohio heading to Canada.[70] In 1855, a writer for *Frederick Douglass' Paper* noted,

> The number of fugitive slaves in Canada is estimated at 40,000, most of whom have settled in the Province within twenty years. There does not appear to be any diminution in the tide, notwithstanding the efforts made to secure and reclaim this uncertain species of property. The fugitives have mostly

come from the Northern Slave States. In so great a number there is room for a wide variety of character, conduct and condition; and this has doubtless given rise to the conflicting statements we so frequently hear in regard to them.[71]

In 1859, and without citing any evidence, Kentucky governor Beriah Magoffin remarked that Ohio had been an outlet for more than one hundred thousand dollars worth of chattel property that escaped from his state alone.[72] Historians Larry Gara, Loren Schweninger, and John Hope Franklin recognize that an amazing number of black refugees crisscrossed Ohio, making the state a virtual highway to freedom.[73]

—

Public appeals and protests against the Fugitive Slave Act notwithstanding, the law went into effect on September 18, 1850. It authorized slave catchers, U.S. marshals, and commissioners to assist in the operation of the fugitive slave law. The Fugitive Slave Act prohibited black captives from giving testimony in court and deprived them of a jury trial. It also made it a crime for anyone to help an escaped slave or to entice a slave to escape. Professional slave catchers roamed Ohio, looking for anyone they could subdue and remove as slaves.[74] As the new law went into effect, an echo of a shocking episode of kidnapping from the previous decade embroiled Ohio, Kentucky, and Virginia until the Civil War. A white gang from Kentucky visited Ohio under cover of night, kidnapped eight children and grandchildren of Peyton Polly, and sold them to slave owners across two states.

The saga of the Polly family was an American success story gone awry. Before January 20, 1849, the family had belonged to David Polly, a struggling white farmer in Pike County, Kentucky. Apparently, David had sorely mismanaged his resources and was on the verge of bankruptcy. Although his slaves had served him dutifully, David put them up for sale, ostensibly to settle his debts. However, his daughter Nancy interceded on behalf of the slave family, especially Mrs. Peyton Polly, who had practically raised her. Attached to her nanny, Nancy persuaded her father to keep the family together. David came upon a plan that would both provide him with badly needed funds and keep the slave family together: he sold them to Douglas Polly, the free brother of Peyton. David had rebuffed Douglas's efforts to purchase his brother until then, and Peyton

Polly held a celebration in Pike County in appreciation of Douglas and in recognition of the family's newly found freedom.[75]

The festivities, however, were interrupted when they learned that David Polly had not satisfied his creditors and that the slaves he had sold were still collateral. Faced with the prospect of his brother and the rest of the family being sold to someone else, Douglas paid David's debt, more than eight hundred dollars. Wearied from the ordeal, Peyton moved his family to Lawrence County, Ohio, just across the Ohio River, hoping for security from his slave past. The family crisis had become well known in Kentucky, according to John Rowe, a white neighbor of David Polly, who indicated that the ordeal of Peyton was the "common talk in the neighborhood for months before he and his family left."[76]

After David Polly suddenly passed away, some of his relatives, including David Justice, "took umbrage because they were not remembered in his will, and [they] contested [it], but the will was sustained."[77] One member of the family took matters into his own hands, tracking the Peyton Polly family to Ohio, claiming to be their lawful owner. Douglas Polly hired an attorney to challenge the claim, but, before he could litigate the matter, a white gang from Kentucky used an ax to chop through the door of the house owned by Peyton, struck him, "grazing the wool on the top of his head," and verbally assaulted "the old man."[78] The Kentucky abductors, including Fildon Isaac, James Sperry, Washington Smith, and Hamilton Willis, then kidnapped the eight Polly children at gunpoint, leaving Peyton and his wife behind, presumably because of their ages or the difficultly of controlling them.

Convinced that Kentucky slave catchers had illegally removed the Polly children, Ohio abolitionists implored Whig governor Seabury Ford to take action. Ford, near the end of his term, issued a requisition to Kentucky, demanding the release of the Polly children and the return of the kidnappers for prosecution. His successor, Reuben Wood, a Democrat, grudgingly accepted the obligation to secure their release. Wood spoke of the children in language that made abolitionists uncomfortable, indicating that he acted on their behalf because it was his duty rather than his passion. Convinced that Kentucky men had violated state law, however, Governor Wood initiated proceedings to apprehend the kidnappers and to secure the release of the children. Wood assigned Ralph Leete, a prominent Whig attorney from Lawrence County, to handle the matter. His early reports were discouraging to Peyton Polly and to sympathetic Ohio residents. The children had been separated: four of them were in neighboring Frankfort and the other four had been sold to a Virginia slave owner. Leete filed complaints in both states, asking the governors in each to appoint counsel for the alleged slaves. Those officials moved slowly, and more than three years elapsed before Leete received any reliable information about the Polly children.[79]

The news that began trickling into Ohio indicated that David Justice had actually kept four of the children in Kentucky. He was notorious for trafficking "slaves and free Negroes and send[ing] them to the southern states for sale."[80] For reasons that are unknown, Justice kept Hilda, Peyton Jr., Mary Jane, and Martha locked up in his private jail for almost three years, using them for his own purposes. Once Ohio officials determined the whereabouts of the Polly children in Kentucky, Leete filed complaints in the appropriate courts for their release. Kentucky officials remained lethargic, prompting Leete to lament to Democratic governor William Medill, "[Ohio abolitionists] continually call on me for explanations as to why the Negroes are not brought back to this state."[81] Finally, in 1853, a Kentucky court ordered Justice to release the children. Although a number of Kentucky men pursued them until they reached the Ohio border, they finally returned to "where they belonged."[82]

Rescuing the children from Virginia proved more difficult. Ohio officials assigned attorney Leroy D. Walton to coordinate the case. Once in Virginia, Walton hired a guide named J. Frey, who apparently knew exactly where the children were being held. William Ratcliffe, a well-known Virginia slave owner, claimed to have been their lawful owner, and he held a bill of sale to bolster his claim. Moreover, the men who sold the children had fled into the hills and sent word that they would do harm to anyone who pursued them. Walton wisely hired Virginia hunters to track them, a move that persuaded Ralph Leete to proclaim that rescuing the children would be difficult. Leete urged the government in Ohio to appropriate additional funds for the effort.[83] As he told Republican governor Salmon P. Chase, if "the federal government could spend $100,000 to reduce one man to slavery, certainly" Ohio should use its resources to secure freedom for the Polly children.[84]

One reason for the difficulty in securing the release of the children was that Virginia officials did not approve of Ohio officials who automatically emancipated slaves brought under their jurisdiction. Virginia officials held the presumption that blacks were slaves, and this perspective helped

William Ratcliffe, although he was a participant in a fraudulent transaction. The litigation for the release of the Polly children, therefore, was a battle between Ohio and Virginia. Ohio attorney Joel Wilson, who later joined Leete and Walton, reported, "It cannot be denied that they [Virginia officials] are strengthening their defense by testimony, but mostly of such persons as were either directly involved in the abduction of their relatives or dependants."[85]

The news worsened for Peyton Polly when he and the family learned that the children were "held in abject servitude."[86] Making matters still worse, an older child had been abused and was pregnant. The laboriously slow way in which Virginia processed the complaint did not improve matters. The effort to free the Polly children suffered a major blow in 1859, when a Virginia court dismissed the case on grounds that the state of Ohio had no standing to sue. The court based its opinion on the claim that only the Polly children could file a suit against Ratcliffe, the slave owner who had effectively rebuffed the state of Ohio; he apparently was cunning enough to brainwash the children. John Laidley, a Virginia resident, admitted that "the colored children are very much attached to Ratcliffe and his family." His comments notwithstanding, Ratcliffe had also intimidated the children, and they seemed to renounce any interest in seeking their freedom. By the time William Dennison, a Republican, was elected governor, Ralph Leete had become disillusioned with the case, informing the governor that Ohio had badly "bungled and shamefully mismanaged it from its commencement."[87]

The four Polly children in Virginia were not restored to their family by the time the Civil War started. The Ohio General Assembly passed a joint resolution in 1860, lamenting that the Polly children "are now held in bondage there."[88] It appropriated additional funds for continuing the litigation and urged the governor to pursue measures that might accomplish the release of the children. The Civil War made the entire question moot, and the Polly children disappeared from public scrutiny. Their ultimate fate escaped the public record, although historians assume that they were emancipated at the end of the war. Federal officials, however, paid little attention to this episode of human suffering or to the many more that followed passage of the Fugitive Slave Act of 1850.

—

As controversial as the fugitive slave issue was in Ohio, New York experienced the first incident of recapture after the 1850 act went into effect, providing another dimension to the disaster looming on the horizon. Thirty-year-old James Hamlet arrived in Brooklyn in 1848. An industrious fellow, he quickly found work as a porter in Tilton and Maloney, a store that sold an assortment of merchandise. Hamlet was also a member of the Methodist Church, and by 1850 he was married and had children. Hamlet's security was threatened on September 26 of that year when Thomas J. Clare, a professional slave catcher, came to town on behalf of Mary Brown, who alleged that Hamlet was a fugitive from Baltimore. In addition to the written document authorizing the recapture, Mrs. Brown sent along her young son, Gustavus, to offer oral testimony. On a warrant issued by U.S. Commissioner Alexander Gardiner, U.S. Marshal Benjamin H. Tallmadge arrested Hamlet.[89]

Just as abolitionists had feared, Commissioner Gardiner made only a cursory examination of the claim before depriving Hamlet of legal counsel and testimony. The commissioner quickly reviewed the case, approved the rendition, and assigned Marshal Tallmadge to escort Clare and his prisoner out of the city. Fortunately, Mrs. Brown agreed to sell Hamlet for eight hundred dollars, and his friends in New York raised money and made the purchase.[90] Free blacks and abolitionists now had empirical evidence of how the act would affect people of color. With the willingness of commissioners to enforce the Fugitive Slave Act, alarm spread among free blacks in the North. The possibility of violence became inevitable. Once again, New York provided a model of what might happen when slave owners and U.S. marshals attempted to forcibly remove an alleged slave. John Long, a violinist, had escaped from Virginia. After he was apprehended, a large crowd of African Americans in the city gathered to protect him. The marshal and the New York police arrested the leaders, and under armed guard a posse provided an escort to the New Jersey state line.[91]

The recovery of alleged slaves from Ohio illustrates how African Americans and abolitionists resisted abduction. Ripley, a town in Brown County on the Ohio River, was the next community to confront the fugitive slave law. After 1850, slave catchers became bolder in their pursuit of slaves, confident in their ability to remove them from Ohio under the new act. Ripley was also the home of John Parker, a former slave who had positioned himself there to aid others fleeing from bondage. Parker, well known among slave owners and slave hunters, was automatically assumed to have been responsible for the escape of slaves from the Kentucky side of the river.[92]

Parker was not alone. African Americans in Ripley joined him in confronting slave hunters who came to town. Their opposition to the new fugitive slave law in the fall of 1850 was responsible for two deaths. In the first instance, Parker and his associates resisted the slave catchers seeking to execute a warrant, and one member of the posse was fatally wounded.[93] In another episode, an Ohio man was killed as he pursued a slave who had escaped from Kentucky and stolen a horse in Ohio. Ultimately, these ordeals embittered feelings between Ohio and Kentucky residents. Abolitionists blamed slaveholding for the deaths of innocent people, and Kentucky blamed Ohio for being friendly to runaway slaves.[94] These feelings were representative of the perils of "slave hunting," and would grow worse as the decade progressed.

Like Ripley, Sandusky, on the shores of Lake Erie, also was home to committed abolitionists willing to defy the Slave Power. Rush R. Sloane had studied law in the office of Cincinnati attorney Francis D. Parrish, an abolitionist who had deliberately contested the removal of a slave in 1847 in order to challenge the Fugitive Slave Act of 1793. It is reasonable to assume that Sloane, having such a mentor, was imbued with the same abolitionist zeal. Upon his return to Sandusky, Sloane immediately opened a law office—and a station on the Underground Railroad. His work quickly caught the attention of slave owners, and Sloane became embroiled in a controversy in 1852, when seven runaway slaves arrived in Sandusky. Tracked by Charles M. Gibbons, a Kentucky slave owner, they were apprehended before they could continue on the Railroad. Elijah Anderson, an African American abolitionist, reported the incident to Sloane, who agreed to defend the alleged slaves pro bono, arguing that their arrest and detention was improper. James O. Patton, an agent appointed by Gibbons, apparently had been the first to apprehend the accused. However, he did not have the appropriate documentation for their arrest. Sloane, a shrewd attorney, effectively used a defect in the warrant against Patton, which did not specifically authorize him to apprehend the alleged fugitives, and the Ohio court immediately ordered the release of the detained individuals. By the time Gibbons produced the required documentation, the individuals he claimed had left town.[95]

Naturally, Gibbons held Sloane responsible and sued under the federal Fugitive Slave Act. Appearing in the district court of Judge Humphrey Howe Leavitt in Columbus, Gibbons, now joined by Lewis F. Weimer, another Kentucky slave owner, accused Sloane of harboring and secreting their slaves. Sandusky was a friendly forum for the defendants, and Judge Leavitt was a renowned antislavery politician, having served in the Ohio house and senate and the U.S. House of Representatives. In his instructions, Leavitt directed the jury to a technical issue raised by the defense—that Patton, not Gibbons, had captured the alleged slaves. Thus, there was only one matter for the jury to resolve: did Patton hold a valid warrant when he captured the alleged slaves? The court concluded that Patton was not identified in the warrant and thus was not authorized to make the arrest. Armed with these instructions, the jury vindicated Sloane on the theory that the individual making the arrest must present an effective warrant. To show appreciation for his work, African Americans in Sandusky gave Sloane a silver-headed cane.[96]

In 1853, a black man named Lewis, who was only sixteen when he fled the farm of Alexander Marshall in Fleming County, Kentucky, precipitated another crisis. Because of his confident manner, many Columbus whites assumed that Lewis had always been free. They came to know him as reliable and industrious. Federal marshals Manuel Dryden and James Black apprehended Lewis in Columbus as a fugitive slave, and they immediately headed south to Kentucky. His recapture did not go unnoticed, although Columbus abolitionists found out too late to stage a rescue. They acted quickly, nonetheless, and telegraphed their friends in Cincinnati, where local abolitionists initiated legal proceedings to intercept the marshals before they crossed the Ohio River. Armed with a warrant, Cincinnati constables arrested Dryden and Black, and abolitionists filed a suit charging them with violating the rights of a free African American.[97]

Dryden and Black then appealed to Commissioner Samuel S. Carpenter to review the case. Abolitionists hired John Jolliffe and Rutherford B. Hayes, future president of the United States. Jolliffe and Hayes attempted to transfer the case to a federal court because they doubted the "competency of the commissioner to adjudicate the question."[98] Commissioner Carpenter explained that he was a duly appointed judicial officer in the federal government, which gave him authority to review claims for runaway slaves. The federal judge in the district agreed. Jolliffe and Hayes, unable to circumvent the hearing with Carpenter, argued that, under Ohio law, a slave became automatically free the moment he entered the state with the knowledge or consent of the claimant. Without citing any evidence, they alleged that Lewis had such consent and by that theory he was freed as soon as he entered Ohio.[99]

Dryden and Black expected favorable treatment from a federal commissioner and presented their arguments without benefit of counsel. They produced an affidavit signed by Alexander Marshall, a Kentucky slave owner, identifying Lewis as his slave. The case took an unexpected turn when Commissioner Carpenter, who apparently sympathized with Lewis, initiated a substantive review of the case. Carpenter pursued the case from the perspective of Ohio law, as suggested by the defense, declaring that in Ohio a person is presumed free until compelling evidence demonstrates the individual is a slave.

The courtroom of Commissioner Carpenter was packed with spectators, both black and white. Their presence weighed heavily on him; contemporaries observed that he looked nervous. He spoke in a low voice that fell to a whisper as the hearing dragged on. Meanwhile, Lewis and his supporters were vigilant, evidently holding the thought that a rescue was still possible. Sympathetic bystanders in the courtroom encouraged Lewis with a touch on his shoulder or a nod of their heads. They beckoned him to edge to the door, which he did, carefully sliding through the crowded courtroom. An abolitionist placed a hat on his head, as others drew their bodies together as a shield. Once Lewis reached the door, he slipped outside into an empty street, where abolitionists guided him to a church. There, they dressed him in women's clothing and escorted him out of town, allowing Lewis to travel the Underground Railroad farther north to Canada.[100]

Dryden and Black, caught up in the trial, lost sight of Lewis temporarily. When Dryden realized what had happened, he shouted, "Lewis is gone." But Dryden engendered little sympathy in a community that had begun to doubt that a slave owner had a legal right to enforce the laws of slavery in a free state. African Americans sitting in the gallery were ecstatic. "In the ecstasy they flung their arms around each other's neck and fairly hugged one another."[101] Commissioner Carpenter was more aware of the change of attitude in Cincinnati. He had assumed that he could enforce the fugitive slave law objectively; however, the case made him a nervous wreck. Carpenter was relieved by Lewis's escape, and he resigned his office in 1854, admitting that he could no longer enforce the fugitive slave policy of the federal government.[102]

The fugitive slave law, therefore, did not work as Congress expected. With each passing year, it became increasingly doubtful that a slave owner could safely pass through Ohio with his or her slaves. When the steamboat *Tropic* docked in Cincinnati in 1853, abolitionists intercepted a Virginia slave owner traveling with two adults, Edward and Hannah, and with Susan, a four-year-old toddler. The slave owner, aware of Ohio's reputation, had boarded the steamer only after the captain assured him that the vessel would dock on the Kentucky side of the Ohio River. Low waters at the Covington harbor, however, made it unsafe to dock, so the captain piloted the boat to Cincinnati. Soon after the Virginia slave owner entered Ohio, abolitionists sought to rescue the slaves. William Troy, a black abolitionist, had secured a writ of habeas corpus from a local judge to examine the detention of the alleged slaves. Troy and his colleagues hired John Jolliffe as counsel, the skillful constitutional lawyer well versed in the theory of automatic emancipation. Jolliffe insisted that the slaves, "being brought by their owners upon free territory were legally free."[103]

During the proceedings, the defense was surprised by Hannah's decision to remain with the slave owner. Jolliffe then entered a motion to the judge to place the toddler in the custody of a guardian. He argued that there was no evidence that Hannah was either the mother or the responsible guardian empowered to decide the fate of the child. As a local newspaper reported, it "appeared from the testimony that Susan was of no relation to the woman." Nevertheless, the court concluded that "the Ohio River was a highway for all the states bordering on it, over which all had concurrent jurisdiction for the purposes necessary to that navigation."[104] Judge Nathaniel Read had established this precedent in *State v. Hoppess* in 1845, when he ruled that the Ohio River was a neutral waterway.[105] The court, therefore, refused to apply to the river the principle that slaves were automatically freed by virtue of Ohio soil. Although abolitionists condemned the ruling, the decision was in line with Ohio precedents so far. However, this decision had not rescinded earlier court rulings regarding automatic emancipation; rather, it simply restated that the river belonged to neither Ohio nor Kentucky.

Not only was Cincinnati a troublesome city for slave owners, but rural Ohio towns also became a thorn in their sides. In Ashtabula County, Quakers had founded Salem in 1806, and they quickly developed a reputation as stalwart conductors on the Underground Railroad. Salem Quakers published the *Bugle,* an antislavery newspaper, and they vigilantly defended alleged slaves who came to town. Salem abolitionists got one such opportunity on August 28, 1854, when a train carrying a fourteen-year-old slave girl stopped at the Fort Wayne station. Its arrival was fortuitous; the Salem chapter of the Ohio Abolitionist Society was meeting at the Hikesite Quaker Church, only one mile from the station. Word that a train from Pittsburgh had arrived in Salem spread quickly. Lawyers among the abolitionists advised that state law prohibited the transporting of slaves over Ohio railroads. On their questionable advice, about thirty abolitionists marched to the railroad depot to rescue the young girl. Charles C. Burleigh, an abolitionist orator from Massachusetts, and Henry B. Blackwell, a black abolitionist from Cincinnati, egged them on. Blackwell entered the train to counsel the child regarding her free status in Ohio. It "was assumed," explains historian Charles Galbreath, "that the girl would be frightened and that she would have confidence in one of her own color."[106] The slave owner explained that he was only traveling through the state and was thus protected by the comity relations among the states. The slave owner exercised his assumed right to forcibly detain the child, but Blackwell persisted, asking her firmly, "Do you desire to be free?" Once she answered in the affirmative, Blackwell walked her out of the railroad car and placed her with Joel McMillan and his wife, a white couple, who agreed to become the guardians. The couple renamed the child Abby Kelly Salem, to honor the famous abolitionist lecturer and the town that had rescued her from bondage.[107]

In that same year, abolitionists in Cincinnati provided refuge for Madeline, who had escaped the plantation of Henry H. Ferguson in Boone County, Kentucky. Ferguson tracked her across the Ohio River and filed a claim with Commissioner Thomas Parker, alleging that Madeline was his chattel, but offered no other evidence to document the claim. Nonetheless, Parker issued a warrant for her arrest, and Madeline was successfully remanded to slavery. For whatever reason, abolitionists did not become involved; they might have gotten word of the proceedings too late to intercede. Nevertheless, it is a certainty that Commissioner Parker recognized that local magistrates, although the *Prigg* ruling did not require them to review a claim for a slave, had a tendency to free the accused whenever the claim appeared in any way deficient. To secure Madeline, therefore, he ordered the marshal to deliver her to his court or that of another federal officer.[108]

By 1854, the courts of Ohio had edged further than before in embracing the theory of automatic emancipation for slaves brought into or allowed to enter the state. Attorneys and abolitionists continually looked for a case to offer the state supreme court a chance to make the theory settled law. With each passing year, slave owners faced continual challenges whenever they brought slaves into Ohio. John Wilson ran into trouble in Cincinnati in 1855 when the *Mediator*, a steamer bound for Virginia, docked at the harbor. He was transporting a woman named Celeste from Louisiana, he told the captain of the vessel, who instinctively doubted the veracity of the assertion. Once in Cincinnati, Wilson temporarily placed Celeste in the custody of the captain while he conducted business in town. Meanwhile, the captain spread the word that a slave was at the harbor, hoping to incite abolitionists to rescue her. Instead of a rescue, abolitionists tested the theory of automatic emancipation by hiring attorney T. J. Gitchell, who then obtained a writ of habeas corpus from Judge Burgoyne to review the detention. Celeste told counsel that the man who held her had actually seized her in Louisiana; however, she had no proof. Influenced by the theory that presumed all Ohio residents were free, the court placed the burden of proof on John Wilson, the claimant. When he showed none, the court declared Celeste free.[109]

Later in the year, a sixteen-year-old mulatto named Rosetta Armstead was brought into Columbus. Rosetta had been the slave of President John Tyler, who made her a gift to his daughter and his son-in-law, Ohio native Henry M. Dennison, an Episcopal minister. Apparently, the couple had planned on moving to Louisville, where slavery was legal, and they hired an agent to deliver Rosetta to their new home. The agent boarded a steamer in Virginia with instructions to travel directly to Kentucky. However, the agent had friends in Columbus and traveled there instead. He faced resistance instantly. Abolitionists secured a writ of habeas corpus, and a local court freed Rosetta and placed her in the care of Lewis Vanslyke, who agreed to serve as guardian.[110]

The agent hired Marshal Hiram H. Robinson, who obtained a warrant from Commissioner John L. Pendery to arrest Rosetta. After conducting a brief hearing, the commissioner approved the removal, and Marshall Robinson "hurried her to the train depot, and started at once for Cincinnati."[111] Vanslyke struck out in pursuit, and once in Cincinnati, he hired Salmon Chase, Rutherford B. Hayes, and Timothy Walker to argue for her release. The attorneys immediately secured a writ of habeas corpus from common pleas judge James Parker to review the claim. The claimant employed George E. Pugh and his law partners from a Louisville firm. Judge Parker ruled that the agent had voluntarily brought Rosetta into Ohio, which freed her from slavery. Chase, anticipating resistance from the claimant, had secured for his client the protection of the sheriff.[112]

Meanwhile, the claimant secured a writ from federal district judge John McLean, who examined the case. Justice McLean's initial ruling alarmed antislavery leaders. As Chase reported it, McLean rebuked the local court "upon the ground that the state court had no jurisdiction to protect the liberty of any individual claimed and seized as a fugitive slave under process authorized by the fugitive slave act."[113] Nonetheless, McLean agreed that the agent had brought the slave into Ohio, which, under state law, made her free. Men who loved liberty, Chase explained, disliked the decision, but their opposition was "less intense than it would have been, had the decision not been followed by practical results."[114]

The case took an uncertain turn when Marshal Hiram Robinson again seized Rosetta on the warrant issued by Commissioner John L. Pendery the following March. Robinson refused to process her in Hamilton County on the grounds that a local court had no jurisdiction in the matter. The federal district court decided this conflict of law question in favor of enforcement of the fugitive slave law.[115]

———

Before 1855, Ohio and federal trial courts had reviewed constitutional challenges to the federal fugitive slave law. The state supreme court had resolved various disputes involving race, but it had not yet offered a ruling on automatic emancipation theory, which the circuit court had approved in the *Farr* case in 1841. The court announced its opinion on the subject in *Anderson v. Poindexter* (1856), when it ruled that a slave, other than a fugitive, automatically became free the moment he or she entered Ohio for any reason.[116]

John Anderson, a Kentucky slave owner, resided in Campbell County, across the Ohio River from New Richmond, in southwestern Ohio. Anderson had owned James P. Poindexter, a twenty-six-year-old man, for eight years. Poindexter made a deal with Anderson to purchase himself and gave him a promissory note signed by his white supporters—Thomas C. Gowdy, Jackson White, and Francis Donaldson—should Poindexter default on the contract. (Poindexter did not sign the agreement.) Later, Poindexter attempted to change the terms of the contract, asking the plaintiff to set him free on the basis of payments already made. The defendants reneged on the notes they had signed for John Anderson to manumit Poindexter. Represented by John Jolliffe, the defendants contended that Poindexter became free when Anderson allowed him to come into Ohio.[117]

Timothy Walker wrote the opinion for the trial court and defined the obligation of Ohio to slave-owning citizens from other states. Judge Walker explained that federal law did not define all Negroes as slaves. "The federal Constitution does not regard slaves as property but simply persons owing labor and service." He pointed out that under state sovereignty, free African Americans had voted in both southern and northern states and also in the Northwest Territory. A state was within its legal rights to decide matters of personal liberty for all individuals who come under its jurisdiction, Walker said. Although slave owners had assumed that the federal Constitution and interstate comity secured their property interest in slaves, the judge rejected the notion that either claim protected the status of a slave in Ohio. "Nothing can be made property in Ohio by being brought hither from another state, which would not be property had it originated here." In a free state, the presumption is for freedom; the burden is on the claimant to prove that the person he claimed escaped from slavery and was returnable under federal law. Comity "is entirely satisfied when we make others equal to ourselves." If a slave enters Ohio, he continued, other than by the terms outlined in the federal fugitive slave law, a slave owner loses control over the person. "If slavery were to exist in this state for one minute it may exist for two minutes, for a day, for a year."[118] Under this theory, the state of Ohio assumed that all individuals on its soil were free, and until a higher court ruled to the contrary the Walker opinion was binding in the state.

Anderson appealed this decision. Writing for the Ohio Supreme Court, Justice Ozias Brown considered it reasonable to infer that the defendants believed that John Anderson had actually owned Poindexter when they signed the promissory notes. He considered the evidence compelling that the owner had allowed Poindexter to enter Ohio at various times. "Some enlightened jurists in the slave States," Bowen continued, "admit that if the master takes his slave into a free State to reside permanently, that he thereby becomes emancipated."[119] Bowen observed that "the common law confers no right of property in persons. It can exist only by municipal authority"[120] Writing separately, but concurring with the majority, Justice Jacob Brinkerhoff considered the controversy a contract question. Kentucky law regarded a slave as incompetent to make contracts, and this plaintiff therefore had no grounds for the complaint. Brinkerhoff had no doubts that a person became free whenever he entered the jurisdiction of Ohio. He regarded the circumstances outlined under federal law—fugitive slaves—to be the only exceptions to this rule of law.[121] Justice Joseph R. Swan, also concurring in the opinion, wrote that, while some states recognized property in human beings, "[i]t has never existed in Ohio."[122] Other justices concurred but made their decisions on other points of law; nevertheless, the state supreme court affirmed the trial court opinion that Poindexter became a freeman under the laws of Ohio upon his entry with the consent of his owner.

That same court, however, acknowledged that, under the federal fugitive slave law, it did not have the authority to set free a slave who escaped into Ohio to interfere with the office of federal commissioner, or to restrain federal marshals. On the other hand, the court made it clear that enforcing the federal fugitive slave law meant dealing with sophisticated Ohio judges and constitutional lawyers, who were sympathetic to the principle that freedom was a natural right and that slavery was a function of statutory law. Federal marshals captured runaway slaves, and commissioners and district judges remanded them, but antislavery men made it difficult for kidnappers and slave catchers to operate in Ohio. So did enslaved blacks, who continually fled bondage to and through Ohio. As the *Cincinnati Daily Commercial* reported in 1856, "The Underground Railroad has recently been doing a great business."[123]

The Ohio Supreme Court, however, did not end the fugitive slave controversy, and the battle over slavery and freedom continued on its discordant course for the rest of the decade. Few events in American history dramatize this more than the desperate effort of the Garner family to secure their freedom in 1856. Fifty-five-year-old Simon Garner and his family fled the farms of Archibald K. Gaines and John Marshall of

Richmond Station, Kentucky, about sixteen miles from Covington. The party included Garner's fifty-year-old wife Mary, their twenty-two-year-old son, Simon Jr., his wife Margaret, and their four children. John Marshall claimed the elder Garners and their son, while Archibald Gaines claimed Margaret and her children.[124]

The Garners made their desperate flight to freedom following a severe midwinter snowstorm. Although snow is a common occurrence in the Midwest, Ohio residents frequently recalled the harshness of the winter of 1856–57. C. H. Cleveland of Cincinnati wrote, "The Ohio is frozen solid, and throughout the West winter reigns and snows."[125] Another observer commented, "[S]ince the Ohio River has been bridged with ice, the slaves living near the border have escaped in great numbers."[126] The storm was not necessarily an obstacle to enslaved blacks; many took it as an opportune time to escape by using the frozen river as a highway.

Simon Garner and his family rode a horse-drawn sleigh to the Ohio River and then walked across the river on foot. Gaines and Marshall assembled a posse, hoping to capture them before they reached Ohio. But they reached the river too late, finding only the horse and sleigh. The posse followed the runaways into Cincinnati. The Garners counted on sympathy in the Queen City from a large community of fugitive slaves who had taken refuge there. They also expected local abolitionists and other workers on the Underground Railroad to provide temporary resources for them, including lodging and provisions.[127]

Joe Kite and his son, Elijah, two runaways, were positioned on the free side of the Ohio River to aid runaway slaves. When Simon and his family arrived in Cincinnati, they were directed to the Kite residence. But because the Garners had left their footprints in the snow, the posse was able to follow them. Once they determined the location of the slaves, Marshall and Gaines obtained a warrant from Commissioner John L. Pendery and enlisted Marshal Hiram H. Robinson and his associates for assistance. Joe Kite and Elijah did not give them easy access, nor did the Garners give themselves up. Simon Jr. fired at the officers, wounding one of them. Margaret swore that she would kill herself and sacrifice her own children to avoid returning to bondage. She plunged a knife into one child and then turned to the other child to do the same, but it was too late for her to accomplish the deed. The marshals and posse captured the family and carried them to jail.[128]

The arrest of the Garner family precipitated one of this nation's most sensational fugitive slave cases. Abolitionists hired antislavery lawyer John Jolliffe, who argued that the slaves had been in Ohio previously with the consent of their masters. Consequently, the Garners, counsel suggested, had actually been illegally held in servitude. Testimony that members of the Garner family had at various times been spotted in Cincinnati was not persuasive, however. Documents presented by the claimants left little doubt that they were still slaves under Kentucky law. When the court rejected the automatic emancipation theory presented by Jolliffe, he resorted to another strategy to block the removal of Margaret Garner.[129]

Jolliffe arranged to have Margaret charged for the murder of her own child. By tying the case up in the courts, Margaret would be free from slavery. When the claimant came to remove Margaret, Cincinnati police chief Edward Hopkins refused to release her on the grounds that a grand jury had indicted the defendant for murder; she was to stand trial in Cincinnati. Cincinnati mayor James J. Faran wrote an open letter to the police chief to remind him of his obligation under local law. The mayor recognized that a claimant had a constitutional right to property in slaves, but thought that the Garner case merited intervention. He thus admonished the chief to be aware of which authority he obeyed—the state of Ohio or the United States.[130]

The federal marshal then appealed to Judge Leavitt for a writ of habeas corpus. The judge faced one fundamental question: Who was entitled to custody of Margaret Garner? The facts disclosed that the police had gained custody of the Garner family while they waited to be processed as fugitive slaves. Once the commissioner approved the rendition of the slaves, Judge Leavitt held, Ohio authorities were obligated to release them to the claimant. Although Jolliffe lost the case, he won the admiration of blacks and whites in Cincinnati who followed the trial. Abolitionists held a public meeting to protest the ruling and to praise Jolliffe for his vigilance. George L. Weed, one of the speakers, commented, "If legal skill, earnest eloquence, and persevering exertion, could have availed in these cases he would have been successful. Nevertheless, truth and justice will ultimately triumph." The abolitionists collected a contribution for Jolliffe, who rarely received compensation for his efforts on behalf of runaway slaves.[131]

The editors of local newspapers sharply disagreed on the defense strategy in the case. The *Cincinnati Enquirer* criticized Jolliffe for abusing the legal system. The editors also accused the abolitionists of inflaming public sentiments by calling a town meeting "to get up an excitement, and thus influence the court of the commissioner in his decision relative to the fugitive slave case now pending before it." The *Cincinnati Daily Commercial* took the opposite position, suggesting that the case involved liberty, "not only of the parties before the court but also of their posterity."[132]

The Margaret Garner case also prompted renewed discussion in Ohio about passing a personal liberty law to secure African American freedom. Salmon P. Chase, now governor of Ohio, urged state representative James Monroe to introduce in the General Assembly legislation for that purpose. Monroe quoted Chase as saying, "You ought to introduce a bill into the House in the morning," and have "it carried through both houses under a suspension of the rules, and have it become a law before you adjourn tomorrow."[133] Monroe studied the matter and, together with Chase, drafted the bill. Essentially, the bill authorized an Ohio judge to issue a writ that would command local authorities to bring before the court anyone detained as a runaway slave. The bill would have given state officers supreme power over runaway slaves. Although the law would not have secured the release of Margaret Garner, it would have protected any person illegally detained in the future. Such a state law, however, would have been in conflict with the *Prigg* decision of 1842 and with the Fugitive Slave Act. The majority in the General Assembly obviously recognized the perils of passing such a law, and the bill died in committee.

Like Margaret Garner, Addison White also was willing to fight to live free. He joined the runaway slave community in Ohio after he fled from Benjamin P. Churchill, of Kentucky. White settled in Mechanicsburg, a town twenty miles west of Columbus, whose residents prided themselves on living in a community intolerant of slavery. Addison White found refuge and employment on the farm of Udney Hyde, a conductor on the Underground Railroad. Churchill tracked down White in 1857. The violent temper of Addison White is the stuff of which legends are made, and Churchill expected resistance.[134] White had vowed not to be taken alive and kept a gun nearby. Abolitionist Levi Coffin later wrote that White "had steady nerves and the skill to use the gun successfully."[135] The claimant was well aware of this capacity and obtained assistance from U.S. Marshal Lewis W. Sifford.

When they arrived at Hyde's farm, Sifford ordered Addison White to surrender. White refused and threatened to fire on anyone who rushed the house. White then ran to the woods, but the heavily armed posse subdued him. Churchill next faced resistance from abolitionists in Mechanicsburg, including ministers, judges, and the sheriff. Marshal Sifford arrested Hyde and other leaders for interfering with the removal of a runaway slave. The arrest of such prominent citizens "created intense excitement," wrote historian Henry Howe; friends of the defendants "secured a writ of *habeas corpus,* which the marshal ignored."[136] Consequently, the posse faced angry abolitionists who dogged their trail as they carried Addison White back to slavery. Once abolitionists in Springfield and Urbana learned of what had happened in nearby Mechanicsburg, they harassed the posse all the way to Cincinnati.

In Cincinnati, the claimant effectively used the legal system to silence their opponents. Marshal Sifford secured from Commissioner Edward R. Newhall a warrant for the arrest of abolitionist Hiram Gatridge and his associates from Champaign County, charging that they had interfered with the removal of Addison White. Meanwhile Sheriff John E. Dayton from Clark County issued a warrant for the arrest of Marshal Sifford, Churchill and nine other men in the posse. The marshal appealed to a justice of the peace who ruled against him; the marshal then carried the matter before Judge Leavitt.[137] Once again the case involved some of the most prominent pro- and antislavery lawyers in Ohio. The claimant hired Stanley Matthews, Clement L. Vallandigham, and George E. Pugh, Democrats who sympathized with slave owners, while abolitionists obtained representation from antislavery attorneys R. Mason and C. P. Wolcott. Judge Leavitt enforced the federal fugitive slave law, rejecting the notion that public passion could override federal law. In a conflict between federal and state officers regarding custody of a slave, federal law was binding. Leavitt ruled that an officer of the law might use reasonable force to maintain control of slaves. The posse, therefore, was within its rights to use force to maintain custody of the runaway slave they had apprehended. Although abolitionists lost the case, they succeeded in freeing Addison White. Churchill grew tired of the proceedings, which lasted almost a year, during which time Addison White was in jail, and

offered to sell Addison for one thousand dollars, a fee to which abolitionists agreed.[138]

Marshal Dennis also faced resistance when he tried to remove James
Worthington, a runaway slave who had lived free in Akron for fifteen
years. Abolitionists in the city staged a rescue, rallying the community by
charging that the marshal had failed to prove that Worthington was a
fugitive slave. Dennis accepted defeat and left town.[139] Lewis Early faced
certain removal too, when George Kilgour captured him in Ross County.
Early claimed to be a freeman, yet he was unable to prove his status.
Though state law no longer required blacks to produce a certificate of
freedom, Early's attorneys argued that he once had one but it had burned
in a house fire in 1859. The claimant scoffed at the argument, suggesting that it was merely a ruse to divest him of his chattel. Ohio law did not
prescribe how its black residents could prove his freedom when challenged. Commissioner C. C. Browne in Cincinnati reviewed the case
and ruled for Kilgour. After verifying his claim, however, Kilgour offered to sell Early to Ohio abolitionists for $1,150, but he later accepted
$425.[140]

Although federal officials in Ohio continually enforced the federal
fugitive slave law, the end of the decade pointed to a new day. State courts
had weakened the federal policy whenever possible, and Ohio communities continually involved themselves in rescues. By the late 1850s, parts
of Ohio had truly become liberated zones. Unlike previous decades,
when Ohio judges meted out harsh punishment to anyone who violated
federal policy, the courts showed leniency to violators. The Connelly case,
decided in 1858, illustrates how Ohio approached fugitive slave disputes.

For many years in Cincinnati, William M. Connelly had used his newspaper, the *Cincinnati Daily Commericial,* to promote abolitionist causes. His
notoriety in Kentucky as a friend to fugitives from labor made Connelly
a target of slave catchers and federal marshals. Whenever slave catchers
came to Cincinnati hunting for fugitive slaves, William Connelly was
automatically a suspect. But the slave catchers knew only the outline of
his involvement; they would learn much more about his participation in
the Underground Railroad in the summer of 1858. The circumstances
leading to this event started on June 13, 1857, when a black man and his
wife escaped from slavery in Covington, Kentucky, to board the Underground Railroad in Cincinnati. Armed with a warrant, federal marshals

went to the offices of the *Cincinnati Daily Commercial,* located in Room 18 on the sixth floor of a downtown office building. Their search initially proved fruitless, and the couple remained in hiding for more than a week. After several days, the marshals, acting on a tip, discovered a back room behind the main newspaper office, which apparently was a station on the Underground Railroad. Upon finding the couple, the marshals faced resistance, as the African American man defended himself and his wife with weapons. After wounding the man in a gunfight, the marshals subdued him and immediately escorted the couple back to Covington, where the injured man died from his wounds.[141]

Fortuitously, Connelly was out of the city when the raid took place at his office. Once he heard the news, he went to New York to delay his arrest and prosecution for violating the federal fugitive slave law. Within a few months he was extradited and subsequently faced prosecution. After his friends arranged bail for him, Connelly hired prominent defense attorneys—former judge J. B. Stallo and Thomas Corwin, a former governor. Stanley Matthews represented the plaintiff in the case. The trial began on May 5, 1858, in the courtroom of federal district judge Humphrey H. Leavitt. While Judge Leavitt enforced the fugitive slave law, his sympathies were clearly against slaveholding. He sentenced Connelly to twenty days in jail and imposed a modest $10 fine. Having challenged the federal fugitive slave law, Connelly left jail with even more renown. He became a popular abolitionist speaker and went on tour throughout the country.[142]

———

Conflict between Ohio and Kentucky intensified throughout the 1850s, as a series of border disputes continually plagued residents on both sides of the Ohio River. North of the river, abolitionists had become steadfast in their belief that slavery was wrong and that to rescue a slave was a badge of honor. South of the river, most whites considered slavery legal and morally legitimate. Conflicting legal systems doubtless existed, and they produced controversy along the Ohio and Kentucky border. It is not surprising that Willis Lago, a freeman of color, precipitated such a legal battle in 1859 when a Kentucky grand jury indicted him of inducing Charlotte, the slave of C. W. Nuckols, to escape. Beriah Magoffin, the governor of Kentucky, issued a requisition to Governor William Dennison of Ohio, asking him to arrest Lago as a fugitive from justice and deliver him to the state of Kentucky. On the advice of C. P. Wolcott, his attorney general, Dennison concluded that only an act of treason, or some other serious crime under federal law, would warrant the delivery of Willis Lago as a fugitive from justice. Moreover, Wolcott explained that though Kentucky considered the conduct of Lago a crime, Ohio was not bound to enforce the laws of a foreign state.[143] Dennison, therefore, refused the requisition for Lago on the grounds that slave stealing was not a crime in Ohio.

Kentucky turned to the U.S. Supreme Court to compel Dennison to return Lago for prosecution. Chief Justice Roger B. Taney chastised Ohio for not returning Lago but concluded that the federal courts lacked the power to require that a state governor extradite someone to another state. On its face the decision was a victory for opponents of slavery, since Lago was not returned to Kentucky for prosecution. However, in the context of when it was decided, February 1861, this case can be seen as a victory for the Southern states, which were now claiming to be independent from the United States.[144]

The common borders of Ohio and Virginia caused a similar problem in 1860, when Virginia officials filed charges against Owen Brown and Francis Merriam for allegedly inciting a slave revolt in the wake of John Brown's raid at Harpers Ferry, Virginia. Like runaway slaves, the men found refuge in Ohio. On the advice of his attorney general, Ohio governor Dennison denied the claim on grounds that there was no evidence that the accused had taken up refuge in Ohio. If the men reached Ohio, state law did not authorize its governor to remand such persons to another state.[145] Obviously, Ohio did not consider giving aid to slaves a crime, though it did extradite bona fide criminals on demand.

—

The Western Reserve was a stronghold of Ohio's antislavery movement, and Oberlin produced some of its most committed leaders, including prominent figures such as Jacob Dolson Cox, a future governor of Ohio. Not surprisingly, Oberlin produced some of the most sensational episodes in the rescue of alleged runaway slaves. The city had never lost an alleged slave to slave catchers since the fugitive policy of the federal government went into effect. In fact, no one had even attempted to remove a slave from Oberlin during the 1850s. John Price, a young runaway slave who had escaped from Kentucky in 1858, had thereby wisely chosen a community that would protect him in the event he was claimed as a fugitive slave.[146]

However, the Oberlin community was not a utopia for African Americans. The 1850s were marked by increased tension between the races, especially among those whites who believed that blacks were competing with them for work. In an election, Anson P. Dayton had lost the position of township clerk to Charles H. Langston, a black man who was the brother of the famous John Mercer Langston. The election angered Dayton, and he wanted to get revenge on blacks in general and the community that helped them. That opportunity came when Anderson P. Jennings came to Oberlin searching for his own slaves and, while there, took an interest in John Price, the slave of his Kentucky neighbor John G. Bacon. Armed with a power of attorney he had obtained from Bacon, Jennings set a trap to capture Price. Jennings and Dayton, now a federal marshal, along with Marshals Lowe and R. P. Mitchell, decided on a plan to lure Price out of Oberlin to a town friendly to slave catching. They hired a fourteen-year-old boy to ask John Price to help him dig potatoes in Wellington, where the slave catchers would snare him. Following behind, the slave catchers subdued John as planned, but a college student who witnessed the crime alerted people in Oberlin, and black and white men struck out in pursuit, strapping on their revolvers and grabbing whatever other weapons they had to intercept Jennings and his men before they boarded a southbound train.[147]

Anderson Jennings and his associates hunkered down in the attic of a Wellington hotel, as the abolitionists approached the building brandishing weapons and repeatedly shouting, "Kidnappers!" According to Jennings, the mob quickly swelled to more than a thousand individuals; other observers, however, estimated the number at only five hundred. As the abolitionist crowd besieged the hotel, they sent Charles Langston to negotiate with Jennings. When that failed, they broke into the building and freed John Price, who emigrated to Canada. This episode became celebrated as the Oberlin-Wellington rescue.[148]

A federal grand jury indicted Simeon Bushnell, John Watson, Charles H. Langston, and thirty-seven local residents for participating in the rescue. The trial began on April 5, 1859, when some of the area's most respected citizens faced prosecution for violating the federal fugitive slave law. Professor Henry E. Peck, antislavery attorney Ralph Plumb, bookseller James M. Fitch, and eleven other blacks headed the list. These men were well known for their active participation in the Underground Railroad, and their opponents seized the opportunity to put them on trial.[149]

The prosecution resulted in a conviction, but only of Langston and Bushnell. Central to the Oberlin-Wellington case was Ohio jury law against enrollment of black jurors. Langston was atypical in Ohio for many reasons—a black schoolteacher, town clerk, and civil rights reformer. For his part in the Oberlin-Wellington rescue, the courts convicted him specifically of not trying to stop the rescue. From reading of his courtroom demeanor, one might conclude that that the court punished him for his years of insolence as a civil rights reformer. Though he had "able counsel," Langston raised the issue of racial fairness before the all-white jury. Langston asserted that he had followed his conscience: "No matter what the laws might be, you would honor yourself for giving aid while your friends and your children to all generations would honor you for doing it, and every good and honest man would say you had done right." The white jury convicted him, in spite of Langston's defense that a jury of his peers did not judge him. The "jurors are well known to have shared largely in these prejudices," Langston argued. He believed that they "'were neither impartial, nor were they a jury of my peers.'"[150] Defending their political principles was vital to both abolitionists and their opponents.

Governor Salmon P. Chase and other Ohio abolitionists condemned the verdict. Chase criticized the decision by invoking state sovereignty and the right of a state to nullify a repugnant federal law. Antislavery leader Benjamin Wade asked the Ohio Supreme Court to issue a writ of habeas corpus to review the case, and if it refused, he suggested that "the people of the Western Reserve must grant it—sword in hand if need be."[151] The court examined the case, but by a 3 to 2 vote it did not challenge federal authority, which would have been a futile act. In *Ableman v. Booth*, the Wisconsin Supreme Court had declared the federal fugitive slave law unconstitutional, only to have its opinion reversed in federal court. The Ohio Supreme Court, therefore, reached the same conclusion as the federal court, ruling that the fugitive slave law was valid. Jacob Brinkerhoff and Milton Sutliff both supported the writ of habeas corpus and were prepared to challenge the federal government on this issue. It was rumored that Governor Chase would have used the militia to enforce the writ if the court had issued it, talk Chase denied in later years.[152]

As the nation drifted toward Civil War, another fugitive slave controversy arose. William S. Goshorn of Wheeling, Virginia, filed a claim for a woman named Lucy Bagby, who lived in Cleveland. Goshorn obtained a warrant from Commissioner Simeon Bushnell and captured Bagby at the home of L. A. Benton, her employer.[153] Ohio judge Joseph R. Swan reviewed the case. Judge Swan explained that for "two generations, the judges of a state court had judicial right to interpose their own individual opinions upon a question thus disposed of." Hence, the citizens of Ohio were constrained by federal law to remain neutral when a federal judge remanded a runaway to slavery. Nonetheless, he understood that the passions of many Ohio citizens ran high and confessed that he was also touched by the plight of runaway slaves. "If a weary, frightened slave should appeal to me to protect him from his pursuers, it is possible I might momentarily forget my allegiance to the law."[154] Yet Judge Swan felt compelled to uphold the law; in effect he would convict himself for allowing his personal feelings to interfere with enforcement of federal law.

Ohio abolitionists did not share his views. Reverend George Gordon of Cincinnati was a minister in the Free Presbyterian Church, a religious body that regarded slavery as a sin in the eyes of God. He was also the president of Iberia College, an Ohio institution that condemned slaveholding. Gordon and his parishioners took action on May 5, 1860, when Kentucky slave owner Isaac Pollock came to town seeking a runaway slave named Grandison Martin. Pollock, under federal law, obtained a warrant from Commissioner Edward R. Newhall. The commissioner ordered U.S. Marshal Joseph S. Barber to make the arrest. Apparently, Gordon and his associates rescued the slave. Unable to recover him, Pollock brought suit in federal district court alleging that Gordon had violated the federal Fugitive Slave Act. Gordon, represented by abolitionist attorney John Jolliffe, argued that resisting slavery was protected in the free exercise of religion clause in the First Amendment. He also argued that the Fugitive Slave Act was contrary to the principles of natural rights and the Constitution and thus invalid. These arguments notwithstanding, Gordon was convicted that November, jailed in Cleveland, and fined three hundred dollars. His attorney immediately petitioned President Lincoln for a pardon, which was granted in April 1862.[155]

The 1850s ended as the decade had begun—in controversy. The revised fugitive slave law was designed to solve problems associated with runaway slaves but instead it only served to exacerbate the problem. At a minimum, Ohio restricted the act's operation in 1855, when the state supreme court held that recapture of an individual was legal only when that person had escaped from slavery and was therefore returnable under federal law. Ohio had weakened the operation of the federal fugitive slave policy, but it had not directly challenged the validity of the law. Matters such as slave transit, temporary visitation, or hiring out slaves, however, were no longer protected.

The Fugitive Slave Act did not end the controversy involving runaway slaves. It inaugurated a period of trial and error. Throughout the 1850s, the federal government sought compromises to end the slavery controversy. Popular sovereignty failed in Kansas, the *Dred Scott* decision caused even greater controversy than the Fugitive Slave Act, and a new political party was formed that called for the restriction of slavery to where it was then legal. Slave owners wanted greater protection for slavery, such as the ability to carry blacks to the western territory. The compromises secured neither abolitionist interests nor those of slave owners. Salmon Chase had anticipated such an outcome: "Compromise measures," he told a colleague, "are apples of discord. It turns out as I predicted that these measures have brought a sword and not peace."[156]

EIGHT

The Limits of Freedom

AFTER SIX DECADES in the Union, Ohio had not yet fully reconciled its laws with the spirit of the Declaration of Independence or the
federal Constitution. Indeed, the Declaration made explicit proclama-
tions about natural rights; the Constitution did so, too, with habeas corpus protections. The Constitution also barred the federal government
from enacting ex post facto laws or bills of attainder, and it guaranteed
a jury trial in criminal prosecutions. The Bill of Rights offered additional guarantees of civil liberties. Together, these documents fostered
an American culture in which its citizens were convinced that liberty and
equality were their birthright. Ohio had also ignored the country's founding principles. To the majority of the whites in America, the culture
excluded African Americans; nevertheless, blacks early benefited from
such protections as habeas corpus, and their quest for recognition of
greater civil rights protections would eventually earn dividends. The African American experience in Ohio followed a similar pattern. The first
state constitution declared that all men are born equal and have certain
natural and unalienable rights, including the enjoyment of life, liberty,

and property.[1] The 1851 Constitution affirmed the principle that "[a]ll men are, by nature, free and independent, and have certain inalienable rights."[2] Civil rights reformers in Ohio faced the challenge of making these principles reality.

Ohio accommodated slave owners until the mid-nineteenth century by allowing them such courtesies as transporting slaves and bringing slaves to Ohio while on holiday. State law did not grant these considerations, yet they were inevitable in a race-based society. Social reformers locally and nationally called on the state to change these policies. The Buckeye State made an astonishing transformation when its trial courts began to prohibit these courtesies.[3] Moreover, the Free-Soil Party of Ohio negotiated a compromise that resulted in the elimination of select provisions in the Black Laws in 1849. Unable to effect the abolition of slavery in the South, abolitionists succeeded in persuading Ohio courts to exercise their power in order to deny slave owners the authority to keep slaves within its borders. Ultimately, the Ohio Supreme Court ruled in *Anderson v. Poindexter* (1856) that a slave became automatically free the moment he or she came into Ohio with the knowledge or consent of a slave owner.[4] Ohio never declared the federal fugitive slave laws unconstitutional, although antislavery lawyers had argued the point for many decades. Nevertheless, Ohio joined other northern states in asserting the automatic emancipation of slaves brought into the state with the consent of the owner.[5]

After decades of toleration, Ohio trial and appellate judges applied a fresh and daring judicial philosophy. However, the notion that federal or state lawmakers could contain slavery had been established in Article VI in the Ordinance of 1787. The history of the Ohio Country suggests that federal policy makers had made the territory a free zone. Ohio merely had subordinated its ban against slavery to accommodate southern planters. Although the vast majority of Ohio whites preferred free labor to slavery, it was bigotry that took center stage—they did not want to live among African Americans and they enacted the Black Laws to that end. The principles of the federal and state constitutions highlighted a glaring contradiction. The free states, especially those that never officially knew slavery, struggled with the many meanings of freedom. Should slavery exist in Ohio? If Ohio prohibited slavery, should African Americans be given full citizenship? Could Ohio rightly use the power of the state to subordinate a group of people solely on account of color? From its territorial period to the Civil War, Ohio lawmakers grappled with the meaning of freedom and the meaning of sovereignty. The debate culminated in a civil rights movement in Ohio and the civil rights revolution in the twentieth century.

The struggle over the meanings of freedom began in earnest when Ohio officials came to realize that black Buckeyes had the right of existence in the state. Indeed, in its report in 1842, a select committee told the members of the Ohio house that "the principles of humanity forbid that we should deny them the right of existence, or the means of sustaining that existence."[6] Talks of expelling African Americans from Ohio had gone on for several decades, but pragmatic lawmakers recognized that they had not made adequate preparation to achieve the colonization of blacks. The Civil War, therefore, compelled Ohio whites to admit that their black neighbors and those destined to enter the state merited more than mere existence. But, even then, whites did not envision an integrated society. Therefore, Ohio lawmakers officially established a segregated society to regulate their racially mixed state. Ohio society under segregation was different from the social construct that existed under the Black Laws. Whereas with the Black Laws, Ohio legislators had attempted to close the state's borders to African Americans by imposing barriers on their entry and subordinated those already in the state, the state's post–Civil War legislature engineered a new Ohio that separated blacks and whites. The Black Laws explicitly had denied runaway slaves entry by requiring black migrants to prove their free status. But in the new Ohio, the General Assembly anticipated that large numbers of African Americans would migrate into the state, especially without racial codes and slavery restraining them. Segregation required legislation that did more than subordinate blacks or impose barriers on those coming into the state. The new Ohio needed to be socially engineered with racial codes that managed race relations in a mixed society. The General Assembly made it inappropriate for blacks and whites to mingle. Ohio whites once again feared that blacks would take away their jobs or would drag down wages and so they accepted the new constraints imposed on African Americans.

Indeed, the Ohio General Assembly had made important changes in 1849. The assembly abolished the state immigration law, the public school law, and the testimony law, which had imposed barriers on black entry into Ohio and deprived them of the same civil rights extended to whites. Although these changes were significant, they obviously were limited. For example, in *State v. Farr,* circuit judges virtually had voided the immigration law—eight years before its abolition by the legislature.[7] Moreover, African Americans and white philanthropists already had established schools for black children. The Ohio General Assembly left in place many laws aimed at segregating blacks, depriving them of suffrage, barring them from the militia and from juries, and depriving them of public relief. The state also established a segregated school system, funded only by the tax dollars of black property owners. In theory, African Americans had most of the same rights as whites; in practice, they remained outcasts in a state that had never known slavery.[8]

The new Ohio experienced another shift in the 1850s. The Democratic Party filled the vacuum that followed the demise of the Whig and Free-Soil parties. For a short time, the Democracy was virtually without rival in Ohio, and it controlled state politics with a free hand. The new Republican Party, founded in 1854, required a few more years to carve out its niche in the state. The Democratic Party took on a more conservative tone over the next few years. Democrats had seen the rise of reform movements in Ohio, with greater emphasis on civil rights and discussions of black equality, especially among abolitionist Christians. These evangelicals invoked the philosophy of natural law to suggest that there should be no distinction between the races. Ohio Democrats wanted to maintain cordial relations with slave owners, and they enacted new restrictions on African Americans. The state senate passed a resolution asserting that the Creator "never intended to place the Negro on equality with the white man."[9] Although social reformers in Ohio advocated universal male suffrage, the state constitutional convention in 1850 and 1851 affirmed "white male suffrage."[10] The ebb and flow between advances and restrictions on black rights continued until the state settled on the course of officially segregating blacks and whites in 1849.

In the early nineteenth century, Ohio embraced the federal policy adopted in the Ordinance of 1787. By prohibiting slavery in the Northwest Territory, the federal government drew a line against its expansion. Yet the federal government made no efforts to protect black civil rights. Instead, it accommodated slave owners by allowing them to recover runaway slaves.

In a sense, Congress envisioned the Northwest Territory as a region for whites only. The state of Ohio adopted this policy. Its constitution prohibited slavery, and in 1803 the General Assembly began codifying the Black Laws, which theoretically walled off the state from its slaveholding neighbors. Ohio officials initially assumed that they could hold down the black population by denying access to runaway slaves. Because only about three hundred African Americans resided in the state in 1803, Ohio officials viewed them as a shrinking population. The founders of Ohio did not envision a multirace society.

Until the late 1830s, Ohio jurists and magistrates had largely sided with slave catchers. When slave owners or their agents came to Ohio hunting for runaway slaves, the courts routinely returned them. Once the abolition movement surfaced, Ohio courts began to experience a transformation. Trial judges denied certificates of removal to slave owners or agents for various reasons, including the theory that if an individual entered Ohio with consent he or she would be freed by that action. The U.S. Supreme Court decision in *Prigg v. Pennsylvania* (1842) sided with local courts that refused to use the instruments of the state to enforce the federal fugitive slave law. However, the opinion simultaneously gave greater protections for slavery by assigning federal officers to enforce the fugitive slave law.

The Fugitive Slave Act of 1850 alarmed black Ohioans, who lived under constant threat of kidnapping or being returned to the masters they escaped from. For several years after passage of the new federal act, blacks and abolitionists urged the Ohio legislature to adopt a personal liberty law. The Republican-controlled assembly did so in 1857, when it made kidnapping a felony punishable by imprisonment for up to nine months and a three-hundred-dollar fine. The statute also forbade constables from using state facilities to hold runaway slaves. Anyone violating this provision, the statute read, faced a minimum of thirty days in jail and a five-hundred-dollar fine.[11] The Democratic assembly repealed the personal liberty law in 1858 and attempted to replace it with a statute that required Ohio to enforce the federal Fugitive Slave Act. Representative Peter Hitchcock challenged the bill, contending that the penalties it would impose on residents who aided runaway slaves were unconscionable. He argued that it was basic human nature to help individuals who were hungry, tired, or cold. "You cannot by law prevent" such aid, he asserted.

Hitchcock also pointed out that the federal Constitution gave Congress the power to enact statutory provisions for the capture and return of runaway slaves. He did not believe it was necessary for Ohio to buttress that law. Should anyone wish to enforce the fugitive slave policy of the United States, he continued, they could do so without state legislation mandating it.[12] Before bringing the bill to a vote, the house established the Committee on Federal Relations to study it as well as other issues relating to runaway slaves. "The legislature has no constitutional power to pass such an act," the committee reported.[13] Endorsing its report, the legislature rejected the bill.

As the Republican Party gained ground in Ohio, its leaders urged voters to defeat racially oppressive laws at the polls. Elected in 1855, Republican governor Salmon Chase advised Ohio voters to elect moderates to protect their interests. Though disenfranchised, African Americans also advocated adoption of laws to secure their civil rights. In 1860, the Ohio State Anti-Slavery Society, an African American organization, urged the assembly to adopt a "personal liberty law for the protection of our wives, children and ourselves against the man stealers and kidnappers." The society demanded a law that would "fully protect every inhabitant of this state in his inalienable right to liberty."[14] Unable to secure a state law, civil rights advocates in Ohio turned to the federal government. Representative James Mitchell Ashley, an Ohio Republican, proposed a federal personal liberty law on January 29, 1861. The Ashley bill did not seek to revoke the fugitive slave law; instead, it would authorize a judge to obtain evidence on the value of the labor owed, to enable the accused to pay the sum in exchange for emancipation. Should the person making the claim refuse, the bill instructed, a court could grant a "certificate of discharge." The personal liberty bill proposed to criminalize kidnapping and, significantly, neutralize the fugitive slave law by purging the clause requiring residents to join a posse comitatus on demand.[15] The Ashley bill died in the U.S. House of Representatives; nonetheless, his fight for freedom ultimately resulted in passage of the Thirteenth Amendment.[16]

The Civil War triggered a series of changes in federal policies regarding fugitive slaves. Early in the war, the administration and the army refused to return runaway slaves who crossed their paths.[17] Furthermore, new federal policies that protected black civil rights eventually included the enlistment of black soldiers, the Emancipation Proclamation, and, of course, the Thirteenth Amendment. The Civil War, however, did not immediately secure black civil rights. African Americans in the Union, particularly those in Ohio, soon learned the limits of freedom. Federal and state statutes announced equality and civil rights protections for all, but these governments simultaneously approved de facto segregation. The Ohio General Assembly enacted a new set of black laws during the Civil War.

Ohio actually started down the slippery slope of civil rights restrictions in 1859, when the state legislature declared, "Be it enacted by the General Assembly of the State of Ohio, That the judge or judges of any election held under the authority of any of the laws of this State, shall reject the vote of any person offering to vote at such elections, and claiming to be a white male citizen of the United States, whenever it shall appear to such judge or judges that the person so offering to vote has a distinct and visible admixture of African blood."[18]

The Ohio Supreme Court earlier had ruled in various cases that an individual with prominent Caucasian features observable by sight was a sufficient basis to recognize that person as being white. The court applied this opinion to anyone seeking access to public schools and to voting booths. Before 1833, the General Assembly had designated three categories of Ohio residents—whites, blacks and mulattoes. However, the legislature did not consider the prospect of an individual whose skin color was lighter than mulatto. The supreme court in *Williams v. Directors of School District* (1834) decided that determination of who was white or black would be decided by the admixture of blood alone and not by sight or mixed racial heritage. An individual with 50 percent or more white blood would enjoy the same privileges of whiteness as any pure white person. The Ohio legislature modified this rule in 1859, when it enacted the visible admixture law, making "light complexion" the criterion for whiteness. Presumably, a magistrate could not legally deprive a person of the privileges of whiteness merely because of his or her mixed heritage.[19]

The supreme court faced the question of who was white in an action brought by Thomas Lane in 1843. As the father of three children, admittedly of mixed races, Lane had considered each of the children to be white. Yet, the defendant, a school director, barred one of the children from the common school on grounds that he was not white. A jury made up entirely of whites found that the Lane child was of Indian, black, and white ancestry, "but of more than one half white blood." After determining these facts, the majority in the court found no reason to alter their judgment expressed in earlier cases and held for the plaintiff because of the visible admixture rule that a preponderance of Caucasian features made an individual white.[20]

By defining whiteness and establishing appearance as the only criterion for determining who is white, the legislature ended a controversy that had lingered for some thirty years. Although it was a subjective standard, "visible admixture" meant that anyone who looked white was white. The Ohio legislature next turned to organizing the races. As many Ohio legislators had expected, blacks fled to Ohio in droves throughout the 1850s, and the trend increased dramatically during the Civil War. The African American population in Ohio increased by 72 percent in the 1860s alone, a net gain of more than twenty-five thousand black people in a ten-year period. Because of its accessibility, southern Ohio continued to experience the largest gain. Approximately two-thirds of all African Americans living in Ohio before 1865 were in its southern region.[21]

Some Ohio politicians responded to this population growth with alarm. Congressman Samuel S. Cox, a Democrat and the owner and editor of the conservative *Ohio Statesman* in Columbus, called for a renewal of the state immigration law in order to deny runaway slaves entry into the state. Cox inflamed the public by suggesting that these black migrants would take away white jobs and pursue social integration.[22] Many white workers assumed that black laborers gladly would accept low wages and thus drag down their pay. Whites therefore organized councils and pushed for legislation that would make distinctions between blacks and whites.[23] Unlike the visible admixture law, which protected whites who might have had African ancestors, the new laws would create two societies in Ohio— white and black. Such laws would discourage social integration and would foster a rigidly segregated culture.

—

The repeal of the Black Laws did not immediately secure political or social equality for black Ohioans. The revision of the Black Laws in 1849 marked a change in the racial codes from the principle of exclusion— restricting the immigration of African Americans into Ohio—to that of official segregation of the races in the state. The school system established exclusively for black children was among the first segregated institutions in state history. The legislature appropriated monies from tax-paying African Americans to fund the school system. It allowed one exception to this policy, permitting mixed classrooms in districts with fewer than twenty children and with the consent of white parents.[24]

Segregation in public education was not new in the North in 1850. The board of education in Boston had already provided for a segregated school system and witnessed the first legal challenge to segregation in 1849. The controversy originated when Benjamin Roberts attempted to enroll his daughter, Sara, in a school reserved for whites. Wishing to end segregation, Roberts contended that his daughter was entitled to attend the school in the district where they lived. Charles Sumner, who was among the first civil rights lawyers in the country, took the case, representing Roberts. His main argument turned on the idea that all individuals are equal before the law. Sumner also raised a number of sociological arguments, emphasizing that the law requiring segregation in public schools injured both black and white children. "With the law as their monitor," Sumner stated, white children "are taught practically to deny that grand revelation of Christianity—the Brotherhood of mankind. Their hearts, while yet tender with childhood, are necessarily hardened by this conduct."[25] Chief Justice Lemuel Shaw had written favorable opinions for African Americans in a few transit cases, such as *Commonwealth v. Aves* (1836); however, he upheld the authority of the board of education to segregate the schools. Shaw based his decision on the fact that the plaintiff had access to an educational facility; thus, she could not have been denied the equal protection of the law. Shaw disagreed with the contention "that men and women are legally clothed with the same civil and political" rights.[26]

Just as Roberts had challenged the board of education in Boston, Enos Van Camp filed a complaint to test the constitutionality of segregation in Ohio. The Ohio Supreme Court had consistently held that individuals who were more than 50 percent white should not be subjected to what it called the disabilities of blackness. Logan County had maintained a segregated school system in compliance with state law. Van Camp was of mixed ancestry, and his children's features were apparently more Caucasian than African. The defendant, however, refused their admission because a school for the education of blacks was available to the plaintiff.

The supreme court turned to the school act of 1853, which provided for the segregation of white and black children. Unlike the 1849 school law, the revised act imposed a duty on the state to provide educational opportunity for all children. The only question before the court was whether the Van Camp children were white under the visible admixture law. Chief Justice William V. Peck wrote, "[C]hildren of three-eights African and five-eights white blood, but who are distinctly colored, and generally treated and regarded as colored children by the community where they reside, are not as of right entitled to admission into the common schools, set apart" for the instruction of white youths.[27] Peck continued,

> Whether consistent with true philanthropy or not, it is nevertheless true, that in many portions, if not throughout the State, there was and still is almost invincible repugnance to such communion and fellowship. It is also to be borne in mind, that a class had grown up among us, which, though partly black had still a preponderance of white blood in their veins, and that the courts, influenced in some degree by the severe and somewhat penal character of the restrictions as to blacks and mulattoes, had held that such persons were not only entitled to vote at elections, and testify in our courts of justice, but were also admissible into the schools for white children.[28]

Peck concluded by observing that the white community abhorred its earlier decisions and that the court could not dispel public sentiments. Although the Peck Court did not reverse earlier opinions, it observed that the plaintiff recognized that whites had considered him to be a person of color. Peck asserted that a person of color was of the African lineage, "mixed or unmixed," and it could not be said that he was entitled to white privilege.

Segregation was the law in Ohio public education, and the *Van Camp* case affirmed it. The General Assembly enacted another black law in 1861, when it passed "an act to prevent the amalgamation of the white and colored races."[29] Just as the state had followed school segregation policies common in much of the North, it did so with sexual and marital relations in mind. Statutes prohibiting interracial marriage in America dated back to 1690s, and could be found in the statute books of most northern and all southern states.[30] Ohio drafted its first statute of this kind in 1861. The act not only made it a crime for a white and a black to marry, it criminalized any interracial sexual intercourse. Moreover, the act made it a crime for a magistrate or minister to issue a marriage license or to perform a marriage ceremony for a racially mixed couple. If convicted, the officiant could be fined a maximum of one hundred dollars or imprisoned for up to three months. However, the marriage law did not prohibit sexual relationships with blacks and mulattoes or anyone who did not look white. Just as the visible admixture law was based on appearance, the marriage law also used a visual test to determine compliance.[31] In 1877, the General Assembly affirmed its prohibition of any sexual relationship involving an individual with "pure white blood with any Negro" or person with a "distinct and visible admixture of African blood."[32] The statute again imposed a fine on anyone who participated in uniting such couples.

As they had done before the Civil War, Southerners continued to accuse Ohio of fostering integration. This sentiment took on greater importance in the South once the Thirteenth Amendment abolished slavery. It was no longer possible for the peculiar institution to separate blacks and whites. Ohio had turned to de facto segregation to replace the Black Laws; Southern states adopted Black Codes immediately after the war, and, after Reconstruction, new segregation laws. In the Jim Crow South, blacks faced statutes that empowered whites to exploit and abuse them as well as prevent them from mingling with their "betters" in public places. The post-Reconstruction South also adopted antimiscegenation laws. In Alabama, the state supreme court upheld a local law that prohibited interracial sex. And state and local municipalities throughout the South enacted hundreds of statutes, city ordinances, and constitutional clauses to keep the races apart. "There is no wonder that we die," an Alabama woman complained. "The wonder is that we persist in living."[33]

The U.S. Supreme Court accepted antimiscegenation laws as valid until it struck down a Virginia statute in 1967.[34] National support for state bans on social integration made Southerners wonder about the commitment of whites in the North. Without any evidence, the *Southern Leader* (Georgia) published a series of articles accusing Ohio of allowing its antimiscegenation law to become "practically a dead letter." Certainly,

Ohio prosecuted violators of its marriage law, but the litigation was aimed at the people who performed the ceremonies; it did not result in the banishment or imprisonment of couples who violated the law.[35] The *Southern Leader* was more pleased with Indiana, with whom Ohio shared a common legacy as part of the original Northwest Territory. In 1884, Indiana convicted Henry Thornton and Mary Stuart for violating the marriage law and fined and jailed them both.[36] Such prosecutions pleased Southern bigots, who wanted to preserve the purity of the white race.

Although Ohio did not jail mixed-race couples, it humiliated African Americans in other ways. The law enforcement and judicial system in Ohio singled out blacks as having a natural tendency for criminality. Prosecutors at the state and local levels had a mania for going after black defendants. They used the powers of the government to keep blacks in their places and deter whites from mingling with them. Although blacks and whites were not always convicted for violating Ohio's 1861 Amalgamation Act, African Americans suffered public humiliation for the mere appearance of criminality. Prosecutors eagerly disgraced blacks, especially the prominent members of the race. They went after sixty-year-old S. J. Howard in Elyria, in northern Ohio, for solicitation. It was common knowledge that many white men had done the same thing that Howard was accused of; indeed, the woman involved had kept a record of the visits of several white men. Yet, the prosecution failed to press charges against the whites, boldly asserting that they did not want to bring them such public humiliation. They publicized the charge against Howard precisely because of his race and good name.[37] Blacks and whites would share the same soil, but the state used its power to keep the races a part.

—

The national civil rights movement influenced Ohio in several important ways. In 1866, Congress passed the nation's first civil rights act, which regarded citizenship as a product of birth and held that every citizen was entitled to equal access to public places. Congress passed a more comprehensive statute in 1875. In addition to these laws, the Civil War Amendments provided for national citizenship, due process, equal protection under the law, suffrage, and various privileges and immunities without regard to color. Furthermore, terrorist groups such as the Ku Klux Klan faced prosecution for interfering with blacks' enjoyment of their civil rights.[38] These policies benefited blacks in Ohio, who rushed to integrate public facilities. For example, in Stark County, blacks integrated restaurants and attended dinner dances without incident. The *Cleveland Gazette* reported, "There was no distinction shown on account of color. Whites and blacks danced together."[39] However, conditions were less favorable in southern Ohio, a region historically inhospitable to blacks.[40] African Americans in southern Ohio asserting that federal law entitled them to the same privileges as whites returned to challenging the segregated education policy of the state.

In *Lewis v. Board of Education of Cincinnati* (1876), the plaintiff, a black child in Cincinnati, alleged that he was denied the equal protection of the law by being forced to walk several miles to a black school when his home was close to a white school. His parents took him to the white school to be enrolled, intending to contest the exclusion of their child solely because of color. The Ohio Supreme Court explained that a school was available for black education and that its very existence rendered moot the notion that separation of the races was unfair.[41] Rebuffed by Ohio courts, black plaintiffs turned to the federal court in 1881. James V. Vines, a sixteen-year-old African American, lived in a township in southern Ohio's Clermont County that had both white and black schools. The white school was located closer to Vines's home, and he argued that, by denying him admission, local law was in violation of federal law. U.S. District Judge John Baxter heard the case in 1881, instructing the jury: "As the law now stands, the colored boy and the white boy are equal and the teacher had no right to discriminate between them. If the colored boy found it more convenient to attend the white school, no one could interfere with his choice."[42] Vines prevailed in the action, and the court awarded him fifty dollars in damages. Obviously, the federal Civil Rights Act of 1866 and the Fourteenth Amendment applied, and the court had little choice in 1881 other than to enforce these laws.[43]

In addition to opening Ohio public schools to black and white youths, federal law also enfranchised African Americans—or at least it discouraged denying them the franchise. The Fifteenth Amendment forbade the states or federal government from denying a citizen the right to vote "on account of race, color or previous condition of servitude."[44] Ohio did not favor enfranchising blacks, and the white electorate had defeated an 1867 referendum on the question.[45] However, federal law prevailed, and elections were opened to African American voters. Moreover, federal law made it clear that state action could not be used to interfere with a citizen in the exercise of his or her civil rights. Ohio congressmen resisted the Civil War Amendments precisely because they did not want them enforced in the North. Republican senator John Sherman persuaded Ohio whites to endorse the amendments by claiming that they applied only to the South. However, the amendments opened Ohio to black participation, just as whites had feared, and the election of black representatives to the assembly was a natural progression. Charles H. Langston and his brother John Mercer Langston held local offices in pre–Civil War Ohio. After the war, other African Americans won public office, and they helped transform the Buckeye State.

Ironically, southern Ohio legislators had produced the original Black Laws and had helped engineer their partial repeal in 1849, and southern Ohio elected some of the first black legislators in the state. It was ironic that these representatives helped write the bill that ultimately abolished those codes. Southern Ohio easily had the largest African American community in Ohio, and black voters joined liberal whites to elect members of their race. Hamilton County voters elected George Washington Williams, a Union war veteran, pioneering historian, and minister.[46] Greene County elected Benjamin William Arnett, a Pennsylvania-born minister who held the doctor of divinity degree. Arnett was also a certified teacher, a member of the National Equal Rights League, and president of Wilberforce University. Cuyahoga County, in the Western Reserve, elected Republican representative Jere A. Brown, who served two terms in the state assembly.[47] John P. Green, a lawyer, was also elected from the Western Reserve, and he joined the black caucus in promoting civil rights reform in Ohio.[48]

The trend toward securing the civil rights of all Ohio residents reached a turning point in 1884, when the legislature passed "an act to protect all citizens in their civil rights." All men are "equal before the law," the statute read, and this "is essential to just government." The statute went on to say that a democratic government should treat each of its citizens in a fair and equitable way. Therefore, under the laws of Ohio all citizens were entitled to the enjoyment of public facilities regardless of "race and color." These facilities included inns, restaurants, barbershops, theaters and other public places.[49] When a Columbus restaurant denied service to Representative George Washington Williams, a black Republican, his colleagues in the General Assembly protested, and the business suffered a temporary financial loss. Governor George B. Hoadly, elected in 1884, although a Democrat, was a leader in supporting civil rights reform. When a Columbus skating rink discriminated against African Americans, Hoadly shut it down in order to force the proprietor to open the facility to blacks as well as whites.[50] These efforts on behalf of blacks in Columbus strengthened the civil rights movement in Ohio. African American representatives in the legislature immediately took steps to extend these friendly gestures of government officials.

In the mid-1880s, Arnett and Brown wrote a bill to abolish the last remnants of the Black Laws, but Representatives Williams and Green were lukewarm in their support for the bill. According to an 1886 article in the black-owned *Cleveland Gazette,* Williams and Green "sat like wooden men during their term and accomplished nothing."[51] The correspondent believed that they, along with other black leaders, were overly concerned with their own interests and did not want to rock the boat. Although Williams had experienced racial discrimination, he did not deliberately set out to boycott establishments that denied service to African Americans. Joining him on the sidelines, the *Gazette* suggested, was Peter H. Clark, a well-known Cincinnati educator who had been engaged in the struggle for equal rights since midcentury. Clark had earned a law degree from the Cincinnati College of Law and served as principal of Gaines High School. The *Gazette* also identified David Branen, a teacher and community leader in Cleveland, who did not openly protest the Black Laws.[52] Clark and Branen did not answer these charges, although it appears that they were uncertain whether "integration" was in the best interest of the black community. Other Ohio blacks joined them—especially educators who worried that integration might be personally and professionally costly.

However, Arnett and Brown pressed the civil rights struggle in Ohio, carefully chipping away at the weakest links in the Black Laws. They attacked segregation in transportation, on railroads and steamboats that traveled through Ohio. Next, they attacked segregation in public places, such as theaters and restaurants. In 1884, after winning victories in these areas, John Littler, a white Republican from Springfield, proposed a bill calling for the end of segregation in public schools. Surprisingly, Peter Clark opposed the bill. The *Cleveland Gazette* and noted civil rights reformers attacked Clark, suggesting that he feared losing his position as a principal in a segregated school as well as other financial benefits he derived from his position as a leader in the black community. Wilberforce University president William Sanders Scarborough also attacked elected officials like Williams and Clark, charging that they "place their own interests over the interests of a race [and] will set aside principle to accomplish their own end."[53]

In its criticism of Williams as a do-nothing lawmaker, the *Cleveland Gazette* ignored his efforts to introduce legislation to abolish the marriage law in 1884, two years before the education bill was proposed. Williams had learned important lessons about black politics in Ohio. Unlike some black officials, Williams doubted the commitment of Ohio Republicans to civil rights reform. He was unwilling to go after the school segregation law in 1884 primarily because he understood that many of his constituents were uneasy about losing control of their school districts. Black leaders had opposed the Littler bill because it did not include a local options clause, which would have given black school boards the choice of keeping their segregated educational system. When John Green had earlier proposed a bill to end segregation in public schools, his black constituents did not support him. Cleveland senator George Ely introduced a bill in 1885 calling for abolition of the Black Laws, but again it did not include a local options clause. Governor Hoadly backed the bill because it called for a complete repudiation of the Black Laws.[54] However, despite his support, the Ely bill failed. Apparently, Williams believed that it was important to at least address the objections of African Americans before putting and end to the institutions they managed.[55] Choosing between integration—for the benefits it offered—and segregation—for the autonomy it offered—was be a decision black leaders would have to make over and over again.

In spite of their enthusiasm for abolishing the Black Laws, the *Cleveland Gazette* was unfair in its criticisms of Clark and his colleagues. Clark had supported civil rights reform since at least 1840, and he had played a vital role in chartering the Cincinnati Colored Orphan Asylum, one of the first institutions to provide educational opportunity and scholarships for black youths. Certainly Clark had motivations other than personal interest when he questioned ending segregated education. Clark did not exactly oppose integration, as the *Gazette* had alleged. On the contrary,

Clark, like his colleagues, was willing to consider the interests of community leaders who feared a loss of jobs. Their fears were not misplaced, as the twentieth-century experience shows. It is highly unlikely that Clark abandoned civil rights reform for personal gain, as his critics claimed. Instead, he urged Ohio lawmakers and educators to make provisions for black educators.[56]

Ohio blacks wanted to improve their lives and those of their children, and their leaders were persistent in their opposition to the Black Laws. Wilberforce University president William Scarborough, who violated the social mores of Ohio when he married a white woman, was an articulate critic of the antimiscegenation law. Scarborough had experienced the benefits of integration at Oberlin, where he had learned firsthand that it was possible for blacks and whites to live in harmony. "I forgot I was a colored boy," he said while reflecting on his college days, "in the genial atmosphere that surrounded me."[57] But it was the editors of the *Cleveland Gazette* who were the most vociferous opponents of the Black Laws. They blasted the political party of Lincoln that had failed to abolish the racial codes. It would not have surprised them if Democrats had been in power, they chided, and failed to abolish the segregation laws. They lamented that they had expected more from Republicans.[58]

Representative Benjamin Arnett, who was among the best-educated men in Ohio, had won the respect of his white colleagues in the state legislature. Arnett was an outspoken advocate of many important social issues of the day, including temperance and the harmful effects of recreational narcotics. He introduced legislation to fund a study of the problem of addiction among young people. Joining him in the crusade for social justice was Jere Brown, who sponsored legislation to prevent insurance companies from charging blacks a higher premium than whites. But Arnett was the point man, and, because of his leadership, the Ohio General Assembly inevitably faced the question of abolishing the Black Laws in 1886.[59]

Arnett introduced the repeal bill on March 10, in the most important performance of his political career. The subject "is of great interest to the people of Ohio," he told the General Assembly. He stood on the shoulders of "great men" who had undertaken this problem earlier in the state's history. Arnett recounted these witnesses, naming James Birney, Martin Van Buren, and John P. Hale as "moral heroes" in the movement for civil rights reform. Let "us repeal these laws," Arnett implored his colleagues, "because the leaders of the forces of Justice of today are in favor of wiping out the color line in State and Church." Arnett pleaded, "Seeing that we are so intimately connected with each other as men and citizens, what wicked prejudice it is to have laws separating our children while learning their duty to themselves, their neighbor, to society, to country and their God; let us do our duty, and in doing this the walls of separation will crumble and fall."[60]

When Representative Brown took the floor, he reminded his colleagues of his duty to race, state, and humanity, which "demands that I should offer some reasons why these statutes should be repealed." Whatever the reasons for enacting these laws in the past, Brown continued, every enlightened mind must admit that they conflict with state and federal civil rights laws. Quizzing his colleagues, Brown demanded, "[W]hy is it that schools must be separate?" The "color of the skin" is not an adequate reason for racial separation, he said. Americans of every race fill positions of importance in government, churches, and civic organizations. Blacks had filled these positions of trust with dignity and honor. The Black Laws were "obsolete," he said; it was time "to inaugurate a new system."[61] The Arnett bill passed the sixty-seventh Ohio General Assembly in 1887 on a vote of 62 to 28, finally repealing the last remnants of the statutes commonly referred to as the Black Laws. These statutes included the school law, public relief law, and the antimiscegenation law.[62]

Civil rights reformers in Ohio had thus shaped the modern civil rights movement. Although many black leaders later followed the controversial Booker T. Washington in advancing vocational occupations and developing businesses, African Americans in Ohio and across the nation did not believe that learning the trades and starting businesses excluded social integration. Arnett, Brown, and others in Ohio did not think so, and they persuaded the legislature to abolish the racial codes.

Feelings ran high throughout Ohio upon the passage of the Arnett bill. Blacks in Salem, a city that had been involved in the civil rights movement since the 1830s, held a meeting to thank the legislature for passing the repeal bill. The *Gazette* published a letter to the editor, putting the repeal bill in perspective ("personal liberty is the inalienable right of all men") and claiming that repealing these racial codes was vital to secure the liberty of African Americans. Other letters to the editor carried titles such as "The Black Laws Struck," apparently celebrating the news that the General Assembly had finally repealed the codes. Still others wrote that they favored the law "wiping out the Black Laws of this state."[63] The modern civil rights movement was thus born, as blacks around the nation looked toward integrating American society.

White reformers were equally pleased. Republican governor Joseph B. Foraker, elected in 1886, had long opposed the Black Laws of Ohio and had urged the legislature to extend greater civil rights protection to people of color. The "colored men of the United States," he said, "are entitled to their citizenship and protection in the enjoyment of it." At an event celebrating the abolition of the Black Laws, Foraker expressed delight that the General Assembly had finally repealed them.[64]

Indeed, just as conservatives in early Ohio had organized to resist the repeal of the original Black Laws, white conservatives in postbellum Ohio opposed civil rights reform. John Hancock led the resistance in Chillicothe, arguing that the repeal law of 1887 had produced strife between blacks and whites. Compelling whites to attend schools with blacks, he argued, would not lead to harmony between the races. He believed the legislature had moved too quickly to bring the races together and advised that it would have been better if it had waited until public sentiments had voluntarily changed.[65] Similar sentiments came from Ripley, in Brown County in southern Ohio. A correspondent for the *United Press* observed that following passage of the Arnett bill, whites were driving blacks away from the community: "In this manner the white farmers gradually, without violence or harsh means, removed the colored people from the community, until there is not one left in some of the school districts and the law, which was intended to benefit, does positive injury to the colored man."[66] Blacks in Clermont County, also in southern Ohio, were not so lucky. "The white people of Felicity," reported a correspondent for the *Cleveland Plain Dealer*, "kept colored children out of the schools by force, and beat and maltreated the colored parents."[67] Violence against blacks occurred elsewhere, in Oxford, New Richmond, Dayton, and Xenia. Civil rights reformers pressed onward with a view that a multicultural America where the races lived in harmony was possible.

Yet they were not naive. Institutional discrimination persisted following the abolition of the state's Black Laws. Representative Brown had addressed the subject of discrimination by insurance companies in 1886, but the General Assembly did not enact legislation on this issue. These companies systematically followed a pattern of discrimination when selling insurance policies to black and white customers. Color was the only criterion for such discrimination, which resulted in blacks paying higher premiums. In 1889, however, the legislature did pass an antidiscrimination law governing insurance companies. The statute set new guidelines. Insurance companies were warned that setting different rates for blacks and whites was a violation of state law. Companies that refused an application for insurance or that set different rates for the insured were required to provide the client with a statement from a medical professional. Only reasons based "solely upon such grounds of the general health and hope of longevity of such person" were a valid explanation for differences in rates. Violators of the statute would pay a maximum fine of two hundred dollars.[68]

——

As the century came to a close, African Americans in Ohio had much to celebrate. Although it had taken nearly a century to accomplish the feat, the Ohio General Assembly completely abolished the Black Laws. There were other reasons for optimism. African Americans could travel the country freely, including moving to Ohio without proving their status. The statute books of the state and nation signaled the dawning of a new day, at least in many northern states. The Fourteenth Amendment recognized everyone born in the United States as a citizen, and federal law prohibited discrimination on account of race, creed, or previous condition of servitude. Blacks supposedly enjoyed the same rights as whites. After passage of the Fourteenth Amendment in 1868, the Southern states risked losing representation in Congress if they discriminated in voting on account of race. Moreover, the Civil Rights Act of 1875 empowered the federal government to enforce the policy of equal protection of the laws regardless of color or previous condition.

Yet there were reasons for pessimism. Race riots, lynching, and state-supported discrimination persisted in Ohio and the rest of the nation well into the twentieth century. The U.S. Supreme Court decision in the *Civil Rights Cases* (1883) limited the scope of these federal laws to state acts of discrimination. The court thus allowed individual acts of discrimination, and whites abridged black rights with impunity. In *Plessy v. Ferguson* (1896), the Supreme Court also recognized segregation as legal, so long as a facility assumed to be equal to those furnished to whites was available to blacks. The legal standard of equality set forth in this decision was specious at best, and the decision set back the gains of the civil rights movement in Ohio, as well as the nation.[69]

The civil rights movement in Ohio struggled against policies that subjugated African Americans with Black Laws and segregated them in a mixed society. At the same time, Ohio banned slavery when it entered the Union and was always seen as a haven by southern blacks seeking to escape bondage and the oppression of a slave society. Blacks who came there established schools, churches, and businesses and struggled with white allies to achieve equality.

As the twentieth century dawned, discrimination in schools, in the workplace, and in the courtroom persisted in Ohio and in virtually every state in the Union. The history of Ohio left an important legacy, illustrating that civil rights reform was possible, even in a state where the legal system approved racial discrimination solely on account of color. This legacy also makes it clear that the vigilance of a conscientious citizenry is required to secure civil rights for all Americans.

NOTES

INTRODUCTION

1. *New York Colored American*, January 23, 1841.

2. *New York Colored American*, March 22, 1838, January 23, 1841; John Malvin, *North into Freedom: The Autobiography of John Malvin, 1795–1880*, ed. Allan Peskin (Cleveland: Press of Western Reserve University, 1966), 6; Charles B. Galbreath, *History of Ohio*, 5 vols. (Chicago: American Historical Society, 1925), 2:198–200.

3. *New York Colored American*, January 23, 1841; Carol Wilson, *Freedom at Risk: The Kidnapping of Free Blacks in America, 1780–1865* (Lexington: University Press of Kentucky, 1994).

4. *New York Colored American*, January 23, 1841.

5. An act to amend the last-named act, "an act to regulate black and mulatto persons," 5 Laws of Ohio 53 (1807), repr. in *The Black Laws in the Old Northwest: A Documentary History*, ed. Stephen Middleton (Westport, Conn.: Greenwood, 1993), 17.

6. *New York Colored American*, January 23, 1841.

7. *Journal of the House of Representatives of the State of Ohio*, 35 (35th Gen. Ass.), 695–98 (March 18, 1837), repr. in S. Middleton, *Black Laws*, 58; *Philanthropist*, July 28, 1837.

8. Preamble, Ohio const. of 1802.

9. An act to regulate black and mulatto persons, 2 Laws of Ohio 63 (1804); An act to regulate black and mulatto persons, 3 Laws of Ohio 356 (1805); An act to amend the last named act "An act to Regulate Black and Mulatto Persons," 5 Laws of Ohio 53 (1807), repr. in S. Middleton, *Black Laws*, 15–18; Malvin, *North into Freedom*, 4–5; Frederick Douglass, "Citizenship and the Spirit of Caste: An Address Delivered in New York," May 11, 1858, in Frederick Douglass, *The Frederick Douglass Papers*, ed. John Blassingame, R. McKivigan, and Peter P. Hinks, 5 vols. (New Haven: Yale University Press, 1979), 3:208–12.

10. Eric Foner, introduction to *The Story of American Freedom* (New York: Norton, 1998), xvi; Joseph Raz, *The Morality of Freedom* (New York: Oxford University Press, 1986), 17–19.

11. State of Ohio v. George, in *Unreported Judicial Decisions Prior to 1823*, ed. Ervin H. Pollack (Indianapolis: Allen Smith, 1952), 185–88; Gray v. Ohio, 4 Ohio 353 (1831); Williams v. Dirs. of Sch. Dist., 1 Wright 578 (1834).

12. *New York Colored American,* January 23, 1841. For an early twentieth-century discussion of color and the law, see Earl Lewis and Heidi Ardizzone, *Love on Trial: An American Scandal in Black and White* (New York: Norton, 2001).

13. *New York Colored American,* January 23, 1841.

14. Benjamin W. Arnett and Jere A. Brown, *The Black Laws! Speeches of Honorable Benjamin W. Arnett of Greene County and Honorable Jere A. Brown of Cuyahoga County, in the House of Representatives, March 10, 1886* (Columbus: Ohio State Journal, 1886).

15. *New York Colored American,* January 23, 1841, emphasis in original; Galbreath, *History of Ohio,* 1:200.

16. Arnett and Brown, *Black Laws;* John Hope Franklin, *George Washington Williams: A Biography* (Chicago: University of Chicago Press, 1985).

CHAPTER 1

1. Paul Finkelman, *Slavery and the Founders: Race and Liberty in the Age of Jefferson,* 2nd ed. (Armonk, N.Y.: M. E. Sharpe, 2001), 58–60; Peter S. Onuf, *Statehood and Union: A History of the Northwest Ordinance* (Bloomington: Indiana University Press, 1987), 109–16.

2. William Samuel Johnson to Roger Sherman, April 20, 1785, in *Letters of Delegates to Congress, 1774–1775,* ed. Ralph M. Gephart and Paul H. Smith, 26 vols. (Washington, D.C.: Library of Congress, 2000), 22:347–50; Richard Henry Lee to James Madison, May 30, 1785, and Lee to Marquis de Lafayette, June 11, 1785, in *The Letters of Richard Henry Lee,* ed. James Curtis Ballagh, 2 vols. (New York: Macmillan, 1914), 2:365, 370; Frederick Stone, "The Ordinance of 1787," *Pennsylvania Magazine of History and Biography* 13, no. 3 (1899): 317–22.

3. Phillip R. Shriver and Clarence E. Wunderlin Jr., eds., *The Documentary Heritage of Ohio* (Athens: Ohio University Press, 2000), 63; Paul Finkelman, "Slavery and the Northwest Ordinance," in *New Perspectives on the Early Republic: Essays from the Journal of the Early Republic, 1981–1991,* ed. Ralph D. Gray and Michael A. Morrison (Urbana: University of Illinois Press, 1994), 81; Samuel A. Drake, *The Making of Ohio Valley States* (New York: Scribner's, 1894), 150–51.

4. Roger G. Kennedy, *Mr. Jefferson's Lost Cause: Land, Farmers, Slavery, and the Louisiana Purchase* (New York: Oxford University Press, 2003), 71; Samuel E. Morrison, introduction to *Sources and Documents Illustrating the American Revolution, 1764–1788, and the Formation of the Federal Constitution,* 2nd ed. (New York: Oxford University Press, 1965), xxxi; Harlan Henthorne Hatcher, *The Buckeye Country: A Page Out of Ohio* (New York: Kinsey, 1940), 78–83; Charles Moore, *The Northwest Territory under Three Flags, 1635–1796* (New York: Harper and Brothers, 1900), 329–30.

5. Finkelman, "Slavery and the Northwest Ordinance," 351–52; E. James Henderson, *Party Politics in the Continental Congress* (New York: McGraw-Hill, 1974), 368–69; Lee to Washington, October 11, 1787, *Letters of Richard Henry Lee,* 5:448; Manasseh Cutler, *The Life, Journals, and Correspondence of Rev. Manasseh Cutler,* ed. William Parker Cutler and Julia Perkins Cutler, 2 vols. (Cincinnati: Robert Clarke, 1888), 1:120; Robert E. Brown, *Manasseh Cutler and the Settlement of Ohio,*

1788 (Marietta, Ohio: Marietta College Press, 1938), 120, 230, 236; Herbert E. Lombard, *Notes by Herbert E. Lombard, 1790–1828,* vol. P, 15–16; Rufus Putnam Papers, American Antiquarian Society, Worcester, Mass.; Arthur St. Clair, *The St. Clair Papers: The Life and Public Services of Arthur St. Clair,* ed. William H. Smith, 2 vols. (Cincinnati: Robert Clarke, 1882), 1:123–26.

6. Nathan Dane to Rufus King, July 16, 1787, in *Letters of Members of the Continental Congress,* ed. Edmund C. Burnett, 8 vols. (Washington, D.C.: Carnegie Institution, 1921–36), 8:621–22.

7. Peter M. Bergman and Jean McCarrol, eds., *The Negro in the Continental Congress* (New York: Bergman, 1969), 137; Worthington C. Ford, et al., *Journals of the Continental Congress, 1774–1789,* 34 vols. (Washington, D.C.: Government Printing Office, 1904–37), 34:314; Roger Bruns, *Am I Not a Man and a Brother: The Antislavery Crusade of Revolutionary America, 1688–1788* (New York: Chelsea House, 1977), 515.

8. Nathan Dane to Rufus King, July 16, 1787, in Gephart and Smith, *Letters of Delegates,* 24:359; Nathan Dane to Rufus King, July 16, 1787, in Burnett, *Letters of Members,* 8:621–22; Daniel J. Ryan, *A History of Ohio, with Biographical Sketches of her Governors and the Ordinance of 1787* (Columbus: A. H. Smythe, 1888), 404–5; Donald Robinson, *Slavery in the Structure of American Politics* (New York: Norton, 1979), 380–82.

9. Richard Henry Lee to Francis Lightfoot Lee, July 14, 1787, and Virginia Delegates to Edmund Randolph, November 3, 1787, in Gephart and Smith, *Letters of Delegates,* 24:354, 355, 538, 539; Theodore C. Pease, "The Ordinance of 1787," *Mississippi Valley Historical Review* 25 (September 1938): 178–79.

10. Quoted in Staughton Lynd, "Slavery and the Founding Fathers," in *Black History: A Reappraisal,* ed. Melvin Drimmer (New York: Anchor Books, 1968), 125; Kate Mason Rowland, *The Life of George Mason, 1725–1792,* 2 vols. (New York: Russell and Russell, 1964), 2:133, 135; Joseph Grady Smoot, "Freedom's Early Ring: The Northwest Ordinance and the American Union" (Ph.D. diss., University of Kentucky, 1964), 81; Robert M. Taylor Jr., ed., introduction to *The Northwest Ordinance, 1787: A Bicentennial Handbook* (Indianapolis: Indiana Historical Society, 1987), x.

11. *Speech of Senator Salmon P. Chase, Delivered at Toledo, May 30, 1851, before a Mass Convention of the Democracy of Northwestern Ohio,* 3, Pamphlet Collection, Cincinnati Historical Society Library.

12. Thomas Hart Benton, introduction to *Historical and Legal Examination of That Part of the Decision of the Supreme Court of the United States in the* Dred Scott *Case, Which Declares the Unconstitutionality of the Missouri Compromise Act and the Self-Extension of the Constitution to Territories, Carrying Slavery along with It* (New York: D. Appleton, 1857), 39; Taylor, *Northwest Ordinance,* x.

13. William Lee Miller, *Arguing about Slavery: The Great Battle in the United States Congress* (New York: Knopf, 1996), 17.

14. *Speech of Senator Salmon P. Chase, Delivered at Toledo,* 3.

15. Burnett, *Letters of Members,* 8:632; Don E. Fehrenbacher, *The Slaveholding Republic: An Account of the United States Government's Relations to Slavery,* completed and ed.

Ward McAfee (Oxford: Oxford University Press, 2001), 224, 255; James H. Rodabaugh, "The Negro in Ohio," *Journal of Negro History* 31 (January 1946): 12; Robinson, *Slavery*, 380–82.

16. Kennedy, *Jefferson's Lost Cause*, 71.

17. James Madison, "Vices of the Political System of the United States," April–June 1787, and "Rule of Representation in the Senate," July 14, 1787, in *The Papers of James Madison: Purchased by Order of the Congress, Being His Correspondence and Reports of Debates during the Congress of the Confederation, and His Reports of Debates in the Federal Convention; Now Published from the Original Manuscripts, Deposited in the Department of State*, ed. Robert A. Rutland, 16 vols. (Chicago: University of Chicago Press, 1962–91), 9:351, 10:102.

18. Kennedy, *Jefferson's Lost Cause*, 75; Merrill D. Peterson, *The Portable Thomas Jefferson* (New York: Viking, 1975), 591; Robinson, *Slavery*, 88–89, 93.

19. Pease, "Ordinance of 1787," 178–79; Francis S. Philbrick, ed., introduction to *The Laws of the Indiana Territory, 1801–1809*, 21 vols. (Springfield: Illinois State Historical Library, 1930), 2:xxxv.

20. Quoted in Walter Havighurst, *The Heartland: Ohio, Indiana, Illinois* (New York: Harper and Row, 1962), 155.

21. Tardiveau to St. Clair, June 30, 1789, *St. Clair Papers*, 2:118.

22. Philip S. Foner, *History of Black Americans*, 3 vols. (Westport, Conn.: Greenwood, 1975), 1:376; *St. Clair Papers*, 1:120; Carrington T. Marshall, *A History of the Courts and Lawyers of Ohio*, 3 vols. (New York: American Historical Society, 1934), 1:60.

23. Tardiveau to St. Clair, June 30, 1789, *St. Clair Papers*, 2:118; John Fiske, *The Critical Period of American History, 1783–1789* (Boston: Houghton Mifflin, 1916), 199, 202–5.

24. Tardiveau to St. Clair, June 30, 1789, *St. Clair Papers*, 2:118; Ryan, *History of Ohio*, 52.

25. Tardiveau to St. Clair, June 30, 1789, *St. Clair Papers*, 2:118; "Memorial in Favor of American Settlers by Barthelemi Tardiveau," August 27, 1787, and "Memorial on Behalf of the French Inhabitants by Barthelemi Tardiveau," September 15, 1787, in *Kaskaskia Records, 1778–1790*, ed. Clarence W. Alvord, 34 vols. (Springfield: Trustees of the Illinois State Historical Library, 1909), 5:445–48.

26. Tardiveau to James Madison, September 25, 1788, *Journals of the Continental Congress*, 34:66, 541; Jacob P. Dunn, *Slavery Petitions and Papers*, 2 vols. (Indianapolis: Bowen-Merrill, 1894), 2:443–529.

27. Tardiveau to St. Clair, June 30, 1789, *St. Clair Papers*, 2:117–19; Frazer Ells Wilson, *Arthur St. Clair, Rugged Ruler of the Old Northwest: An Epic of the American Frontier* (Richmond, Va.: Garrett and Massie Publishers, 1944), 157.

28. Tardiveau to St. Clair, June 30, 1789, Arthur St. Clair Papers, box 3, folder 3, Ohio Historical Society, Columbus (hereafter, OHS); Tardiveau to St. Clair, June 30, 1789, *St. Clair Papers*, 2:117–19; *Journals of the Continental Congress*, 34:541; Ryan, *History of Ohio* (1888), 52.

29. Clarence E. Carter, ed., *Territorial Papers of the United States,* 24 vols. (Washington, D.C.: Government Printing Office, 1934), 2:248; Judge Turner to St. Clair, June 14, 1794, St. Clair to Judge Turner, December 14, 1794, and St. Clair to Secretary Sargent, April 28, 1795, in *St. Clair Papers,* 2:325, 2:330, 2:342; Richard F. O'Dell, "The Early Antislavery Movement in Ohio" (Ph.D. diss., University of Michigan, 1948), 76; B. A. Hinsdale, *The Old Northwest: With a View of the Thirteen Colonies as Constituted by the Royal Charters* (New York: Townsend MacCoun, 1888), 335–36; Daniel Owen, "Circumvention of Article VI of the Ordinance of 1787," *Indiana Magazine of History* 36 (June 1940): 112.

30. William H. English Papers, "Examination of Henry Vanderburgh before Judge George Turner, Knox County, Territory of the United States Northwest of the Ohio," August 8, 1794; Writ of Habeas Corpus ad Subjiciendum for Henry Vanderburgh, and Peter and Queen McNelly Turner for the Appearance of Henry Vanderburgh, Peter and Queen McNelly Turner for Henry Vanderburgh, Peter and Queen McNelly, September 30, 1794, Special Collections Research Center, University of Chicago Library; Jacob P. Dunn, *Indiana: A Redemption from Slavery* (Boston: Houghton, Mifflin, 1896), 223–25.

31. Dunn, *Indiana,* 223–24; Finkelman, "Slavery and the Northwest Ordinance," 366–67; Eugene H. Berwanger, *The Frontier against Slavery: Western Anti-Negro Prejudice and the Slavery Extension Controversy* (Urbana: University of Illinois Press, 1967), 19; Alfred Byron Sears, *Thomas Worthington: Father of Ohio Statehood* (Columbus: Ohio State University Press, 1958), 50.

32. Judge Parsons to St. Clair, August 23, 1789, in *St. Clair Papers,* 2:121; *Annals of Congress,* 4th Cong., 1st sess., 1170–71 (April 25, 1796), 1349 (May 12, 1796), and 9th Cong., 1st sess., 293, 848 (December 18, 1804); Owen, "Circumvention of Article VI," 113–14; Ryan, *History of Ohio,* 53–54; Berwanger, *Frontier,* 9.

33. Courts in Kentucky, Missouri, and Louisiana also held that residence in the territory after the passage of the ordinance led to immediate freedom. See Paul Finkelman, *An Imperfect Union: Slavery, Federalism, and Comity* (Chapel Hill: University of North Carolina Press, 1981).

34. Merrily Pierce, "Luke Decker and Slavery: His Cases with Bob and Anthony, 1817–1822," *Indiana Magazine of History* 85 (March 1989): 31–48; John D. Barnhart and Dorothy L. Riker, *Indiana to 1816: The Colonial Period* (Indianapolis: Indiana Historical Bureau, 1971), 57–93.

35. Quoted in A. Leon Higginbotham Jr., *In the Matter of Color: The Colonial Period,* vol. 1 of Race and the American Legal Process (New York: Oxford University Press, 1978), 608.

36. Beverly W. Bond Jr., *The Civilization of the Old Northwest: A Study of Political, Social, and Economic Development, 1788–1812* (New York: Macmillan, 1934), 333.

CHAPTER 2

1. William T. McClintock, "Ohio's Birth Struggle," *Ohio History* 11 (July 1902): 44–52; Jefferson and his followers were not abolitionists, yet they favored

emancipation. Indeed, he believed that blacks were innately inferior and could not live in harmony with whites. Jefferson wanted to colonize African Americans upon their emancipation. Short of that, he believed that slavery should be restricted. See Thomas Jefferson, *Thomas Jefferson: Writings*, ed. Merrill D. Peterson (New York: Literary Classics, 1984), 288–89.

2. "Republican" was the designation commonly used by the followers of Thomas Jefferson, though their opponents offered other party labels to describe them. Many political leaders linked the label "Democrat" to anarchy, until the word evolved into a positive appellation. Some Republicans came to use the label Democrat interchangeably, and a few states used Democratic Republican. Because Republican was the label preferred by Jeffersonians, it is the one used in this study. See Noble E. Cunningham Jr., "The Jeffersonian Republican Party," in *History of U.S. Political Parties, 1789–1860: From Factions to Parties*, ed. Arthur M. Schlesinger Jr., 4 vols. (New York: Chelsea House, 1973), 1:240.

3. Donald J. Ratcliffe, *Party Spirit in a Frontier Republic: Democratic Politics in Ohio, 1793–1821* (Columbus: Ohio State University Press, 1998), 14–18; James H. Rodabaugh, "The Negro in Ohio," *Journal of Negro History* 31 (January 1946): 9.

4. John Cummings and Joseph A. Hill, eds., *Negro Population, 1790–1915* (Washington, D.C.: Government Printing Office, 1918), 44–45; J. Reuben Sheeler, "The Struggle of the Negro for Freedom in Ohio," *Journal of Negro History* 31 (April 1946): 210; Rodabaugh, "Negro in Ohio," 13.

5. Eric Hinderaker, *Elusive Empires: Constructing Colonialism in the Ohio Valley, 1673–1800* (Cambridge: Cambridge University Press, 1997), 238–40.

6. Ohio const. of 1802, art. IV, § 1.

7. Andrew R. L. Cayton, *Ohio: The History of a People* (Columbus: Ohio State University Press, 2002), 13–16.

8. Washington County (Ohio) Pioneer Association, *The Coming Centennial, April 7, 1888: The Ninety-eighth Anniversary of the Settlement of Ohio and the Northwest Territory, Celebrated at Marietta, Ohio, April 7, 1886* (Marietta, Ohio: Marietta Register Power Print, 1886), 7; Julia Perkins Cutler, *The Founders of Ohio: Brief Sketches of the Forty-eight Pioneers Who, under Command of General Rufus Putnam, Landed at the Mouth of the Muskingum River on the Seventh of April, 1788, and Commenced the First White Settlement in the Northwest Territory* (Cincinnati: R. Clarke, 1888), 7; *Scioto Gazette*, November 20, 1800; Nahum Ward to Thomas W. Ward, November 10, 1810, May 21, 1812, June 7, 1814, Ward Family Papers, American Antiquarian Society, Worcester, Mass.; Robert Chaddock, "Ohio before 1850: A Study of the Early Influence of Pennsylvania and Southern Populations in Ohio" (Ph.D. diss., Columbia University, 1908), 28–29.

9. Quoted in Hinderaker, *Elusive Empires*, 254.

10. Richard T. Farrell, "Cincinnati: 1800–1830: Economic Development through Trade and Industry," *Ohio History* 77 (Autumn 1968): 3–29; Walter Havighurst, *Ohio: A Bicentennial History* (New York: Norton, 1976), 12; John S. Abbott, *The History of the State of Ohio: From the Discovery of the Great Valley to the Present Time* (Detroit: Northwestern Publishing, 1875), 160; Samuel Adams Drake, *The Making of the Ohio Valley States, 1660–1837* (New York: Scribner's, 1894), 142; Caleb Atwater, *History*

of the State of Ohio, Natural and Civil (Cincinnati: Glezen and Shepard, 1838), 131; Rodabaugh, "Negro in Ohio," 9–10.

11. Randolph C. Downes, *Frontier Ohio, 1788–1803* (Columbus: Ohio State Archaeological Society, 1935), 201; William Cheek and Aimee Lee Cheek, *John Mercer Langston and the Fight for Black Freedom, 1829–1865* (Urbana: University of Illinois Press, 1989), 30; Beverly W. Bond Jr., *The Foundations of Ohio*, vol. 1 of *The History of the State of Ohio*, ed. Carl Wittke (Columbus: Ohio State Archaeological and Historical Society, 1941), 120; Edgar Allen Holt, "The Election of 1840 in Ohio," *Ohio Archaeological and Historical Society Publications* 37 (July 1928): 442.

12. For a comprehensive list of election returns, see the Philip J. Lampi Collection, Election Returns, 1789–1808, American Antiquarian Society, Worcester, Mass.

13. McClintock, "Birth Struggle," 54–56; Linden F. Edwards, "Governor Edward Tiffin: Pioneer Doctor," *Ohio History* 56 (October 1947): 351–52, 358; Alfred B. Sears, "Thomas Worthington, Pioneer Business Man of the Old Northwest," *Ohio History* 58 (January 1949): 70.

14. Paul Finkelman, *Slavery and the Founders: Race and Liberty in the Age of Jefferson*, 2nd ed. (Armonk, N.Y.: M. E. Sharpe, 2001); Eugene H. Berwanger, *The Frontier against Slavery: Western Anti-Negro Prejudice and the Slavery Extension Controversy* (Urbana: University of Illinois Press, 1967), 9–10; Daniel J. Ryan, *A History of Ohio, with Biographical Sketches of Her Governors and the Ordinance of 1787* (Columbus: A. H. Smythe, 1888), 53–54; Philip S. Foner, *History of Black Americans*, 3 vols. (Westport, Conn.: Greenwood, 1975), 1:376; Daniel Owen, "Circumvention of Article VI of the Ordinance of 1787," *Indiana Magazine of History* 36 (June 1940): 113.

15. Thomas Posey to John Gibson, March 13, 1813, William H. English Papers, Illinois Historical Society, Chicago; *Scioto Gazette*, October 16, 1802; John Thornton Posey, *General Thomas Posey: Son of the American Revolution* (East Lansing: Michigan State University Press, 1992), 208–9; Charles Jay Wilson, "The Negro in Early Ohio," *Ohio Archaeological and Historical Publications* 39 (July 1930): 193; Lyle S. Evans, ed., *A Standard History of Ross County, Ohio, an Authentic Narrative of the Past, with Particular Attention to the Modern Era in the Commercial, Industrial, Civic and Social Development*, 2 vols. (Chicago: Lewis Publishing, 1917), 1:241.

16. *Journal of the House of Representatives of the Territory of United States, Northwest of the Ohio River* (Chillicothe, Ohio: Winship and Willis, 1800), 6, 19, 108, 117, 121; Beverly W. Bond Jr., *The Civilization of the Old Northwest: A Study of Political, Social, and Economic Development, 1788–1812* (New York: Macmillan, 1934), 96–97; *Freeman's Journal* (New York), March 5, 1799; *Cincinnati Western Spy*, March 12, 1800; Rufus King, *Ohio: First Fruits of the Ordinance of 1787* (New York: Houghton Mifflin, 1903), 180.

17. *Annals of Congress*, 4th Cong., 1st sess., 1170–71 (April 25, 1796), 1349 (May 12, 1796), and 9th Cong., 1st sess., 293, 848 (December 18, 1804); Clarence E. Carter, ed., *Territorial Papers of the United States*, 24 vols. (Washington, D.C.: Government Printing Office, 1934), 3:112; Owen, "Circumvention of Article VI," 113–14; William Cohen, "Thomas Jefferson and the Problem of Slavery," *Journal*

of American History 56 (December 1969): 511; Julian Boyd, ed., *The Papers of Thomas Jefferson*, 22 vols. (Princeton: Princeton University Press, 1950), 7:118–19.

18. *St. Clair Papers*, 1:121; Owen, "Circumventing of Article VI," 112.

19. Jacob Burnet, *Notes on the Early Settlement of the North-Western Territory* (Cincinnati: Derby, Bradley, 1847), 306–7.

20. Bond, *Foundations*, 445; Harry R. Stevens, *The Early Jackson Party in Ohio* (Durham, N.C.: Duke University Press, 1957), 6.

21. Although there is no explicit evidence that Ohio politicians solicited the votes of blacks, they needed the votes of every eligible man. It was important to Republican candidates that they had sympathetic voters, which included blacks. Moreover, two new states, Vermont (1791) and Tennessee (1796), had enfranchised free black men.

22. Hinderaker, *Elusive Empires*, 255.

23. St. Clair to Samuel Huntington, July 15, 1802, Manuscripts Relating to the Western Reserve, folder 18, container 10, Western Reserve Historical Society, Cleveland (hereafter, WRHS); *Scioto Gazette*, March 20, 1802; Ratcliffe, *Party Spirit*, 13–14; Charles M. Walker, *History of Athens County, Ohio, and Incidentally of the Ohio Land Company and the First Settlement of the State of Marietta, with Personal and Biographical Sketches of the Early Settlers, Narratives of Pioneer Adventurers* (Cincinnati: Robert Clarke, 1869), 389–90.

24. VFM 1172 ms., Arthur St. Clair Scattered Papers, 1772–1802, OHS.

25. Eugene H. Roseboom, *A History of Ohio* (New York: Prentice Hall, 1934), 103–4; Isaac F. Patterson, ed., *The Constitutions of Ohio and Allied Documents* (Cleveland: Arthur H. Clark, 1912), 53; Thomas R. Swisher, introduction to *Ohio Constitution Handbook* (Cleveland: Banks-Baldwin Law Publishing, 1990), xii; William O. Lynch, *Fifty Years of Party Warfare, 1789–1837* (Indianapolis: Bobbs-Merrill, 1931), 143; Chaddock, "Ohio before 1850," 61; A Citizen of Wayne County, Indiana, *History of Federal and Democratic Parties in the United States from their Origin to the Present Time* (Richmond, Ind.: Richmond Democratic Association, 1837), 25; James H. Perkins, *The Memoir and Writings of James H. Perkins*, ed. William Henry Channing, 2 vols. (Cincinnati: Ruman and Spofford, 1851), 2:335–36; Ratcliffe, *Party Spirit*, 14, 21–25.

26. *Journal of the House of Representatives of the United States*, 7th Cong., 1st sess., 184 (April 7, 1802); *Journal of the Senate of the United States*, 7th Cong., 1st sess., 219 (April 23, 1802); Jeffrey P. Brown, "The Political Culture of Early Ohio," introduction to *The Pursuit of Public Power: Political Culture in Ohio, 1787–1861*, ed. Jeffrey P. Brown and Andrew R. L. Cayton (Kent, Ohio: Kent State University Press, 1994), viii, 1; Barbara A. Terzian, "'Effusions of Folly and Fanaticism': Race, Gender, and Constitution-Making in Ohio, 1802–1923" (Ph.D. diss., Ohio State University, 1999), 53; Randolph C. Downes, "Ohio's First Constitution," *Northwest Ohio Quarterly* 24–25 (Winter 1952–53): 14; J. F. Laning, "The Evolution of Ohio Counties," *Ohio Archaeological and Historical Quarterly* 5 (August 1897): 345; John Fiske, *The Critical Period of American History, 1783–1789* (Boston: Houghton Mifflin, 1916), 218–21; Abbott, *History of Ohio*, 523; Patterson, *Constitutions of Ohio*,

56; *Scioto Gazette*, March 20, 1802; William A. Taylor, *Ohio Statesmen and Annals of Progress, from the Year 1788 to the Year 1900*, 2 vols. (Columbus: Press of Westbote, 1899), 1:34.

27. Edward Tiffin to George Todd, July 25, 1802, Edward Tiffin Papers, box 1, folder 1, OHS; Zabdiel Sampson, *Republican Celebration of American Independence: An Oration, Pronounced in the New Meeting House at Plymouth, July 4, 1806* (Boston: Chronicle Office, 1806), 7; William Nisbet Chambers, *Political Parties in A New Nation: The American Experience, 1776–1809* (New York: Oxford University Press, 1963), 53–174; James Edwin Campbell, "Recent Addresses of James Edwin Campbell," *Ohio Archaeological and Historical Quarterly* 34 (January 1925): 31–34; Patterson, *Constitutions of Ohio*, 2:56.

28. William Goforth to Thomas Worthington, Charles E. Rice Collection, box 1, folder 2, p. 3, OHS; Chaddock, "Ohio before 1850," 33, 82; Richard F. O'Dell, introduction to "The Early Antislavery Movement in Ohio" (Ph.D. diss., University of Michigan, 1948), i–ii; Ryan, *History of Ohio*, 111; George W. Rightmire, "Ohio in McGuffey's Time," *Ohio Archaeological and Historical Quarterly* 50 (April–June 1941): 115–19; Frank U. Quillin, *The Color Line in Ohio: A History of Race Prejudice in a Typical Northern State* (Ann Arbor, Mich.: George Wahr, 1913), 17.

29. Dromgoole to W. P. Pelham, February 20, 1807; Pelham to Dromgoole, April 28, 1807, March 8, 1808, Edward Dromgoole Papers, box 1, folder 230, Southern Historical Collection, University of North Carolina, Chapel Hill.

30. Samuel W. Compton, "Reminiscences of Samuel W. Compton," Samuel W. Compton Papers, book 14, pp. 1–3, 22–23, Rare Book, Manuscript, and Special Collections Library, Duke University, Durham, N.C.; Caleb Atwater, *The General Character, Present and Future Prospects of the People of Ohio: An Address Delivered at the United States' Court House, during the term of the United States' Circuit Court, in Columbus, December, 1826* (Columbus: P. H. Olmsted, 1827), 3.

31. *Norfolk and Portsmouth Herald*, September 6, 1822, repr. from *National Gazette*; Andrew C. Lenner, *The Federal Principle in American Politics, 1790–1833* (New York: Rowman and Littlefield, 2001), 133.

32. Pelham to Dromgoole, March 8, 1808, Dromgoole Papers.

33. Daniel McBride to Zebina Eastman, April 7, 1874, Zebina Eastman Papers, folder 1841–61, Chicago Historical Society (hereafter, ChiHS); *Ohio Gazette*, October 4, 1802; *Cincinnati Western Spy*, August 7, 1802; Kenneth Winkle, *The Politics of Community in Antebellum Ohio* (Cambridge: Cambridge University Press, 1988), 14–15, 26; Don R. Leet, *Population Pressure and Human Fertility Response: Ohio, 1810–1860* (New York: Arno Press, 1978), 157–60.

34. Julia Perkins Cutler, *Life and Times of Ephraim Cutler Prepared from His Journals and Correspondence, with Biographical Sketches of Jervis Cutler and William P. Cutler* (Cincinnati: Robert Clarke, 1890), 60, 66–67; Terzian, "Folly and Fanaticism," 60–66.

35. *Scioto Gazette*, August 7, September 11, 1802; J. Brown, "Political Culture," 4–5; Ratcliffe, *Party Spirit*, 15–16, 38–39; Terzian, "Folly and Fanaticism," 60–66.

36. *Cincinnati Western Spy*, August 28, 1802; Terzian, "Folly and Fanaticism," 59–66.

37. Lenner, *Federal Principle*, 125–27; Hinderaker, *Elusive Empires*, 247–48; Linda K. Kerber, "The Federalist Party," in *History of U.S. Political Parties, 1789–1860: From Factions to Parties*, ed. Arthur M. Schlesinger Jr., 4 vols. (New York: Chelsea House, 1973), 1:22–23.

38. Kerber, "Federalist Party," 1:22.

39. *Cincinnati Western Spy*, June 26, July 24, August 28, 1802; *Scioto Gazette*, September 18, 1802; Ratcliffe, *Party Spirit*, 49; Bond, *Old Northwest*, 123.

40. *Scioto Gazette*, July 17, 1802; J. Brown, "Political Culture," 4–5; L. Evans, *Ross County*, 1:242.

41. *Scioto Gazette*, August 28, September 11, 1802; L. Evans, *Ross County*, 1:242.

42. *Scioto Gazette*, September 11, 1802; *Cincinnati Western Spy*, September 11, 1802.

43. *Scioto Gazette*, September 11, 18, 1802; L. Evans, *Ross County*, 1:242–44.

44. *Scioto Gazette*, August 23–24, September 11, 18, October 16, November 6, 1802; *Cincinnati Western Spy*, September 11, 1802; *Ohio Gazette*, September 28, 1802; Andrew R. L. Cayton, "Language Gives Way to Feelings," in *The Pursuit of Public Power: Political Culture in Ohio, 1787–1861*, ed. Jeffrey P. Brown and Andrew R. L. Cayton (Kent, Ohio: Kent State University Press, 1994), 38; L. Evans, *Ross County*, 1:242–43; William A. Taylor, *Ohio in Congress from 1803–1901, with Notes and Sketches of Senators and Representatives and Other Historical Data* (Columbus: Century Publishing, 1900), 38–39, 275; Simeon D. Fess, ed., *Ohio: A Four-Volume Reference Library on the History of a Great State* (New York: Lewis Publishing, 1937), 1:268; Downes, "Ohio's First Constitution," 15; Cornelius G. Comegys, *Reminiscences of the Life and Public Services of Edward Tiffin, Ohio's First Governor* (Chillicothe, Ohio: J. R. S. Bond and Son, 1869), 1–7; William Edward Gilmore, *Life of Edward Tiffin: First Governor of Ohio* (Chillicothe, Ohio: Horney and Son, 1897), 4–6; Frazer Ells Wilson, *Arthur St. Clair, Rugged Ruler of the Old Northwest: An Epic of the American Frontier* (Richmond, Va.: Garrett and Massie Publishers, 1944), 157.

45. Emancipation Record of Negroes, 1804–55, clerk of courts, Ross County, microfilm, frame 98, 8–9, OHS.

46. *Scioto Gazette*, September 18, 1802; Fess, *Ohio*, 1:19; Compton, "Reminiscences," book 14, 23.

47. *Scioto Gazette*, August 28, 1802; L. Evans, *Ross County*, 1:242–43; John D. Barnhardt, "The Southern Influence in the Formation of Ohio," *Journal of Southern History* 3 (February 1937): 29–30; Ruhl Jacob Bartlett, "The Struggle for Statehood in Ohio," *Ohio Archaeological and Historical Quarterly* 32 (July 1923): 495; William T. Utter, "Chillicothe Junto: A Stolen March on the Opposition That Cleared the Way for Ohio's Statehood," *American Heritage* 38 (Spring 1953): 70.

48. Biographical Sketches and Autographs of James Sargent and Philip Gatch, January 18, 1895, Rice Collection, box 1, folder 1. This document is not attributed to its author, though it is assumed that Charles Rice wrote it. Also see Charles E. Rice to Judge Eli P. Evans, September 10, 1906, ibid., box 8, folder 7.

49. Patterson, *Constitutions of Ohio*, 2:66; Manuscripts Relating to the Early History of the Connecticut Western Reserve, folder 2, container 19, vol. 23,

1795–1860, Western Reserve Historical Society, Cleveland, Ohio (hereafter, Connecticut Western Reserve); A. P. Miller, *Remarks of Mr. A. P. Miller of Butler County, on House Bill 242, to Prevent Persons Who Are of African Descent in Whole or in Part from Exercising the Privilege of Voting at Elections*, 2–3, Ohio Historical Society, Columbus.

50. *Cincinnati Western Spy*, November 17, 1802; *Ohio Gazette*, September 28, 1802; Winthrop D. Jordan, *White over Black: American Attitudes toward the Negro, 1550–1812* (Chapel Hill: University of North Carolina Press, 1968), 412; Stephen A. Siegel, "The Federal Government's Power to Enact Color-Conscious Laws: An Originalist Inquiry," *Northwestern University Law Review* 92 (Winter 1998): 496–97.

51. *Philanthropist*, November 25, 1836.

52. Report on Petitions to Repeal the Black Laws, December 4, 1837, *Ohio House Journal*, 35 (35th Gen. Ass., 1st sess.), 695–98 (March 18, 1837), repr. in *The Black Laws in the Old Northwest: A Documentary History*, ed. Stephen Middleton (Westport, Conn.: Greenwood, 1993), 58.

53. State Convention of Colored Men, *Address to the Constitutional Convention of Ohio from the State Convention of Colored Men, Held in the City of Columbus, January 15th, 16th, 17th and 18th, 1851* (Columbus: E. Glover, 1851), 5–8.

54. Terzian, "Folly and Fanaticism," 54.

55. O'Dell, "Antislavery Movement," 70; Betty M. Culpepper, "The Negro and the Black Laws, 1803–1860" (master's thesis, Kent State University, 1965), 4; Burnet, *Early Settlement*, 355; Rodabaugh, "Negro in Ohio," 13; Gary E. French, *Men of Color: An Historical Account of the Black Settlement on Wilberforce Street and Oro Township, Simcoe County, 1819–1949* (Stroud, Ontario: Kaste Books, 1978), 19.

56. Terzian, "Folly and Fanaticism," 73–77; *Journal of the First Constitutional Convention* (1802), in Daniel J. Ryan, "From Charter to Constitution: Being a Collection of Public Documents Pertaining to the Territory of the Northwest and the State of Ohio, From the Charters of James I, to and Including the First Constitution of Ohio, and the State Papers," *Ohio Archaeological and Historical Society Publications* 5 (August 1897); Ryan, *History of Ohio*, 111; Chaddock, "Ohio before 1850," 62–63; Bond, *Old Northwest*, 124–25; Marietta College, Library, *The Sesquicentennial of Ohio's Statehood, 1803–1953: An Exhibition of Manuscript and Other Materials in the Library of Congress, June 5, 1953, to June 12, 1953* (Marietta, Ohio: Marietta College, 1953), 10; Taylor, *Ohio Statesmen*, 1:22; Sears, *Thomas Worthington*, 94, 100, 102; Helen Thurston, "The 1802 Constitutional Convention and the Status of the Negro," *Ohio History* 81 (Winter 1972): 16–17; O'Dell, "Antislavery Movement," 104; Quillin, *Color Line*, 16–17; Roberta Rivera, ed., *Ohio Almanac* (Lorain, Ohio: Lorain Journal, 1977), 14; John D. Barnhart, "Southern Influence in the Formation of Ohio," *Journal of Southern History* 3 (February 1937): 32–33.

57. Charles B. Galbreath, *Constitutional Conventions of Ohio* (Columbus: Stoneman Press, 1911); J. Cutler, *Life and Times*, 70; *Norfolk and Portsmouth Herald*, September 6, 1822 (repr. from *National Gazette*); Marietta College, *Sesquicentennial of Statehood, 1803–1953*, 10.

58. *Journal of the First Constitutional Convention* (1802), 80–84; Carrington T. Marshall, *A History of the Courts and Lawyers of Ohio*, 4 vols. (New York: American

Historical Society, 1934), 2:87; Compton, "Reminiscences," book 14, 30. Other committees included Preamble and First Article, Stationary and Printing, Style (to revise journal), the Executive, Judiciary, Civil Servants, Militia, Regulations and Provisions, Acceptance or Rejection, and Qualifications and Electors.

59. *Journal of the First Constitutional Convention* (1802), 87–88; *Cincinnati Western Spy*, November 17, 1802; Bond, *Old Northwest*, 125; Burnet, *Early Settlement*, 350–53.

60. Evan P. Middleton, ed., *History of Champaign County, Ohio, Its Peoples, Industries and Institutions* (Indianapolis: B. F. Bowen, 1917), 39; Frank Theodore Cole, "Thomas Worthington," *Ohio History* 12 (October 1903): 347.

61. *Journal of the First Constitutional Convention* (1802), 90, 95; Galbreath, *History of Ohio*, 2:15; J. Cutler, *Life and Times*, 74.

62. Thurston, "Constitutional Convention," 19–20.

63. *Journal of the First Constitutional Convention* (1802), 105

64. Ibid., 95; J. Cutler, *Life and Times*, 77; Bartlett, "Struggle," 499–500; Otto A. Lovett, "Black Laws of Ohio" (master's thesis, Ohio State University, 1929), 6; Galbreath, *History of Ohio*, 1:273; Quillin, *Color Line*, 16; Thurston, "Constitutional Convention," 21.

65. J. Cutler, *Life and Times*, 74–77, 122; Burnet, *Early Settlement*, 355; Terzian, "Folly and Fanaticism," 94.

66. J. Cutler, *Life and Times*, 74–77, 122; Burnet, *Early Settlement*, 355; Terzian, "Folly and Fanaticism," 94.

67. J. Cutler, *Life and Times*, 74; C. B. Galbreath, "Thomas Jefferson's Views on Slavery," *Ohio Archaeological and Historical Quarterly* 34 (April 1925): 184–86; William T. Utter, *The History of the State of Ohio: The Frontier State, 1803–1825* (Columbus: Ohio State Archaeological and Historical Society, 1942), 18–19; J. Cutler, *Life and Times*, 69, 74, 77; Benjamin F. Morris, *The Life of Thomas Morris: Pioneer and Long a Legislator of Ohio, and U.S. Senator from 1833–1839* (Cincinnati: Moore, Wilstach, Keys and Overend, 1856), 29; Bartlett, "Struggle," 500.

68. J. Cutler, *Life and Times*, 74–77; Lovett, "Black Laws," 6; Utter, *History*, 20; Quillin, *Color Line*, 15; Terzian, "Folly and Fanaticism," 94–95

69. *Journal of the First Constitutional Convention* (1802), 27, 95, 111.

70. Ibid., 27, 95, 111; Thurston, "Constitutional Convention," 21; Ohio, *Biographical Annals of Ohio: A Handbook of the Government and Institutions of the State of Ohio*, Comp. under the Authority of the Act of April 19, 1904 (Springfield, Ohio: State Printers, 1905), 82; C. Walker, *Athens County*, 390.

71. Thurston, "Constitutional Convention," 21; J. Cutler, *Life and Times*, 76–77, 82; Chaddock, "Ohio before 1850," 79–80.

72. *Cincinnati Western Spy*, November 24, 1802; Alfred Mathews, *Ohio and Her Western Reserve: With a Story of Three States* (New York: D. Appleton, 1902), 254; Rodabaugh, "Negro in Ohio," 14.

73. *Journal of the First Constitutional Convention* (1802), 27, 110–11; Terzian, "Folly and Fanaticism," 98–102.

74. *Journal of the First Constitutional Convention* (1802), 110; letter from William Starling, February 7, 1793, Sullivant-Starling Papers, ms. 459, box 1, folder 1, OHS.

75. Indentured Agreement, September 13, 1837, Larwill Family Collection, ms. 154, box 6, folder 1, OHS.

76. *Journal of the First Constitutional Convention* (1802), 96, 100, 113; Terzian, "Folly and Fanaticism," 103–4; Emil Pocock, "A 'Candidate I'll Surely Be': Election Practices in Early Ohio, 1798–1825," in Brown and Cayton, *Pursuit of Public Power*, 54; Quillin, *Color Line*, 13.

77. *Journal of the First Constitutional Convention* (1802), 114; Sears, *Thomas Worthington*, 101; Marshall, *Courts and Lawyers*, 2:87; Ryan, *History of Ohio*, 118; Utter, *History*, 2:21.

78. *Journal of the First Constitutional Convention* (1802), 114; Terzian, "Folly and Fanaticism," 103–4; Rodabaugh, "Negro in Ohio," 14; Sears, *Thomas Worthington*, 101; Ryan, *History of Ohio*, 118; Bartlett, "Struggle for Ohio," 499–500.

79. *Journal of the First Constitutional Convention* (1802), 122; Terzian, "Folly and Fanaticism," 104–10.

80. *Journal of the First Constitutional Convention* (1802), 122; Wilson, "Negro in Early Ohio," 723; "Recent addresses of James Edwin Campbell," 36; Galbreath, *History of Ohio*, 2:15–16; Burnet, *Early Settlement*, 354–55; O'Dell, "Antislavery Movement," 105; Bond, *Old Northwest*, 126; Thurston, "Constitutional Convention," 23.

81. *Journal of the First Constitutional Convention* (1802), 122.

82. Ibid., 115–16; Sears, *Thomas Worthington*, 101; Bond, *Old Northwest*, 126–27; Burnet, *Early Settlement*, 355; Utter, *History*, 2:21.

83. *Journal of the First Constitutional Convention* (1802), 115–16.

84. Lowell Dwight Black, "The Negro Volunteer Militia Units of the Ohio National Guard, 1870–1954: The Struggle for Military Recognition and Equality in the State of Ohio" (Ph.D. diss., Ohio State University, 1976), 2–3.

85. An act to provide for calling forth the militia to execute the laws of the Union, 1 Stat. 424, 424–25; An act to amend the act calling forth the militia to execute the laws of the Union, 12 Stat. 597, 597–99; Lowell Dwight Black, "The Negro Volunteer Militia Units of the Ohio National Guard, 1870–1954: The Struggle for Military Recognition and Equality in the State of Ohio" (Ph.D. diss., Ohio State University, 1976), 3, 4, 6, 14; John F. Callan, *Laws of the United States, for the Government of the Militia of the District of Columbia, and the United States Rules and Articles of War* (Baltimore: J. Murphy, 1861).

86. Ohio const. of 1802, art. VIII, §§ 7, 25.

87. Quoted in Lyle Koehler, ed., *Cincinnati's Black Peoples: A Chronology and Bibliography, 1787–1982* (Cincinnati: Arts Consortium, 1986), 1; Ohio const. of 1802, art. I, § on Indentured Servitude, art. IV, § on White Suffrage, art. IV, § 5, art. VIII, § 2; Connecticut Western Reserve, folder 2, container 19, 23, WRHS.

88. *Journal of the First Constitutional Convention* (1802), 97–98, 131.

89. An act to provide for the due execution of the laws of the United States, within the State of Ohio, *Annals of Congress*, 7th Cong., 2d sess., 1559 (February 19, 1803).

CHAPTER 3

1. A Declaration of the Rights of the Inhabitants of the State of Vermont, Vermont const. of 1777, 1786, 1793, ch. 1; A Declaration of the Rights of the Inhabitants of the Commonwealth of Pennsylvania, constitution, September 28, 1776.

2. Indiana const. of 1816, art. VIII, § 1; Illinois const. of 1818, art. VI, § 1; Elmer Gertz, "The Black Laws of Illinois," *Journal of the Illinois State Historical Society* 56 (Autumn 1963): 454–73.

3. Ohio const. of 1802, art. VIII, § 2.

4. Samuel Shepherd, ed., *The Statutes at Large of Virginia, from October Session 1792, to December Session 1807*, 3 vols. (Richmond, Va.: Printed by S. Shepherd, 1836–37), 2:300; W. Edwin Hemphill, "Examinations of George Wythe Swinney for Forgery and Murder: A Documentary Essay," *William and Mary Quarterly* 12 (October 1955): 567.

5. See *Report of the Debates and Proceedings of the Convention for the Revision of the Constitution of the State of Ohio, 1850–1851*, 2 vols. (Columbus: S. Medary, printer to the Convention, 1851), 1:337; Edgar F. Love, "Registration of Free Blacks in Ohio: The Slaves of George C. Mendenhall." *Journal of Negro History* 69 (Winter 1984): 38.

6. "Race Hate in Early Ohio," *Negro History Bulletin* 10 (June 1946): 203; Otto A. Lovett, "Black Laws of Ohio" (master's thesis, Ohio State University, 1929); Thomas C. Nelson, "The Aliened American: The Free Negro in Ohio" (master's thesis, University of Toledo, 1969), 1, 5–8, 13–14; John Mercer Langston, *From the Virginia Plantation to the National Capitol* (Hartford, Conn.: American Publishing, 1894), 91.

7. *Scioto Gazette*, March 19, October 16, November 6, 1803; Francis Weisenburger, *History of the State of Ohio: The Passing of the Frontier, 1825–1850*, 3 vols. (Columbus: Ohio State Archaeological and Historical Society, 1941), 3:42; An act to regulate black and mulatto persons, 2 Laws of Ohio 63 (1804), repr. in *The Black Laws in the Old Northwest: A Documentary History*, ed. Stephen Middleton (Westport, Conn.: Greenwood, 1993), 16–17.

8. Jacob Burnet, *Notes on the Early Settlement of the North-Western Territory* (Cincinnati: Derby, Bradley, 1847), 355–56.

9. Staughton Lynd, "Slavery and the Founding Fathers," in *Black History: A Reappraisal*, ed. Melvin Drimmer (New York: Anchor Books, 1968), 117; Chisholm v. Georgia, 2 U.S. (2 Dall.) 419, 472 (1793).

10. Lydia M. Child, *An Appeal in Favor of That Class of Americans Called Africans* (Boston: Allen and Ticknor, 1833), 123; Elmer Gertz, "The Black Laws of Illinois," *Journal of the Illinois State Historical Society* 56 (Autumn 1963): 455–56.

11. David A. Gerber, *Black Ohio and the Color Line, 1860–1915* (Urbana: University of Illinois Press, 1976), x, 3, 9.

12. Harold E. Davis, "The Economic Basis of Ohio Politics, 1820–1840," *Ohio Archaeological and Historical Quarterly* 47 (October 1938): 288; Samuel S. Cox, "Emancipation and Its Results: Is Ohio to Be Africanized?" Speech of Hon. S. S. Cox Delivered in the House of Representatives, June 6, 1862, 5; Carter G.

Woodson, "The Negroes of Cincinnati Prior to the Civil War," *Journal of Negro History* I (January 1916): 4; Carter G. Woodson, ed., *The Mind of the Negro as Reflected in Letters Written during the Crisis, 1800–1860* (repr., New York: Russell and Russell, 1969), 483; Charles B. Galbreath, *History of Ohio*, 5 vols. (Chicago: American Historical Society, 1925), 2:200; Leonard Erickson, "The Color Line in Ohio Public Schools, 1829–1890" (Ph.D. diss., Ohio State University, 1959), 28; James Monroe, *Oberlin Thursday Lectures, Addresses, and Essays* (Oberlin, Ohio: Edward J. Goodrich, 1897), 112; Robert Chaddock, "Ohio before 1850: A Study of the Early Influence of Pennsylvania and Southern Populations in Ohio" (Ph.D. diss., Columbia University, 1908), 82; William Cheek and Aimee Lee Cheek, *John Mercer Langston and the Fight for Black Freedom, 1829–1865* (Urbana: University of Illinois Press, 1989), 60.

13. Chaddock, "Ohio before 1850," 82–83.

14. An act to provide for organizing and disciplining the militia, 2 Laws of Ohio 5 (1803); An act for disciplining the militia, 5 Laws of Ohio 1 (1807); *Journal of the House of Representatives of the State of Ohio*, I (1st Gen. Ass.), 12 (March 4, 1803), repr. in S. Middleton, *Black Laws*, 13–14; Lowell Dwight Black, "The Negro Volunteer Militia Units of the Ohio National Guard, 1870–1954: The Struggle for Military Recognition and Equality in the State of Ohio" (Ph.D. diss., Ohio State University, 1976), 17–18; *Philanthropist*, March 20, 1838.

15. An act to provide for the organizing and disciplining the militia, 2 Laws of Ohio 5, 5–55 (1803–4); An act to regulate black and mulatto persons, 2 Laws of Ohio 63 (1804); J. Reuben Sheeler, "The Struggle of the Negro for Freedom in Ohio," *Journal of Negro History* 31 (April 1946): 211.

16. Ohio const. of 1802, art. I, § 7; An act regulating the mode of taking the enumeration of the white male inhabitants above twenty-one years of age, 1 Laws of Ohio 72, 72–74 (1803); An act making additional provision for taking the enumeration of white male inhabitants of this state, over the age of twenty-one years, 30 Laws of Ohio 5, 5–6 (1831), repr. in S. Middleton, *Black Laws*, 11–12; *Ohio House Journal*, 6 (6th Gen. Ass.), 45 (December 12, 1807).

17. An act to regulate black and mulatto persons, 2 Laws of Ohio 63 (1804), repr. in S. Middleton, *Black Laws*, 13–18 *Ohio House Journal*, 2 (1st Gen. Ass.), 33 (December 14, 1803), 43, 45, 47 (December 22, 1803); *Philanthropist*, June 12, 1844.

18. An act to regulate black and mulatto persons, 2 Laws of Ohio 63 (1804), repr. in S. Middleton, *Black Laws*, 15–18; Barbara A. Terzian, "'Effusions of Folly and Fanaticism': Race, Gender, and Constitution-Making in Ohio, 1802–1923" (Ph.D. diss., Ohio State University, 1999), 114–15.

19. An act to regulate black and mulatto persons, 2 Laws of Ohio 63 (1804), repr. in S. Middleton, *Black Laws*, 15–18; Russell H. Davis, *Black Americans in Cleveland from George Peake to Carl B. Stokes, 1796–1969* (Washington, D.C.: Associated Publishers, 1972), 63–64.

20. An act to regulate black and mulatto persons, 2 Laws of Ohio 63 (1804); *Ohio House Journal*, 2 (1st Gen. Ass.), 43, 47 (December 22, 1803), repr. in S. Middleton, *Black Laws*, 15–18; Terzian, "Folly and Fanaticism," 114–15.

21. An act to regulate black and mulatto persons, 2 Laws of Ohio 63 (1804); William A. Taylor, *Ohio Statesmen and Annals of Progress, from the Year 1788 to the Year 1900*, 2 vols. (Columbus: Press of Westbote, 1899), 1:45; *Philanthropist*, November 25, 1836, May 26, 1841; James J. Burns, *Educational History of Ohio: A History of Its Progress since the Formation of the State, Together with the Portraits and Biographies of Past and Present State Officials* (Columbus: Historical Publications, 1905), 195–96; Eugene H. Berwanger, *The Frontier against Slavery: Western Anti-Negro Prejudice and the Slavery Extension Controversy* (Urbana: University of Illinois Press, 1967), 22; Erickson, "Color Line," 26.

22. Eugene H. Roseboom, *A History of Ohio* (New York: Prentice Hall, 1934), 210–11; Grace Julian Clarke, ed., "A Letter of Dr. Gamaliel Bailey to Joshua R. Giddings," *Documents, Indiana Magazine of History* 26 (March 1930): 33, 37–38; Ohio Antislavery Society (hereafter, OAS), *Memorial of the Ohio Antislavery Society, to the General Assembly of the State of Ohio* (Cincinnati: Pugh and Dodd, 1838), 4.

23. Roseboom, *History of Ohio*, 210–11; Clarke, "Letter," 33, 37–38; OAS, *Memorial*, 4.

24. *Ohio House Journal*, 2 (1st Gen. Ass.), 37–38 (December 17, 1803), 40, 42, (December 19, 1803); Clarke, "Letter," 37–38; *Scioto Gazette*, January 9, 1804.

25. An act to amend the last named act, "an act to regulate black and mulatto persons," 5 Laws of Ohio 53 (1807), repr. in S. Middleton, *Black Laws*, 17; Terzian, "Folly and Fanaticism," 115.

26. Ohio Antislavery Society, "Report on the Black Laws," in *Proceedings of the Ohio Antislavery Convention, Held at Putnam, Ohio, April 22–24, 1835* (Putnam, Ohio: American Antislavery Society, 1835), 18; *Anti-Slavery Examiner*, no. 13 (1839): 7–8; Salmon Chase, ed., *The Statutes of Ohio and of the Northwest Territory, 1788–1833*, 3 vols. (Cincinnati: Corey and Fairbank, 1833–35), 1:393; OAS, "Black Laws," 36–37; *Philanthropist*, November 25, 1836.

27. An act to amend the last named act, "an act to regulate black and mulatto persons," 5 Laws of Ohio 53 (1807); Sheeler, "Struggle," 210.

28. An act to amend the last named act, "an act to regulate black and mulatto persons," 5 Laws of Ohio 53, 53–54 (1807); *Philanthropist*, March 20, 1838; *Ohio State Journal*, February 5, 1845; OAS, *Memorial*, 6; George W. Knepper, *Ohio and Its People* (Kent, Ohio: Kent State University Press, 1989), 205; Berwanger, *Frontier*, 22; Erickson, "Color Line," 26; OAS, "Black Laws," 38–39; *Anti-Slavery Examiner*, no. 13 (1839): 7; James G. Birney, *The American Churches: Bulwarks of Slavery* (repr., Concord, N.H.: P. Pillsbury, 1885), 5; W. Taylor, *Ohio Statesmen*, 1:54–55; Philip S. Foner, *History of Black Americans*, 3 vols. (Westport, Conn.: Greenwood, 1975), 2:195.

29. An act to punish kidnapping, 17 Laws of Ohio 159, 159–61 (1819), repr. in S. Middleton, *Black Laws*, 26.

30. An act to prevent kidnapping, 29 Laws of Ohio 442 (1831); An act to prevent kidnapping, 54 Laws of Ohio 221, 221–22 (1857); An act to prevent slaveholding and kidnapping in Ohio, 54 Laws of Ohio 186 (1857); An act to prohibit the confinement of fugitives from slavery in the jails of Ohio, 54 Laws of Ohio 170 (1857), repr. in S. Middleton, *Black Laws*, 27–32.

31. An act for the relief of the poor, 22 Laws of Ohio 331, 331–35 (1819); An act to amend the act entitled "an act for the relief of the poor," 27 Laws of Ohio 54 (1829); An act for the relief of the poor, 29 Laws of Ohio 72 (1831); An act for the relief of the poor, 51 Laws of Ohio 466 (1853), repr. in Chase, *Statutes*, 3:18–32; Sheeler, "Struggle," 211; Terzian, "Folly and Fanaticism," 117.

32. William Cox Cochran, "Ohio from 1802 to 1851: The Black Laws—The Three-Fifths Rule," in *The Western Reserve and the Fugitive Slave Law: A Prelude to the Civil War* (Cleveland: Western Reserve Historical Society, 1920), 61.

33. An act to regulate black and mulatto persons, 2 Laws of Ohio 63 (1804), repr. in S. Middleton, *Black Laws*, 16–17; Betty M. Culpepper, "The Negro and the Black Laws, 1803–1860" (master's thesis, Kent State University, 1965), 22; Stephen E. Maizlish, *The Triumph of Sectionalism: The Transformation of Ohio Politics, 1844–1856* (Kent, Ohio: Kent State University Press, 1983), 7; "Civil Condition of the Colored People of Ohio," *New York Colored American*, January 9, 1841.

34. OAS, "Black Laws," 38; T. Nelson, "Aliened American," 9–10.

35. Culpepper, "Negro and Black Laws," 22; Indiana Yearly Meeting of Friends, *Address to the Citizens of the State of Ohio Concerning What Are Called the Black Laws, Issued in Behalf of the Society of Friends of Indiana Yearly Meeting* (Cincinnati: A. Pugh, 1848), 9–10; Leon F. Litwack, "Free Blacks in the Antebellum North," in *America's Black Past: A Reader in Afro-American History*, ed. Eric Foner (New York: Harper and Row, 1970), 145–46; Richard W. Pih, "Negro Self-Improvement Efforts in Ante-Bellum Cincinnati, 1836–1850," *Ohio History* 78 (Summer 1969): 180; OAS, "Black Laws," 38.

36. John Malvin, *North into Freedom: The Autobiography of John Malvin, 1795–1880,* ed. Allan Peskin (Cleveland: Press of Western Reserve University, 1966), 38–40, also quoted in T. Nelson, "Aliened American," 49

37. OAS, "Black Laws," 19; Lenwood G. Davis, "Nineteenth-Century Blacks in Ohio: An Historical Overview," in *Blacks in Ohio History*, ed. Rubin F. Weston (Columbus: Ohio Historical Society, 1976), 4; Frank U. Quillin, *The Color Line in Ohio: A History of Race Prejudice in a Typical Northern State* (Ann Arbor, Mich.: George Wahr, 1913), 28; Galbreath, *History of Ohio*, 1:200; Malvin, *North into Freedom*, 6; Culpepper, "Negro and Black Laws," 20; Litwack, "Free Blacks," 48; OAS, *Black Laws*, 20–21; Benjamin Drew, *A Northside View of Slavery; the Refugee: or, the Narratives of Fugitive Slaves in Canada; Related by Themselves, with an Account of the History and Condition of the Colored Population of Upper Canada* (Boston: J. P. Jewett, 1856), 358.

38. *Philanthropist*, May 26, 1841; Pih, "Negro Self-Improvement," 181–82.

39. Cox, "Emancipation," 5; Galbreath, *History of Ohio*, 1:200; Malvin, *North into Freedom*, 9–11; Woodson, "Negroes of Cincinnati," 4; Woodson, *Mind of the Negro*, 483; Erickson, "Color Line," 28; Monroe, *Oberlin Lectures*, 112.

40. An act regulating juries, 14 Laws of Ohio 386, 386–98 (1816); Sheeler, "Struggle," 211; Carter G. Woodson, *A Century of Negro Migration* (New York: Association for the Study of Negro Life and History, 1969), 3; Malvin, *North into Freedom*, 5.

41. An act in addition to an act to establish a fund for the support of common schools, 28 Laws of Ohio 56, 56–57 (1829), repr. in S. Middleton, *Black Laws*, 34–38; *New York Colored American*, November 2, 1839, January 9, 1841.

42. An act to authorize the establishment of separate schools for the education of colored children, and for other purposes, 47 Laws of Ohio 17 (1849); *Ohio Senate Journal,* 27 (27th Gen. Ass.) 63 (December 12, 1828), 152 (December 27, 1828); *Ohio House Journal,* 32 (32nd Gen. Ass.) 435–36 (January 20, 1834); *The School Officers' Guide, for the State of Ohio; Containing the Laws on the Subject of Common Schools, the School Fund, and etc., Together with Instructions for the Information and Government of School Officers, Printed by Authority of the General Assembly* (Columbus: Samuel Medary, State Printer, 1842), 3.

43. An act to provide for the support and better regulation of common schools, 27 Laws of Ohio 72, 73–79 (1828); An act in addition to the act entitled, An act to incorporate and establish the city of Cincinnati, and for repealing all laws and parts of laws heretofore enacted on that subject, passed the twenty-sixth day of January in the year eighteen hundred and twenty-seven, 27 Laws of Ohio 33, 34–51 (1829); An act to provide for the support and better regulation of common schools, 29 Laws of Ohio 414, 414–23 (1831); *Ohio Senate Journal,* 35 (35th Gen. Ass.), 148, 149 (January 7, 1837), repr. in S. Middleton, *Black Laws,* 34.

44. An act for the support and better regulation of common schools and to create permanently the office of superintendent, 36 Laws of Ohio 21, 21–37 (1838); Child, *Appeal,* 123.

45. State v. George, in Pollack, *Unreported Decisions,* 185–87.

46. R. Davis, *Black Americans;* Charles W. Wadelington, "Ohio's Visible Admixture Principle, 1802–1970" (master's thesis, Miami University, 1977).

47. Gray v. Ohio, 4 Ohio 353 (1831); Terzian, "Folly and Fanaticism," 118.

48. Gray v. Ohio, 4 Ohio at 353–54; Terzian, "Folly and Fanaticism," 118–22.

49. Gray v. Ohio, 4 Ohio at 353–54.

50. John A. Caldwell, *History of Belmont and Jefferson Counties, Ohio, and Incidental Historical Collections Pertaining to Border Warfare and the Early Settlement of the Adjacent Portion of the Ohio Valley,* ed. J. H. Newton (Wheeling, W. Va.: Historical Publication, 1880), 174.

51. Ibid., 428.

52. N. Dwight Harris, *The History of Negro Servitude in Illinois and of the Slavery Agitation in that State, 1719–1864* (Chicago: A. C. McClurg, 1904), 25; Gertz, "Black Laws," 463–64; Mason M. Fishback, "Illinois Legislation on Slavery and Free Negroes, 1818–1856," *Illinois State Historical Society Transactions,* no. 9 (1904): 421–27; Illinois, *Revised Statutes of the State of Illinois* (1844–45), 386–91; Berwanger, *Frontier,* 22, 25, 32, 40–45; Vernon L. Volpe, *Forlorn Hope of Freedom: The Liberty Party in the Old Northwest, 1838–1848* (Kent, Ohio: Kent State University Press, 1990), 151; "Settlement of Springfield and Slavery in Springfield," *Transactions of the Illinois State Historical Society,* no. 14 (1909): 197–98.

53. Indiana const. of 1816, art. III, § 2, art. VI, § 1, art. VII, § 2. For an analysis of other northern states that enacted black laws, see "Race Hate," 203–4.

54. Illinois const. of 1818, art. II, § 5.

55. Ibid., art. II, § 27.

56. Ibid., art. V, § 1; Getz, "Black Laws," 463–64.

57. Fishback, "Illinois Legislation," 414–20.

58. Michigan const. of 1835, art. XI, § 1.

59. Ibid., art. X, § 3.

60. Wisconsin const. of 1848, art. III, § 1; Ray A. Brown, "The Making of the Wisconsin Constitution," *Wisconsin Law Review* 1949 (July 1949): 655, 685–89; Brown, "The Making of the Wisconsin Constitution," *Wisconsin Law Review* 1952 (January 1952): 23, 57–60; Wisconsin const. of 1846, art. XVI; Milo Milton Quaife, *The Convention of 1846* (Madison: State Historical Society of Wisconsin, 1919), 215, 732–35.

61. Emancipation Record, 1805–1844, Greene County clerk of courts, microfilm, roll 55, OHS; Records of Black and Mulatto Persons, Greene, Logan, Miami and Montgomery Counties, 1805–1844, microfilm ed., roll 55, WRHS; James Buchanan, comp., *The Blacks of Pickaway County, Ohio, in the Nineteenth Century* (Bowie, Md.: Heritage Books, 1988), iii.

62. Emancipation Record, 1805–1844, roll 55, OHS; Black, "Negro Volunteers," 22; Malvin, *North into Freedom,* 19.

63. Records of Black and Mulatto Persons, Greene, Logan, Miami and Montgomery Counties, 1805–1844, microfilm ed., roll 55, WRHS.

64. Emancipation Record, 1805–1844, microfilm, roll 55, OHS.

65. "Records of Black and Mulatto Persons, Greene County, Logan, Miami and Montgomery Counties, 1805–1844," microfilm ed., roll 55, WRHS.

66. Maxey to Droomgoole, July 27, 1807, also quoted in Andrew R. L. Cayton, "Language Gives Way to Feelings," in *The Pursuit of Public Power: Political Culture in Ohio, 1787–1861,* ed. Jeffrey P. Brown and Andrew R. L. Cayton (Kent, Ohio: Kent State University Press, 1994), 38; William Warren Sweet, ed., *The Methodists: A Collection of Source Materials,* vol. 4 of *Religion on the American Frontier, 1783–1840* (Chicago: University of Chicago Press, 1931; repr. New York: Coover Square Publishers, 1964), 160; Gatch to Dromgoole, June 1, 1805, ibid., 4:156–57.

67. Gatch to Droomgoole, June 1, 1805, also quoted in Cayton, "Language Gives Way," 38. Also see John Sale to Edward Dromgoole, February 20, 1807, in "The Edward Dromgoole Letters, 1778–1812," in Sweet, *Methodists,* 4:160; Frederick Bonner to Dromgoole, June 19, 1807, ibid., 4:171; Maxey to Dromgoole, July 27, 1807, ibid., 4:175.

68. Cayton, "Language Gives Way," 38; John Sale to Dromgoole, February 20, 1807, "The Edward Dromgoole Letters, 1778–1812," 4:160; Gatch to Dromgoole, June 1, 1805, ibid., 4:156–57; Frederick Bonner to Dromgoole, June 19, 1807, ibid., 4:171; Maxey to Dromgoole, July 27, 1807, ibid., 4:175.

69. William R. Coates, *A History of Cuyahoga County and the City of Cleveland* (Chicago: American Historical Society, 1924), 67.

70. Henry Todd, VFM 3282, OHS; Court of Common Pleas, Columbiana County, Bond of $500 with Approved Security entered into by Edward Moins, a black man, New Lisbon, July 24, 1807, WRHS; OAS, "Black Laws," 38.

71. Emancipation Record of Negroes, 1804–1855, clerk of courts, Ross County, microfilm, roll 55, pp. 2–3, OHS.

72. Ibid., 1–2.

73. Ibid.

74. Ibid., 26–29, 42–43.

75. Emancipation Record, 1805–1844, clerk of courts, Greene County, microfilm, roll 55, OHS.

76. Emancipation Record of Negroes, 1804–1855, clerk of courts, Ross County, microfilm, roll 55, p. 20, OHS.

77. Ohio const. of 1802, Bill of Rights, art. VIII, § 2.

78. Emancipation Record, 1804–1855, clerk of courts, Ross County, microfilm, roll 55, pp. 30–31, 38–39, OHS; Joan Turpin, *Register of Black, Mulatto, and Poor Persons in Four Ohio Counties, 1791–1861* (Bowie, Md.: Heritage Books, 1985), 4–5.

79. Emancipation Record, 1804–1855, clerk of courts, Ross County, microfilm ed., roll 55, pp. 30–31, 38–39, OHS; Turpin, *Register of Blacks,* 4–5.

80. Emancipation Record, 1804–1855, clerk of courts, Ross County, microfilm, roll 55, p. 111, OHS.

81. *Ohio House Journal,* 33 (33rd Gen. Ass.), 787–92 (February 20, 1835); Quillin, *Color Line,* 25, 55; Berwanger, *Frontier,* 32; Simeon D. Fess, ed., *Ohio: A Four-Volume Reference Library on the History of a Great State* (New York: Lewis Publishing, 1937), 1:268; Weisenburger, *History of Ohio,* 242; Lovett, "Black Laws," 1.

82. R. Davis, *Black Americans,* 7–8.

83. Quoted in Western Biographical Publishing Company, *A History and Biographical Cyclopedia of Butler County, Ohio, With Illustrations and Sketches of Its Representative Men and Pioneers* (Cincinnati: Western Biographical Publishing, 1882), 326.

84. A few years later, a Dayton newspaper predicted, "The State will be thronged with runaway Negroes." See *Dayton Transcript,* March 17, 1841.

85. Henry Howe, *Historical Collections of Ohio, Containing Collection of the Most Interesting Facts, Traditions, Biographical Sketches, Anecdotes, etc., Relating to Its General and Local History; with Descriptions of its Counties, Cities, Towns, and Villages* (Cincinnati: Derby, Bradley, 1847), 71, 356; Stephen E. Haller and Robert H. Smith Jr., eds., *Registers of Blacks in the Miami Valley: A Name Abstract in the Miami Valley, 1804–1857* (Dayton: Wright State University, 1977), 10–28; Moritz Busch, *Travels between the Hudson and the Mississippi, 1851–1852* (repr., Lexington: University Press of Kentucky, 1971), 122–23.

86. Marion B. Lucas, *A History of Blacks in Kentucky: From Slavery to Segregation, 1760–1891,* 2 vols. (Frankfort: Kentucky Historical Society, 1992), 62–64; *Freedom's Journal* (New York), January 16, 1829; "The John Parker Story," Rankin-Parker Papers, Manuscript Department, Perkins Library, Duke University; Louis Weeks, "John P. Parker: Black Abolitionist Entrepreneur, 1827–1900," *Ohio History* 80 (Spring 1971): 159–61.

87. Quoted in James Walker, *Identity: The Black Experience in Canada* ([Toronto]: Ontario Educational Communications, 1979), 18; *Freedom's Journal,* January 9, 1829; William H. Pease and Jane H. Pease, *Black Utopia: Negro Communal Experiments in America* (Madison: State Historical Society of Wisconsin, 1963), 8–12, 103–5.

88. Ohio Antislavery Society, *American Antislavery Almanac for 1841* (Cincinnati: Published for the OAS, 1841), 9, 11, 13. The man had been kidnapped and resold as a slave. He paid six hundred dollars for his liberty on three separate occasions. See also OAS, *Report of the Third Anniversary of the Ohio Antislavery Society, Held in Granville, Licking County, Ohio, May 30, 1838* (Cincinnati: Ohio Antislavery Society, Samuel Alley, printer, 1838), 13–14.

89. OAS, *Antislavery Almanac* (1841), 11, 13. See also OAS, *Third Anniversary*, 13–14.

90. *Scioto Gazette*, February 12, 1803.

91. *Scioto Gazette*, January 23, 1804.

92. *Scioto Gazette*, July 17, 29, August 5, 12, October 31, 1805; September 23, 1808, September 25, 1809; September 24, 1810; *Cincinnati Western Spy*, August 10, 17, 1807; *Chillicothe Fredonian*, March 30, 1808; *Marietta Commentator*, August 25, 1808.

93. *Marietta Commentator*, August 25, 1808.

94. *Scioto Gazette*, July 17, 29, 1805; August 5, 12, October 31, 1805; September 23, 1808; September 25, 1809; September 24, 1810; *Cincinnati Western Spy*, August 10, 17, 1807; *Chillicothe Fredonian*, March 30, 1808; *Marietta Commentator*, August 25, 1808; Nelson W. Evans, ed., *A History of Scioto County, Ohio, Together with A Pioneer Record of Southern Ohio* (Portsmouth, Ohio: Nelson W. Evans, 1903), 612; Richard F. O'Dell, "The Early Antislavery Movement in Ohio" (Ph.D. diss., University of Michigan, 1948), 144–45. See also Billy G. Smith and Richard Wojtowicz, eds., *Blacks Who Stole Themselves: Advertisements for Runaways in the Pennsylvania Gazette, 1728–1790* (Philadelphia: University of Pennsylvania Press, 1989); Freddie L. Parker, *Running for Freedom: Slave Runaways in North Carolina* (New York: Garland Publishing, 1993); Henry Todd, VFM 3282, OHS; Culpepper, "Black Laws," 47; Records of Black and Mulatto Persons, Greene County, WRHS; Drew, introduction to *Northside View*, v; Samuel P. Orth, *A History of Cleveland, Ohio*, 3 vols. (Cleveland: S. J. Clarke Publishing, 1910), 1:297.

95. John Cummings and Joseph A. Hill, eds., *Negro Population, 1790–1915* (Washington, D.C.: Government Printing Office, 1918), 57.

96. Wendell P. Dabney, *Cincinnati's Colored Citizens: Historical, Sociological and Biographical* (Cincinnati: Dabney Publishing, 1926), 33; Lyle Koehler, ed., *Cincinnati's Black Peoples: A Chronology and Bibliography, 1787–1982* (Cincinnati: Arts Consortium, 1986), 3, 6; Berwanger, *Frontier*, 23, 31; Richard Wade, "The Negro in Cincinnati, 1800–1830," *Journal of Negro History* 39 (January 1954): 43–44; Patrick Allen Folk, "The Queen City Mobs" (Ph.D. diss., University of Toledo, 1978), 43–44; *Anti-Slavery Examiner*, no. 13 (1839), 8; Quillin, *Color Line*, 25; Malvin, *North into Freedom*, 7–8; L. Davis, "Nineteenth-Century Blacks," 7–8; Culpepper, "Black Laws," 20, 22; Cox, "Emancipation," 7.

97. "Race Hate," 203.

98. OAS, *Proceedings*, 18; Fess, *Ohio*, 1:268; "Race Hate," 203; Philip S. Foner, *Frederick Douglass: A Biography* (New York: Citadel Press, 1964), 108; Culpepper, "Black Laws," 26–27; Knepper, *Ohio*, 205; Leon Litwack, *North of Slavery: The Negro*

in the *Free States, 1790–1860* (Chicago: University of Chicago Press, 1961), 73–74; Malvin, *North into Freedom*, 4; *Cincinnati Daily Gazette*, September 6, 1841; Levi Coffin, *Reminiscences of Levi Coffin, the Reputed President of the Underground Railroad: Being a Brief History of the Labors of a Lifetime in Behalf of the Slave, with the Stories of Numerous Fugitives, Who Gained Their Freedom through His Instrumentality, and Many Other Incidents* (Cincinnati: Robert Clarke, 1880), 528–33; Wade, "Negro in Cincinnati," 50.

99. *Cincinnati Daily Gazette*, July 4, 1829; *Friend*, November 28, 1829; William Mills, Benjamin Hopkins, and George Lee, "Banishment of the People of Color from Cincinnati," Documents, *Journal of Negro History* 8 (July 1923): 331–32; Marilyn Baily, "From Cincinnati, Ohio, to Wilberforce, Canada: A Note on Antebellum Colonization," *Journal of Negro History* 58 (October 1973): 428–29.

100. *Ohio House Journal*, 28 (28th Gen. Ass.), 51, 184–85 (December 14, 1829); J. Walker, *Identity*, 17–18; William Renwick Riddell, "Additional Notes on Slavery," *Journal of Negro History* 17 (July 1932): 368; Baily, "From Cincinnati," 429; Gary E. French, *Men of Color: An Historical Account of the Black Settlement on Wilberforce Street and Oro Township, Simcoe County, 1819–1949* (Stroud, Ontario: Kaste Books, 1978), 2–3.

101. French, *Men of Color*, 20–21; "Race Hate," 203; William Wilberforce, an English abolitionist, also denounced the international slave trade. See David Christy, "A Lecture on African Colonization, Including a Brief Outline of the Slave Trade, Emancipation, the Relation of the Republic of Liberia to England," speech, Ohio House of Representatives (Cincinnati: J. A. and U. P. James, 1849), 6–7; OAS, *Memorial*, 28–30; James Freeman Clarke, *Present Condition of the Free Colored People of the United States* (New York: American Anti-Slavery Society, 1859), 377–78; "Relief of Fugitive Slaves in Canada," November 11, 1850, December 7, 1850, Zebina Eastman Papers, folder 1841–61, Chicago Historical Society; Malvin, *North into Freedom*, 40–42; OAS, *Proceedings*, 19; Culpepper, "Black Laws," 26–27; Fess, *Ohio*, 1:268; C. Peter Ripley, *The Black Abolitionist Papers*, 5 vols. (Chapel Hill: University of North Carolina Press, 1985), 1:55–56. Race riots broke out sporadically throughout Ohio in the nineteenth century. See Flamen Ball to S. P. Chase, September 4, 1841, Salmon P. Chase Papers, Historical Society of Pennsylvania, Philadelphia (hereafter, HSP); Sheeler, "Struggle," 213; Carter G. Woodson, *Negro in Our History* (Washington, D.C.: Associated Publishers, 1927), 262.

102. *Friend*, November 28, 1829; Mills, Hopkins, and Lee, "Banishment," 332.

103. Quillin, *Color Line*, 32; Lovett, "Black Laws," 20; N. Evans, *Scioto County*, 613; Knepper, *Ohio*, 205; Malvin, *North into Freedom*, 5, 41–42; Sheeler, "Struggle," 213.

104. Dabney, *Colored Citizens*, 49.

105. *Colored American*, November 2, 1839; *Ohio Free Press* (Xenia), March 16, 1839; Erickson, "Color Line," 29.

106. Knight to Thomas Hodgkins, July 17, 1844, VF ms., CinHS.

107. Ibid.

108. An act to punish kidnapping, 17 Laws of Ohio 56 (1819).

109. An act to prevent kidnapping, 29 Laws of Ohio 422 (1831).

CHAPTER 4

1. An act relating to juries, 14 Laws of Ohio 386, 386–98 (1816); An act relating to juries, 29 Laws of Ohio 94 (1831); *Philanthropist*, August 7, 1838; *New York Colored American*, November 2, 1839. For an overview of the Black Laws, see Stephen Middleton, ed., *The Black Laws in the Old Northwest: A Documentary History* (Westport, Conn.: Greenwood, 1993), 3–141.

2. Stephen E. Maizlish, *The Triumph of Sectionalism: The Transformation of Ohio Politics, 1844–1856* (Kent, Ohio: Kent State University Press, 1983), 7.

3. Thomas Foraker Scrapbook, 3, Cincinnati Historical Society; Ohio Antislavery Society (hereafter, OAS), *Memorial of the Ohio Antislavery Society, to the General Assembly of the State of Ohio* (Cincinnati: Pugh and Dodd, 1838), 14–15, 16–17.

4. Leo Alilunas, "Fugitive Slave Cases in Ohio Prior to 1850," *Ohio Archaeological and Historical Quarterly* 49 (April 1940): 160–61; Charles Wesley, *Negro Americans in Ohio: A Sesquicentennial View* (Wilberforce, Ohio: Central State College, 1953), 7; *Philanthropist*, March 6, 1838; Francis Weisenburger, *History of the State of Ohio: The Passing of the Frontier, 1825–1850,* 3 vols. (Columbus: Ohio State Archaeological and Historical Society, 1941), 3:364.

5. *Western-Union Republican*, November 15, 1839; *Philanthropist*, March 6, 1838; *Senate Journal*, 18th Cong., 1st sess., 245 (March 23, 1824); Henry Wilson, *History of the Rise and Fall of the Slave Power*, 3 vols. (Boston: J. R. Osgood, 1872–77), 1:2, 13, 14; William Birney, *James G. Birney and His Times: The Genesis of the Republican Party with Some Account of Abolition Movements in the South before 1828* (New York: D. Appleton, 1890), 74–86, 382–414.

6. Autograph file, Arthur Tappan folder, Oberlin College Library Archives, Oberlin, Ohio.

7. McBride to Eastman, April 7, 1874, Zebina Eastman Papers, folder 1841–61, Chicago Historical Society (hereafter, ChiHS); George Clary Wing, ed., *Early Years on the Western Reserve: With Extracts from Letters of Ephraim Brown and Family, 1805–1845* (Cleveland: Printed by the Arthur H. Clark Company, 1916), 23–26; Autobiography, Samuel Compton Papers, book 12, 7–8, 12–13, Duke University Archives, Durham, N.C.; Russell D. Parker, "The Philosophy of Charles G. Finney: Higher Law and Revivalism," *Ohio History* 82 (Summer–Autumn 1973): 142–47.

8. Charlotte Ludlow-Jones to John S. Whitter, January 7, 1874, Zebina Eastman Papers, folder 1869–74, ChiHS.

9. Ohio State Antislavery Society (African American organization), *Declaration of Sentiments and the Constitution of the Ohio State Anti-Slavery Society* (Cincinnati: Samuel A. Alley, Printer, 1839), 5–7; McBride to Eastman, April 7, 1874, Zebina Eastman Papers, folder 1841–61, ChiHS; Frank U. Quillin, *The Color Line in Ohio: A History of Race Prejudice in a Typical Northern State* (Ann Arbor, Mich.: George Wahr, 1913), 35.

10. Marius Robinson to Emily Robinson (wife), December 29, 1836, Marius Robinson Papers, folder 1, Western Reserve Historical Society (hereafter, WRHS), Cleveland; Russell B. Nye, "Marius Robinson, A Forgotten Abolitionist Leader," *Ohio History* 55 (April–June 1946): 138–46.

11. Canton Ladies Antislavery Society Papers, records (1836), pp. 1–6, WRHS; Thomas E. Thomas, ed., *Correspondence of Thomas E. Thomas, Mainly Relating to the Antislavery Conflict in Ohio, Especially in the Presbyterian Church* (Dayton, Ohio: Published by his son, 1909), 1.

12. John M. Myers, "Antislavery Activities of Five Lane Seminary Boys, 1835–1836," *Bulletin of the Historical and Philosophical Society of Ohio* 21 (April 1963): 95.

13. Thomas Jefferson, *Notes on the State of Virginia* (Boston: Printed by David Carlisle, 1801).

14. Lydia M. Child, *An Appeal in Favor of That Class of Americans Called Africans* (Boston: Allen and Ticknor, 1833), 123; William M. Malehorn, "The Fugitive Slave Law of 1850: Its Enforcement in Ohio" (master's thesis, Ohio State University, 1928), 28.

15. *Proceedings of the Cincinnati Colonization Society, at the Annual Meeting, January 14, 1833* (Cincinnati, F. S. Benton, 1833); *New York Colored American,* September 25, 1841; Child, *Appeal,* 127–28; Eugene H. Roseboom, *A History of Ohio* (New York: Prentice Hall, 1934), 211–12; Merton L. Dillon, *The Abolitionists: The Growth of a Dissenting Minority* (DeKalb: Northern Illinois University Press, 1974), 59.

16. "Who Is [James] Birney?" Pamphlet Collection, ChiHS; James G. Birney, *Letter on Colonization, Addressed to Rev. Thornton J. Mills* (New York: Antislavery Reporter, 1834), 3–10, 46; "Resolution on Colonization," *Kentucky House Journal* (1828–29), January 21, 1829, 347–64; John Malvin, *North into Freedom: The Autobiography of John Malvin, 1795–1880,* ed. Allan Peskin (Cleveland: Press of Western Reserve University, 1966), 2.

17. "Who Is Judge Wade?" *Washington (D.C.) National Era* (March 27, 1851); Dillon, *Abolitionists,* 58. See Salmon P. Chase to John T. Trowbridge, March 21, 1864, box Letters and Drafts, 1864–73, Historical Society of Pennsylvania, Philadelphia.

18. Resolution on colonization, 16 Laws of Ohio 198 (1818); Resolution on colonization, 22 Laws of Ohio 160 (1824); Resolution of January 24, 1828, 26 Laws of Ohio 177 (1828), repr. in S. Middleton, *Black Laws,* 19–22; Governor Hutchins G. Burton, Letter Book, February 8, 1825, GLB, vol. 26, 1824–27, 11, Ohio Historical Society; Samuel A'Court Ashe, *History of North Carolina,* 7 vols. (Raleigh, N.C.: C. L. Van Noppen, 1925), 1:302; David Holmes to Jeremiah Morrow, January 23, 1826, Morrow Papers, box 1, folder 2, Ohio Historical Society; Governor of Delaware to Jeremiah Morrow, June 30, 1824, ibid.

19. Thomas C. Nelson, "The Aliened American: The Free Negro in Ohio" (master's thesis, University of Toledo, 1969), 22–23, 48–49.

20. "Colonization, January 1817," Leon Gardener Papers, American Negro Historical Society Papers, Historical Society of Pennsylvania; Jane H. Pease and William H. Pease, *They Who Would Be Free: Blacks' Search for Freedom, 1830–1861* (New York: Atheneum, 1974), 25–26.

21. For a comprehensive review of Whig politics see Michael F. Holt, *The Rise and Fall of the American Whig Party: Jacksonian Politics and the Onset of the Civil War* (New York: Oxford University Press, 1999); also see John Julius Reed, *The Emergence of the Whig Party in the North: Massachusetts, New York, Pennsylvania, and Ohio* (Ann Arbor, Mich.: University microfilms, 1953).

22. *Journal of the Senate of the State of Ohio* 30 (30th Gen. Ass.), 10 (December 5, 1831), 225 (December 13, 1832), 223 (January 14, 1832), 316 (January 19, 1832); Leonard Erickson, "The Color Line in Ohio Public Schools, 1829–1890" (Ph.D. diss., Ohio State University, 1959), 141; Franklin Johnson, *The Development of State Legislation Concerning the Free Negro* (New York: Arbor Press, 1919), 16, 27, 162; *Philanthropist*, January 22, 1839.

23. *Journal of the House of Representatives of the State of Ohio,* 30 (30th Gen. Ass.), 232–35 (January 13, 1832); Erickson, "Color Line," 141; T. Nelson, "Aliened American," 49.

24. An act to amend the act entitled "an act to provide for the support and better regulation of common schools," 30 Laws of Ohio 4, 5 (1831); Salmon Chase, ed., *The Statutes of Ohio and of the Northwest Territory, 1788–1833,* 3 vols. (Cincinnati: Corey and Fairbank, 1833–35), 2:1832, 1867, 1878; T. Nelson, "Aliened American," 49.

25. Cassius M. Clay, *The Life of Cassius Marcellus Clay: Memoirs, Writings, and Speeches, Showing His Conduct in the Overthrow of American Slavery, the Salvation of the Union, and the Restoration of the Autonomy of the States,* 2 vols. (Cincinnati: J. F. Brennan, 1866), 1:180; Lowell H. Harrison, *The Antislavery Movement in Kentucky* (Lexington: University Press of Kentucky, 1978), 40–44.

26. Somerset v. Stuart [also spelled Stewart], 98 Eng. Rep. 499 (KB 1772); Commonwealth v. Aves, 35 Mass. 193 (1836); Jackson v. Bulloch, 12 Conn. 38 (1837); Paul Finkelman, *An Imperfect Union: Slavery, Federalism, and Comity* (Chapel Hill: University of North Carolina Press, 1981), 16–17, 106–7, 110–11; William M. Wiecek, *The Sources of Antislavery Constitutionalism in America, 1760–1848* (Ithaca: Cornell University Press, 1977), 28–39, 40–45.

27. Charles G. Finney, *Memoirs* (New York: A. S. Barnes, 1876), 324; Betty L. Fladeland, "James G. Birney's Anti-slavery Activities in Cincinnati, 1835–1837," *Bulletin of the Historical and Philosophical Society of Ohio* 9 (October 1951): 252; R. Parker, "Philosophy of Finney," 142–47.

28. *Statement of the Reasons Which Induced the Students of Lane Seminary to Dissolve Their Connection with That Institution* (1834), Pamphlet Collection, Cincinnati Historical Society; Writers' Program (Ohio), *Cincinnati: A Guide to the Queen City and Its Neighbors,* comp. Workers of the Writer's Program of the Work Projects Administration in the State of Ohio, sponsored by the City of Cincinnati (Cincinnati: Wiesen-Hart Press, 1943), 30–32; Victor B. Howard, *Conscience and Slavery: The Evangelistic Calvinist Domestic Missions, 1837–1861* (Kent, Ohio: Kent State University Press, 1990), 13–14; R. Parker, "Philosophy of Finney," 144–45.

29. Quoted in Wing, *Western Reserve,* 23–26.

30. Robert Samuel Fletcher, *A History of Oberlin College: From Its Foundation through the Civil War,* 2 vols. (New York: Arno Press, 1971), 1:533–35.

31. William G. Ballantine, *The Oberlin Jubilee, 1833–1883* (Oberlin, Ohio: E. J. Goodrich, 1883), 15–16, 62.

32. Connie Perdreau, *A Black History of Athens County and Ohio University* (Athens: Ohio University Press, 1988), 1–7.

33. Ohio Antislavery Society, *American Antislavery Almanac for 1841* (Cincinnati: Published for the OAS, 1841), 6–7. Bradley labored for five years and saved $855. He bought himself for $655.

34. An act for the support of common schools, 36 Laws of Ohio 21 (1838); William C. Cochran, "Ohio from 1802 to 1851: The Black Laws—The Three-Fifths Rule," in *The Western Reserve and the Fugitive Slave Law: A Prelude to the Civil War* (Cleveland: Western Reserve Historical Society, 1920), 59–61; T. Nelson, "Aliened American," 10–14.

35. C. Peter Ripley, *The Black Abolitionist Papers,* 5 vols. (Chapel Hill: University of North Carolina Press, 1985), 1:140–41; *People's Church Journal* (1831–1953), 1:54, CinHS.

36. Betty M. Culpepper, "The Negro and the Black Laws, 1803–1860" (master's thesis, Kent State University, 1965), 47; Wesley, *Negro Americans,* 10. Decades later, Oberlin College continued to produce African American leaders. William S. Scarborough earned a degree in 1875. Armed with a letter from the president of his alma mater, Scarborough, "a man of high character, good scholarship and successful experience," became a professor and the president of Wilberforce University. See James H. Fairchild to William S. Scarborough, February 10, 1875; C. H. Churchill to Scarborough, November 24, 1872; W. H. Rader to Scarborough, November 26, 1872; B. F. Lee to Scarborough, July 2, 1877, William S. Scarborough Papers, box 8, correspondences folder, 1872–79, Wilberforce University, Wilberforce, Ohio.

37. George Washington Williams, *History of the Negro Race in America, 1619–1880* (repr., New York: Arno Press, 1968), 171; T. Nelson, "Aliened American," 9. For an extensive discussion of the political activity of nineteenth-century blacks, see Howard H. Bell, "A Survey of the Negro Convention Movement, 1830–1861" (Ph.D. diss., Northwestern University, 1953).

38. *New York Colored American,* November 2, 1839; Malvin, *North into Freedom,* 65; Society of Friends, report, monthly meeting, Benjamin Hopkins, secretary, box 1, folder 3, 1813–39, OHS; *Philanthropist,* February 14, 1839; Culpepper, "Black Laws," 32–33; Erickson, "Color Line," 61–62.

39. *Ohio Senate Journal* 35 (35th Gen. Ass.), 143, 144, 148 (January 4, 1837), 36 (36th Gen. Ass.), 551–86 (March 3, 1838); Erickson, "Color Line," 150–51.

40. Williams v. Dirs. of Sch. Dist., 1 Wright 578, 578–80 (1834); Carter G. Woodson, ed., *The Mind of the Negro as Reflected in Letters Written during the Crisis, 1800–1860* (repr., New York: Russell and Russell, 1969), 276; James G. Birney, *The American Churches: Bulwarks of Slavery* (repr., Concord, N.H.: P. Pillsbury, 1885), 5.

41. Historians Earl Lewis and Heidi Ardizzone suggest the theory of a black individual being socially white in the Rhineland case decided in New York. See

Earl Lewis and Heidi Ardizzone, *Love on Trial: An American Scandal in Black and White* (New York: Norton, 2001).

42. Woodson, *Mind of the Negro*, 276; 26 Laws of Ohio 61 (1839); Culpepper, "Black Laws," 29–30; *Philanthropist*, March 30, 1838; Quillin, *Color Line*, 23; Malvin, *North into Freedom*, 8; Simeon D. Fess, ed., *Ohio: A Four-Volume Reference Library on the History of a Great State* (New York: Lewis Publishing, 1937), 1:268; OAS, "Black Laws," 38; Barbara A. Terzian, "'Effusions of Folly and Fanaticism': Race, Gender, and Constitution-Making in Ohio, 1802–1923" (Ph.D. diss., Ohio State University, 1999), 122.

43. Williams v. Dirs. of Sch. Dist., 1 Wright at 580.

44. Ibid., 578–80; 56 Laws of Ohio 120–21 (1859).

45. Williams v. Dirs. of Sch. Dist., 1 Wright at 578–80; Terzian, "Folly and Fanaticism," 123.

46. "Distribution of the Colored Population," *Washington National Era*, April 19, 1849; *New York Colored American*, November 2, 1839; Lenwood G. Davis, "Nineteenth-Century Blacks in Ohio: An Historical Overview," in *Blacks in Ohio History*, ed. Rubin F. Weston (Columbus: Ohio Historical Society, 1976), 8; William H. Siebert, *The Mysteries of Ohio's Underground Railroads* (Columbus: Long's College Book Co., 1951), 156, 160–64; Malvin, *North into Freedom*, 9–12.

47. Richard W. Pih, "Negro Self-Improvement Efforts in Ante-Bellum Cincinnati, 1836–1850," *Ohio History* 78 (Summer 1969): 182; *Cincinnati Business Directory*, 1840, 467–77; *Philanthropist*, December 28, 1842.

48. *Cincinnati Daily Gazette*, August 5, 1836.

49. Marius Robinson to Emily Robinson (wife), July (n.d.), 1837, Robinson Papers, folder 1, WRHS.

50. *Philanthropist*, November 25, 1836; Malvin, *North into Freedom*, 17–18.

51. OAS, *Memorial*, 6.

52. Ibid., 4–6; Harold B. Barth, *History of Columbiana County, Ohio*, 2 vols. (Topeka, Kan.: Historical Publishing, 1926), 1:118.

53. OAS, *Memorial*, 6–15; T. Nelson, "Aliened American," 9–10

54. James Buchanan, comp., *The Blacks of Pickaway County, Ohio, in the Nineteenth Century* (Bowie, Md.: Heritage Books, 1988), iii.

55. Pih, "Negro Self-Improvement," 182; L. Davis, "Nineteenth-Century Blacks," 6–7; Malvin, *North into Freedom*, 11–12; Culpepper, "Black Laws," 25; *Cincinnati Daily Atlas*, November 3, 1843.

56. OAS, *Memorial*, 6–15; OAS, *Report of the Third Anniversary of the Ohio Antislavery Society, Held in Granville, Licking County, Ohio, May 30, 1838* (Cincinnati: Ohio Antislavery Society, Samuel Alley, printer, 1838), 13–14.

57. John H. Dunn to Hiram Wilson, January 28, 1837, in OAS, *Memorial*, 31.

58. Allen Johnson, "The Constitutionality of the Fugitive Slave Acts," *Yale Law Journal* 31 (December 1921): 162–64; David Sheppard to Beverly Randolph, May 9, 1791, 5:301–2; Randolph to Thomas Mifflin, June 20, 1791, 5:329 and July 8, 1791, 5:340–341; and Mifflin to George Washington, July 18, 1791, 5:343, in *Calendar of Virginia State Papers and Other Manuscripts, Preserved in the Capitol at*

Richmond, arr. William P. Palmer, II vols. (Richmond: published by Virginia State Library, 1885); Paul Finkelman, "The Kidnapping of John Davis and the Adoption of the Fugitive Slave Law of 1793," *Journal of Southern History* 56 (August 1990): 397–422; Alfred H. Kelly, Winfred A. Harbison, and Herman Belz, *The American Constitution: Its Origins and Development* (New York: Norton, 1976), 246–49; William R. Leslie, "A Study in the Origins of Interstate Rendition: The Big Beaver Creek Murders," *American Historical Review* 57 (October 1951): 63–76.

59. An act to regulate black and mulatto persons, 2 Laws of Ohio 63 (1804), repr. in S. Middleton, *Black Laws*, 16.

60. An act to punish kidnapping, 22 Laws of Ohio 338 (1824); An act to prevent kidnapping, 29 Laws of Ohio 442 (1830).

61. An act to prevent the forcible abduction of the citizens of Ohio, 33 Laws of Ohio 5 (1835), repr. in Joseph R. Swan, ed., *Statutes of the State of Ohio of a General Nature* (Columbus: Samuel Medary, State Printer, 1841), 276.

62. *Philanthropist*, June 10, 1836.

63. *Philanthropist*, June 17, 1836; Benjamin F. Morris, *The Life of Thomas Morris: Pioneer and Long a Legislator of Ohio, and U.S. Senator from 1833–1839* (Cincinnati: Moore, Wilstach, Keys and Overend, 1856), 237–38.

64. Birney to Leavitt, January 10, 1842, in *Letters of James Gillespie Birney*, ed. Dwight L. Dumond, 2 vols. (New York: Appleton-Century, 1938), 2:651.

65. Wendell P. Dabney, *Cincinnati's Colored Citizens: Historical, Sociological and Biographical* (Cincinnati: Dabney Publishing, 1926), 63–64.

66. *Philanthropist*, June 17, 1836.

67. *Philanthropist*, June 26, 1836.

68. Joseph Vance, "Slave Stealing," November 18, 1837, p.1, Joseph Vance Papers, box 2, folder 3, OHS; "Eliza Jane Johnson," April 7, 1838, ibid., box 3, folder 4; *Philanthropist*, January 30, 1838, February 29, 1838.

69. Douglass to Garrison, September 17, 1847, in Woodson, *Mind of the Negro*, 482–83.

70. *Philanthropist*, January 11, 12, 13, 16, 30, December 4, 1838.

71. *Philanthropist*, February 19, 1839.

72. *Philanthropist*, February 13, November 27, 1838; *Journal of the House of Representatives of the State of Ohio*, 36 (36th Gen. Ass.), 3–9 (December 20, 1837); "Address to the Citizens of Ohio: The Black Laws," in Paul Finkelman, ed. *Statutes on Slavery: The Pamphlet Literature*, 2 vols. (New York: Garland, 1988), 2:104, 109; Society of Friends, report of the monthly meeting, Benjamin Hopkins, secretary, pp. 9, 16, 21, box 1, folder 3, 1813–39 CinHS.

73. *Ohio House Journal* 36 (36th Gen. Ass.), appendix no. 6, 3–9 (December 20, 1837); OAS, *Proceedings*, April 23–24, 1835 (New York, 1835), 6, 9–10. See also David Root to Nathaniel Wright, December 20, 1834, Nathaniel Wright Papers, no. 59, CinHS.

74. Indiana Yearly Meeting of Friends, *Address to the Citizens of the State of Ohio, Concerning What Are Called the Black Laws, Issued in Behalf of the Society of Friends of Indiana*

Yearly Meeting (Cincinnati: A. Pugh, 1848), 3–4; William A. Taylor, *Ohio Statesmen and Annals of Progress, from the Year 1788 to the Year 1900*, 2 vols. (Columbus: Press of Westbote, 1899), 138

75. OAS, *Memorial*, 3–4; *Ohio House Journal*, 33 (33rd Gen. Ass.), 787–92 (February 20, 1835).

76. *Ohio House Journal*, 37 (37th Gen. Ass.), 491 (February 19, 1839), 499 (February 19, 1839), 527 (February 21, 1839); Malvin, *North into Freedom*, 43–44; J. Reuben Sheeler, "The Struggle of the Negro for Freedom in Ohio," *Journal of Negro History* 31 (April 1946): 212; Richard Wade, "The Negro in Cincinnati, 1800–1830," *Journal of Negro History* 39 (January 1954): 47–53.

77. *Ohio Senate Journal*, 27 (27th Gen. Ass.), 63 (December 12, 1828), 30 (30th Gen. Ass.), 232–35 (January 13, 1832); Culpepper, "Black Laws," 52–56.

78. *Ohio House Journal*, 32 (32nd Gen. Ass.), 435–36, 437 (January 20, 1834); James Freeman Clarke, *Present Condition of the Free Colored People of the United States* (New York: American Anti-Slavery Society, 1859), 9; *Philanthropist*, January 12, 22, 1839; Weisenburger, *History of Ohio*, 3:381; Leon Litwack, *North of Slavery: The Negro in the Free States, 1790–1860* (Chicago: University of Chicago Press, 1961), 74.

79. *Ohio House Journal*, 37 (37th Gen. Ass.), 208 (January 11, 1839), quoted in *Philanthropist*, January 22, 1839.

80. *Ohio House Journal*, 37 (37th Gen. Ass.), 220–21 (February 14, 1839); Clarke, *Free People of Color*, 10–11, 379; *Philanthropist*, January 2, March 30, April 3, 1838; Malvin, *North into Freedom*, 43; *Philanthropist*, January 22, 29, 1839.

81. OAS, *Proceedings*, 6–10.

82. *Philanthropist*, January 16, February 3, 27, 30, April 3, 1838.

83. "Who Is Judge Wade?" *Washington National Era*, March 27, 1851; *Philanthropist*, January 5, 1838.

84. Joshua Giddings to Milton Sutliff, December 15, 1838, Milton Sutcliff Letters, folder 1, WRHS; *Philanthropist*, January 5, 13, 16, February 3, 5, 8, 13, 27, 1838; Roseboom, *History of Ohio*, 215; Daniel and Sally Hoit to Enoch P. Sherman, March 3, 1837, Ira Bean Letters, no. 10, CinHS; *Philanthropist*, January 19, 1839; Weisenburger, *History of Ohio*, 3:380, 383.

85. *Ohio Senate Journal*, 32 (32nd Gen. Ass.), 504–7 (January 27, 1834); "Report on Petitions to Repeal the Black Laws," December 4, 1837, repr. in S. Middleton, *Black Laws*, 49–50.

86. *Philanthropist*, February 6, 1838; OAS, *Third Anniversary*, 16–17.

87. *Ohio House Journal*, 38 (38th Gen. Ass.), appendix no. 6, 3 (February 20, 1840); "Report on Petitions," repr. in S. Middleton, *Black Laws*, 50–55.

88. Repr. in S. Middleton, *Black Laws*, 50–55.

89. Repr. in S. Middleton, *Black Laws*, 57–62; *Philanthropist*, February 19, 1839.

90. *Ohio Senate Journal*, 36 (36th Gen. Ass.), 446–50 (January 3, 1838); "Report on the Repeal of the Black Laws," February 7, 1838, repr. in S. Middleton, *Black Laws*, 85–86.

91. Repr. in S. Middleton, *Black Laws,* 86. John Malvin comments on an incident in which "a public, daylight murder of a Negro by a white man went unpunished, since only Negroes were available as witnesses." See Malvin, *North into Freedom,* 6.

92. "Report on the Repeal of the Black Laws," February 7, 1838, repr. in S. Middleton, *Black Laws,* 86–88; *Ohio Senate Journal,* 36 (36th Gen. Ass.), 551–86 (March 3, 1838).

93. Lawson v. Perry, 1 Wright 242 (1833).

94. Woods v. Green, 1 Wright 504 (1834).

95. Ibid.

96. *New York Colored American,* March 22, 1838.

97. Office of the American Anti-Slavery Society, A. B. Stanton to Edward Sturges, July 20, 1838, Sturges Family Papers, box 1, folder 2, OHS; *Cincinnati Daily Gazette,* August 4, 1836; *Louisville City Gazette,* August 1, 1836.

98. M. G. Williams to Erasmus Gest, July 14, August 2, 1836, Erasmus Gest Papers, Letter Book, vol. 1, OHS; Oran Follett to Thurlow Weed, December 4, 1837, Follett Papers, box 2, 49, CinHS.

99. Fladeland, "Birney's Activities," 254–57; Patrick Allen Folk, "The Queen City Mobs" (Ph.D. diss., University of Toledo, 1978), 89–91.

100. Alpha to Birney, July 1836, in J. Birney, *Letters,* 1:342; *Philanthropist,* July 15, 1836; *Cincinnati Daily Gazette,* July 20, 1836; Charles T. Greve, *Centennial History of Cincinnati and Representative Citizens,* 2 vols. (Chicago: Biographical Co., 1904), 1:598; W. Birney, *James Birney,* 249; *Liberty Hall and Cincinnati Gazette,* July 28, 1836; Folk, "Queen City Mobs," 86–87; *Cincinnati Daily Evening Post* (July 14, 1836; *Cincinnati Advertiser and Ohio Phoenix,* September 23, 1835.

101. Follett to Weed, December 4, 1837, Follett Papers, box 2, p. 49, CinHS; *Cincinnati Whig and Commercial Intelligencer,* July 16, 1836.

102. Birney to Tappan, July 22, 1836, in J. Birney, *Letters,* 1:345–47.

103. *Cincinnati Whig and Commercial Register,* July 18, 1836; *Philanthropist,* July 22, 1836.

104. *Liberty Hall and Cincinnati Gazette,* July 28, 1836; R. Carlyle Buley, *The Old Northwest: Pioneer Period, 1815–1840,* 2 vols. (Indianapolis: Indiana Historical Society, 1950), 2:621; W. Birney, *James Birney,* 242; *Cincinnati Daily Evening Post,* July 21, 1836.

105. Henry A. Ford and Kate B. Ford, *History of Cincinnati and Hamilton County* (Cleveland: S. B. Nelson, 1881), 86–87, 364–65; *Cincinnati Daily Evening Post,* August 2, 1836; Folk, "Queen City Mobs," 89–91; *Liberty Hall,* August 4, 1836; *Cincinnati Daily Gazette,* August 4, 5, 1836; *Cincinnati Whig and Commercial Intelligencer,* April 10, 1836; Pih, "Negro Self-Improvement," 179.

106. Birney to Tappan, August 10, 1836, in J. Birney, *Letters,* 1:349.

107. *Cincinnati Whig and Commercial Intelligencer,* August 1, 1836; W. Birney, *James Birney,* 245–47; Morris, *Thomas Morris,* 270–71.

108. *Liberty Hall and Cincinnati Gazette,* August 4, 1836.

109. *Cincinnati Daily Gazette,* August 3, 1836.

110. Augustus Wattles v. George Hartwell, February 15, 1838, transcript of case, CinHS.

111. Ibid.; Birney to Tappan, September 26, 1836; Gamaliel Bailey to Birney, May 27, 1837, both in J. Birney, *Letters,* 1:358, 385.

112. *Philanthropist,* January 9, June 19, 26, 1838; Birney to Lewis Tappan, July 17, 1838; Fladeland, "Birney's Activities," 146.

113. David Root to Nathaniel Wright, December 20, 1834, Nathaniel Wright Papers, no. 59, CinHS; Ohio Antislavery Society to Presbyterian Trustees, July 4, 1836, Sturges Family Papers, box 1, folder 2, OHS; *Cincinnati Daily Gazette,* March 2, 4, 1839; Weisenburger, *History of Ohio,* 332.

114. State v. Birney, 8 Ohio 230 (1837); Birney to Lewis Tappan, April 29, May 2, 1836, in J. Birney, *Letters,* 1:318–22, 324–25; Clarisson to Erasmus Gest, August 2, 1836, Gest Papers, OHS; Clay, *Life,* 1:180; Finkelman, *Imperfect Union,* 160–64; Frederick J. Blue, *Salmon P. Chase: A Life in Politics* (Kent, Ohio: Kent State University Press, 1987), 33–34.

115. Lawrence v. Matilda, reported in the *Daily Republican,* March 16, 1837; John Niven, *Salmon P. Chase: A Biography* (New York: Oxford University Press, 1995), 50–51; Finkelman, *Imperfect Union,* 160–64.

116. Salmon P. Chase, *Speech of Salmon P. Chase in the Case of the Colored Woman Matilda, Who Was Brought before the Court of Common Pleas in Hamilton County, Ohio, by Writ of Habeas Corpus March 11, 1837* (Cincinnati: Pugh and Dodd, 1837), 3–5, 7–35; Niven, *Salmon P. Chase,* 50–51; Finkelman, *Imperfect Union,* 160–64.

117. Niven, *Salmon P. Chase,* 56; Chase, *Address to the Citizens of Ohio,* 7, 9; Finkelman, *Imperfect Union,* 160–64.

118. Birney v. Ohio, 8 Ohio 230 (1837).

CHAPTER 5

1. I am using *progressive* to indicate that these Whigs were liberal-minded. Dr. Norton S. Townshend, who lived during this period, also used *progressive* to describe party men who favored reform. See Norton S. Townshend, "Salmon P. Chase," *Ohio History* 1 (September 1887): 119; Edgar Allan Holt, "Party Politics in Ohio, 1840–1850," *Ohio Archaeological and Historical Society Publications* 37 (July 1928): 440.

2. Jacob Bruce, "The Color Line in Ohio," Jacob Bruce Collection, Schomburg Center for Research in Black Culture, New York, 1–4; Emilius O. Randall and Daniel J. Ryan, *History of Ohio: The Rise and Progress of an American State,* 5 vols. (New York: Century History Co., 1912), 3:143.

3. The General Assembly later made token concessions to liberal Whigs, such as approving legislative reviews of repeal petitions in order to placate them. See Stephen Middleton, ed., *The Black Laws in the Old Northwest: A Documentary History* (Westport, Conn.: Greenwood, 1993), 49–110.

4. An act to regulate black and mulatto persons, 2 Laws of Ohio 63 (1804), repr. in S. Middleton, *Black Laws,* 15–17; *New York Colored American,* November 2, 1839; "The Ohio Black Laws," *Rochester North Star,* May 5, 1848; Holt, "Party

Politics," 38:134; Townshend, "Salmon P. Chase," 119; William Siebert, "Beginnings of the Underground Railroad in Ohio," *Ohio History* 56 (January 1947): 70–71.

5. Ohio Antislavery Society, *American Antislavery Almanac for 1838* (Cincinnati: Published for the OAS, 1838), 28; Paul Finkelman, *An Imperfect Union: Slavery, Federalism, and Comity* (Chapel Hill: University of North Carolina Press, 1981), 155; Richard Wade, *The Urban Frontier: The Rise and Fall of Western Cities, 1790–1830* (Cambridge, Mass.: Harvard University Press, 1967), 196–97, 220–21; James H. Fairchild, *The Underground Railroad,* Western Reserve Historical Society Tracts, vol. 4, no. 87 (Cleveland: Western Reserve Historical Society, 1895), 97–98.

6. McArthur won the election by 482 votes. Charles Thomas Hickok, "The Negro in Ohio, 1802–1870" (Ph.D. diss., Case Western Reserve University, 1896), 135; William Birney, *James G. Birney and His Times: The Genesis of the Republican Party with Some Account of Abolition Movements in the South before 1828* (New York: D. Appleton, 1890), 209; Donald J. Ratcliffe, "Captain James Riley and Antislavery Sentiment in Ohio, 1819–1824," *Ohio History* 81 (Spring 1972): 92–93.

7. *Cincinnati Whig,* December 21, 1836.

8. Russell H. Davis, *Black Americans in Cleveland from George Peake to Carl B. Stokes, 1796–1969* (Washington, D.C.: Associated Publishers, 1972), 9; David Brion Davis, *The Problem of Slavery in the Age of Revolution, 1770–1823* (Ithaca: Cornell University Press, 1975), 152–53; Ruhl Jacob Bartlett, "The Struggle for Statehood in Ohio," *Ohio Archaeological and Historical Quarterly* 32 (July 1923): 475; Leonard Erickson, "The Color Line in Ohio Public Schools, 1829–1890" (Ph.D. diss., Ohio State University, 1959), 15.

9. Congressman Samuel S. Cox went as far as saying that the ability to exclude blacks from Ohio was "compatible with our system of state sovereign and federal supremacy." See Samuel Sullivan Cox, *Emancipation and Its Results—Is Ohio to Be Africanized?* (Washington, D.C.: L. Towers, 1862), 7.

10. Finkelman, *Imperfect Union,* 164–67.

11. Francis Weisenburger, *History of the State of Ohio: The Passing of the Frontier, 1825–1850,* 3 vols. (Columbus: Ohio State Archaeological and Historical Society, 1941), 3:383; Erickson, "Color Line," 129–38.

12. "Who Is Judge Wade," *Washington National Era,* March 27, 1851; *Journal of the House of Representatives of the State of Ohio,* 33 (33rd Gen. Ass.), 787–92 (February 20, 1835), 868 (February 27, 1835); *Journal of the Senate of the State of Ohio,* 33 (33rd Gen. Ass.), 446–50 (January 23, 1835), 36 (36th Gen. Ass.), 551–86 (March 3, 1886); *Rochester North Star,* March 17, 1851; Hans L. Trefousse, *Benjamin Franklin Wade* (New York: Twayne Publishers, 1963), 31, 34, 41; Erickson, "Color Line," 150–51; Weisenburger, *History of Ohio,* 3:386.

13. *Philanthropist,* January 1, 16, February 6, 1838; Joshua Giddings to Milton Sutliff, December 15, 1838, Milton Sutliff Letters, container 1, folder 1, Western Reserve Historical Society (hereafter, WRHS), Cleveland; Eugene H. Roseboom, *A History of Ohio* (New York: Prentice Hall, 1934), 215; *Philanthropist,* January 5, 16, February 6, 1838, October 8, 1839.

14. *Cleveland Herald*, September 26, 1846; J. Reuben Sheeler, "The Struggle of the Negro for Freedom in Ohio," *Journal of Negro History* 31 (April 1946): 220.

15. *Rochester North Star*, June 2, 1818; *New York Colored American*, January 21, 1841.

16. Leon F. Litwack, "Free Blacks in the Antebellum North," in *America's Black Past: A Reader in Afro-American History*, ed. Eric Foner (New York: Harper and Row, 1970), 142–44.

17. *Cincinnati Post and Anti-Abolitionist*, January 22, 1842; *Philanthropist*, January 22, 1839; Weisenburger, *History of Ohio*, 3:381.

18. *Cincinnati Post and Anti-Abolitionist*, January 22, 1842; *Philanthropist*, January 22, 1839; Weisenburger, *History of Ohio*, 3:381.

19. *Ohio House Journal*, 37 (37th Gen. Ass.), 234 (January 15, 1839); *Ohio Senate Journal*, 35 (35th Gen. Ass.), 568, 569 (March 4, 1837); *Cincinnati Post and Anti-Abolitionist*, January 22, 1842; Weisenburger, *History of Ohio*, 3:382.

20. William B. McCord, ed., *History of Columbiana County, Ohio, and Representative Citizens* (Chicago: Biographical Publishing, 1905), 109–10, 150, 240, 401.

21. Greathouse v. Dunlap, 10 F. Cas. 1062, 1063 (C.C.D. Ohio 1843) (No. 5,742); letter from Joseph Vance, October, 5, 1838, Joseph Vance Papers, ms. 295, folder 3, Ohio Historical Society; *Freedom's Journal*, November 16, 1839.

22. *Philanthropist*, March 27, 1838; *Ohio State Journal*, October 17, 24, 1838; *Ohio Statesman*, October 10, 1838; *Cincinnati Gazette*, March 2, 4, 1839; Weisenburger, *History of Ohio*, 3:350, 382; Giddings to Sutliff, July 4, 1840, Sutliff Letters, container 1, folder 1, WRHS; Theodore Clark Smith, *The Liberty and Free Soil Parties in the Northwest* (New York: Russell and Russell, 1967), 30; Weisenburger, *History of Ohio*, 214.

23. James Walker, *Identity: The Black Experience in Canada* ([Toronto]: Ontario Educational Communications, 1979), 17–20; Robin W. Winks, "The Canadian Negro: A Historical Assessment: The Negro in the Canadian-American Relationship," part 1, *Journal of Negro History* 53 (October 1968): 291–92; William Renwick Riddell, "The Slave in Canada," *Journal of Negro History* 5 (July 1920): 320–21.

24. David Grimsted, *American Mobbing, 1828–1861: Toward Civil War* (New York: Oxford University Press, 1998), 34–37; T. Smith, *Liberty and Free Soil Parties*, 16.

25. *Philanthropist*, July 24, 1838.

26. *Dayton Transcript*, January 27, 1841.

27. *Philanthropist*, February 3, 10, 1841; *Cincinnati Daily Gazette*, January 29, 1841.

28. *Philanthropist*, February 10, 1841; *Cincinnati Daily Gazette*, January 29, 1841.

29. *Cleveland Herald*, September 26, 1846; Sheeler, "Struggle," 220.

30. Sheeler, "Struggle," 220–21; John Malvin, *North into Freedom: The Autobiography of John Malvin, 1795–1880*, ed. Allan Peskin (Cleveland: Press of Western Reserve University, 1966), 66–67.

31. T. Smith, *Liberty and Free Soil Parties*, 27–28; *Philanthropist*, October 28, 1836, May 19, 1837; W. Birney, *James Birney*, 232; John Niven, *Salmon P. Chase: A Biography* (New York: Oxford University Press, 1995), 61.

32. *Philanthropist*, June 11, 1839; *Ohio Statesman*, June 25, 1839.

33. Giddings to Oran Follett, November 14, 1844, June 16, 1845, "Selections from the Follett Papers I," *Historical and Philosophical Society of Ohio Quarterly* [hereafter, *HPSOQ*] 3 (April–June 1910): 20, 29; *Washington National Era*, September 30, 1847.

34. Daniel Walker Howe, *The Political Culture of the American Whigs* (Chicago: University of Chicago Press, 1979): 167–73; James McPherson, "The Fight against the Gag Rule: Joshua Leavitt and Antislavery Insurgency in the Whig Party, 1839–1842," *Journal of Negro History* 48 (July 1963): 179.

35. *Cincinnati Weekly Herald and Philanthropist*, October 14, 1846; Erickson, "Color Line," 169–70; Chase to Giddings, October 20, 1846, in *The Salmon P. Chase Papers*, ed. John Niven, 5 vols. (Kent, Ohio: Kent State University Press, 1993–98), 2:134.

36. Joshua Leavitt to James Birney, October 1, 1840, and Birney to Leavitt, January 10, 1842, *Letters of James Gillespie Birney*, ed. Dwight L. Dumond, 2 vols. (New York: Appleton-Century, 1938), 2:603–4, 645–46; *Philanthropist*, January 21, 1840; Holt, "Party Politics," 37:476–77, 38:134.

37. *Ohio State Journal*, February 5, 1845; *Ohio Senate Journal*, 43 (43rd Gen. Ass.), appendix, 26–27 (December 14, 1844); Leonard Erickson, "Politics and Repeal of Ohio's Black Laws, 1837–1849," *Ohio History* 82 (Summer–Autumn 1973): 155–59.

38. *Ohio House Journal*, 44 (44th Gen. Ass.), 476 (February 9, 1846), repr. in S. Middleton, *Black Laws*, 90–93.

39. *Report of the Committee on the Judiciary Relative to the Repeal of the Black Laws* (Columbus, n.d.), 3, repr. in S. Middleton, *Black Laws*, 92–94.

40. *Ohio Senate Journal*, 46 (46th Gen. Ass.), appendix, 185–98 (February 11, 1848); *Ohio House Journal*, 38 (38th Gen. Ass.), appendix no. 6, 3–4 (February 20, 1840); William A. Taylor, *Ohio Statesmen and Annals of Progress, from the Year 1788 to the Year 1900*, 2 vols. (Columbus: Press of Westbote, 1899), 1:199, 212, 214.

41. *Ohio House Journal*, 45 (45th Gen. Ass.), 96 (December 28, 1846), 46 (December 17, 1846); Ohio, *Executive Documents* (1845), vol. 10, part 1, no. 1, 2; Holt, "Party Politics," 38:134; Taylor, *Ohio Statesmen*, 199, 212, 214; Erickson, "Color Line," 167–68; *Ohio Statesman*, February 13, 21, 1845; *Ohio State Journal*, February 12, 19, 1845.

42. *Cincinnati Weekly Herald and Philanthropist*, September 30, October 14, 1846; *Cincinnati Weekly Herald*, February 17, 24, March 30, 1847.

43. *Ohio House Journal*, 37 (37th Gen. Ass.), 630 (March 4, 1839), 39 (39th Gen. Ass.), 1–6 (February 9, 1841); *Ohio Statesman*, December 29, 1841; Taylor, *Ohio Statesmen*, 199.

44. *New York Colored American*, April 17, 1841; *Ohio House Journal*, 40, Part II (40th Gen. Ass.), appendix 19, 1–7, 740 (March 3, 1842), 39 (39th Gen. Ass.), appendix C, 1–6 (February 9, 1841).

45. Jeffries v. Ankeny, 11 Ohio 372, 372–76 (1842); Charles H. Wesley, "The Participation of Negroes in Anti-slavery Political Parties," *Journal of Negro History* 29 (January 1944): 37–38.

46. State v. George, *Ohio Unreported Judicial Decisions Prior to 1823*, ed. Ervin H. Pollack (Indianapolis: Allen Smith, 1952), 185–87; Gray v. Ohio, 4 Ohio 353, 353–54 (1831); Barbara A. Terzian, "'Effusions of Folly and Fanaticism': Race, Gender, and Constitution-Making in Ohio, 1802–1923" (Ph.D. diss., Ohio State University, 1999), 118–21.

47. Jeffries v. Ankeny, 11 Ohio at 372–76.

48. Thacker v. Hawk, 11 Ohio 376, 376–86 (1842).

49. Jordan v. Smith, 14 Ohio 199, 201–2 (1846).

50. Ibid., 201–3.

51. Terzian, "Folly and Fanaticism," 134–35; Woodson v. State, 17 Ohio 161, 162–63, 168–69 (1848).

52. Jordan v. Smith, 14 Ohio 199, 199–204 (1846).

53. Chalmers v. Stewart, 11 Ohio 386, 387–88 (1842); Terzian, "Folly and Fanaticism," 132.

54. Giddings to Follett, July 12, 1844, November 18, 1844, and June 16, 1845, *HPSOQ*, 3:15–16, 20, 27; Erickson, "Color Line," 164.

55. Democratic Party (Ohio), *Proceedings of the Democratic State Convention of the State of Ohio: Held in Columbus on the Eighth of January, 1840—With an Address to the People of Ohio* (Columbus: S. and M. H. Medary, 1840), "Address to the People," 14.

56. *Cincinnati Weekly Herald and Philanthropist*, February 18, 1846; Weisenburger, *History of Ohio*, 210–11.

57. *Philanthropist*, January 28, September 29, 1840.

58. Clay to Thomas B. Stevenson, August 14, 1848, Thomas B. Stevenson Papers, box 1, vol. 1, p. 49a, CinHS.

59. James A. Briggs to Oran Follett, July 26, 1843, Follett to Briggs, August 9, 1843, Giddings to Follett, July 18, 27, 1843, *HPSOQ*, 3:9–13.

60. *Ohio State Journal*, October 24, 1838; also quoted in Weisenburger, *History of Ohio*, 350.

61. *Philanthropist*, December 16, 1846; *Ohio House Journal*, 43 (43rd Gen. Ass.), appendix, 17–24 (January 18, 1845), 44 (44th Gen. Ass.), appendix, 54–61 (January 9, 1846).

62. Giddings to Follett, June 6, November 14, 1844, *HPSOQ*, 3:17, 19–20; Erwin H. Price, "The Election of 1848 in Ohio," *Ohio Archeological and Historical Society Publications* 36 (April 1927): 194.

63. Weisenburger, *History of Ohio*, 218–22; Giddings to Sutliff, July 15, 1845, Sutliff Letters, container 1, folder 1, WRHS.

64. *Ohio Statesman*, May 29, 1844; also quoted in *Cincinnati Enquirer*, May 8, 1844, and Stephen E. Maizlish, "Ohio and the Rise of Sectional Politics," in *The Pursuit of Public Power: Political Culture in Ohio, 1787–1861*, ed. Jeffrey P. Brown and Andrew R. L. Cayton (Kent, Ohio: Kent State University Press, 1994), 120.

65. Quoted in Maizlish, "Sectional Politics," 120.

66. Quoted in Erickson, "Politics and Repeal," 157; *Ohio House Journal*, 41 (41st Gen. Ass.), 724–25 (February 24, 1843), 43 (43rd Gen. Ass.), 25–35 (January

18, 1845); *Ohio State Journal,* February 19, 1845; *Ohio Statesman,* February 7, 8, 13, 21, 1845.

67. Weisenburger, *History of Ohio,* 224; Daniel J. Ryan, *A History of Ohio, with Biographical Sketches of Her Governors and the Ordinance of 1787* (Columbus: A. H. Smythe, 1888), 144; Holt, "Party Politics," 38:135.

68. Holt, "Party Politics," 38:136–37; *Ohio State Journal,* October 8, 1846; *Ohio Statesman,* October 9, 1846; Weisenburger, *History of Ohio,* 224–27; Vernon L. Volpe, "The Ohio Election of 1838: A Study in the Historical Method," *Ohio History* 95 (Summer–Autumn 1986): 85.

69. Quoted in *Ohio State Journal,* August 20, 27, November 5, 1846; *Washington Daily Union,* November 2, 1846; *Cincinnati Daily Gazette,* January 1, 1846; Holt, "Party Politics," 38:135.

70. Holt, "Party Politics," 38:136; *Ohio State Journal,* September 26, October 3, 1846; Norton S. Townshend to Benjamin W. Arnett, April 8, 1886, in *Speeches and Papers by Ohio Men,* ed. Emilius O. Randall, 5 vols. (Columbus: n.p., 1903), 4:34; *Philanthropist,* December 30, 1846, January 13, 1847.

71. "Message of the Governor of Ohio," *Washington National Era,* December 30, 1847; Randall, *Speeches and Papers,* 4:34; also quoted in Ryan, *History of Ohio,* 144, and *Liberty Hall and Cincinnati Gazette,* November 16, 1848.

72. *Salem Anti-Slavery Bugle,* February 20, March 13, 1846; Erickson, "Politics and Repeal," 157.

73. Erickson, "Politics and Repeal," 157, 159; *Salem Anti-Slavery Bugle,* January 23, 1846; *Ohio Statesman,* September 9, October 7, 9, 1846; *Weekly Ohio State Journal,* September 16, November 10, 1846; *Cincinnati Weekly Herald and Philanthropist,* October 14, 1846.

74. *Washington National Era,* January 7, November 18, 1847.

75. *Washington National Era,* January 7, 1847.

76. *Ohio State Journal,* February 10, 1846; Thomas C. Nelson, "The Aliened American: The Free Negro in Ohio" (master's thesis, University of Toledo, 1969), 58–59.

77. *Ohio State Journal,* February 10, 1846; Holt, "Party Politics," 38:136; Erickson, "Politics and Repeal," 160; Townshend to Arnett, April 8, 1886, in Randall, *Speeches and Papers,* 4:34.

78. *Ohio State Journal,* February 10, 1846; T. Nelson, "Aliened American," 60.

79. *Ohio House Journal,* 45 (45th Gen. Ass.), 123–27, 135–36 (January 2, 1847); T. Nelson, "Aliened American," 65; Holt, "Party Politics," 38:171–72; Hal A. Bochin, "Tom Corwin's Speech against the Mexican War: Courageous but Misunderstood," *Ohio History* 90 (Winter 1981): 48; Price, "Election of 1848," 193.

80. *Xenia Torch-Light,* May 21, 28, 1846; Holt, "Party Politics," 38:151; *Ohio State Journal,* September 11, 1847.

81. Anthony Gene Carey, "The Second Party System Collapses: The 1853 Maine Law Campaign in Ohio," *Ohio History* 100 (Summer–Autumn 1991): 130; D. Howe, *American Whigs,* 146–47; Victor B. Howard, *Conscience and Slavery: The Evan-*

gelistic Calvinist Domestic Missions, 1837–1861 (Kent, Ohio: Kent State University Press), 77–80.

82. Quoted in Stephen E. Maizlish, The Triumph of Sectionalism: The Transformation of Ohio Politics, 1844–1856 (Kent, Ohio: Kent State University Press, 1983), 102.

83. David M. Potter, The Impending Crisis, 1848–1861 (New York: Harper and Row, 1976), 96–105, 107–12; Don E. Fehrenbacher, "Lincoln, Douglas, and the 'Freeport Question,'" American Historical Review 66 (April 1961): 606; Reinhard H. Luthin, "Some Demagogues in American History," American Historical Review 57 (October 1951): 30–35.

84. Quoted in Maizlish, Triumph of Sectionalism, 102.

85. Eric Foner, Free Soil, Free Labor, Free Men: The Ideology of the Republican Party before the Civil War (New York: Oxford University Press, 1970), 190; Joshua Giddings to Follett, July 26, 1847, Oran Follett Papers, box 2, p. 137, CinHS; Thomas Corwin to Bebb, June 28, 1847, Thomas Corwin, VFM 3569 (1847), OHS; Corwin to Briggs, August 8, 1848, Thomas Corwin, VFM 1397, OHS; John McLean to John Teesdale, September 26 and 27, 1846, box 1, folder 1, ms. 39, John McLean Papers, OHS; National Press and Cincinnati Weekly Herald, May 5, 1847; Weisenburger, History of Ohio, 218–19; Niven, Salmon P. Chase, 62.

86. T. Smith, Liberty and Free Soil Parties, 98–104; Lysander Spooner, The Unconstitutionality of Slavery (Boston: B. Marsh, 1845); Maizlish, "Sectional Politics," 128.

87. Quoted in Maizlish, "Sectional Politics," 128–29; Washington National Era, August 2, 1849; Eric Foner, "Politics and Prejudice: The Free Soil Party and the Negro, 1849–1852," Journal of Negro History 50 (October 1965): 239–40.

88. Benjamin Bofinger to Chase, November 4, 1844, Chase Papers, HSP; "The Free Soil Men of Ohio," Washington National Era, February 8, 1849.

89. Corwin to Stevenson, July 25, 1849, vol. 1, 85b; August 21, 1849, vol. 1, 87a; August 26, 1849, vol. 1, 87b, Stevenson Papers, CinHS.

90. "Colored National Convention at Cleveland," Rochester North Star, September 15, 1848; Howard H. Bell, "National Negro Conventions of the Middle 1840's: Moral Suasion vs. Political Action," Journal of Negro History 42 (October 1957): 248, 249, 253; National Emigration Convention of Colored People, Proceedings, August 24–26, 1854, Cleveland (Pittsburgh: A. A. Anderson, 1854); Howard, Conscience and Slavery, 32–33.

91. Howard B. Bell, "The National Negro Convention, 1848," Ohio Historical Quarterly 67 (October 1958): 356–57; D. Howe, American Whigs, 17; Wesley, "Participation of Negroes," 35–36; "The Whig Party in the South," William and Mary Quarterly 23 (July 1914): 1–5; Charles Grier Sellers Jr., "Who Were the Southern Whigs?" American Historical Review 59 (January 1954).

92. Wesley, "Participation of Negroes," 37.

93. D. Howe, American Whigs, 18; E. Foner, "Politics and Prejudice," 241; Akron Free Democratic Standard, January 10, 1850.

94. Philip S. Foner and George E. Walker, eds., Proceedings of the Black State Conventions, 1840–1865, 2 vols. (Philadelphia: Temple University Press, 1979–80), 2:218–19, 229.

95. *Liberty Hall and Cincinnati Gazette,* January 4, 1849; *Cincinnati Weekly Globe,* November 23, 1848, January 4, 1849; *Philanthropist,* December 16, 1846.

96. *Cincinnati Daily Gazette,* February 2, 1849; *Ohio State Journal,* January 13, 1849; Malvin, *North into Freedom,* 28–29; Richard C. Minor, "James Preston Poindexter: Elder Statesman of Columbus," *Ohio Historical Quarterly* 56 (July 1947): 267–76; William J. Simmons, *Men of Mark: Eminent, Progressive and Rising* (Cleveland: G. M. Rewell, 1887), 394–403, 978–89; William H. Siebert, *The Mysteries of Ohio's Underground Railroads* (Columbus: Long's College Book Co., 1951), 160–61.

97. William H. Seward, *The Works of William H. Seward,* ed. George E. Baker, 5 vols. (New York: Houghton, Mifflin, 1884–89), 3:301.

98. *Rochester North Star,* November 3, 1848; E. Foner, "Politics and Prejudice," 241–42.

99. *Rochester North Star,* May 18, 1849.

100. David Walker, *David Walker's Appeal, in Four Articles, together with a Preamble, to the Coloured Citizens of the World, but in Particular, and Very Expressly, to Those of the United States of America* (Boston: D. Walker, 1830); *An Address to the State Convention of Ohio from the State Convention of Colored Men* (Columbus: E. Glover, 1851), 18; Howard H. Bell, "Expressions of Negro Militancy in the North, 1840–1860," *Journal of Negro History* 45 (January 1960): 13.

101. *Washington National Era,* January 7, 1847.

102. The Colored Citizens of Ohio, *Minutes of the State Convention, of the Colored Citizens of Ohio, Convened at Columbus, January 15, 16, 17, 18* (Oberlin, Ohio: E. Glover, Printer, 1851), 5–13, 17–25; *Liberty Hall and Cincinnati Gazette,* January 25, 1849; Sheeler, "Struggle," 222–23; *Washington National Era,* February 8, 1849.

103. *Washington National Era,* February 8, 1849; *Rochester North Star,* March 23, 26, 1849.

104. State Convention of Colored Men, *Address to the Constitutional Convention,* 17–25; Sheeler, "Struggle," 223.

105. *Rochester North Star,* December 1, 1848; James J. Burns, *Educational History of Ohio: A History of Its Progress since the Formation of the State, Together with the Portraits and Biographies of Past and Present State Officials* (Columbus: Historical Publications, 1905), 350; William A. Joiner, comp., *A Half Century of Freedom of the Negro in Ohio* (Xenia, Ohio: Smith Adv. Co., 1915; repr. Freeport, N.Y.: Books for Libraries Press, 1972), 41–43.

106. Quoted in *Washington National Era,* February 8, 1849; E. Foner, "Politics and Prejudice," 241.

107. *Liberty Hall and Cincinnati Gazette,* October 19, 26, November 11, 1848; *Daily Cincinnati Gazette,* October 6, 7, 1848; Michael F. Holt, *The Rise and Fall of the American Whig Party: Jacksonian Politics and the Onset of the Civil War* (New York: Oxford University Press, 1999), 399.

108. *Rochester North Star,* January 21, February 25, 1848; *Washington National Era,* February 4, 1847.

109. *Cincinnati Weekly Globe,* October 25, 1848; *Liberty Hall and Cincinnati Gazette,* November 30, December 21, 1848.

110. *Washington National Era*, November 9, 1848; *Rochester North Star*, October 13, 1848; Thomas Matijasic, "The Reaction of the Ohio General Assembly to the Fugitive Slave Law of 1850," *Northwest Ohio Quarterly* 55 (Spring 1982–83): 40–41; *Ohio Repository*, December 9, 1850.

111. *Cincinnati Weekly Globe*, October 25, 1848; *Liberty Hall and Cincinnati Gazette*, November 30, December 21, 1848; Seward to Follett, December 28, 1848, *HPSOQ*, 4:35.

112. Townshend, "Salmon P. Chase," 118–20; *Washington National Era*, November 9, 1848; *Liberty Hall and Cincinnati Gazette*, October 19, 26, 1848; T. Smith, *Liberty and Free Soil Parties*, 163; Benjamin H. Pershing, "Membership in the General Assembly of Ohio," *Ohio Archaeological and Historical Publications* 40 (April 1931): 232, 242; Edgar Allen Holt, "The Reapportionment Bill of February, 1848," *Ohio Archaeological and Historical Publications* 38 (January 1930): 319–53.

113. Chase to Stanley Matthews, December 23, 1848, in "Some Letters of Salmon P. Chase," *American Historical Review* 34 (April 1929): 536–37; *Washington National Era*, October 25, 1849.

114. Holt, *American Whig Party*, 398–99; Niven, *Salmon P. Chase*, 116. Chase discussed the 1849 Ohio election in his speech at a Republican political rally in 1855. See Salmon P. Chase, *Speech of the Honorable Salmon P. Chase, Delivered at the Republican Mass Meeting in Cincinnati, August 21, 1855* (Columbus: Ohio State Journal, 1855), 4.

115. Townshend, "Salmon P. Chase," 120; *Washington National Era*, February 22, 1849; Chase to Stanley Matthews, January 13, 1849, in "Some Letters of Salmon P. Chase," 538; Holt, *American Whig Party*, 400–402.

116. Chase to August Belmont, May 30, 1868, in Chase, *Papers*, 5:xxi, 221; Chase, *Speech of the Honorable Salmon P. Chase*, 4; Townshend to Arnett, April 8, 1886, in Randall, *Speeches and Papers*, 4:32–33.

117. Chase to Matthews, December 23, 1848, in "Some Letters of Salmon P. Chase," 536–37; Chase to E. S. Hamlin, January 12, 1850, in *Diary and Correspondence of Salmon P. Chase*, 2 vols. (reprint of the 1903 Annual Report of the American Historical Association; New York: Da Capo Press, 1971), 2:195–97.

118. *Rochester North Star*, January 26, 1849; Wesley, "Participation of Negroes," 59; Leo Alilunas, "Fugitive Slave Cases in Ohio Prior to 1850," *Ohio Archaeological and Historical Quarterly* 49 (April 1940): 163–65.

119. An act to provide for the establishment of common schools for the education of children of black and mulatto persons, and to amend an act entitled "an act for the support and better regulation of common schools, and to create permanently the office of superintendent," passed March 7, 1838, and the acts amendatory thereto, 46 Laws of Ohio 81, 82–83 (1848); An act to authorize the establishment of separate schools for the education of colored children, and for other purposes, 47 Laws of Ohio 17, 18 (1849); *Rochester North Star*, February 9, 16, May 25, 1849; *Cincinnati Weekly Globe*, December 6, 20, 1848; *Liberty Hall and Cincinnati Gazette*, November 2, 1848; *Daily Cincinnati Gazette*, October 7, 1848; William C. Cochran, "Ohio from 1802 to 1851: The Black Laws—The Three-Fifths Rule," in *The Western Reserve and the Fugitive Slave Law: A Prelude to the Civil War*

(Cleveland: Western Reserve Historical Society, 1920), 57; Alilunas, "Fugitive Slaves," 163, 164; Chase to Caldwell, July 25, 1849, Chase Papers, CinHS; Jere A. Brown's speech appeared in Benjamin W. Arnett, *The Black Laws! Speeches of Honorable B. W. Arnett of Greene County, and Honorable J. A. Brown of Cuyahoga County, in the Ohio House of Representatives, March 10, 1886* (Columbus: Ohio State Journal, 1886), 32–33; Erickson, "Color Line," 172; T. Smith, *Liberty and Free Soil Parties*, 163–75; A. G. Riddle, "Recollections of the Forty-seventh General Assembly of Ohio, 1847–1848," *Magazine of Western History* 6 (August 1887): 341–51; Norton S. Townshend, "The Forty-seventh General Assembly—Comments on Mr. Riddle's Paper," *Magazine of Western History* 6 (October 1887): 623–28.

120. *Speech of Senator Salmon P. Chase, Delivered at Toledo, May 30, 1851, Before a Mass Convention of the Democracy of Northwestern Ohio*, Pamphlet Collection, CinHS, 1; *Speech of the Honorable Salmon P. Chase*, August 21, 1855, 4–5.

121. *Washington National Era*, May 3, 1849; "Letter from Samuel Lewis," July 16, 1849, in *Washington National Era*, August 2, 1849; John F. Cunningham, "An Early American Crusader: Norton Strange Townshend," *Ohio Archeological and Historical Society Publications* 53 (October–December 1944): 359–60.

122. *Rochester North Star*, June 29, July 6, 1849.

123. *Rochester North Star*, March 2, 23, 1849.

124. *Rochester North Star*, March 9, 1849.

125. *Rochester North Star*, March 23, 1849.

126. *Rochester North Star*, March 2, 23, 1849; An act to prescribe the duties of judges of elections in certain cases, and preserve the purity of elections, 56 Laws of Ohio 120, 121 (1859); *Washington National Era*, September 16, 1852, January 13, 1853, repr. in S. Middleton, *Black Laws*, 133–34.

127. *Washington National Era*, February 8, 22, 1849; *Rochester North Star*, March 23, 1849.

128. State v. Cincinnati, 19 Ohio 178, 179–83, 188–91, 196–97 (1850).

CHAPTER 6

1. Northwest Ordinance of 1787, art. VI, 1 Stat. 51, 53; Fugitive Slave Act of 1793, 1 Stat. 302; also quoted in *The Public Statutes at Large of the State of Ohio: From the Close of Chase's Statutes, February, 1833, to the Present Time, with References to the Judicial Decisions Construing Those Statutes, and a Supplement Containing All Laws Passed Prior to February 1833, Which Are Now in Force*, ed. Maskell E. Curwen, 4 vols. (Cincinnati: Maskell E. Curwen, 1853–53), 2:93–95.

2. Fugitive Slave Act of 1793, 1 Stat. 302; Paul Finkelman, "Fugitive Slaves, Midwestern Racial Tolerance, and the Value of 'Justice Delayed,'" *Iowa Law Review* 78 (October 1992): 105; Jordan M. Smith, "The Federal Courts and the Black Man in America, 1800–1883: A Study of Judicial Policy Making" (Ph.D. diss., University of North Carolina, 1977), 144–49; Charles August Banker, "Salmon P. Chase, Legal Counsel for Fugitive Slaves: Antislavery Ideology as a Lawyer's Creation" (master's thesis, Rice University, 1986), 52–54.

3. An act to regulate black and mulatto persons, 2 Laws of Ohio 63 (1804); An act to amend the last named act "An act to regulate black and mulatto persons," 5 Laws of Ohio 53 (1807), repr. in *The Black Laws in the Old Northwest: A Documentary History*, ed. Stephen Middleton (Westport, Conn.: Greenwood, 1993),15–18.

4. Charles T. Greve, *Centennial History of Cincinnati and Representative Citizens*, 2 vols. (Chicago: Biographical, 1904), 1:598.

5. Proceedings of Brooke Court on the Trial of the Negro Woman Slave Jane, Daniel L. Hylton, clerk of the executive council, October 22, 1808, Executive Papers, Governor William H. Cabell, box 157, folder January 1808, Virginia State Library and Archives (hereafter, VSLA), Richmond; Bell to Samuel Huntington, February 24, 1810, Samuel Huntington Papers, box 1, folder 8, Ohio Historical Society; William H. Smith, "The First Fugitive Slave Case of Record in Ohio," *Senate Miscellaneous Documents*, vol. 4, no. 104, 53d Cong., 2d sess., 94; Charles B. Galbreath, *History of Ohio*, 5 vols. (Chicago: American Historical Society, 1925), 1:173–74

6. Executive Papers of William H. Cabell, November 14, 1808, box 157, folder, November 1808, VSLA. See also trial of James, January 4, 1808, trial of Will, December 21, 1807, and trial of Reuben, January 25, 1808, Executive Papers of Cabell, box 152, folder January 1808, VSLA; John Atkinson to A. Douglas, re trial of Tom, John Tyler Papers, box 164, folder 1–10, 1810, VSLA.

7. Moses Congleton to Cabell, December 23, 1808, Executive Papers of Cabell, box 158, folder December 12–31, 1808, VSLA; Tyler to Jacob Beeson, June 23, 1810, Executive Letter Book, 46, VSLA; Bell to Huntington, February 24, 1810, Huntington Papers, VSLA; W. Smith, "First Fugitive Slave," 96–97; Galbreath, *History of Ohio*, 1:175.

8. Bell to Huntington, February 24, 1810, Huntington Papers, VSLA; Tyler to Beeson, April 26, 1810, Executive Letter Book, 46, VSLA; Beeson to Tyler, January 31, 1810, Tyler Papers, VSLA; W. Smith, "First Fugitive Slave," 96–97; Galbreath, *History of Ohio*, 1:175.

9. Bell to Huntington, February 24, 1810, Huntington to John Tyler, February 5, 1810, Tyler to Huntington, February 5, 1810, J. W. Sam to Huntington, March 7, 1810, Huntington Papers, VSLA; Tyler to Huntington, April 26, 1810, Executive Letter Book, 45, VSLA; W. Smith, "First Fugitive Slave," 98–99; Galbreath, *History of Ohio*, 1:175.

10. Ward to Tyler, December 12, 17, 1808, Executive Papers of Cabell, box 158, folder December 12–31, 1808, VSLA.

11. Sally E. Hadden, *Slave Patrols: Law and Violence in Virginia and the Carolinas* (Cambridge, Mass.: Harvard University Press, 2001).

12. VFM ms. 2626, OHS.

13. Prigg v. Pennsylvania, 41 U.S. (16 Pet.) 539 (1842); Finkelman, "Slaves, Tolerance," 91; Paul Finkelman, *Slavery and the Founders: Race and Liberty in the Age of Jefferson*, 2d ed. (Armonk, N.Y.: M. E. Sharpe, 2001).

14. Alfred Kelly, *The American Constitution: Its Origins and Development* (New York: Norton, 1976), 246–48.

15. An act to regulate black and mulatto persons, 2 Laws of Ohio 63 (1804); An act to amend the last named act, "an act to regulate black and mulatto persons," 5 Laws of Ohio 53 (1807), repr. in S. Middleton, *Black Laws*, 15–18.

16. Edward Coles to Jeremiah Morrow, April 10, 1823, Jeremiah Morrow Papers, mic. roll 1, box 1, folder 2, Ohio Historical Society.

17. The resolution of the Ohio legislature is quoted in Emmett D. Preston, "The Fugitive Slave Acts in Ohio," *Journal of Negro History* 28 (October 1943): 426.

18. Quoted in Samuel A'Court Ashe, *History of North Carolina*, 7 vols. (Raleigh: C. L. Van Noppen, 1925), 2:302; *North Carolina House Journal*, 100; *House Journal*, "Black Laws," 5.

19. Ohio governor, 1832–1836 (Robert Lucas), *Report No. 1, Annual Message of Governor Lucas, with Accompanying Documents, Dec. 6, 1836*, in *Reports Including Messages, and Other Communications, Made to the Thirty-fifth General Assembly of the State of Ohio* (Columbus: James B. Gardiner, 1836), 1:23. This imprint is also available at various libraries, including the Ohio Historical Society. See Robert Lucas, *Message of the Governor of Ohio, to the Thirty-fourth General Assembly, Begun and Held in the City of Columbus, Monday, December 7, 1835* (Columbus: James B. Gardiner, Printer to the State, 1835), 1–17.

20. Ohio governor, 1836–1838 (Joseph Vance), *Report No. 28, Annual Message of Governor Vance, Dec. 25, 1837*, in *Documents Including Messages, and Other Communications, Made to the Thirty-sixth General Assembly of the State of Ohio* (Columbus: Samuel Medary, 1837), 2:3–4.

21. An Act to regulate black and mulatto persons, 2 Laws of Ohio 63 (1804); An Act to amend the last named act "An Act to regulate black and mulatto persons," 5 Laws of Ohio 53 (1807), repr. in S. Middleton, *Black Laws*, 16–18.

22. James Walker, *Identity: The Black Experience in Canada* ([Toronto]: Ontario Educational Communications, 1979), 17–20; Martin Van Buren to William T. Barry, August 12, 1829, James Taylor Papers, Manuscript Department, Filson Club Historical Society, Louisville, Ky.; Resolutions, requesting the attention of the General Government to the subject of slaves belonging to citizens of the United States, who have or may have escaped into Canada, 32 Ky. Acts 487, 488 (1823); James G. Birney to Lewis Tappan, February 27, 1837, in James Birney, *Letters of James Gillespie Birney, 1831–1857*, ed. Dwight L. Dumond, 2 vols. (New York: D. Appleton-Century, 1938), 1:376.

23. Quoted in J. Walker, *Identity*, 18; Robin Winks, *The Blacks in Canada: A History* (New Haven: Yale University Press, 1971), 168–71.

24. Resolutions, 32 Ky. Acts 487 (1823); Ohio Antislavery Society, *American Antislavery Almanac for 1838* (Cincinnati: Published for the OAS, 1838), 20; Christy, *African Colonization*, 20.

25. James Clark, governor of Kentucky, to governor of Ohio, October 18, 1837, VFM 2399, OHS; William Renwick Riddell, "The Slave in Canada," *Journal of Negro History* 5 (July 1920): 335–36.

26. Stephen Middleton, "Cincinnati and the Fight for the Law of Freedom in Ohio, 1830–1856," *Locus: An Historical Journal of Regional Perspectives* 4 (Fall 1991):

66–67; *Liberty Hall and Cincinnati Gazette,* November 10, 1836, January 11, 1838; *Philanthropist,* November 11, 18, 1836; *Cincinnati Daily Gazette,* January 18, 1838.

27. *Liberty Hall and Cincinnati Gazette,* November 10, 1836; *Philanthropist,* November 11, 1836; *Cincinnati Daily Gazette,* January 11, 18, 1838.

28. Somerset v. Stuart [also spelled Stewart], 98 Eng. Rep. 499 (KB 1772); Paul Finkelman, *An Imperfect Union: Slavery, Federalism, and Comity* (Chapel Hill: University of North Carolina Press, 1981), 34–40; William M. Wiecek, *The Sources of Antislavery Constitutionalism in America, 1760–1848* (Ithaca: Cornell University Press, 1977), 28–39, 40–45; A. Leon Higginbotham Jr., *In the Matter of Color: The Colonial Period,* vol. 1 of Race and the American Legal Process (New York: Oxford University Press, 1978), 333–68.

29. Louise v. Marot, 8 La. 475 (1835), 9 La. 473 (1836); Phillis v. Gentin, 9 La. 208 (1836); Smith v. Smith, 13 La. 441 (1839); *Philanthropist,* November 11, 18, 1836; *Liberty Hall and Cincinnati Gazette,* January 11, 1838; William M. Wiecek, "Somerset: Lord Mansfield and the Legitimacy of Slavery in the Anglo-American World," *University of Chicago Law Review* 42 (Fall 1974): 86–146; Judith Kelleher Schafer, *Slavery, the Civil Law, and the Supreme Court of Louisiana* (Baton Rouge: Louisiana State University Press, 1994).

30. Rankin v. Lydia, 9 Ky. 467 (1820); Finkelman, *Imperfect Union,* 190–98; William C. Cochran, "Ohio from 1802 to 1851: The Black Laws—The Three Fifths Rule," in *The Western Reserve and the Fugitive Slave Law: A Prelude to the Civil War* (Cleveland: Western Reserve Historical Society, 1920), 72–74.

31. Frederick J. Blue, *Salmon P. Chase: A Life in Politics* (Kent, Ohio: Kent State University Press, 1987), 33–34; Finkelman, *Imperfect Union,* 163–64; William Birney, *James G. Birney and His Times: The Genesis of the Republican Party with Some Account of Abolition Movements in the South before 1828* (New York: D. Appleton, 1890), 240; Greve, *Centennial History,* 1:598; Ohio Antislavery Society, *Narrative of the Late Riotous Proceedings against the Liberty of the Press in Cincinnati* (Cincinnati: Ohio Antislavery Society, 1836), 12.

32. *Philanthropist,* March 17, 1837, May 19, 1841; *Daily Cincinnati Republican and Commercial Register,* March 28, 1837; Charles B. Galbreath, "Ohio's Fugitive Slave Law," *Ohio Archaeological and Historical Quarterly* 34 (April 1925): 216–17.

33. *Covington (Ky.) Daily News,* February 9, 1837.

34. Letter from Governor Wilson Shannon, January 19, 1838, Wilson Shannon Collection, MIC 999, roll 10, OHS.

35. *Philanthropist,* August 14, 1838.

36. *Philanthropist,* September 25, 1838.

37. *Niles' National Register,* September 14, 1839; Galbreath, *History of Ohio,* 1:233.

38. *Philanthropist,* January 8, 1839.

39. Ralph, a Colored Man v. Montgomery, reported in the *Philanthropist,* August 6, 1839.

40. *Philanthropist,* March 20, 1838.

41. Ibid.

42. Resolutions, 32 Ky. Acts 487 (1823); OAS, *Antislavery Almanac,* (1838), 20.

43. Martin Van Buren to William T. Barry, August 12, 1829, James Taylor Papers, Manuscript Department, Filson Club Historical Society, Louisville, Ky.; *Journal of the House of Representatives of the United States,* 20th Cong., 2d sess., 29 (December 5, 1828); Resolutions, 32 Ky. Acts 487 (1823); Samuel Gridley Howe, *The Refugees from Slavery in Canada West* (Boston: Wright and Potter, 1864), 12–14.

44. James T. Morehead and John S. Smith to Gov. Charles A. Wickliffe, Report from the Commissioners to Ohio, *Kentucky House Journal,* 103 (November 20, 1839) (volumes of the Kentucky *House Journal* published in the nineteenth century were not always numbered but were arranged chronologically by date of publication); Benjamin F. Morris, *The Life of Thomas Morris: Pioneer and Long a Legislator of Ohio, and U.S. Senator from 1833–1839* (Cincinnati: Moore, Wilstach, Keys and Overend, 1856), 237–38.

45. Morehead and Smith to Wilson Shannon, January 26, 1839, *Kentucky House Journal,* 112; N. S. Townshend, "Black Laws of 1807," in *Speeches and Papers by Ohio Men,* ed. Emilius O. Randall, 5 vols. (Columbus: n.p., 1903), 5:33; Beverly W. Bond Jr., *The Civilization of the Old Northwest: A Study of Political, Social, and Economic Development, 1788–1812* (New York: Macmillan, 1934), 136; *Philanthropist,* January 22, March 5, 1839.

46. Wilson Shannon, "To the General Assembly of the State of Ohio," January 21, 1839, Wilson Shannon Papers, microfilm, roll 11, OHS; James S. Morehead and John S. Smith to Gov. Charles A. Wickliffe, Report from the Commissioners to Ohio, 103; Asa Earl Martin, *The Antislavery Movement in Kentucky* (Louisville, Ky.: Standard Printing Co., 1918), 110; Emilius O. Randall and Daniel J. Ryan, *History of Ohio: The Rise and Progress of an American State* (New York: Century History Co., 1912), 93–94; Simeon D. Fess, ed. *Ohio: A Four-Volume Reference Library on the History of a Great State,* 5 vols. (New York: Lewis Publishing, 1937), 4:95; B. Morris, *Thomas Morris,* 237–38; Edgar Allen Holt, "Party Politics in Ohio, 1840–1850," *Ohio Archeological and Historical Society Publications* 37 (July 1928): 203; Galbreath, "Fugitive Slave Law," 217; Society of Friends, *Address to the Citizens of the State of Ohio, Concerning What Are Called the Black Laws, Issued in Behalf of the Society of Friends of Indiana Yearly Meeting* (Cincinnati: A. Pugh, 1848),7.

47. An act relating to fugitives from labor or service from other states, 37 Laws of Ohio 38 (1839), repr. in S. Middleton, *Black Laws,* 111–16; Fugitive Slave Act of 1793, 1 Stat. 302, 302–5; OAS, *Antislavery Almanac* (1838), 27–28; Carter G. Woodson, *The Mind of the Negro as Reflected in Letters Written during the Crisis, 1800–1860* (repr., New York: Russell and Russell, 1969), 483; B. Morris, *Thomas Morris,* 237–38.

48. B. Morris, *Thomas Morris,* 237–38.

49. *Philanthropist,* November 20, 27, 1838, October 22, 1839.

50. B. Morris, *Thomas Morris,* 123–24.

51. An act relating to fugitives from labor or service from other states, 37 Laws of Ohio 38 (1839), repr. in S. Middleton, *Black Laws,* 111–16; Joseph R. Swan, ed., *Statutes of the State of Ohio of a General Nature* (Columbus: Samuel Medary, State Printer, 1841), 595–600; Fugitive Slave Act of 1793, 1 Stat. 302, 302–5;

OAS, *Antislavery Almanac* (1838), 27–28; Woodson, *Mind of the Negro*, 483; B. Morris, *Thomas Morris*, 237–38; Preston, "Fugitive Slave Acts," 427.

52. Henry Bushnell, *The History of Granville, Licking County, Ohio* (Columbus: Press of Hann and Adair, 1889), 307–8; Galbreath, *History of Ohio*, 2:234.

53. Samuel P. Orth, *A History of Cleveland Ohio*, 3 vols. (Cleveland: S. J. Clarke Publishing Co., 1910), 1:291.

54. *Freedom's Journal*, January 16, 1829.

55. Treaty of Ghent, art. I, 8 Stat. 218 (1814).

56. Ibid., art. X; The Webster-Ashburton Treaty: Treaty to Settle and Define the Boundaries between the Territories of the United States and the Possessions of Her Britannic Majesty in North America, for the Final Suppression of the African Slave Trade, and for the Giving up of Criminals Fugitive from Justice, in Certain Cases, Signed at Washington August 9,1842. Ratified by the United States August 22, 1842, 8 Stat. 572; Winks, *Blacks in Canada*, 172–73.

57. Webster-Ashburton Treaty, art. X; *Montreal Gazette*, December 21, 1842; Winks, *Blacks in Canada*, 173.

58. State v. Farr, reported in *Lower Sandusky Whig*, May 27, 1841.

59. Commonwealth v. Aves, 35 Mass. 193 (1836); S. Middleton, "Cincinnati," 60–62; Paul Finkelman, ed., *The Law of Freedom and Bondage: A Casebook* (New York: Oceana Publications, 1986), 73, 75.

60. *Philanthropist*, May 19, 1841.

61. *Philanthropist*, May 19, June 9, July 7, 1841; *Cincinnati Daily Gazette*, June 1, 1841; Finkelman, *Imperfect Union*, 164–65.

62. State v. Farr, reported in *Lower Sandusky Whig*, May 27, 1841.

63. *Philanthropist*, May 19, 1841; *Cincinnati Daily Gazette*, June 3, 1841

64. *Niles' National Register* (Baltimore), March 1841–September 1841, 206; *Lower Sandusky Whig*, May 27, 1841.

65. *Philanthropist*, May 19, 1841.

66. Ibid.; *Cincinnati Daily Gazette*, May 21, 1841.

67. *Philanthropist*, May 19, 1841; *Cincinnati Daily Gazette*, May 21, 1841.

68. *Philanthropist*, September 20, 1843.

69. "Report of Fugitive Slaves," January 18, 1841, repr. in S. Middleton, *Black Laws*, 116; *Journal of the House of Representatives of the State of Ohio*, 36 (36th Gen. Ass.), 429 (February 7, 1838).

70. "Report of Fugitive Slaves," January 18, 1841, repr. in S. Middleton, *Black Laws*, 117.

71. Ibid., 118.

72. Ibid.

73. Ibid., 119–20.

74. Ibid., 124–28.

75. An act to repeal the act entitled, "an act relating to fugitives from labor and service from other states," 41 Laws of Ohio 13 (1843), repr. in S. Middleton, *Black Laws*, 129.

76. *Philanthropist*, May 12, 26, 1841.

77. Carol Wilson, "Freedom at Risk: The Kidnapping of Free Blacks in America, 1780–1865" (Ph.D. diss., West Virginia University, 1991), 25.

78. Wilbur H. Siebert and Albert B. Hart, *The Underground Railroad from Slavery to Freedom* (New York: Macmillan, 1898), 39.

79. Preston, "Fugitive Slave Acts," 427–28.

80. "Report of Fugitive Slaves," January 18, 1841, repr. in S. Middleton, *Black Laws,* 124.

81. Gibbons v. Ogden, 22 U.S. (9 Wheat.) 1 (1824).

82. R. Kent Newmyer, *The Supreme Court under Marshall and Taney* (New York: Crowell, 1968), 101.

83. New York v. Miln, 36 U.S. (11 Pet.) 102 (1837).

84. Newmyer, *Supreme Court,* 102–3.

85. Groves v. Slaughter, 40 U.S. (15 Pet.) 449 (1841).

86. Newmyer, *Supreme Court,* 122–23.

87. A Supplement to "An act Concerning Slaves," 51 N.J. Laws 90 (1826); Paul Finkelman, "State Constitutional Protections of Liberty and the Antebellum New Jersey Supreme Court: Chief Justice Hornblower and the Fugitive Slave Law of 1793," *Rutgers Law Journal* 23 (Winter 1992): 753–87; Paul Finkelman, "Chief Justice Hornblower and the Fugitive Slave Law of 1793," in *Slavery and the Law,* ed. Paul Finkelman (Madison, Wis.: Madison House, 1997), 113–34.

88. *Pennsylvania State Journal* (1825–26), 353–54, 466, 481, 494, 511, 516–17, 522; Thomas D. Morris, *Free Men All: The Personal Liberty Laws of the North, 1780–1861* (Baltimore: Johns Hopkins University Press, 1974), 50–58.

89. Jane H. Pease and William H. Pease, *The Fugitive Slave Law and Anthony Burns: A Problem in Law Enforcement* (Philadelphia: Lippincott, 1975); T. Morris, *Free Men All,* 166–67, 172–73.

90. Paul Finkelman, "Sorting out *Prigg v. Pennsylvania,*" *Rutgers Law Journal* 24 (Spring 1993): 605–65; "The Great Slave Case between Pennsylvania and Maryland," *Philanthropist,* March 30, 1842; Robert J. Cottrol, "Commentary: Perspectives on Fugitive Slaves from Legal and Social History," *Rutgers Law Journal* 24 (Spring 1993): 695–98.

91. Scott v. Sandford, 60 U.S. (19 How.) 393 (1857); Paul Finkelman, ed., *Dred Scott v. Sandford: A Brief History with Documents* (Boston: Bedford Books, 1997); Don E. Fehrenbacher, *The Dred Scott Case: Its Significance in American Law and Politics* (New York: Oxford University Press, 1978).

92. Prigg v. Pennsylvania, 41 U.S. (16 Pet.) 539 (1842); Paul Finkelman, "Story Telling on the Supreme Court: *Prigg v. Pennsylvania* and Justice Joseph Story's Judicial Nationalism," *Supreme Court Review* (1995): 247–94.

93. "Report of Fugitive Slaves," January 18, 1841, repr. in S. Middleton, *Black Laws,* 118, 121.

94. Salmon P. Chase, *The Address and Reply on the Presentation of a Testimonial to S. P. Chase* (Cincinnati: H. W. Derby, 1845), 4–8; *Philanthropist,* February 19, 1845.

95. Chase, *Address and Reply,* 8.

96. *Philanthropist,* February 19, 1845.

97. Chase, *Address and Reply*, 9.

98. Ibid., 8; State v. Hoppess, 2 Western L.J. 279 (1845); 2 Western L.J. 333 (1845).

99. Commonwealth v. Garner, 44 Va. 624 (1846); *Cincinnati Weekly Herald and Philanthropist*, July 23, August 13, 20, December 31, 1845, February 11, 1846.

100. James McDowell to Mordecai Bartley, December 13, 1845, Bartley Papers, box 2, folder 4, OHS; *Cincinnati Weekly Herald and Philanthropist*, February 25, 1846; William B. Neff, *Bench and Bar of Northern Ohio: History and Biography* (Cleveland: Historical Publishing, 1921), 55.

101. *Cincinnati Weekly Herald and Philanthropist*, August 13, 1845.

102. Emerson to Bartley, July 30, 1845, Bartley Papers, box 2, folder 3b, OHS; *Cincinnati Weekly Herald and Philanthropist*, September 1, 3, 1845.

103. An Ohio grand jury indicted Francis Lewis, Wyatt Lewis, James Coe, Nimrod Coe, and Calvin Rockingham for kidnapping. A Virginia grand jury indicted Peter Garner, Joseph Romini, Titus Shotwell, and Berton Staunton for violating the federal law. See *Cincinnati Weekly Herald and Philanthropist*, October 15, November 19, 26, December 17, 24, 1845.

104. *Executive Documents*, vol. 10, 44th Gen. Ass. (Columbus: Scott, 1846); Bartley to McDowell, October 11, 1845, 28–29; McDowell to Bartley, October 21, 1845, 30–31.

105. Samuel F. Vinton, *Substance of an Argument of Samuel F. Vinton, for the Defendants, in the Case of the* Commonwealth of Virginia v. Peter M. Garner and Others, *for an Alleged Abduction of Certain Slaves, Delivered before the General Court of Virginia, at Its December Term, A.D. 1845* (Marietta, Ohio: printed at the Intelligencer office, 1846), 1–32.

106. Ibid.; Executive Office of Ohio, January 17, 1846, Bartley Papers, box 3, folder 1, OHS.

107. *Cincinnati Weekly Herald and Philanthropist*, February 11, 1846.

108. Neff, *Bench and Bar*, 55; *Cincinnati Weekly Herald and Philanthropist*, February 11, 1846.

109. *Frankfort Commonwealth*, April 7, 14, 1846; State of Ohio v. Forbes and Armitage, Arrested upon Requisition of the Government of Ohio, on Charge of Kidnapping Jerry Phinney, and Tried before the Franklin Circuit Court of Kentucky, April 10, 1846, CinHS, 13; Graham v. Strader, 44 Ky. 173 (1844); Young's Adm'r v. Small, 43 Ky. 220 (1843).

110. *Frankfort Commonwealth*, April 14, 1846; *Liberty Hall and Cincinnati Gazette*, April 9, 1846; "The John Parker Story," pp. 2–3, John Rankin Collection, Duke University Manuscript Department, William Perkins Library, Durham, N.C. Parker claimed to have devoted his life to helping slaves. See also Henry L. Taylor, "Spatial Organization and the Residential Experience: Black Cincinnati in 1850," *Social Science History* 10 (Spring 1986): 61; Ira Berlin, "The Structure of the Free Negro Caste in the Antebellum United States," *Journal of Social History* 9 (Spring 1976): 302–3; *Cincinnati Daily Gazette*, April 3, 1846; Ohio v. Forbes and Armitage, 8–9; Finkelman, *Imperfect Union*, 172–73.

111. Judge Mason Brown to Mordecai Bartley, April 13, 1846, Mordecai Bartley Collection, OHS. Slave owners generally listed two quotes for reward

advertisements in newspapers. The smallest reward went to slave catchers who apprehended and jailed runaways in the city where they lived, while the highest reward went to those who returned runaways to the city from whence they fled. See *Scioto Gazette,* January 1804; *Cincinnati Western Spy,* August 1807; *Chillicothe Fredonian,* March 1808; *Philanthropist,* April 1, 1846; *Liberty Hall and Cincinnati Gazette,* April 2, 1846; *Frankfort Commonwealth,* April 7, 1846; Rankin v. Lydia, 9 Ky. 467 (1820); Finkelman, *Imperfect Union,* 190–95.

112. *Frankfort Commonwealth,* April 7, 1846.

113. Ibid.; *Dayton Journal and Advertiser,* April 14, 1846.

114. Siebert and Hart, *Underground Railroad,* 160–64; *Frankfort Commonwealth* (Lexington), April 7, 1846.

115. *Dayton Journal and Advertiser,* April 14, 1846.

116. *Ohio Press,* April 1, 1846.

117. *Ohio State Journal,* March 28, 1846; *Xenia Torch-Light,* April 2, 1846; *Germantown Gazette and Miami Valley Advertiser,* April 3, 1846; *Ohio Statesman,* April 1, 1846; *Ohio State Journal,* April 2, 1846.

118. *Frankfort Commonwealth,* March 31, April 7, 1846; *Licking Valley Register,* April 4, 1846.

119. Kentucky, *Executive Journal,* April 9, 1846, William Owsley Papers, drawer 53, box 1, Kentucky Historical Society, Frankfort; Ohio v. Forbes and Armitage, 8.

120. Ohio v. Forbes and Armitage, 4–5; "Fugitives," *Digest of the Statutes of Kentucky,* 2 vols. (Frankfort, Ky.: A. G. Hodges, 1834), 1:745–47; *Dayton Journal and Advertiser,* April 14, 1846.

121. *Ohio v. Forbes and Armitage,* 6–7; *Licking Valley Register,* April 18, 1846.

122. William Johnston to Bartley, April 18, 1846, Bartley Papers; *Dayton Transcript,* April 18, 1846; *Ohio State Journal,* April 23, 25, 1846; Ohio v. Forbes and Armitage, 10; *Licking Valley Register,* April 18, 1846; *Philanthropist,* May 6, 1846.

123. Henderson v. Ohio, reported in *Philanthropist,* January 27, 1847; *Cincinnati Weekly Herald,* January 27, 1847; *Cincinnati Daily Enquirer,* January 25, 30, 1847; *Liberty Hall and Cincinnati Gazette,* January 28, 1847; *Frankfort Commonwealth,* February 27, 1847.

124. *Rochester North Star,* April 21, 1848.

125. James H. Fairchild, "The Underground Railroad," 4 Western Reserve Historical Society (1894), 107.

126. Gates to Birney, December 11, 1841, in J. Birney, *Letters,* 2:602.

127. Jones v. Van Zandt, 13 F. Cas., 1040, 1040–41, 1046–47, 1052, 1057 (C.C.D. Ohio 1843) (No. 7,501); Salmon P. Chase, *An Argument for the Defendant, Submitted to the Supreme Court of the United States in the Case of* Wharton Jones v. John Van Zandt (Cincinnati: R. P. Donogh, 1847), 3–4; Chase to John T. Trowbridge, March 18, 1864, in *The Law in Southwestern Ohio,* ed. George P. Stimson and comp. Frank G. Davis (Cincinnati: Cincinnati Bar Association, 1972), 65–67; *Cincinnati Daily Enquirer,* March 16, 1847; *Liberty Hall,* August 10, 1843.

128. Jones v. Van Zandt, 13 F. Cas. 1040 at 1052–54; Chase, *Argument,* 3–4; *Cincinnati Daily Enquirer,* March 16, 1847; *Liberty Hall,* August 10, 1843.

129. Jones v. Van Zandt, 5 U.S. 215 (1847); Chase, *Argument*, 6–11; *National Press and Cincinnati Weekly*, April 14, 21, 1847; *Liberty Hall*, March 11, 1847; Finkelman, "Slaves, Tolerance," 115.

130. Driskell v. Parish, 7 F. Cas. 1100 (C.C.D. Ohio 1845) (No. 4,089); 7 F. Cas. 1093 (C.C.D. Ohio 1847) (No. 4,087); 7 F. Cas. 1095 (C.C.D. Ohio 1849) (No. 4,088). Quotes at 1094–95, 1100.

131. Chase Papers, folder Legal File, 575, HSP; Driskell v. Parrish, 7 F. Cas. at 1093–96.

132. *Rochester North Star*, October 12, 1849; *Washington National Era*, October 4, 1849.

133. Miller v. McQuerry, 17 F. Cas. 335 (C.C.D. Ohio 1853) (No. 9,583); *Miller v. McQuerry*, reported in 10 *Western Law Journal* 528 (1853); *Cincinnati Daily Gazette*, September 16, 1853; Levi Coffin, *Reminiscences of Levi Coffin, the Reputed President of the Underground Railroad: Being a Brief History of the Labors of a Lifetime in behalf of the Slave, with the Stories of Numerous Fugitives, Who Gained Their Freedom through His Instrumentality, and Many Other Incidents* (Cincinnati: Robert Clarke and Co., 1880), 542–44; Campbell v. Kirkpatrick, 4 F. Cas. 1174 (C.C.D. Ohio 1850) (No. 2,363); Samuel May, *The Fugitive Slave Law and Its Victims* (New York: American Anti-Slavery Society, 1861), 20; Robert M. Cover, *Justice Accused: Antislavery and the Judicial Process* (New Haven: Yale University Press, 1975), 183.

134. Miller v. McQuerry, 17 F. Cas. at 335, 336; *Philanthropist*, October 22, 1839; Coffin, *Reminiscences*, 542–44; William H. Siebert, *The Mysteries of Ohio's Underground Railroads* (Columbus: Long's College Book Co., 1951), 241; Greve, *Centennial History*, 1:759–60; May, *Slave Law and Victims*, 20.

135. Miller v. McQuerry, 17 F. Cas. 335 at 335–36; Coffin, *Reminiscences*, 542–48; Greve, *Centennial History*, 1:759–60; Chase to Charles Sumner, September 3, 1853, *AHA*, 252; Cover, *Justice Accused*, 183.

136. Repr. in *Liberty Hall and Cincinnati Gazette*, May 27, 1839.

CHAPTER 7

1. Prigg v. Pennsylvania, 41 U.S. (16 Pet.) 539 (1842); William E. Nelson, "The Impact of the Antislavery Movement upon Styles of Judicial Reasoning in Nineteenth-Century America," in *Essays in Nineteenth-Century American Legal History*, ed. Wythe Holt (Westport, Conn.: Greenwood, 1976), 172–73.

2. Alfred Kelly, *The American Constitution: Its Origins and Development* (New York: Norton, 1976), 246–48.

3. Chase to J. W. Smith, November 14, 1851, Salmon P. Chase Papers, Letters and Drafts, box 1, Historical Society of Pennsylvania.

4. Prigg v. Pennsylvania, 41 U.S. (16 Pet.) 539 (1842). The *Prigg* case was also reported in the *Cincinnati Gazette*, November 1, 1850.

5. Fugitive Slave Act of 1850, 9 Stat. 464; Marion G. McDougall, *Fugitive Slaves, 1619–1865* (Boston: Ginn, 1891), 30–31; Jehiel Brooks, ed., *A Compilation of the Laws of the United States, and of States, in Relation to Fugitives from Labor, with the Clauses of*

the Constitution of the United States Involved in the Execution of the Same (Washington, D.C.: Taylor and Maury, 1860); William Breyfogle, *Make Free: The Story of the Underground Railroad* (Philadelphia: Lippincott, 1958), 205–6.

6. Fugitive Slave Act of 1850, 9 Stat. 464; McDougall, *Fugitive Slaves*, 30–31; Paul Finkelman, ed., *Fugitive Slaves and American Courts*, (New York: Garland, 1988); Breyfogle, *Make Free*, 205–6.

7. *Cincinnati Enquirer*, October 23, 1850; *Cincinnati Gazette*, October 21, 1850; Robert J. Scarry, *Millard Fillmore* (Jefferson, N.C.: McFarland, 2001), 178–81; Robert J. Rayback, *Millard Fillmore: Biography of a President* (Buffalo, N.Y.: Buffalo Historical Society, 1959), 268–73; William Elliot Griffis, *Millard Fillmore, Constructive Statesman, Defender of the Constitution, President of the United States* (Ithaca: Andrus and Church, 1915), 69–76.

8. "The privilege of the writ of habeas corpus shall not be suspended, unless when in cases of rebellion or invasion the public safety may require it." U.S. Const., art. I, § 9; *Clermont Courier*, November 14, 1850.

9. *Dayton Evening Empire*, October 22, 1850.

10. *Dayton Evening Empire*, October 19, 1850.

11. *Dayton Evening Empire*, October 22, 1850; *Clermont Courier*, November 14, 1850; Cover, *Justice Accused*, 175; *Dayton Evening Empire*, October 18, 22, 1850; Mrs. Chapman Coleman, ed., *The Life of John J. Crittenden, with Selections from His Correspondence and Speeches* (Philadelphia: J. B. Lippincott, 1871), 377; Emmett D. Preston, "The Fugitive Slave Acts in Ohio," *Journal of Negro History* 28 (October 1943): 433.

12. *Cincinnati Enquirer*, October 23, 1850.

13. John White Chadwick, *Theodore Parker, Preacher and Reformer* (New York: Houghton, 1901); Henry Steele Commager, *Theodore Parker: Yankee Crusader* (Gloucester, Mass.: Peter Smith, 1960); Theodore Parker, *The Trial of Theodore Parker: For the "Misdemeanor" of a Speech in Faneuil Hall against Kidnapping, before the Circuit Court of the United States* (Boston: published for the author, 1855).

14. See William Cullen Bryant, "The Death of Slavery," in *An American Anthology, 1787–1900: Selections, Illustrating the Editor's Critical Review of American Poetry in the Nineteenth Century,* ed. Edmund Clarence Stedman (Boston: Houghton Mifflin, 1900).

15. January Searle [pseud.], *Emerson, His Life and Writings* (London: Holyoake, 1855); Merton L. Dillon, *The Abolitionists: The Growth of a Dissenting Minority* (DeKalb: Northern Illinois University Press, 1974), 59.

16. A. D. Mayo, *An Address to the Legislature and People of New York* (Albany, N.Y.: Weed, Parsons, Printers, 1859), 3–4, 12–13.

17. *Speech of Mr. Robert Rantoul of Massachusetts on the Constitutionality of the Fugitive Slave Law, Delivered in the House of Representatives, June 11, 1852,* Pamphlet Collection, Cincinnati Historical Society, 2–4; *Frederick Douglass' Paper,* June 17, 1852.

18. *Rochester North Star,* September 5, October 3, 1850, March 20, 1851; Stanley Campbell, *Slave Catchers: Enforcement of the Fugitive Slave Law, 1850–1860* (Chapel Hill: University of North Carolina Press, 1970), 50–53; *Rochester North Star,* April 3, 1851.

19. Samuel S. Cox, *Three Decades of Federal Legislation, 1855 to 1885: Personal and Historical Memories of Events Preceding, during, and since the American Civil War, Involving Slavery and Secession, Emancipation and Reconstruction; with Sketches of Prominent Actors during These Periods* (Providence, R.I.: J. A. and R. A. Reid, 1885), 48–49, also quoted in Preston, "Fugitive Slave Acts," 429, 431; David Lindsey, *"Sunset" Cox: Irrepressible Democrat* (Detroit: Wayne State University Press, 1959).

20. *Congressional Globe*, 32d Cong., 1st sess., 774–75 (March 16, 1852, 1123 (August 26, 1852); *Journal of the House of Representatives of the United States*, 31st Cong., 1st sess., 992 (June 8, 1850), 1268 (August 15, 1850), 67 (December 17, 1850); *Journal of the Senate of the United States*, 31st Cong., 1st sess., 307–8 (April 25, 1850), 351 (May 23, 1850).

21. Preston, "Fugitive Slave Acts," 457.

22. *Congressional Globe*, 32d Cong., 1st sess., 53, (February 11, 1852), 773–74 (March 16, 1852); *House Journal*, 31st Cong., 1st sess., 36 (December 10, 1850); *Senate Journal*, 31st Cong., 1st sess., 384 (June 8, 1850), 556–67 (August 20, 1850).

23. *House Journal*, 32d Cong., 1st sess., 543 (April 5, 1852); *Western Reserve Chronicle*, December 25, 1850; quoted in Preston, "Fugitive Slave Acts," 465.

24. *House Journal*, 32d Cong., 1st sess., 309–10 (April 5, 1852); Preston, "Fugitive Slave Acts," 431.

25. *Senate Journal*, 31st Cong., 1st sess., 277 (April 12, 1850), 308–9 (April 25, 1850), 351–52 (May 23, 1850), 384 (June 8, 1850); *House Journal*, 32d Cong., 1st sess., 258 (August 15, 1850). "Omnibus bill" was a relatively new term at the time. Because such bills contained a multitude of provisions, critics likened them to an omnibus, a public conveyance that carries all sorts of passengers.

26. *Speech of Senator Chase, Delivered at Toledo, May 30, 1851, before a Mass Convention of the Democracy of Northwestern Ohio*, Pamphlet Collection, CinHS, 1–2.

27. *Cincinnati Enquirer*, October 16, 1850; *Cincinnati Gazette*, October 21 and 22, 1850; *Dayton Journal and Advertiser*, October 29, 1850; James Monroe, *Oberlin Thursday Lectures, Addresses, and Essays* (Oberlin, Ohio: Edward J. Goodrich, 1897), 104.

28. *Ohio State Journal*, April 8, 1850.

29. *Journal of the Senate of the State of Ohio*, 49 (49th Gen. Ass.), 47, 48, 71, 206–7 (December 11, 1850).

30. Resolution Relative to Slavery and the Fugitive Law, 49 Laws of Ohio 814 (1851), repr. in *The Black Laws in the Old Northwest: A Documentary History*, ed. Stephen Middleton (Westport, Conn.: Greenwood, 1993), 129–30; Preston, "Fugitive Slave Acts," 466.

31. *Ohio Senate Journal*, 52 (52d Gen. Ass.), 421 (April 8, 1856).

32. *Frederick Douglass' Paper*, December 24, 1852; *Rochester North Star*, April 3, 1851; Albert G. Riddle, *The Life of Benjamin Wade* (Cleveland: W. W. Williams, 1886), 167; Preston, "Fugitive Slave Acts," 465–66.

33. Thomas Matijasic, "The Reaction of the Ohio General Assembly to the Fugitive Slave Law of 1850," *Northwest Ohio Quarterly* 55 (Spring 1982–83): 40–41.

34. For the text of Wood's address see *Western Reserve Chronicle*, December 25, 1850, also quoted in Preston, "Fugitive Slave Acts," 464–65.

35. *Cincinnati Gazette*, September 19, 1850.

36. James Birney to Christian Antislavery Convention, April 2, 1850, in James Gillespie Birney, *Letters of James Gillespie Birney, 1831–1857*, ed. Dwight L. Dumond, 2 vols. (New York: D. Appleton-Century Co., 1938), 2:1131; *Cincinnati Gazette*, October 21, 1850.

37. Birney to Gerrit Smith, April 17, 1852, J. Birney, *Letters*, 2:1144–46; Don E. Fehrenbacher, *The Slaveholding Republic: An Account of the United States Government's Relations to Slavery*, completed and ed. Ward McAfee (Oxford: Oxford University Press, 2001), 231; *Dayton Journal and Advertiser*, December 3, 1850; *Cincinnati Gazette*, October 21, 22, 1850.

38. *Speech of Senator Chase, Delivered at Toledo*, 4; William H. Patton, *Conscience and Law; or, A Discussion of Our Comparative Responsibility to Human and Divine Government; with an Application to the Fugitive Slave Law* (New York: M. H. Newman, 1850), 49.

39. See J. A. Collins to James Monroe, January 4, 1842, and James Gibson to Monroe, January 5, 1842, James Monroe Papers, box 1, Oberlin College Archives; Frederick Blue, "Oberlin's James Monroe: Forgotten Abolitionist," *Civil War History* 35 (December 1989): 285–301; Eugene D. Schmiel, "The Congressional Career of James Monroe of Ohio," unpublished essay, Ohio State University, 1967; Catherine M. Rokicky, *James Monroe: Oberlin's Christian Statesman and Reformer, 1821–1898* (Kent, Ohio: Kent State University Press, 2002).

40. *Ohio Statesman*, October 30, 1850, also quoted in Preston, "Fugitive Slave Acts," 467.

41. Resolutions reported in *Western Reserve Chronicle*, April 20, 1859, also quoted in Preston, "Fugitive Slave Acts," 467.

42. Resolutions reported in *Toledo Daily Blade*, July 20, 1859, also quoted in Preston, "Fugitive Slave Acts," 467–68.

43. Resolutions reported in *Ashtabula Sentinel*, December 21, 1850; also quoted in Preston, "Fugitive Slave Acts," 468, emphasis in original.

44. *Western Reserve Chronicle*, September 11, 1850; *Dayton Journal and Advertiser*, December 3, 1850; Preston, "Fugitive Slave Acts," 462–63.

45. *Ashtabula Sentinel*, October 6, 1850, also quoted in Preston, "Fugitive Slave Acts," 463.

46. *Cleveland Herald*, October 22, 1850; *Western Reserve Chronicle*, October 30, November 6, December 4, 1850; *Washington National Era*, December 5, 1850, also quoted in Preston, "Fugitive Slave Acts," 468.

47. *Cincinnati Enquirer*, October 10, 1850; *Cincinnati Gazette*, September 19, 1850; *Ohio State Journal*, April 8, 1850; Campbell, *Slave Catchers*, 53.

48. *Dayton Evening Empire*, October 17, 1850; *Dayton Journal and Advertiser*, December 3, 1850.

49. *Cincinnati Gazette*, September 19, 1850.

50. *Cincinnati Gazette*, October 17, 1850.

51. Philip S. Foner, and George E. Walker, eds., *Proceedings of the Black State Conventions, 1840–1865*, 2 vols. (Philadelphia: Temple University Press, 1979–80), 1:215

52. *Clermont Courier*, September 19, 1850.

53. *Dayton Journal and Advertiser*, October 29, November 12, December 3, 13, 1850; *Salem Anti-Slavery Bugle*, August 2, 1856; *Cincinnati Enquirer*, October 26, 1850; *Clermont Courier*, September 19, 1850; Leo Alilunas, "Fugitive Slave Cases in Ohio Prior to 1850," *Ohio Archaeological and Historical Quarterly* 49 (April 1940): 169.

54. *Salem Anti-Slavery Bugle*, August 2, 1856.

55. Ibid.; *Frederick Douglass' Paper*, August 6, 1852.

56. James Walker, *Identity: The Black Experience in Canada* ([Toronto]: Ontario Educational Communications, 1979), 17–20; *Washington National Era*, May 29, 1851; *Provincial Freeman*, July 25, 1857; Jason H. Silversmith, *Unwelcome Guests: Canada West's Response to American Fugitive Slaves, 1800–1865* (Millwood, N.Y.: Associated Faculty Press, 1985); "Canada," p. 206, John Kirk Collection, Letter Books, box 1, vol. 1 (1850–53), ChiHS.

57. *Ohio State Journal*, November 26, 1850; "Fugitive Slave Law," p. 204, John Kirk Collection, box 1, vol. 1, 1850–53, ChiHS; *Cincinnati Enquirer*, February 8, 1850.

58. *Dayton Journal and Advertiser*, October 29, 1850; *Dayton Evening Empire*, October 18, 1850; *Cincinnati Enquirer*, October 26, 1850.

59. *Cincinnati Enquirer*, October 10, 1850; *Ohio State Journal*, October 24, 1850; Eugene H. Roseboom, "Southern Ohio and the Union in 1863," *Mississippi Valley Historical Review* 39 (June 1952): 29–44; Frank L. Klement, *The Limits of Dissent: Clement L. Vallandigham and the Civil War* (Lexington: University Press of Kentucky, 1970).

60. Political Speeches of Thomas Corwin (1859), 67, Newspaper Clippings, CinHS.

61. Dennison to John Laidly, September 29, 1860, William Dennison Papers, OHS; Frederick J. Blue, *Salmon P. Chase: A Life in Politics* (Kent, Ohio: Kent State University Press, 1987), 122, 135, 244.

62. Douglass was quoted in the *Dayton Evening Empire*, October 17, 1850; Frederick Douglass, "Frederick Douglass and the Negro Convention Movement," in *The Life and Writings of Frederick Douglass*, ed. Philip S. Foner, 4 vols. (New York: International Publishers, 1950), 2:28–29.

63. Frederick Douglass, "Aggressions of the Slave Power: An Address Delivered in Rochester, NY" May 22, 1856, in *The Frederick Douglass Papers*, ed. John Blassingame, R. McKivigan, and Peter P. Hinks, 5 vols. (New Haven: Yale University Press, 1979), 3:127–28; "West India Emancipation Speech Delivered at Canandaigua, New York," August 4, 1857; "The Fugitive Slave Law Delivered to the National Free Soil Convention at Pittsburgh," August 11, 1852, in Foner, *Life and Writings of Frederick Douglass*, 2:207, 437; Monroe, *Oberlin Thursday Lectures*, 101–2, 117; *Dayton Evening Empire*, October 17, 1850.

64. Nell to W. L. Garrison, February 19, 1852, in Carter G. Woodson, ed., *The Mind of the Negro as Reflected in Letters Written during the Crisis, 1800–1860* (repr., New York: Russell and Russell, 1969), 334; p. 206, John Kirk Collection, Letter Books, vol. 1, box 1, 1852–53, ChiHS; Marion B. Lucas, *A History of Blacks in Kentucky: From Slavery to Segregation, 1760–1891*, 2 vols. (Frankfort: Kentucky Historical Society, 1992), 1:62–64; Fairchild, "Underground Railroad," 114; *Dayton Evening Empire*, November 1, 1850.

65. *Dayton Evening Empire*, October 17, 1850; *Ohio Statesman*, October 15, 1850; Howard H. Bell, "Expressions of Negro Militancy in the North, 1840–1860," *Journal of Negro History* 45 (January 1960): 15–16; Preston, "Fugitive Slave Acts," 471–72.

66. Oversized Volumes, ms. 1807, John Means Collection, OHS.

67. Vertical File Manuscripts, ms. 2920, Rachel Myers Papers, OHS.

68. *Dayton Evening Empire*, October 31, 1850.

69. C. Peter Ripley, ed., *The Black Abolitionist Papers*, 5 vols. (Chapel Hill: University of North Carolina Press, 1985), 2:11–12; *Cincinnati Gazette*, October 26, 1850.

70. *Cincinnati Gazette*, October 26, 1850; *Washington National Era*, November 15, 1855; Douglass, *Life and Writings*, 2:28–29; Lucas, *Blacks in Kentucky*, 1:62–64; *Frederick Douglass' Paper*, June 10, 1852, August 24, 1855.

71. *Frederick Douglass' Paper*, August 24, 1855.

72. *Message of Governor Magoffin to the General Assembly of Kentucky, December Session, 1859, Journal of the House of Representatives of the Commonwealth of Kentucky, Begun and Held in the Town of Frankfort, on Monday, the Fifth Day of December, in the Year of our Lord 1859, and of the Commonwealth the Sixty-eight.* (Frankfort, Ky.: Printed at the Yeoman Office, John B. Major, State Printer, 1859), 36–38, 59–61.

73. Larry Gara, "The Fugitive Slave Law in the Eastern Ohio Valley," *Ohio History* 72 (April 1963): 116–18; Gara, *The Liberty Line: The Legend of the Underground Railroad* (Lexington: University Press of Kentucky, 1961); Gara, "The Underground Railroad: A Re-evaluation," *Ohio Historical Quarterly* 69 (July 1960); Gara, John Hope Franklin and Loren Schweninger, *Runaway Slaves: Rebels on the Plantation* (New York: Oxford University Press, 1999).

74. *Rochester North Star*, January 23, March 20, April 10, 1851.

75. Copy of Proofs and Exhibits in the *Peyton Polly* Case, April 7, 1848–May 17, 1851, Reuben Wood Papers, folder 10, Ohio Historical Society; Office of Prosecuting Attorney Burlington Lawrence, Columbus, June 1, 1851, Wood Papers, folder 6.

76. Copy of Proofs and Exhibits, April 7, 1848–May 17, 1851, Wood Papers, folder 10; Depositions of Jacob Heaberling and Coleman Walker in Peyton Polly v. John Watson, Louisville Chancery Court Records, Kentucky Department of Libraries and Archives, Louisville, Ky.; Carol Wilson, "Freedom at Risk," 83.

77. Office of Prosecuting Attorney, June 1, 1851; Resolution, Relative to the Abduction of the Children and Grand Child of Peyton Polly, 49 Local Laws of Ohio 811 (1851); Carol Wilson, *Freedom at Risk*, 76.

78. John S. George to Wood, February 22, 1851, Wood Papers, folder 3.

79. Seabury Ford to Lewis Sheppard, July 2, 1850, Seabury Ford Papers, box 2, OHS; Ralph Leete to Governor Wood, March 1, 1851, Wood Papers, folder 4; McCormick to Wood, February 28, 1851, Wood Papers, folder 3.

80. J. Harlan to Medill, September 17, 1853, William Medill Papers, box 1, folder 4, OHS.

81. Leete to Medill, August 1, 1853, Medill Papers, box 1, folder 3.

82. George B. Kinkead to J. W. Wilson, August 9, 12, 1853, Medill Papers, box 1, folder 3; Wood to Leete, March 3, 1851, Medill Papers, folder 4; Leete to Chase, March 31, 1856, Salmon P. Chase Papers, microfilm, series 2, box 1, folder 11, OHS; J. Laidly to Chase, April 25, 1856, Chase Papers, microfilm, series 2, box 2, folder 2.

83. Leroy D. Walton to Wood, March 15, 1851, Wood Papers, box 1, folder 4; Wilson to Wood, October 21, 1851, Wood Papers, box 2, folder 2.

84. Wilson to Wood, August 5, 1851, Wood Papers, box 1, folder 10; Chase to H. S. Neal, March 15, 1856, Chase Papers, microfilm, series 2, box 2, folder 3; Chase to Laidly, March 18, 1856, Chase Papers, microfilm, series 2, box 1, folder 10; C. Wilson, "Freedom at Risk," 78.

85. Wilson to Wood, August 18, 1852, box 1, folder 10 Wood Papers; C. Wilson, "Freedom at Risk," 78.

86. Joel W. Wilson to Medill, April 13, 1854, Medill Papers, box 2, folder 2.

87. William Dennison to John Laidly, September 29, 1860, William Dennison Papers, OHS; C. Wilson, "Freedom at Risk," 80.

88. Joint Resolution, Relative to the Kidnapping of the Polly Family, 57 Laws of Ohio 149–50 (1860); see also Ratcliff v. Polly, 53 Va. 528 (1855).

89. Lewis Tappan, *The Fugitive Slave Bill: Its History and Unconstitutionality; with an Account of the Seizure and Enslavement of James Hamlet, and His Subsequent Restoration to Liberty* (New York: William Harned, 1850), 1–5; *Cincinnati Gazette*, October 9, 1850, January 14–15, 1851; *Cincinnati Enquirer*, October 10, 1850.

90. *Dayton Journal and Advertiser*, October 15, 29, 1850; McDougall, *Fugitive Slaves*, 43–44.

91. *Cincinnati Gazette*, January 4, 14–15, 1851; *Dayton Journal and Advertiser*, November 12, 1850.

92. William M. Malehorn, "The Fugitive Slave Law of 1850: Its Enforcement in Ohio" (master's thesis, Ohio State University, 1928), 28, 106; Louis Weeks, "John P. Parker: Black Abolitionist Entrepreneur, 1827–1900," *Ohio History* 80 (Spring 1971): 155–62.

93. Samuel May, *The Fugitive Slave Law and Its Victims* (New York: American Anti-Slavery Society, 1861), 18, 11.

94. Ibid., 18, 13; *Cincinnati Enquirer*, October 27, 30, 1850.

95. Gibbons v. Sloane, 10 F. Cas. 294 (C.C.D. Ohio 1854) (No. 5,382); Weimer v. Sloane, 29 F. Cas. 599 (C.C.D. Ohio 1854) (No. 17,363); Charles Thomas Hickok, "The Negro in Ohio, 1802–1870" (Ph.D. diss., Case Western Reserve University, 1896), 175.

96. *Washington National Era,* November 9, 1854; Levi Coffin, *Reminiscences of Levi Coffin, the Reputed President of the Underground Railroad: Being a Brief History of the Labors of a Lifetime in Behalf of the Slave, with the Stories of Numerous Fugitives, Who Gained Their Freedom through His Instrumentality, and Many Other Incidents* (Cincinnati: Robert Clarke and Co., 1880), 548; Hickok, "Negro in Ohio," 75.

97. Coffin, *Reminiscences,* 549; "Fugitive Slave Case," James G. Birney Scrapbook, 43–44, CinHS; Charles T. Greve, *Centennial History of Cincinnati and Representative Citizens,* 2 vols. (Chicago: Biographical Co., 1904), 1:549, 760–61.

98. "Fugitive Slave Case," Birney Scrapbook, 43; Greve, *Centennial History,* 760–61.

99. Newspaper clippings, Thomas Foraker Scrapbook, 43–44, CinHS; Coffin, *Reminiscences,* 549; Greve, *Centennial History,* 1:760–61.

100. Coffin, *Reminiscences,* 550–54; Greve, *Centennial History,* 1:760–61.

101. "Fugitive Slave Case," Birney Scrapbook, 44.

102. Coffin, *Reminiscences,* 549; *Cincinnati Gazette,* August 27, 1853.

103. *Cincinnati Gazette,* August 27, 1853; May, *Slave Law and Its Victims,* 21.

104. *Cincinnati Gazette,* August 27, September 16, 1853.

105. State v. Hoppess, 2 Western L.J. 279 (1845), and 2 Western L.J. 333 (1845); Paul Finkelman, *An Imperfect Union: Slavery, Federalism, and Comity* (Chapel Hill: University of North Carolina Press, 1981), 167–72, 173, 175.

106. Charles B. Galbreath, "Antislavery Movement in Columbiana County," *Ohio Archaeological and Historical Quarterly* 30 (October 1921): 383.

107. Harold B. Barth, *History of Columbiana County Ohio,* 2 vols. (Topeka, Kan.: Historical Publishing Co., 1926), 1:118.

108. Warrant for the Arrest of Madeline, a Fugitive from Labor, U.S. District Court for the Southern District of Ohio, 1854, CinHS.

109. *Cincinnati Daily Gazette,* July 7, 1855; May, *Slave Law and Victims,* 34.

110. "Rosetta Case," Chase Papers, box 1, HSP; May, *Slave Law and Its Victims,* 32; Greve, *Centennial History,* 1:760–62; Cover, *Justice Accused,* 184.

111. Cover, *Justice Accused,* 184.

112. "Rosetta Case," box 1, Chase Papers.

113. Ibid.

114. Ibid.; Cover, *Justice Accused,* 184; William C. Cochran, "Ohio from 1802 to 1851: The Black Laws—The Three Fifths Rule," in *The Western Reserve and the Fugitive Slave Law: A Prelude to the Civil War* (Cleveland: Western Reserve Historical Society, 1920), 112–13.

115. Ex parte Robinson, 20 F. Cas. 969 (C.C.S.D. Ohio 1856) (No. 11,934). See also Campbell v. Kirkpatrick, 4 F. Cas. 1174 (C.C.D. Ohio 1850) (No. 2,363).

116. Anderson v. Poindexter, 6 Ohio St. 622, 622–24 (1856); Richard C. Minor, "James Preston Poindexter: Elder Statesman of Columbus," *Ohio Historical Quarterly* 56 (July 1947): 266–86.

117. Timothy Walker Papers, Record Book, box 2, CinHS, 185; *Daily Cincinnati Commercial,* March 19, April 2, 1855.

118. Timothy Walker Papers, Record Book, box 2, CinHS, 185; *Daily Cincinnati Commercial*, March 19, 1855, April 2, 1855.

119. Anderson v. Poindexter, 6 Ohio St. at 626–32. See also Rankin v. Lydia, 9 Ky. 467 (1820); Marie Louise v. Marat, 9 La. 473 (1836); Frank v. Powell, 11 La. 499 (1838); Smith v. Smith, 18 La. 341 (1839).

120. Anderson v. Poindexter, 6 Ohio St. at 627.

121. Ibid., 633–35.

122. Ibid., 639.

123. *Cincinnati Daily Commercial*, January 31, 1856.

124. Ex parte Robinson, 20 F. Cas. 969 (C.C.S.D. Ohio 1856) (No. 11,934); *American Law Register* 4, 617; Julius Yanuck, "The Garner Fugitive Slave Case," *Mississippi Valley Historical Review* 40 (June 1953): 47–66; *Cincinnati Daily Commercial*, January 29, 1856; May, *Slave Law and Victims*, 37–48. For a fictionalized account of this episode, see Toni Morrison, *Beloved: A Novel* (New York: Knopf, 1987).

125. Letter from C. H. Cleveland, February 6, 1856, VFM ms. 975, OHS.

126. *Cincinnati Daily Commercial*, January 31, 1856.

127. *Cincinnati Daily Commercial*, January 29, 1856.

128. Salmon P. Chase to John Trowbridge, March 13, 1864, Chase Papers, Letters and Drafts; Greve, *Centennial History*, 1:762; Frederick Douglass, "West India Emancipation Speech," August 4, 1857, in Foner, *Douglass Papers*, 2:457; Frederick Douglass, "Freedom in the West Indies: An Address Delivered in Poughkeepsie, NY," August 2, 1858, ibid., 3:214–42; Monroe, *Oberlin Thursday Lectures*, 117.

129. McDougall, *Fugitive Slaves*, 30–31; Patton, *Conscience and Law*, 49; May, *Slave Law and Victims*, 1–2; Cover, *Justice Accused*, 175; Yanuck, "Garner Case," 49.

130. "Proclamation by the Mayor of Cincinnati to the Chief of Police," *Cincinnati Daily Commercial*, February 8–9, 11–12, 29, 1856; *Washington National Era*, March 20, 1856.

131. *Cincinnati Daily Commercial*, January 29, 31, February 1–2, 10–11, 29, March 3, 6, 1856; *Harpers Weekly*, July 18, 1857, 454; Richard C. Schneider, *African-American History in the Press, 1851–1899: From the Coming of the Civil War to the Rise of Jim Crow as Reported and Illustrated in Selected Newspapers of the Time*, 2 vols. (Detroit: Gale, 1996), 1:71.

132. *Cincinnati Daily Enquirer*, February 1, 1856; *Cincinnati Daily Commercial*, February 9, 29, March 1, 3, 1856; *Cincinnati Daily Republican*, March 6, 1856.

133. Monroe, *Oberlin Thursday Lectures*, 117–19; Monroe Papers, box 19, folder, Amendment to the Habeas Corpus Act.

134. "The Slave Case in Ohio," Chase Papers, box 1, Slavery; Alden P. Steele and Oscar T. Martin, *The History of Clark County, Ohio* (Chicago: W. H. Beers, 1881), 287–90; Henry Howe, *Historical Collections of Ohio, an Encyclopedia of the State: History Both General and Local, Geography with Descriptions of Its Counties, Cities and Villages, Its Agricultural, Manufacturing, Mining and Business Development, Sketches of Eminent and Interesting*

Characters, etc., with Notes of a Tour over It in 1886, 2 vols. (Norwalk: Published by the State of Ohio, Laning Printing, 1896), 1:384–85, 486.

135. Howe, *Historical Collections,* 1:485–86; Steele and Martin, *Clark County,* 287–90.

136. Howe, *Historical Collections,* 1:384–85; Cochran, *Western Reserve,* 114–15.

137. Ex parte Sifford, 22 F. Cas. 105 (S.D. Ohio 1857) (No. 12,848).

138. Howe, *Historical Collections,* 1:485–86; Wilbur H. Siebert and Albert B. Hart, *The Underground Railroad from Slavery to Freedom* (New York: Macmillan, 1898), 241.

139. "Arrest of Fugitive Slave," Birney Scrapbook, 43, 45, CinHS; newspaper clippings, Thomas Foraker Scrapbook, 45, CinHS.

140. Cochran, *Western Reserve,* 114–15; Greve, *Centennial History,* 1:764–65.

141. *Cincinnati Daily Commercial,* May 7, 10, and 24, 1858; Walter P. Herz, "Such a Glaring Inconsistency: The Unitarian Laity and Antislavery in Antebellum Cincinnati," Let Freedom Ring: First Unitarian Journey of Reconstruction Project, First Unitarian Church of Cincinnati Library, Cincinnati, Ohio, 2003, 13; Coffin, *Reminiscences,* 342–46.

142. *Cincinnati Daily Enquirer,* June 14, 15, and 16, 1857, May 5 and 22, 1858; *Liberator,* July 2, 1858; Coffin, *Reminiscences,* 342–46.

143. Ohio Attorney General, *Biennial Report of the Attorney General, 1860–62* (Columbus: Richard Nevins, 1862), 10; Kentucky v. Dennison, 65 U.S. (24 How.) 66 (1860).

144. Ohio Attorney General, *Biennial Report, 1860–62,* 10; Kentucky v. Dennison, 65 U.S. at 66, 73; Yanuck, "Garner Case," 49

145. John C. Hurd, *The Law of Freedom and Bondage in the United States* (New York: Negro Universities Press, 1968), 391.

146. James Fairchild, *The Underground Railroad* (Cleveland: Western Reserve Historical Society, 1895), 112–14; Hickok, "Negro in Ohio," 176–78; Nat Brandt, *The Town That Started the Civil War* (Syracuse, N.Y.: Syracuse University Press, 1990).

147. "Meeting of the Colored Freemen of Columbus," *Rochester North Star,* June 29, 1849; Campbell, *Slave Catchers,* 164–65. For a contemporary review of the incident, see Jacob R. Shipherd, comp., *History of the Oberlin-Wellington Rescue* (Boston: J. P. Jewett, 1859); William Cheek and Aimee Lee Cheek, *John Mercer Langston and the Fight for Black Freedom, 1829–1865* (Urbana: University of Illinois Press, 1989), 316–19; Eugene D. Schmiel, "The Career of Jacob Dolson Cox, 1828–1900: Soldier, Scholar, Statesman" (Ph.D. diss., Ohio State University, 1969), 36.

148. Hickok, "Negro in Ohio," 178; Schmiel, "Cox," 47; Cheek and Cheek, *Langston,* 318–19; Foner and Walker, *Proceedings,* 2:392–93.

149. Campbell, *Slave Catchers,* 165; Cheek and Cheek, *Langston,* 329; Schmiel, "Cox," 47.

150. William H. Pease and Jane H. Pease, *They Who Would Be Free: Blacks' Search for Freedom, 1830–1861* (New York: Atheneum, 1974), 157–58, 231; *Liberty,* June 3, 1859; Charles H. Langston, *Should Colored Men Be Subject to the Pains and Penalties of the*

Fugitive Slave Law? Speech before the U.S. District Court Delivered When about to be Sentenced for Rescuing a Man from Slavery (Cleveland: E. Cowles, 1859), 16.

151. Thomas D. Morris, *Free Men All: The Personal Liberty Laws of the North, 1780–1861* (Baltimore: Johns Hopkins University Press, 1974), 187.

152. Ex parte Bushnell, 9 Ohio St. 77 (1859); Joseph R. Swan, *Opinion of J. R. Swan in the Case of Bushnell and Langston on Habeas Corpus* (Columbus: Osgood and Pearce, 1859), 7–8. See also the Wisconsin Supreme Court's decision In re Booth, 3 Wis. 157 (1854), *rev'd sub nom.* Ableman v. Booth, 62 U.S. (21 How.) 506 (1859).

153. John E. Vacha, "The Case of Sarah Lucy Bagby: A Late Gesture," *Ohio History* 76 (Autumn 1967): 222.

154. Swan, *Opinion in Bushnell and Langston*, 10–16.

155. John Jolliffe, *In the Matter of George Gordon's Petition for Pardon* (Cincinnati: Gazette Company Steam Printing House, 1862), 1–56.

156. Chase to E. S. Hamlin, February 3, 1852, in *Diary and Correspondence of Salmon P. Chase*, 2 vols. (reprint of the 1903 Annual Report of the American Historical Association; New York: Da Capo Press, 1971), 2:240.

CHAPTER 8

1. Ohio const. of 1802, bill of rights, art. VIII, § 1. See Betty L. Fladeland, "James G. Birney's Anti-Slavery Activities in Cincinnati, 1835–1837," *Bulletin of the Historical and Philosophical Society of Ohio* 9 (October 1951): 251.

2. Ohio const. of 1851, bill of rights, art. I, § 1.

3. Prigg v. Pennsylvania, 41 U.S. (16 Pet.) 539 (1842); Paul Finkelman, "Fugitive Slaves, Midwestern Racial Tolerance, and the Value of 'Justice Delayed,'" *Iowa Law Review* 78 (October 1992): 105.

4. Anderson v. Poindexter, 6 Ohio St. 622 (1856); Stephen Middleton, "Cincinnati and the Fight for the Law of Freedom in Ohio, 1830–1856," *Locus: An Historical Journal of Regional Perspectives* 4 (Fall 1991): 72–73.

5. Commonwealth v. Aves, 35 Mass. 193 (1836); Jackson v. Bulloch, 12 Conn. 38 (1837); Leonard W. Levy, *The Law of the Commonwealth and Chief Justice Shaw* (Cambridge, Mass.: Harvard University Press, 1957; repr. New York: Oxford University Press, 1987); Paul Finkelman, *An Imperfect Union: Slavery, Federalism, and Comity* (Chapel Hill: University of North Carolina Press, 1981).

6. "Report of the Select Committee, to Which Was Referred Petitions and Memorials Relating to the Disabilities of Persons of Color," March 3, 1842, reprinted in *The Black Laws in the Old Northwest: A Documentary History*, ed. Stephen Middleton (Westport, Conn.: Greenwood, 1993), 92.

7. State v. Farr, reported in *Lower Sandusky Whig*, May 27, 1841; Finkelman, *Imperfect Union*, 165–66.

8. Benjamin W. Arnett and Jere A. Brown, *The Black Laws! Speeches of Honorable Benjamin W. Arnett of Greene County and Honorable Jere A. Brown of Cuyahoga County, in the*

House of Representatives, March 10, 1886 (Columbus: Ohio State Journal, 1886), 37–40; An act to prevent the amalgamation of the white and colored races, 58 Laws of Ohio 6 (1861), repr. in S. Middleton, *Black Laws*, 135–36.

9. *Toledo Blade*, September 19, 1859, also quoted in Emmett D. Preston, "The Fugitive Slave Acts in Ohio," *Journal of Negro History* 28 (October 1943): 474.

10. *Report of the Debates and Proceedings of the Convention for the Revision of the Constitution of the State of Ohio, 1850–1851*, 2 vols. (Columbus: S. Medary, 1851).

11. Ohio Anti-Slavery Society, *Proceedings of the First Annual Meeting of the Ohio State Anti-Slavery Society* (Xenia, Ohio, January 3–5, 1860), 1, 7; 54 Laws of Ohio 170 (1856); William C. Cochran, "Ohio from 1802 to 1851: The Black Laws—the Three-Fifths Rule," *The Western Reserve and the Fugitive Slave Law: A Prelude to the Civil War* (Cleveland: Western Reserve Historical Society, 1920), 115; James Monroe, Speech in the Ohio House of Representatives, January 12, 1858, James Monroe Papers, box 27, Oberlin College Library Archives.

12. Speech of Honorable Peter Hitchcock of Geauga, on the "Bill to Prevent Giving Aid to Fugitive Slaves," in the House of Representatives, February 23, 1861 (Columbus: Richard Nevins' Steam Printing House, 1861), 4, 5.

13. Report of the Committee on Federal Relations, Ohio General Assembly, 1859, 1, Documents Collection, OHS.

14. Ohio Anti-Slavery Society, *Proceedings of the First Annual Meeting of the Ohio State Anti-Slavery Society*, Xenia, Ohio, January 3–5, 1860).

15. *Toledo Blade*, February 8, 1861, also quoted in Preston, "Fugitive Slave Acts," 475–77.

16. Robert F. Horowitz, *Great Impeacher: A Political Biography of James M. Ashley* (New York: Brooklyn College Press, 1979); Maxine B. Kahn, "Congressman Ashley in the Post–Civil War Years," *Northwest Ohio Quarterly* 36 (Summer 1964): 116–33, 194–210.

17. See John Hope Franklin and Alfred A. Moss, *From Slavery to Freedom: A History of African Americans*, 8th ed. (Boston: McGraw-Hill, 2000), 181–85.

18. The law was passed to amend an act entitled "an act to amend the act to provided for the maintenance and better regulation of the common school in the city of Cincinnati," 56 Laws of Ohio 117, 118 (1856); Quillin, *Color Line*, 97.

19. See Williams v. Dirs. of Sch. Dist., 1 Wright 578 (1834); Jeffries v. Ankeny, 11 Ohio 372 (1842); Thacker v. Hawk, 11 Ohio 376 (1842).

20. Lane v. Baker, 12 Ohio 237, 238–39, 251–52 (1843).

21. David A. Gerber, *Black Ohio and the Color Line, 1860–1915* (Urbana: University of Illinois Press, 1976), 26–27; Felice A. Bonadio, *North of Reconstruction: Ohio Politics, 1865–1870* (New York: New York University Press, 1970), 81.

22. Samuel S. Cox, *Emancipation and Its Results—Is Ohio to Be Africanized?* (Washington, D.C.: L. Towers, 1862), 15; Gerber, *Black Ohio*, 28.

23. Bonadio, *North of Reconstruction*, 81.

24. Arnett and Brown, *Black Laws!* 37–40; An act to prevent the amalgamation of the white and colored races, 58 Laws of Ohio 6 (1861), repr. in S. Middleton, *Black Laws*, 135–36.

25. Roberts v. City of Boston, 59 Mass. 198 (1849); Charles Sumner, *Argument of Charles Sumner, Esq. against the Constitutionality of Separate Colored Schools, in the Case of Sara Roberts vs. the City of Boston before the Supreme Court of Massachusetts, December 4, 1849* (Boston: B. F. Roberts, 1849); Leonard Williams Levy, *Jim Crow in Boston: The Origin of the Separate but Equal Doctrine* (New York: Da Capo Press, 1974); Levy, *Law of the Commonwealth*, 109–13.

26. Levy, *Law of the Commonwealth*, 114.

27. Van Camp v. Logan, 9 Ohio 406 (1859); Frank U. Quillin, *The Color Line in Ohio: A History of Race Prejudice in a Typical Northern State* (Ann Arbor, Mich.: George Wahr, 1913), 89–91.

28. Van Camp v. Logan, 9 Ohio at 410–12.

29. An act to prevent the amalgamation of the white and colored races, 58 Laws of Ohio 6 (1861), repr. in S. Middleton, *Black Laws*, 135.

30. Barbara C. Cruz and Michael J. Berson, "The American Melting Pot? Miscegenation Laws in the United States." *OAH Magazine of History* 15 (Summer 2001): 80–83.

31. An act to prevent the amalgamation of the white and colored races, 58 Laws of Ohio 6 (1861), repr. in S. Middleton, *Black Laws*, 136; Franklin Johnson, *The Development of State Legislation Concerning the Free Negro* (New York: Arbor Press, 1919), 163; Speech of Peter Hitchcock, 4.

32. An act to prevent the amalgamation of the white and colored races, 58 Laws of Ohio 6, 74 (1861), repr. in S. Middleton, *Black Laws*, 136.

33. "The Negro Problem," *Independent*, September 18, 1902.

34. Loving v. Virginia, 388 U.S. 1 (1967); Peter Wallenstein, "Race, Marriage, and the Supreme Court from *Pace v. Alabama* (1883) to *Loving v. Virginia* (1967)," *Journal of Supreme Court History* 2 (1998): 66, 73, 79–84.

35. Quoted in *Cleveland Gazette*, January 30, 1886.

36. *Cleveland Gazette*, August 30, 1884.

37. *Cleveland Gazette*, January 23, 1886.

38. C. Vann Woodward, *The Strange Career of Jim Crow* (New York: Oxford University Press, 1955); Charles A. Lofgren, *The Plessy Case: A Legal-Historical Interpretation* (New York: Oxford University Press, 1987); Gerber, *Black Ohio*, 26; Lou Falkner Williams, *The Great South Carolina Ku Klux Klan Trials, 1871–1872* (Athens: University of Georgia Press, 1996).

39. *Cleveland Gazette*, January 1, 1887; Gerber, *Black Ohio*, 56.

40. Gerber, *Black Ohio*, 57.

41. State ex rel. Lewis v. Bd. of Educ. of Cincinnati, 1876 WL 6031 (Ohio); Quillin, *Color Line*, 92.

42. *Ohio State School Commissioner's Report*, 1881, 138; Quillin, *Color Line*, 92–93.

43. Civil Rights Act of 1866, 14 Stat. 27; Robert P. Green Jr., ed., *Equal Protection and the African American Constitutional Experience: A Documentary History* (Westport, Conn.: Greenwood, 2000).

44. "The right of citizens of the United States to vote shall not be denied or abridged by the United States or by any state on account of race, color, or previous condition of servitude." U.S. Const. amend. XV, § 1.

45. *Ohio State Journal*, October 21, 1867; Quillin, *Color Line*, 98–99; Victor B. Howard, *Religion and the Radical Republican Movement, 1860–1870* (Lexington: University Press of Kentucky, 1990), 171–73.

46. John Hope Franklin, *George Washington Williams: A Biography* (Chicago: University of Chicago Press, 1985); George Washington Williams, *History of the Negro Race in America, 1619–1880* (repr., New York: Arno Press, 1968).

47. Representative Jere A. Brown, Hallie Q. Brown and Frances Brown Hughes Collection, National Afro-American Museum and Cultural Center, Wilberforce, Ohio.

48. Hallie and Frances Brown Collection, nos. 87–86, National Afro-American History Museum and Cultural Center, "Sketches of Life Members," *Ohio Archaeological and Historical Society Publications* 4 (1895): 452–53; Gerber, *Black Ohio*, 17.

49. An act to protect all citizens in their civil and legal rights, 81 Laws of Ohio 15, 16, 90 (1884); An act to amend section 1 of an act "to protect all citizens in their civil and legal rights," 81 Laws of Ohio 90 (1884); repr. in S. Middleton, *Black Laws*, 137–38; Gerber, *Black Ohio*, 46.

50. Gerber, *Black Ohio*, 54, 238; *Cleveland Gazette*, February 14, 1885.

51. *Cleveland Gazette*, March 13, 1886.

52. *Cleveland Gazette*, March 13, May 5, 1886.

53. Gerber, *Black Ohio*, 237; *Cleveland Gazette*, April 12, 1884, February 24, 1885.

54. Gerber, *Black Ohio*, 54, 238; *Cleveland Gazette*, February 14, 1885.

55. Williams to Green, December 24, 1879, John P. Green Papers, box I, folder I, Western Reserve Historical Society; *Cleveland Gazette*, March 13, 1886; Gerber, *Black Ohio*, 237.

56. Gerber, *Black Ohio*, 237–38.

57. *Cleveland Gazette*, February 14, 1885; Gerber, *Black Ohio*, 55.

58. *Cleveland Gazette*, September 15, 1883, February 2, 1885, May 15, 1886.

59. An act to repeal the Black Laws of Ohio, 84 Laws of Ohio 34 (1887); *Cleveland Gazette*, March 13, 1886; Brown Collection, National Afro-American Museum and Cultural Center, nos. 86–87.

60. Speech of Honorable B. W. Arnett in the Ohio House of Representatives, in *The Black Laws!* 1, 16, 17; Benjamin W. Arnett, "Sermons and Addresses," *Wilberforce Alumni, 1841–1881*.

61. Speech of Honorable Jere A. Brown, in the Ohio House of Representatives, in *The Black Laws!* 19–20, 28; Arnett, "Sermons and Addresses."

62. Speech of Arnett, in *The Black Laws!* 40; Gerber, *Black Ohio*, 243; Quillin, *Color Line*, 93.

63. *Cleveland Gazette*, March 12, 1887.

64. Speech of Hon. Joseph B. Foraker at Hamilton County, Ohio, Emancipation Day, September 22, 1899, 1, Pamphlet Collection, CinHS; *Cleveland Gazette*, April 1, March 13, May 15, 1886, March 12, 1887.

65. *Ohio Educational Monthly*, January 1888, 59; Quillin, *Color Line*, 93–94.

66. Reported in *Cincinnati Enquirer,* February 15, 1889; Quillin, *Color Line,* 94.

67. *Cleveland Plain Dealer,* January 17, 1889; Quillin, *Color Line,* 94–95.

68. An act to prevent discrimination by life insurance companies against persons of color, 86 Laws of Ohio 34 (1889), repr. in S. Middleton, *Black Laws,* 139–40.

69. The Civil Rights Cases, 109 U.S. 3 (1883); Plessy v. Ferguson, 163 U.S. 537 (1896); Paul Oberst, "The Strange Career of *Plessy v. Ferguson,*" *Arizona Law Review* 15, no. 1 (1993): 389–418.

SELECTED BIBLIOGRAPHY

ABBREVIATIONS

ChiHS	Chicago Historical Society
CinHS	Cincinnati Historical Society
HPSOQ	*Historical and Philosophical Society of Ohio Quarterly*
HSP	Historical Society of Pennsylvania
OAS	Ohio Anti-Slavery Society
OHS	Ohio Historical Society
VFM	Vertical File Manuscript
VSLA	Virginia State Library and Archives
WRHS	Western Reserve Historical Society

MANUSCRIPT COLLECTIONS

American Antiquarian Society, Worcester, Mass.

Funk Family Papers
Philip J. Lampi Collection
Rufus Putnam Papers
Ward Family Papers

Chicago Historical Society

Zebina Eastman Papers
John Kirk Papers

Cincinnati Historical Society

James Gillespie Birney Scrapbook
Salmon Portland Chase Papers
Henry M. Ernest Papers
Female Association of Cincinnati Record Book

Oran Follett Papers
Thomas Foraker Scrapbook
Gwynne Family Papers
List of Negroes Emancipated by the Will of John Randolph
People's Church Record Book, 1831–1953
Thomas B. Stevenson Papers
Timothy Walker Papers
Nathaniel Wright Papers
Union Humane Society

Duke University Library, Manuscript Department, Durham, N.C.

Samuel Compton Papers

Filson Historical Society, Louisville, Ky.

Barthelemi Tardiveau Papers
James Taylor Papers

Frankfort (Ky.) Historical Society

William Owsley Papers

Historical Society of Pennsylvania, Philadelphia

Salmon Portland Chase Papers
Leon Gardener Papers

Library of Congress, Manuscript Division, Washington, D.C.

Thomas Worthington Papers

New York Historical Society, Manhattan

Rufus King Papers

Oberlin College Archives, Oberlin, Ohio

James Monroe Papers

Ohio Historical Society, Columbus

Mordecai Bartley Papers

William Dennison Papers
Seabury Ford Papers
Erasmus Gest Papers
Charles Hammond Papers
William Henry Harrison Papers
Samuel Huntington Papers
Manumission Record (VFM)
John McLean Papers
William Medill Papers
Jeremiah Morrow Papers
Daniel Parker Diary, 1846
Priscilla M. Parker (VFM)
Delia Peck Letter (VFM)
Peyton Polly Collection
Charles E. Rice Collection
Arthur St. Clair Papers
Arthur St. Clair Scattered Papers (VFM)
Winthrop Sargent Papers
Wilson Shannon Papers
Sturges Family Papers
William Starling Sullivant Collection
Edward Tiffin Papers
Joseph Vance Papers
Micajah T. Williams Papers (VFM)
Reuben Wood Papers

Schomburg Center for Research in Black Culture, New York

Jacob Bruce Collection

Southern Historical Collection, University of North Carolina, Chapel Hill

Edward Dromgoole Papers

University of Chicago Library, Special Collections Research Center

William H. English Papers

Virginia State Library and Archives, Richmond

William H. Cabell Executive Papers, 1811
Executive Letterbook (Governors)
John Tyler Papers

Western Reserve Historical Society, Cleveland

Canton Ladies Antislavery Society Papers
Connecticut Western Reserve Papers
Caleb Emerson Family Papers
John P. Green Papers
Marius Robinson Papers
Allen Trimble Executive Papers, 1819–1822
Elisha Whittlesey Papers

Wilberforce University Library Archives, Wilberforce, Ohio

William S. Scarborough Papers

LEGAL CASES

Augustus Wattles v. George Hartwell, February 15, 1838. Official Transcript. Cincinnati Historical Society.
Augustus Wattles v. Joseph Graham, reported in *Philanthropist*, February 27, 1838.
Anderson v. Poindexter, 6 Ohio St. 622 (1856).
Campbell v. Kirkpatrick, 4 F. Cas. 1174 (C.C.D. Ohio 1850) (No. 2,363).
Chalmers v. Stewart, 11 Ohio 386 (1842).
Commonwealth v. Aves, 35 Mass. 193 (1836.)
Commonwealth v. Garner, 44 Va. 624 (1846).
Driskell v. Parish, 7 F. Cas. 1100 (C.C.D. Ohio 1845) (No. 4,089); 7 F. Cas. 1093 (C.C.D. Ohio 1847) (No. 4,087); 7 F. Cas. 1095 (C.C.D. Ohio 1849) (No. 4,088).
Ex parte Bushnell, 9 Ohio St. 77 (1859).
Ex parte Robinson, 20 F. Cas. 969 (C.C.S.D. Ohio 1856) (No. 11,934).
Ex parte Sifford, 22 F. Cas. 105 (S.D. Ohio 1857) (No. 12,848).
Gibbons v. Ogden, 22 U.S. (9 Wheat.) 1 (1824).
Gibbons v. Sloane, 10 F. Cas. 294 (C.C.D. Ohio 1854) (No. 5,382).
Graham v. Strader, 44 Ky. 173 (1844).
Gray v. Ohio, 4 Ohio 353 (1831).
Greathouse v. Dunlap, 10 F. Cas. 1062 (C.C.D. Ohio 1843) (No. 5,742).
Groves v. Slaughter, 40 U.S. (14 Pet.) 449 (1841).
Henderson v. Ohio, reported in *Philanthropist*, January 27, 1847.
Jackson v. Bulloch, 12 Conn. 38 (1837).
Jeffries v. Ankeny, 11 Ohio 372 (1842).
Jones v. Van Zandt, 13 F. Cas. 1040 (C.C.D. Ohio 1843) (No. 7,501).
Jones v. Van Zandt, 46 U.S. (5 How.) 215 (1847).
John Lawrence v. Matilda, a Colored Girl, reported in *Daily Republican*, March 16, 1837.
Kentucky v. Dennison, 65 U.S. (24 How.) 66 (1861).

Lane v. Baker, 12 Ohio 237 (1843).

Lawson v. Perry, 1 Wright 242 (1833).

Loving v. Virginia, 388 U.S. 1 (1967).

Marie Louise v. Marat, 9 La. 473 (1836).

Miller v. McQuerry, 17 F. Cas. 335 (C.C.D. Ohio 1853) (No. 9,583).

New York v. Miln, 36 U.S. (11 Pet.) 102 (1837).

Peyton Polly v. John Watson, depositions of Jacob Heaberling and Coleman Walker in Louisville Chancery Court Records, Kentucky Department of Libraries and Archives, Frankfort.

Plessy v. Ferguson, 163 U.S. 537 (1896).

Prigg v. Pennsylvania, 41 U.S. (16 Pet.) 539 (1842).

Ralph, a Colored Man v. Montgomery, reported in *Philanthropist*, August 6, 1839.

Rankin v. Lydia, 9 Ky. 467 (1820).

Roberts v. City of Boston, 59 Mass. 198 (1849).

Scott v. Sandford, 60 U.S. (19 How.) 393 (1857).

State v. Birney, 8 Ohio 230 (1837).

State v. Cincinnati, 19 Ohio 178 (1850).

State v. Farr, reported in *Lower Sandusky Whig*, May 27, 1841.

State v. Forbes and Armitage, Arrested upon Requisition of the Government of Ohio, on Charge of Kidnapping Jerry Phinney, and Tried before the Franklin Circuit Court of Kentucky, April 10, 1846. Pamphlet, Cincinnati Historical Society.

State v. Hoppess, 2 Western L.J. 279 (1845); 2 Western L.J. 333 (1845).

Thacker v. Hawk, 11 Ohio 376 (1842).

Van Camp v. Logan, 9 Ohio 406 (1859).

Weimer v. Sloane, 29 F. Cas. 599 (C.C.D. Ohio 1854) (No. 17,363).

Williams v. Directors of School District, 1 Wright 578 (1834).

Woods v. Green, 1 Wright 504 (1834).

Woodson v. State, 17 Ohio 161 (1848).

Young's Administrator v. Small, 43 Ky. 220 (1843).

NEWSPAPERS

Akron Free Democratic Standard
Ashtabula Sentinel
Chillicothe Fredonian
Cincinnati Advertiser and Ohio Phoenix
Cincinnati Daily Enquirer
Cincinnati Daily Evening Post
Cincinnati Daily Gazette
Cincinnati Enquirer
Cincinnati Herald and Philanthropist (1843–46)
Cincinnati Post and Anti-Abolitionist
Cincinnati Weekly Globe

Cincinnati Weekly Herald (1846–48)
Cincinnati Western Spy
Cincinnati Whig
Cincinnati Whig and Commercial Intelligencer
Clermont Courier
Cleveland Gazette
Cleveland Herald
Cleveland Plain Dealer
Covington (Ky.) Daily News
Daily Cincinnati Enquirer (1841–43)
Daily Cincinnati Commercial
Daily Cincinnati Republican and Commercial Register
Daily Evening Post (Cincinnati)
Dayton Evening Empire
Dayton Journal and Advertiser
Dayton Transcript
Frankfort Commonwealth (Lexington)
Frederick Douglass' Paper (NYC)
Freedom's Journal (NYC)
Germantown Gazette and Miami Valley Advertiser (Dayton)
Liberator (Boston)
Liberty Hall (Cincinnati)
Liberty Hall and Cincinnati Gazette
Licking Valley Register (Covington, Ky.)
Louisville City Gazette
Lower Sandusky Whig
Marietta Commentator
Montreal Gazette
Mt. Pleasant Philanthropist
National Gazette
National Press and Cincinnati Weekly
New York Colored American (NYC)
Norfolk and Portsmouth (Va.) Herald
Niles' National Register (Baltimore)
Ohio Educational Monthly
Ohio Gazette
Ohio Press (Columbus)
Ohio Repository
Ohio State Journal (Columbus)
Ohio Statesman (Columbus)
Philanthropist (Cincinnati)
Provincial Freeman (Canada West [now Ontario])
Rochester (N.Y.) North Star
Salem Anti-Slavery Bugle

Scioto Gazette (Chillicothe)
Toledo Daily Blade
Washington (D.C.) National Era
Weekly Ohio State Journal (Columbus)
Western Reserve Chronicle (Warren, Ohio)
Western-Union Republican
Xenia Torch-Light

BOOKS AND ARTICLES

Abbott, John S. C. *The History of the State of Ohio: From the Discovery of the Great Valley to the Present Time.* Detroit: Northwestern Publishing Co., 1875.

Abernathy, Thomas P. *Western Lands and the American Revolution.* New York: D. Appleton-Century Co., 1937.

Adams, Henry. *History of the United States of America.* 9 vols. New York: Charles Scribner's Sons, 1889–91.

Alilunas, Leo. "Fugitive Slave Cases in Ohio Prior to 1850." *Ohio Archaeological and Historical Quarterly* 49 (April 1940): 160–84.

Aptheker, Herbert. *A Documentary History of the Negro People in the United States.* New York: Citadel Press, 1951.

Arnett, Benjamin W., and Jere A. Brown. *The Black Laws! Speeches of Honorable Benjamin W. Arnett of Greene County and Honorable Jere A. Brown of Cuyahoga County, in the House of Representatives, March 10, 1886.* Columbus: Ohio State Journal, 1886.

Ashe, Samuel A'Court. *History of North Carolina.* 7 vols. (Raleigh, N.C.: C. L. Van Noppen, 1925.

Atwater, Caleb. *The General Character, Present and Future Prospects of the People of Ohio: An Address Delivered at the United States Court House, during the term of the United States Circuit Court, in Columbus, Ohio, December, 1826.* Columbus: P. H. Olmstead and Co., 1827.

——. *History of the State of Ohio, Natural and Civil.* Cincinnati: Glezen and Shepard, 1838.

Aumann, F. R. "Judicial Law Making and Stare Decisis." *Kentucky Law Journal* 21 (November 1932): 156–71.

Baily, Marilyn. "From Cincinnati, Ohio, to Wilberforce, Canada: A Note on Antebellum Colonization." *Journal of Negro History* 58 (October 1973): 427–40.

Banker, Charles August. "Salmon P. Chase, Legal Counsel for Fugitive Slaves: Antislavery Ideology as a Lawyer's Creation." Master's thesis, Rice University, Houston, 1986.

Barnhart, John D. "The Migration of Kentuckians Across the Ohio River." *Filson Club Historical Quarterly* 25 (January 1951): 24–32.

——. "Southern Influence in the Formation of Ohio." *Journal of Southern History* 3 (February 1937): 28–42.

Barnhart, John D., and Dorothy L. Riker. *Indiana to 1816: The Colonial Period.* Indianapolis: Indiana Historical Bureau and Indiana Historical Society, 1971.

Barth, Harold B. *History of Columbiana County Ohio.* 2 vols. Topeka, Kan.: Historical Publishing Co., 1926.

Bartlett, Ruhl Jacob. "The Struggle for Statehood in Ohio." *Ohio Archaeological and
Historical Quarterly* 32 (July 1923): 472–505.

Beard, Charles A., and Mary R. Beard. *A Basic History of the United States.* New York:
Doubleday, 1950.

Bell, Howard H. "Expressions of Negro Militancy in the North, 1840–1860."
Journal of Negro History 45 (January 1960): 11–20.

Benton, Thomas Hart. *Examination of the Dred Scott Case.* New York: D. Appleton
and Co., 1858.

Benton, Wilbourn E. *1787: Drafting the United States Constitution.* 2 vols. College Station: Texas A and M University Press, 1986.

Bergman, Peter M., and Jean McCarroll, eds. *The Negro in the Continental Congress.*
New York: Bergman, 1969.

Berlin, Ira. "The Structure of the Free Negro Caste in the Antebellum United
States." *Journal of Social History* 9 (Spring 1976): 297–318.

Bernstein, Richard B, with Jerome Agel. *Amending America: If We Love the Constitution
So Much, Why Do We Keep Trying to Change It?* New York: Times Books, 1993.

Berwanger, Eugene H. *The Frontier against Slavery: Western Anti-Negro Prejudice and the
Slavery Extension Controversy.* Chicago: University of Illinois Press, 1967.

Biographical Annals of Ohio: A Handbook of the Government and Institutions of the State of Ohio.
Compiled under the authority of the Act of April 19, 1904 (Springfield,
Ohio: State Printers, 1905).

Birney, James Gillespie. *The American Churches: Bulwarks of Slavery.* Reprint, Concord, N.H.: P. Pillsbury, 1885.

———. *Letters of James Gillespie Birney, 1831–1857.* Ed. Dwight L. Dumond. 2 vols. New
York: D. Appleton-Century Co., 1938.

Birney, William. *James G. Birney and His Times: The Genesis of the Republican Party with Some
Account of Abolition Movements in the South before 1828.* New York: D. Appleton and
Co., 1890.

Black, Lowell Dwight. "The Negro Volunteer Militia Units of the Ohio National
Guard, 1870–1954: The Struggle for Military Recognition and Equality in
the State of Ohio." Ph.D. diss., Ohio State University, 1976.

Blanchard, Rufus. *The Discovery and Conquests of the Northwest Territory.* Chicago: Cush-
ing, Thomas and Co., 1880.

Blue, Frederick J. *Salmon P. Chase: A Life in Politics.* Kent, Ohio: Kent State University Press, 1987.

Bochin, Hal W. "Tom Corwin's Speech against the Mexican War: Courageous
but Misunderstood." *Ohio History* 90 (Winter 1981): 33–54.

Bodley, Temple. *Our First Great West: In Revolutionary War, Diplomacy and Politics.*
Louisville, Ky.: John P. Merton and Co., 1938.

Bonadio, Felice A. *North of Reconstruction: Ohio Politics, 1865–1870.* New York: New
York University Press, 1970.

Bond, Beverly W., Jr. *The Civilization of the Old Northwest: A Study of Political, Social, and Economic Development, 1788–1812.* New York: Macmillan, 1934.

———. *The History of the State of Ohio: The Foundations of Ohio.* Columbus: State Archaeological and Historical Society, 1941.

Brandt, Nat. *The Town That Started the Civil War.* Syracuse, N.Y.: Syracuse University Press, 1990.

Brisbane, William H., et. al. *Church Abolitionism, or the Legitimate Tendency of the Doctrines of Modern Abolitionism.* First Baptist Church of Cincinnati. Cincinnati: William H. Brisbane, 1841.

Brooke, John. "Anthony Wayne: His Campaign against the Indians of the Northwest." *Pennsylvania Magazine of History and Biography* 19, no. 3 (1895–96): 387–96.

Brooks, Jehiel, ed. *A Compilation of the Laws of the United States, and of States, in Relation to Fugitives from Labor, with the Clauses of the Constitution of the United States Involved in the Execution of the Same.* Washington, D.C.: Taylor and Maury, 1860.

Brown, Jeffrey P., and Andrew R. L. Cayton, eds. *The Pursuit of Public Power: Political Culture in Ohio, 1787–1861.* Kent, Ohio: Kent State University Press, 1994.

Brown, Ray A. "The Making of the Wisconsin Constitution." *Wisconsin Law Review* 1949 (July 1949): 648–94.

Brown, Robert Elliot. *Manasseh Cutler and the Settlement of Ohio, 1788.* Marietta, Ohio: Marietta College Press, 1938.

Buchanan, James, comp. *The Blacks of Pickaway County, Ohio, in the Nineteenth Century.* Bowie, Md.: Heritage Books, 1988.

Burnet, Jacob. *Notes on the Early Settlement of the North-Western Territory.* Cincinnati: Derby, Bradley and Co., 1847.

Burnett, Edmund C. *The Continental Congress.* New York: Macmillan, 1941.

———, ed. *Letters of Members of the Continental Congress.* 8 vols. Washington, D.C.: Carnegie Institution of Washington, 1921–36.

Burns, James J. *Educational History of Ohio: A History of Its Progress since the Formation of the State, together with the Portraits and Biographies of Past and Present State Officials.* Columbus: Historical Publications Co., 1905.

Bushnell, Henry. *The History of Granville, Licking County, Ohio.* Columbus: Press of Hann and Adair, 1889.

Caldwell, John A. *History of Belmont and Jefferson Counties, Ohio, and Incidentally Historical Collections Pertaining to Border Warfare and the Early Settlement of the Adjacent Portion of the Ohio Valley.* Ed. J. H. Newton. Wheeling, W. Va.: Historical Publication Co., 1880.

Calkins, David L. "Chronological Highlights of Cincinnati's Black Community." *Cincinnati Historical Quarterly* 28 (Winter 1970): 344–53.

Callan, John F. *Laws of the United States, for the Government of the Militia of the District of Columbia, and the United States Rules and Articles of War.* Baltimore: J. Murphy and Co., 1861.

Campbell, Stanley. *Slave Catchers: Enforcement of the Fugitive Slave Law, 1850–1860.* Chapel Hill: University of North Carolina Press, 1970.

Carey, Anthony Gene. "The Second Party System Collapses: The 1853 Maine Law Campaign in Ohio." *Ohio History* 100 (Summer–Autumn 1991): 129–53.

Caruso, John. *The Great Lakes Frontier: An Epic of the Old Northwest*. New York: Bobbs-Merrill, 1961.

Cayton, Andrew R. L. *The Frontier Republic: Ideology and Politics in the Ohio Country, 1780–1825*. Kent, Ohio: Kent State University Press, 1986.

———. *Ohio: The History of a People*. Columbus: Ohio State University Press, 2002.

Chaddock, Robert E. "Ohio Before 1850: A Study of the Early Influence of Pennsylvania and Southern Populations in Ohio." Ph.D. diss., Columbia University, 1908.

Chambers, William Nisbet. *Political Parties in a New Nation: The American Experience, 1776–1809*. New York: Oxford University Press, 1963.

Chase, Salmon P. *The Address and Reply on the Presentation of a Testimonial to S. P. Chase*. Cincinnati: Henry W. Derby and Co., 1845.

———. *An Argument for the Defendant, Submitted to the Supreme Court of the United States in the Case of Wharton Jones v. John Van Zandt*. Cincinnati: R. P. Donogh and Co., 1847.

———. *Diary and Correspondence of Salmon P. Chase*. 2 vols. Reprint of the 1903 Annual Report of the American Historical Association. New York: Da Capo Press, 1971.

———. *The Salmon P. Chase Papers*. Ed. John Niven. 5 vols. Kent, Ohio: Kent State University Press, 1993–98.

———. *Speech of Salmon P. Chase in the Case of the Colored Woman Matilda, Who Was Brought before the Court of Common Pleas of Hamilton Co., Ohio, by Writ of Habeas Corpus, March 11, 1837*. Cincinnati: Pugh and Dodd, 1837.

———. *Maintain Plighted Faith. Speech of the Honorable Salmon P. Chase, of Ohio, in the Senate, February 3, 1854, against the Repeal of the Missouri Prohibition of Slavery North of 36, 30*. Washington, D.C.: J. T. and L. Towers, 1854.

———, ed. *The Statutes of Ohio and of the Northwestern Territory, 1787–1833*. 3 vols. Cincinnati: Corey and Fairbank, 1833–35.

Cheek, William, and Aimee Lee Cheek. *John Mercer Langston and the Fight for Black Freedom, 1829–1865*. Urbana: University of Illinois Press, 1989.

Child, Lydia M. *An Appeal in Favor of That Class of Americans Called Africans*. Boston: Allen and Ticknor, 1833.

Christy, David. *A Lecture on African Colonization, Including a Brief Outline of the Slave Trade, Emancipation, the Relation of the Republic of Liberia to England, & etc., Delivered in the Hall of the House of Representatives of the State of Ohio*. Cincinnati: J. A. and U. P. James, 1849.

Cincinnati Colonization Society. *Proceedings of the Cincinnati Colonization Society, at the Annual Meeting, January 14, 1833*. Pamphlet. Cincinnati: F. S. Benton, 1833.

Clarfield, Gerard H. *Timothy Pickering and the American Republic*. Pittsburgh: University of Pittsburgh Press, 1980.

Clarke, Grace Julian, ed. "A Letter of Dr. Gamaliel Bailey to Joshua R. Giddings." Documents, *Indiana Magazine of History* 26 (March 1930): 43–46.

Clarke, James Freeman. *Present Condition of the Free Colored People of the United States*. New York: American Anti-Slavery Society, 1859.

Clay, Cassius M. *The Life of Cassius Marcellus Clay: Memoirs, Writings, and Speeches, Showing His Conduct in the Overthrow of American Slavery, the Salvation of the Union, and the Restoration of the Autonomy of the States.* 2 vols. Cincinnati: J. F. Brennan and Co., 1886.

Coates, William R. *A History of Cuyahoga County and the City of Cleveland.* Chicago: American Historical Society, 1924.

Cochran, William C. "Ohio from 1802 to 1851: The Black Laws—The Three-Fifths Rule," in *The Western Reserve and the Fugitive Slave Law: A Prelude to the Civil War.* Cleveland: Western Reserve Historical Society, 1920.

———. *The Western Reserve and the Fugitive Slave Law: A Prelude to the Civil War.* Cleveland: Western Reserve Historical Society, 1920.

Coffin, Levi. *Reminiscences of Levi Coffin, the Reputed President of the Underground Railroad: Being a Brief History of the Labors of a Lifetime in behalf of the Slave, with the Stories of Numerous Fugitives, Who Gained Their Freedom through His Instrumentality, and Many Other Incidents.* Cincinnati: Robert Clarke and Co., 1880.

Cohen, William. "Thomas Jefferson and the Problem of Slavery." *Journal of American History* 56 (December 1969): 503–26.

Comegys, C. G.. *Reminiscences of the Life and Public Services of Edward Tiffin, Ohio's First Governor.* Chillicothe, Ohio: J. R. S. Bond and Son, 1869.

Conlin, Mary Lou. *Simon Perkins of the Western Reserve.* Cleveland: Western Reserve Historical Society, 1968.

Constitutional Convention. *Journal of the Constitutional Convention of Ohio.* Ed. Daniel Ryan. Chillicothe, Ohio: N. Willis, 1802.

Corwin, Thomas. *Free Soil vs. Slavery: Speech of Thomas Corwin of Ohio against the Compromise Bill, Delivered in the Senate of the United States, July 24, 1848.* Washington, D.C.: Printed by Buell and Blanchard, 1848.

Cover, Robert M. *Justice Accused: Antislavery and the Judicial Process.* New Haven: Yale University Press, 1975.

Cox, Samuel S. *Eight Years in Congress, from 1857–1865: Memoir and Speeches.* New York: D. Appleton and Co., 1865.

———. *Emancipation and Its Results: Is Ohio to Be Africanized? Speech of Hon. S. S. Cox Delivered in the House of Representatives, June 6, 1862.* Washington, D.C.: n.p., 1862.

———. *Emancipation and Its Results—Is Ohio to Be Africanized?* Washington, D.C.: L. Towers, 1862.

———. *Free Debate in Congress Threatened—Abolition Leaders and Their Revolutionary Schemes Unmasked. Speech of the Honorable Samuel S. Cox Delivered in the House of Representatives, April 6, 1864.* Washington, D.C.: n.p., 1864

Crouse, D. F. *The Ohio Gateway.* New York: Charles Scribner's Sons, 1938.

Crum, Fred Stephen. "Edward Coles, with Special Reference to His Influence against Slavery in the Northwest." Master's thesis, Cornell University, 1893.

Cruz, Barbara C., and Michael J. Berson, "The American Melting Pot? Miscegenation Laws in the United States." *OAH Magazine of History* 15 (Summer 2001): 80–84.

Culpepper, Betty M. "The Negro and the Black Laws of Ohio, 1803–1860." Master's thesis, Kent State University, 1965.

Cummings, John, and Joseph A. Hill, eds. *Negro Population, 1790–1915.* Washington, D.C.: Government Printing Office, 1918.

Curtis, George T. *History of the Origins, Formation, and Adoption of the Constitution of the United States with Notices of Its Principal Framers.* 2 vols. New York: Harper and Brothers, 1863.

Cutler, Julia Perkins. *The Founders of Ohio: Brief Sketches of the Forty-eight Pioneers Who, under Command of General Rufus Putnam, Landed at the Mouth of the Muskingum River on the Seventh of April, 1788, and Commenced the First White Settlement in the Northwest Territory.* Cincinnati: R. Clarke and Co., 1888.

———. *The Life and Times of Ephraim Cutler: Prepared from His Journals and Correspondence.* With biographical sketches of Jervis Cutler and William P. Cutler. Cincinnati: Robert Clarke and Co., 1890.

Cutler, Manasseh. "Contemporary Description of Ohio." *Ohio Archaeological and Historical Quarterly* 3 (1891): 82–108.

———. *The Life, Journals, and Correspondence of Rev. Manasseh Cutler.* Ed. William Parker Cutler and Julia Perkins Cutler. 2 vols. Cincinnati: Robert Clarke and Co., 1888.

Cutler, William P. "The Ordinance of July 13, 1787." *Ohio Archaeological and Historical Publications* 1 (June 1887): 10–37.

Dabney, Wendell P. *Cincinnati's Colored Citizens: Historical, Sociological and Biographical.* Cincinnati: Dabney Publishing Co., 1926.

Davis, David Brion. *The Problem of Slavery in the Age of Revolution, 1770–1823.* Ithaca: Cornell University Press, 1975.

Davis, Harold E. "Economic Basis of Ohio Politics, 1820–1840." *Ohio Archaeological and Historical Quarterly* 47 (October 1938): 288–318.

Davis, Lenwood G. "Nineteenth-Century Blacks in Ohio: An Historical Overview." In *Blacks in Ohio History,* ed. Rubin F. Weston. Columbus: Ohio Historical Society, 1976.

Davis, Russell H. *Black Americans in Cleveland from George Peake to Carl B. Stokes, 1796–1969.* Washington, D.C.: Associated Publishers, 1972.

Democratic Party (Ohio). *Proceedings of the Democratic State Convention Held in Columbus on the Eighth of January, 1838, with an Address to the People of Ohio.* Columbus: Printed at the office of the Ohio Statesman, 1838.

Descriptive Sketch of the State of Ohio, with the Contract of Co-Partnery of the Glasgow Ohio Company and Letters of Correspondence between the Company and Their Managers Now in Ohio. Glasgow: Printed for R. Malcolm, Trongate, 1824.

Dillon, Merton L. *The Abolitionists: The Growth of a Dissenting Minority.* DeKalb: Northern Illinois University Press, 1974.

Douglass, Frederick. *The Frederick Douglass Papers.* Ed. John Blassingame, R. McKivigan, and Peter P. Hinks. 5 vols. New Haven: Yale University Press, 1979.

Douglass, Frederick. *The Life and Writings of Frederick Douglass.* Ed. Philip S. Foner. 4 vols. New York: International Publishers, 1950.

Downes, Randolph C. *Frontier Ohio, 1788–1803.* Columbus: Ohio State Archaeological Society, 1935.

——. "Ohio's First Constitution." *Northwest Ohio Quarterly* 24–25 (Winter 1952–53): 12–21.

Drake, Samuel Adams. *The Making of the Ohio Valley States, 1660–1837.* New York: Scribner's, 1894.

Drew, Benjamin. *A Northside View of Slavery; the Refuge; or, the Narratives of Fugitive Slaves in Canada; Related by Themselves, with an Account of the History and Condition of the Colored Population of Upper Canada.* Boston: J. P. Jewett and Co., 1856.

Dunn, Jacob P. *Indiana: A Redemption from Slavery.* Boston: Houghton, Mifflin, 1896.

Elkins, Stanley, and Eric McKitrick. *The Age of Federalism: The Early American Republic, 1788–1900.* New York: Oxford University Press, 1993.

Emancipation Record of Negroes, 1804–1855. Clerk of Courts, Ross County. Microfilm, frame 98. Ohio Historical Society, Columbus.

Erickson, Leonard Ernest. "The Color Line in Ohio Public Schools, 1829–1890." Ph.D. diss., Ohio State University, 1959.

——. "Politics and Repeal of Ohio's Black Laws, 1837–1849." *Ohio History* 82 (Summer–Autumn 1973): 154–75.

Ernest, Robert. *Rufus King: American Federalist.* Chapel Hill: University of North Carolina Press, 1968.

Evans, Lyle S., ed. *A Standard History of Ross County, Ohio, an Authentic Narrative of the Past, with Particular Attention to the Modern Era in the Commercial, Industrial, Civic and Social Development.* 2 vols. Chicago: Lewis Publishing Co., 1917.

Evans, Nelson W., ed. *A History of Scioto County, Ohio, Together with A Pioneer Record of Southern Ohio.* Portsmouth, N.H.: Nelson W. Evans, 1903.

Fairchild, James H. "The Underground Railroad." Western Reserve Historical Society Tract no. 87, Cleveland, 1895.

Farrand, Max, ed. *The Records of the Federal Convention of 1787.* 4 vols. New Haven: Yale University Press, 1966.

Farrell, Richard T. "Cincinnati, 1800–1830: Economic Development through Trade and Industry." *Ohio History* 77 (Autumn 1968): 111–29.

Fehrenbacher, Don E. *The Dred Scott Case: Its Significance in American Law and Politics.* New York: Oxford University Press, 1978.

——. *The Slaveholding Republic: An Account of the United States Government's Relations to Slavery.* Completed and ed. Ward McAfee. Oxford: Oxford University Press, 2001.

Fess, Simeon D., ed. *Ohio: A Four-Volume Reference Library on the History of a Great State.* 5 vols. New York: Lewis Publishing, 1937.

Fielder, George. *The Illinois Law Courts in Three Centuries, 1675–1875: A Documentary History.* Berwyn, Ill.: Physicians' Record Co., 1973.

Finkelman, Paul. "Chief Justice Hornblower and the Fugitive Slave Law of 1793." In *Slavery and the Law,* ed. Finkelman. Madison, Wis.: Madison House, 1997.

——. *Dred Scott v. Sandford: A Brief History with Documents.* Boston: Bedford Books, 1997.

——. *Fugitive Slaves.* 6 vols. New York: Garland, 1989.

——. "Fugitive Slaves, Midwestern Racial Tolerance, and the Value of 'Justice Delayed.'" *Iowa Law Review* 78 (October 1992): 89–141.

——. *An Imperfect Union: Slavery, Federalism, and Comity.* Chapel Hill: University of North Carolina Press, 1981.

——. "*Prigg v. Pennsylvania:* Understanding Justice Story's Pro-Slavery Nationalism." *Journal of Supreme Court History* 2 (1997): 51–64.

——. "*Prigg v. Pennsylvania* and Northern State Courts: Anti-Slavery Use of a Pro-Slavery Decision." *Civil War History* 25 (March 1979): 5–35.

——. *Slavery and the Founders: Race and Liberty in the Age of Jefferson.* 2d ed. Armonk, N.Y.: M. E. Sharpe, 2001.

——. "Slavery and the Northwest Ordinance: A Study in Ambiguity." *Journal of the Early Republic* 6 (Winter 1986): 343–70.

——. "Sorting Out *Prigg v. Pennsylvania,*" *Rutgers Law Journal* 24 (Spring 1993): 605–65.

——. "State Constitutional Protections of Liberty and the Antebellum New Jersey Supreme Court: Chief Justice Hornblower and the Fugitive Slave Law of 1793." *Rutgers Law Journal* 23 (Summer 1992): 753–87.

——. *Statutes on Slavery: The Pamphlet Literature.* 2 vols. New York: Garland Publishing, 1988.

——. "Story Telling on the Supreme Court: *Prigg v. Pennsylvania* and Justice Joseph Story's Judicial Nationalism." *Supreme Court Review* (1994): 247–94.

——, ed. *The Law of Freedom and Bondage: A Casebook.* New York: Oceana Publications, 1986.

Fishback, Mason M. "Illinois Legislation on Slavery and Free Negroes, 1818–1856." *Illinois State Historical Society Transactions* 9 (1904).

Fiske, John. *The Critical Period of American History, 1783–1789.* Boston: Houghton Mifflin, 1916.

Fladeland, Betty L. "James G. Birney's Anti-Slavery Activities in Cincinnati, 1835–1837." *Bulletin of the Historical and Philosophical Society of Ohio* 9 (October 1951): 250–65.

——. *Men and Brothers: Anglo-American Antislavery Cooperation.* Urbana: University of Illinois Press, 1972.

Fletcher, Robert Samuel. *A History of Oberlin College: From Its Foundation through the Civil War.* 2 vols. New York: Arno Press, 1971.

Folk, Patrick Allen. "The Queen City Mobs." Ph.D. diss., University of Toledo, 1978.

Foner, Eric. *Free Soil, Free Labor, Free Men: the Ideology of the Republican Party before the Civil War.* New York: Oxford University Press, 1970.

——. "Politics and Prejudice: The Free Soil Party and the Negro, 1849–1852." *Journal of Negro History* 50 (October 1965): 239–56.

——. *The Story of American Freedom.* New York: Norton, 1998.

Foner, Philip S. *Frederick Douglass: A Biography.* New York: Citadel Press, 1964.

——. *History of Black Americans.* 3 vols. Westport, Conn.: Greenwood, 1975.

Foner, Philip S., and George E. Walker, eds. *Proceedings of the Black State Conventions, 1840–1865.* 2 vols. Philadelphia: Temple University Press, 1979–80.

Franklin, Isaac, ed. *The Constitutions of Ohio: Amendments and Proposed Amendments.* Cleveland: Arthur H. Clark Co., 1912.

French, Gary E. *Men of Color: An Historical Account of the Black Settlement on Wilberforce Street and Oro Township, Simcoe County, 1819–1949.* Stroud, Ont.: Kaste Books, 1978.

Galbreath, Charles B. "Antislavery Movement in Columbiana County." *Ohio Archaeological and Historical Quarterly* 30 (October 1921): 355–95.

——. *History of Ohio.* 5 vols. Chicago: American Historical Society, 1925.

——. "Ohio's Fugitive Slave Law." *Ohio Archaeological and Historical Quarterly* 34 (April 1925): 216–40.

——. "Thomas Jefferson's Views on Slavery," *Ohio Archaeological and Historical Quarterly* 34 (April 1925): 184–202.

Gara, Larry. "The Fugitive Slave Law in the Eastern Ohio Valley." *Ohio History* 72 (April 1963): 116–28.

——. *The Liberty Line: The Legend of the Underground Railroad.* Lexington: University Press of Kentucky, 1961.

——. "The Underground Railroad: A Re-evaluation." *Ohio Historical Quarterly* 69 (July 1960): 217–30.

Gerber, David A. *Black Ohio and the Color Line, 1860–1915.* Urbana: University of Illinois Press, 1976.

Gertz, Elmer. "The Black Laws of Illinois." *Journal of the Illinois State Historical Society* 56 (Autumn 1963): 454–73.

Gilmore, William Edward. *Life of Edward Tiffin: First Governor of Ohio.* Chillicothe, Ohio: Horney and Son, 1897.

Graham, A. A. "Legislation in the Northwest Territory." *Ohio Archaeological and Historical Quarterly* 1 (March 1888): 303–18.

Grant, John N. "Black Immigrants into Nova Scotia, 1776–1815." *Journal of Negro History* 58 (July 1973): 253–70.

Greve, Charles T. *Centennial History of Cincinnati and Representative Citizens.* 2 vols. Chicago: Biographical Co., 1904.

Haller, Stephen E., and Robert H. Smith Jr. *Registers of Blacks in the Miami Valley: A Name Abstract in the Miami Valley, 1804–1857.* Dayton, Ohio: Wright State University, 1977.

Harris, N. Dwight. *The History of Negro Servitude in Illinois and of the Slavery Agitation in That State, 1719–1864.* Chicago: A. C. McClurg and Co., 1904.

Harrison, Lowell H. *The Antislavery Movement in Kentucky.* Lexington: University Press of Kentucky, 1978.

Hart, Edgar Allan. *Party Politics in Ohio.* Columbus: F. J. Heery, 1931.

Hatcher, Harlan H. *The Buckeye Country: A Page Out of Ohio.* New York: H. C. Kinsey and Co., 1940.

Havighurst, Walter. *The Heartland: Ohio, Indiana, Illinois.* New York: Harper and Row, 1962.

——. *Ohio: A Bicentennial History.* New York: Norton, 1976.

Henderson, Archibald, ed. *North Carolina: The Old State and the New.* 2 vols. Chicago: Lewis Publishing Co., 1941.

Henderson, E. James. *Party Politics in the Continental Congress.* New York: McGraw-Hill, 1974.

Herz, Walter P. "Such a Glaring Inconsistency: The Unitarian Laity and Anti-slavery in Antebellum Cincinnati." First Unitarian Church of Cincinnati Library, Cincinnati, Ohio, 2003.

Hickok, Charles Thomas. "The Negro in Ohio, 1802–1870." Ph.D. diss., Case Western Reserve University, 1896.

Higginbotham, A. Leon. *In the Matter of Color:, The Colonial Period.* Race and the American Legal Process. New York: Oxford University Press, 1978.

Hinderaker, Eric. *Elusive Empires: Constructing Colonialism in the Ohio Valley, 1673–1800.* Cambridge: Cambridge University Press, 1997.

Hinsdale, B. A. *The Old Northwest.* Boston: Silver Burdett and Co., 1899.

——. *The Old Northwest: With a View of the Thirteen Colonies as Constituted by the Royal Charters.* New York: Townsend MacCoun, 1888.

Holt, Edgar Allen. "The Election of 1840 in Ohio." *Ohio Archaeological and Historical Society Publications* 38 (January 1929): 47–182.

——. "Party Politics in Ohio, 1840–1850." *Ohio Archeological and Historical Society Publications* 37 (July 1928): 439–591.

Holt, Michael F. *The Rise and Fall of the American Whig Party: Jacksonian Politics and the Onset of the Civil War.* New York: Oxford University Press, 1999.

Horowitz, Robert F. *Great Impeacher: A Political Biography of James M. Ashley.* New York: Brooklyn College Press, 1979.

Howard, Victor B. *Conscience and Slavery: The Evangelistic Calvinist Domestic Missions, 1837–1861.* Kent, Ohio: Kent State University Press, 1990.

——. *Religion and the Radical Republican Movement, 1860–1870.* Lexington: University Press of Kentucky, 1990.

Howe, Daniel Walker. *The Political Culture of the American Whigs.* Chicago: University of Chicago Press, 1979.

Howe, Henry. *Historical Collections of Ohio, an Encyclopedia of the State: History both General and Local, Geography with Descriptions of Its Counties, Cities and Villages, Its Agricultural, Manufacturing, Mining and Business Development, Sketches of Eminent and Interesting Characters, etc., with Notes of a Tour over It in 1886.* 2 vols. Norwalk: Published by the State of Ohio, Laning Printing Co., 1896.

——. Historical Collections of Ohio, Containing a Collection of the Most Interesting Facts, Traditions, Biographical Sketches, Anecdotes, etc., Relating to Its General and Local History; with Descriptions of its Counties, Cities, Towns, and Villages. Cincinnati: Derby, Bradley and Company, 1847.

Howe, Samuel Gridley. *The Refugees from Slavery in Canada West.* Boston: Wright and Potter, 1864.

Hulbert, Arthur Butler. *Ohio in the Time of the Confederation.* 3 vols. Marietta, Ohio: Marietta Historical Commission, 1918.

——, ed. *The Records of the Original Proceedings of the Ohio Company.* 2 vols. Marietta, Ohio: Marietta Historical Commission, 1917.

Hurd, John C. *The Law of Freedom and Bondage in the United States.* New York: Negro Universities Press, 1968.

Hutchinson, Thomas. *A Brief Sketch of the State of Ohio, One of the United States in North America.* Glasgow: A. Penman and Co., 1822.

Hyman, Harold M., and William M. Wiecek. *Equal Justice under the Law: Constitutional Development, 1835–1875.* New York: Harper and Row, 1982.

Indiana. *The Laws of the Indiana Territory, 1801–1809.* Ed. Francis S. Philbrick. 21 vols. Springfield: Illinois State Historical Library, 1930.

Indiana Yearly Meeting of Friends. *Address to the Citizens of the State of Ohio, Concerning What Are Called the Black Laws, Issued in Behalf of the Society of Friends of Indiana Yearly Meeting.* Cincinnati: A. Pugh, 1848.

Illinois Historical Collections, 34 volumes. *Kaskaskia Records, 1789–1790,* vol. 5. Ed. Clarence W. Alvord. (Springfield, Ill.: Illinois State Historical Library, 1909.

James, John Henry. *Ohio in 1788: A Description of the Soil, Productions of that Portion of the United States Situated between Pennsylvania, the Rivers Ohio and Scioto, and Lake Erie.* Columbus: A. H. Symthe, 1888.

Jay, John. *The Correspondence and Public Papers of John Jay.* Ed. Henry P. Johnston. 4 vols. New York: G. P. Putnam's Sons, 1890–93.

Jefferson, Thomas. *The Papers of Thomas Jefferson.* Ed. Julian Boyd. 22 vols. Princeton, N.J.: Princeton University Press, 1950.

Jenks, William L. "Territorial Legislation by Governor and Judges." *Mississippi Valley Historical Review* 5 (June 1918–19): 36–50.

Jensen, Merrill. "The Creation of the National Domain, 1781–1784." *Mississippi Valley Historical Review* 26 (December 1939): 323–42.

———. *The New Nation: A History of the United States during the Confederation, 1781–1789.* New York: Knopf, 1950.

Johnson, Allen. "The Constitutionality of the Fugitive Slave Acts." *Yale Law Journal* 31 (December 1921): 161–84.

Johnson, Franklin. *The Development of State Legislation Concerning the Free Negro.* New York: Arbor Press, 1919.

Joiner, William A., comp. *A Half Century of Freedom of the Negro in Ohio.* Xenia, Ohio: Smith Adv. Co., 1915. Repr. Freeport, N.Y.: Books for Libraries Press, 1972.

Jolliffe, John. *In the Matter of George Gordon's Petition for Pardon.* Cincinnati: Gazette Company Steam Printing House, 1862.

Jordan, Winthrop D. *White over Black: American Attitudes toward the Negro, 1550–1812.* Chapel Hill: University of North Carolina Press, 1968.

Kaczorowski, Robert J. "The Enforcement Provision of the Civil Rights Act of 1866: A Legislative History in Light of *Runyon v. McCrary.*" *Yale Law Journal* 98 (January 1989).

Kahn, Maxine B. "Congressman Ashley in the Post–Civil War Years." *Northwest Ohio Quarterly* 36 (Summer 1964): 116–33.

Kelly, Alfred. *The American Constitution: Its Origins and Development.* New York: Norton, 1976.

Kennedy, Aileen E. *The Ohio Poor Law and Its Administration.* Chicago: University of Chicago Press, 1934.

Kennedy, Roger G. *Mr. Jefferson's Lost Cause: Land, Farmers, Slavery, and the Louisiana Purchase.* Oxford: Oxford University Press, 2003.

Kerber, Linda K. "The Federalist Party." In *History of U.S. Political Parties,* ed. Schlesinger.

King, Leicester. *Report of the Select Committee of the Senate: On the Petitions of Sundry Citizens, Praying the Repeal of Certain Laws Restricting the Rights of Persons of Color: and for Securing to All Persons within the Jurisdiction of the State, the Right of Trial by Jury: Senate, March 3, 1838.* Pamphlet, Cincinnati Historical Society.

King, Rufus. *First Fruits of the Ordinance of 1787.* New York: Houghton Mifflin, 1903.

———. "Speech Delivered by Rufus King in the Senate on the Subject of the Missouri Bill." *North American Review* 10 (January 1820): 137–68.

Klingaman, David C., and Richard K. Vedder. *Essays on the Economy of the Old Northwest.* Athens: Ohio University Press, 1987.

Knepper, George W. *Ohio and Its People.* Kent, Ohio: Kent State University Press, 1989.

Koehler, Lyle, ed. *Cincinnati's Black Peoples: A Chronology and Bibliography, 1787–1982.* Cincinnati: Arts Consortium, 1986.

Kohlmeier, A. L. *The Old Northwest as the Keystone of the Arch of American Federal Union: A Study in Commerce and Politics.* Bloomington, Ind.: Principia Press, 1938.

Kolchin, Peter. *American Slavery, 1619–1877.* New York: Hill and Wang, 1993.

Konig, David T., ed. *Devising Liberty: Preserving and Creating Liberty in the New American Republic.* Stanford: Stanford University Press, 1995.

Krout, John Allen. *Dixon Ryan Fox, The Coming of Independence, 1790–1830.* New York: Macmillan, 1944.

Langston, Charles H. *Should Colored Men Be Subject to the Pains and Penalties of the Fugitive Slave Law? Speech before the U.S. District Court for the Northern Dist. of Ohio, May 12, 1859, Delivered When about to be Sentenced for Rescuing a Man from Slavery.* Cleveland: E. Cowles and Co., 1859.

Lasser, Carol. *Educating Men and Women Together: Coeducation in a Changing World.* Urbana: University of Illinois Press, 1987.

Lee, Richard Henry. *The Letters of Richard Henry Lee.* Ed. James Curtis Ballagh. 2 vols. New York: Macmillan, 1914.

Leet, Don R. *Population Pressure and Human Fertility Response: Ohio, 1810–1860.* New York: Arno Press, 1978.

Lenner, Andrew C. *The Federal Principle in American Politics, 1790–1833.* New York: Rowman and Littlefield, 2001.

Levy, Leonard. *Judgments: Essays on American Constitutional History.* Chicago: Quadrangle Books, 1972.

———. *The Law of the Commonwealth and Chief Justice Shaw.* Cambridge, Mass.: Harvard University Press, 1957. Repr. New York: Oxford University Press, 1986.

Lewis, Anthony Marc. "Jefferson and Virginia's Pioneers, 1774–1781." *Mississippi Valley Historical Review* 34 (March 1948): 551–88.

Litwack, Leon. "Free Blacks in the Antebellum North." In *America's Black Past: A Reader in Afro-American History,* ed. Eric Foner, New York: Harper and Row, 1970.

——. *North of Slavery: The Negro in the Free States, 1790–1860.* Chicago: University of Chicago Press, 1961.

——. "Trouble in Mind: The Bicentennial and the Afro-American Experience." *Journal of American History* 74 (September 1987): 315–37.

Livingston, William. *The Papers of William Livingston.* Ed. Carl E. Prince. 5 vols. New Brunswick, N.J.: Rutgers University Press, 1988.

Lovett, Otto Arnold. "Black Laws of Ohio." Master's thesis, Ohio State University, 1929.

Lucas, Marion B. *A History of Blacks in Kentucky: From Slavery to Segregation, 1760–1891.* 2 vols. Frankfort: Kentucky Historical Society, 1992.

Luthin, Reinhard H. "Some Demagogues in American History." *American Historical Review* 57 (October 1951): 22–46.

Lynch, William O. *Fifty Years of Party Warfare, 1789–1837.* Indianapolis: Bobbs-Merrill, 1931.

Lynd, Staughton. "Slavery and the Founding Fathers." In *Black History: A Reappraisal,* ed. Melvin Drimmer. New York: Anchor Books, 1968.

Madison, James. *The Papers of James Madison: Purchased by Order of the Congress, Being His Correspondence and Reports of Debates during the Congress of the Confederation, and His Reports of Debates in the Federal Connection; Now Published from the Original Manuscripts Deposited in the Department of State.* Ed. Robert A. Rutland. 16 vols. Chicago: University of Chicago Press, 1962–91.

Maizlish, Stephen E. *The Triumph of Sectionalism: The Transformation of Ohio Politics, 1844–1856.* Kent, Ohio: Kent State University Press, 1983.

Malehorn, William M. "The Fugitive Slave Law of 1850: Its Enforcement in Ohio." Master's thesis, Ohio State University, 1928.

Malvin, John. *North into Freedom: The Autobiography of John Malvin, 1795–1880.* Ed. Allan Peskin. Cleveland, Leader Print. Co., 1879. Repr. Cleveland: Press of Western Reserve University, 1966.

Marietta College Library. *The Sesquicentennial of Ohio's Statehood, 1803–1953: An Exhibition of Manuscript and Other Materials in the Library, June 5, 1953, to June 12, 1953.* Marietta, Ohio: Marietta College, 1953.

Marshall, Carrington T. ed. *A History of the Courts and Lawyers of Ohio.* 4 vols. New York: American Historical Society, 1934.

Martin, Asa Earl. *The Antislavery Movement in Kentucky.* Louisville, Ky.: Standard Printing Co., 1918.

Matijasic, Thomas. "The Reaction of the Ohio General Assembly to the Fugitive Slave Law of 1850." *Northwest Ohio Quarterly* 55 (Spring 1983): 40–60.

Mathews, Alfred. *Ohio and Her Western Reserve, with a Story of Three States Leading to the Latter, from Connecticut, by Way of Wyoming, Its Indian Wars and Massacre.* New York: D. Appleton and Co., 1902.

May, Samuel. *The Fugitive Slave Law and Its Victims.* New York: American Anti-Slavery Society, 1861.

McDonald, Forrest M. *E Pluribus Unum: The Formation of the American Republic, 1776–1790.* Indianapolis: Liberty Fund, 1965.

McDougall, Marion G. *Fugitive Slaves, 1619–1865.* Boston: Ginn and Co., 1891.

M'Clintock, William T. "Ohio's Birth Struggle." *Ohio History* 11 (July 1902): 44–70.

McPherson, James M. "The Fight against the Gag Rule: Joshua Leavitt and Antislavery Insurgency in the Whig Party, 1839–1842." *Journal of Negro History* 48 (July 1963): 177–95.

Meade, Robert Douthat, ed. *Patrick Henry.* 2 vols. Philadelphia: Lippincott, 1957–69.

Meinig, D. W. *The Shaping of America: A Geographical Perspective on 500 Years of History.* 4 vols. New Haven: Yale University Press, 1993.

Middleton, Evan P., ed. *History of Champaign County, Ohio, Its Peoples, Industries and Institutions.* Indianapolis: B. F. Bowen, 1917.

Middleton, Stephen. "Cincinnati and the Fight for the Law of Freedom in Ohio, 1830–1856." *Locus: An Historical Journal of Regional Perspectives* 4 (Fall 1991): 59–73.

———, ed. *The Black Laws in the Old Northwest: A Documentary History.* Westport, Conn.: Greenwood, 1993.

Miller, Helen Hill. *George Mason: Gentleman Revolutionary.* Chapel Hill: University of North Carolina Press, 1975.

Miller, William Lee. *Arguing about Slavery: The Great Battle in the United States Congress.* New York: Knopf, 1996.

Mills, William, Benjamin Hopkins, and George Lee. "Banishment of the People of Color from Cincinnati." Documents, *Journal of Negro History* 8 (July 1923): 331–32.

Minor, Richard C. "James Preston Poindexter: Elder Statesman of Columbus." *Ohio Historical Quarterly* 56 (July 1947): 266–86.

Monroe, James. *Oberlin Thursday Lectures, Addresses, and Essays.* Oberlin, Ohio: Edward J. Goodrich, 1897.

Moore, Charles. *The Northwest under Three Flags, 1635–1796.* New York: Harper and Brothers, 1900.

Morris, Benjamin F. *The Life of Thomas Morris: Pioneer and Long a Legislator of Ohio, and U.S. Senator from 1833–1839.* Cincinnati: Moore, Wilstach, Keys and Overend, 1856.

Morris, Richard. *The Forging of the Union, 1781–1789.* New York: Harper and Row, 1987.

Morris, Thomas D. *Free Men All: The Personal Liberty Laws of the North, 1780–1861.* Baltimore: Johns Hopkins University Press, 1974.

Morrison, Samuel E. *Sources and Documents Illustrating the American Revolution, 1764–1788, and the Formation of the Federal Constitution.* 2d ed. New York: Oxford University Press, 1965.

Nash, Gary B. *Race and the Revolution*. Madison, Wis.: Madison House, 1990.

National Emigration Convention of Colored People. *Proceedings of the National Emigration Convention of Colored People Held at Cleveland, Ohio, on Thursday, Friday and Saturday, the 24th, 25th and 26th of August, 1854.* Pittsburgh: A. A. Anderson, 1854.

Neff, William B. *Bench and Bar of Northern Ohio: History and Biography.* Cleveland: Historical Publishing Co., 1921.

Nelson, Thomas C. "The Aliened American: The Free Negro in Ohio." Master's thesis, University of Toledo, 1969.

Nelson, William E. *The Fourteenth Amendment: From Political Principle to Judicial Doctrine.* Cambridge, Mass.: Harvard University Press, 1988.

Nevins, Allen. *The American States: During and After the Revolution, 1775–1789.* New York: Macmillan, 1924.

Nieman, Donald G. *Promises to Keep: African-Americans and the Constitutional Order, 1776 to the Present.* New York: Oxford University Press, 1991.

Niven, John. *Salmon P. Chase: A Biography.* New York: Oxford University Press, 1995.

Nye, Russell B. "Marius Robinson, A Forgotten Abolitionist Leader." *Ohio History* 55 (April–June 1946): 138–54.

Oberst, Paul. "The Strange Career of *Plessy v. Ferguson.*" *Arizona Law Review* 15, no. 1 (1993): 389–418.

O'Dell, Richard F. "The Early Antislavery Movement in Ohio." Ph.D. diss., University of Michigan, 1948.

Ohio. *Public Statutes at Large of the State of Ohio: From the Close of Chase's Statutes, February, 1833, to the Present Time, with References to the Judicial Decisions Construing Those Statutes, and a Supplement Containing All Laws Passed Prior to February 1833, Which Are Now in Force.* 4 vols. Cincinnati: Maskell E. Curwen, 1853–61.

———. *Official Reports of the Debates and Proceedings of the Ohio State Convention Called to Alter, Revise or Amend the Constitution of the State, 1850–1851.* Columbus: Scott and Bascom, 1851.

———. *Report of the Debates and Proceedings of the Convention for the Revision of the Constitution of the State of Ohio, 1850–1851.* 2 vols. Columbus: S. Medary, Printer to the Convention, 1851.

———. *The School Officers' Guide, for the State of Ohio; Containing the Laws on the Subject of Common Schools, the School Fund, and etc., Together with Instructions for the Information and Government of School Officers, Printed by Authority of the General Assembly.* Columbus: S. Medary, State Printer, 1842.

———. Attorney General. *Biennial Report of the Ohio Attorney General, 1860–62.* Columbus: Richard Nevins, 1862.

———. Governor. *Annual Message of Governor Vance, Tuesday, December 5, 1837.* Columbus: n.p., 1838.

———. *Annual Message of the Governor of Ohio, to the Fifty-second General Assembly.* Columbus: Statesman Steam Press, 1856.

———. *Annual Message of the Governor of Ohio, to the Forty-eighth General Assembly: December 31, 1849.* Columbus: Scott and Bascom, 1849.

———. *Annual Message of the Governor of Ohio, Transmitted to Both Branches of the Forty-third General Assembly, Tuesday, December 3, 1844.* Columbus: Samuel Medary, State Printer, 1848.

———. *Communication from the Governor Relating to the Abduction of a Negro.* Columbus: n.p., 1838.

———. *Message of the Governor of Ohio, to the Thirty-fourth General Assembly of the State of Ohio.* Columbus: James B. Gardiner, Printer to the State, 1835.

———. *Report No. 1, Annual Message of Governor Lucas, with Accompanying Documents, Dec. 6, 1836,* in *Reports Including Messages, and Other Communications, Made to the Thirty-fifth General Assembly of the State of Ohio.* Columbus: James B. Gardiner, 1836.

———. *Report No. 28, Annual Message of Governor Vance, Dec. 5, 1837,* in *Documents Including Messages, and other Communications, Made to the Thirty-sixth General Assembly of the State of Ohio.* Columbus: Samuel Medary, 1837.

Ohio Anti-Slavery Society. *Memorial of the Ohio Anti-Slavery Society, to the General Assembly of the State of Ohio.* Cincinnati: Pugh and Dodd, 1838.

———. *Narrative of the Late Riotous Proceedings against the Liberty of the Press in Cincinnati.* Cincinnati: Ohio Anti-Slavery Society, 1836.

———. *Report of the Third Anniversary of the Ohio Anti-Slavery Society, Held in Granville, Licking County, Ohio, on the 30th of May, 1838.* Cincinnati: Ohio Anti-Slavery Society, Samuel A. Alley, printer, 1838.

———. "Report on the Black Laws." In *Proceedings of the Ohio Antislavery Convention Held at Putnam, April 23–24, 1835.* New York: American Anti-Slavery Society, 1835.

Ohio State Anti-Slavery Society. *Declaration of Sentiments and Constitution of the Ohio State Anti-Slavery Society.* Cincinnati: Ohio Anti Slavery Society, Samuel A. Alley, printer, 1839.

———. *Proceedings of the First Annual Meeting of the Ohio State Anti-Slavery Society.* Xenia, Ohio: January 3–5, 1860.

Okey, George B., and John D. Morten. *The Constitutions of the State of Ohio, 1802 and 1851, with Notes to the Decisions Construing Them, and References to the Constitutional Debates.* Columbus: Nevins and Myers, 1873.

Onuf, Peter S. *The Origins of the Federal Republic: Jurisdictional Controversies in the United States, 1775–1787.* Philadelphia: University of Pennsylvania Press, 1983.

———. *Statehood and Union: A History of the Northwest Ordinance.* Bloomington: Indiana University Press, 1987.

Orth, Samuel P. *A History of Cleveland, Ohio.* 3 vols. Cleveland: S. J. Clarke Publishing Co., 1910.

Owen, Daniel. "Circumvention of Article VI of the Ordinance of 1787." *Indiana Magazine of History* 36 (June 1940): 110–16.

Padover, Saul K. *Thomas Jefferson and the Foundations of American Freedom.* New York: Van Nostrand, 1965.

Parker, Russell D. "The Philosophy of Charles G. Finney: Higher Law and Revivalism." *Ohio History* 82 (Summer–Autumn 1973): 142–53.

Patterson, Isaac F., comp. *The Constitutions of Ohio, Amendments, and Proposed Amendments, Including the Ordinance of 1787, the Act of Congress Dividing the Northwest Territory, and* the Acts of Congress Creating and Recognizing the State of Ohio. Cleveland: Arthur H. Clark Co., 1912.

———, ed. The Constitutions of Ohio and Allied Documents. Cleveland: Arthur H. Clark Co., 1912.

Patton, William H. Conscience and Law; or, A Discussion of Our Comparative Responsibility to Human and Divine Government; with an Application to the Fugitive Slave Law. New York: M. H. Newman, 1850.

Paxson, Frederic L. History of the American Frontier, 1763–1893. New York: Houghton Mifflin, 1924.

Pease, Theodore C. "The Ordinance of 1787." Mississippi Valley Historical Review 25 (September 1938): 167–80.

Pease, William H., and Jane H. Pease. Black Utopia: Negro Communal Experiments in America. Madison: State Historical Society of Wisconsin, 1963.

———. They Who Would Be Free: Blacks' Search for Freedom, 1830–1861. New York: Atheneum, 1974.

Perdreau, Connie. A Black History of Athens County and Ohio University. Athens: Ohio University, 1988.

Perkins, James H. The Memoir and Writings of James H. Perkins. Ed. William Henry Channing. 2 vols. Cincinnati: Truman and Spofford, 1851.

Pershing, Benjamin H. "Membership in the General Assembly of Ohio." Ohio Archaeological and Historical Publications 40 (April 1931): 222–83.

Peters, William. A More Perfect Union. New York: Crown Publishers, 1987.

Peterson, Merrill D. The Jefferson Image in the American Mind. New York: Oxford University Press, 1962.

———. Thomas Jefferson: Writings. New York: Literary Classics, 1984

Phillips, Ulrich B. American Negro Slavery: A Survey of the Supply, Employment and Control of Negro Labor as Determined by the Plantation Regime. New York: D. Appleton and Co., 1918.

Pierce, Merrily. "Luke Decker and Slavery: His Cases with Bob and Anthony, 1817–1822." Indiana Magazine of History 85 (March 1989): 31–48.

Pih, Richard W. "Negro Self-Improvement Efforts in Ante-Bellum Cincinnati, 1836–1850." Ohio History 78 (Summer 1969): 179–87.

Pollack, Ervin H., ed. Unreported Judicial Decisions Prior to 1823. Indianapolis: Allen Smith Co., 1952.

Porter, George H. Ohio Politics during the Civil War Period. New York: Columbia University, 1911.

Potter, David M. The Impending Crisis, 1848–1861. New York: Harper and Row, 1976.

Preston, Emmett D. "The Fugitive Slave Acts in Ohio." Journal of Negro History 28 (October 1943): 422–77.

Price, Erwin H. "The Election of 1848 in Ohio." Ohio Archeological and Historical Society Publications 36 (April 1927): 188–311.

Proceedings of Brooke Court on the Trial of the Negro Woman Slave Jane. Daniel L. Hylton, Clerk of the Executive Council, October 22, 1808. Executive Papers, Virginia State Library and Archives, Richmond.

Purcell, Richard J. *The American Nation.* New York: Ginn and Co., 1929.

Putnam, Rufus. *The Memoirs of Rufus Putnam and Certain Official Papers and Correspondence.* Boston: Houghton Mifflin, 1903.

Quaife, Milo M. "The Significance of the Ordinance of 1787." *Journal of the Illinois State Historical Society* 30 (January 1938): 415–28.

Quillin, Frank U. *The Color Line in Ohio: A History of Race Prejudice in a Typical Northern State.* Ann Arbor, Mich.: George Wahr, 1913.

"Race Hate in Early Ohio." *Negro History Bulletin* 10 (June 1946): 203–10.

Randall, Emilius O., ed. *Speeches and Papers by Ohio Men.* 5 vols. Columbus: n.p., 1903.

Randall, Emilius O., and Daniel J. Ryan. *History of Ohio: The Rise and Progress of an American State.* New York: Century History Co., 1912.

Raphael, Ray. *A People's History of the American Revolution: How Common People Shaped the Fight for Independence.* New York: New Press, 2001.

Ratcliffe, Donald J. "Captain James Riley and Antislavery Sentiment in Ohio, 1819–1824." *Ohio History* 81 (Spring 1972).

———. *The Party Spirit in a Frontier Republic: Democratic Politics in Ohio, 1793–1821.* Columbus: Ohio State University Press, 1998.

———. *The Politics of Long Division: The Birth of the Second Party System in Ohio, 1818–1828.* Columbus: Ohio State University Press, 2000.

Reed, George Irving. *Bench and Bar of Ohio: A Compendium of History and Biography.* Chicago: Century Publishing and Engraving Co., 1897.

Riddell, William Renwick. "Additional Notes on Slavery." *Journal of Negro History* 17 (July 1932): 368–77.

———. "The Slave in Canada." *Journal of Negro History* 5 (July 1920): 261–62.

Riddle, Albert G. "Recollections of the Forty-seventh General Assembly." *Magazine of Western History* 6 (August 1887): 341–51.

Ripley, C. Peter, ed. *The Black Abolitionist Papers.* 5 vols. Chapel Hill: University of North Carolina Press, 1985.

Rivera, Roberta, ed. *Ohio Almanac.* Lorain, Ohio: Lorain Journal Co., 1977.

Robinson, Donald. *Slavery in the Structure of American Politics.* New York: Norton, 1979.

Rodabaugh, James H. "The Negro in Ohio." *Journal of Negro History* 31 (January 1946): 9–29.

Rokicky, Catherine M. *James Monroe: Oberlin's Christian Statesman and Reformer, 1821–1898.* Kent, Ohio: Kent State University Press, 2002.

Roseboom, Eugene H. *A History of Ohio.* New York: Prentice Hall, 1934.

Ross, Steven J. *Workers on the Edge: Work, Leisure, and Politics in Industrializing Cincinnati, 1788–1790.* New York: Columbia University Press, 1985.

Rowland, Kate Mason, ed. *The Life of George Mason, 1725–1792.* 2 vols. New York: Russell and Russell, 1964.

Ryan, Daniel J. "From Charter to Constitution: Being a Collection of Public Documents Pertaining to the Territory of the Northwest and the State of Ohio, from the Charters of James I, to and Including the First Constitution of Ohio, and the State Papers Relating to Its Admission to the Union, Show-

ing Thereby the Historical Chain of Title of Said State from 1606 to 1803."
Ohio Archaeological and Historical Society Publications 5 (August 1897): 1–164.

——. *A History of Ohio, with Biographical Sketches of Her Governors and the Ordinance of 1787.*
Columbus: A. H. Smythe, 1888.

——. *History of Ohio: The Rise and Progress of an American State.* New York: Century History Co., 1912.

Schafer, Judith Kelleher. *Slavery, the Civil Law, and the Supreme Court of Louisiana.* Baton Rouge: Louisiana State University Press, 1994.

Schlesinger, Arthur M., Jr., ed. *History of U.S. Political Parties, 1789–1860: From Factions to Parties.* 4 vols. New York: Chelsea House, 1973.

Schmiel, Eugene D. "The Career of Jacob Dolson Cox, 1828–1900: Soldier, Scholar, Statesman." Ph.D. diss., Ohio State University, 1969.

Schweninger, Loren. *Black Property Owners in the South, 1790–1915.* Urbana: University of Illinois Press, 1990.

Sears, Alfred Byron. *Thomas Worthington: Father of Ohio Statehood.* Columbus: Ohio State University Press, 1958.

Shannon, Fred A. *Economic History of the People of the United States.* New York: Macmillan, 1934.

Sheeler, J. Reuben. "The Struggle of the Negro for Freedom in Ohio." *Journal of Negro History* 31 (April 1946): 208–26.

Shepherd, Samuel, ed. *The Statutes at Large of Virginia, from October Session 1792, to December Session 1807.* 3 vols. Richmond, Va.: Printed by S. Shepherd, 1835–36.

Shriver, Phillip R., and Clarence E. Wunderlin Jr., eds. *The Documentary Heritage of Ohio.* Athens: Ohio University Press, 2000.

Siebert, William H. *The Mysteries of Ohio's Underground Railroads.* Columbus: Long's College Book Co., 1951.

Siebert, Wilbur H., and Albert B. Hart, *The Underground Railroad from Slavery to Freedom.* New York: Macmillan, 1898.

Siegel, Stephen A. "The Federal Government's Power to Enact Color-Conscious Laws: An Originalist Inquiry." *Northwestern University Law Review* 92 (Winter 1998).

Smith, John David. *Black Judas: William Hannibal Thomas and the American Negro.* Athens: University of Georgia Press, 2000.

Smith, Jordan M. "The Federal Courts and the Black Man in America, 1800–1883: A Study of Judicial Policy Making." Ph.D. diss., University of North Carolina, 1977.

Smith, Theodore Clark. *The Liberty and Free Soil Parties in the Northwest.* New York: Russell and Russell, 1967.

Smith, William H. "The First Fugitive Slave Case of Record in Ohio." *Senate Miscellaneous Documents,* no. 104, 53d Cong., 2d sess., vol. 4.

Smoot, Joseph Grady. "Freedom's Early Ring: The Northwest Ordinance and the American Union." Ph.D. diss., University of Kentucky, 1964.

Solomon, Barbara Miller. *In the Company of Educated Women: A History of Women and Higher Education in America.* New Haven: Yale University Press, 1985.

State Convention of Colored Men. *Address to the Constitutional Convention of Ohio, from the State Convention of Colored Men, Held in the City of Columbus, January 15th, 16th, 17th and 18th, 1851.* Columbus: E. Glover, 1851.

State Independent Free Territory Convention. *Addresses and Proceedings of the State Independent Free Territory Convention of the People of Ohio, Held at Columbus, June 20 and 21, 1848.* Cincinnati: Herald Office, 1848; pamphlet collection, American Antiquarian Society, Worcester, Mass.

A Statement of the Reasons Which Induced the Students of Lane Seminary to Dissolve Their Connection with That Institution. Cincinnati, 1834. Pamphlet, Cincinnati Historical Society.

St. Clair, Arthur. *The St. Clair Papers: The Life and Public Services of Arthur St. Clair.* Ed. William H. Smith. 2 vols. Cincinnati: Robert Clarke and Co., 1882.

Steele, Alden P., and Oscar T. Martin. *The History of Clark County, Ohio, Containing a History of the County; Its Cities, Towns, etc.; General and Local Statistics; Portraits of Early Settlers and Prominent Men; History of the Northwest Territory; History of Ohio; Map of Clark County; Constitution of the United States, Miscellaneous Matters.* Chicago: W. H. Beers and Co., 1881.

Stevens, Harry R. *The Early Jackson Party in Ohio.* Durham, N.C.: Duke University Press, 1957.

Stille, Charles J. *The Life and Times of John Dickinson, 1732–1800.* Philadelphia: Historical Society of Pennsylvania, 1891.

Stone, Frederic. "The Ordinance of 1787." *Pennsylvania Magazine of History and Biography* 13, no. 3 (1889): 309–40.

Sumner, Charles. *Argument of Charles Sumner, Esq. against the Constitutionality of Separate Colored Schools, in the Case of Sara Roberts vs. the City of Boston before the Supreme Court of Mass., December 4, 1849.* Boston: B. F. Roberts, 1849.

Swan, Joseph R. *Opinion of J. R. Swan, C.J., in the Cases of Bushnell and Langston on Habeas Corpus.* Columbus: Osgood and Pearce, 1859.

———, ed. *Statutes of the State of Ohio of a General Nature.* Columbus: Samuel Medary, State Printer, 1841.

Swisher, Thomas R., ed. *Ohio Constitution: Handbook.* Cleveland: Banks-Baldwin Law Publishing Co., 1990.

Taylor, Henry L. "Spatial Organization and the Residential Experience: Black Cincinnati in 1850." *Social Science History* 10 (Spring 1986): 45–69.

Taylor, Robert M., Jr., ed. *The Northwest Ordinance, 1787, A Bicentennial Handbook.* Indianapolis: Indiana Historical Society, 1987.

Taylor, William A. *Ohio in Congress from 1803 to 1901, with Notes and Sketches of Senators and Representatives and Other Historical Data.* Columbus: Century Publishing Co., 1900.

———. *Ohio Statesmen and Annals of Progress, from the Year 1788 to the Year 1900.* 2 vols. Columbus: Press of Westbote Co., 1899.

———. *Ohio Statesman and Hundred Year Book, from 1788 to 1892.* Columbus: Westbote Co., State Printers, 1892.

Terzian, Barbara A. "'Effusions of Folly and Fanaticism': Race, Gender, and Constitution-Making in Ohio, 1802–1923." Ph.D. diss., Ohio State University, 1999.

Thurston, Helen. "The 1802 Constitutional Convention and the Status of the Negro." *Ohio History* 81 (Winter 1972): 15–37.

Townshend, Norton S. "The Forty-seventh General Assembly: Comments on Mr. Riddle's Paper." *Magazine of Western History* 6 (October 1887): 623–28.

———. "Salmon P. Chase." *Ohio History* 1 (September 1887).

Trefousse, Hans L. *Benjamin Franklin Wade*. New York: Twayne Publishers, 1963.

Trotter, Joe William, Jr. *The African American Experience*. New York: Houghton Mifflin, 2001.

Turpin, Joan. *Register of Black, Mulatto, and Poor Persons in Four Ohio Counties, 1791–1861*. Bowie, Md.: Heritage Books, 1985.

United States. *Territorial Papers of the United States*. Ed. Clarence E. Carter. 24 vols. Washington, D.C.: Government Printing Office, 1934.

———. *Warrant for the Arrest of Madeline, a Fugitive from Labor*. United States, Southern District, 1854. CinHS.

———. Continental Congress. *Journals of the Continental Congress, 1774–1789*, 34 vols. Washington, D.C.: Government Printing Office, 1904–1937.

U.S. Senators from 1833–1839. Cincinnati: Moore, Wilstach, Keys and Overend, 1856.

Utter, William T. "Chillicothe Junto: A Stolen March on the Opposition That Cleared the Way for Ohio's Statehood." *American Heritage* 38 (Spring 1953): 38–39, 70–71.

———. *The History of the State of Ohio: The Frontier State, 1803–1825*. 6 vols. Columbus: Ohio State Archaeological and Historical Society, 1942.

Venable, W. H. "Cincinnati, Historical and Descriptive." *New England Magazine* 6 (September 1888): 423–46.

Vinton, Samuel F. *Substance of an Argument of Samuel F. Vinton, for the Defendants, in the Case of the Commonwealth of Virginia vs. Peter M. Garner and Others, for an Alleged Abduction of Certain Slaves, Delivered before the General Court of Virginia, at Its December Term, A.D. 1845*. Marietta, Ohio: Printed at the Intelligencer Office, 1846.

Wade, Richard. "The Negro in Cincinnati, 1800–1830." *Journal of Negro History* 39 (January 1954): 43–57.

———. *The Urban Frontier: The Rise and Fall of Western Cities, 1790–1830*. Cambridge, Mass.: Harvard University Press, 1967.

Walker, Charles M. *History of Athens County, Ohio and Incidentally of the Ohio Land Company and the First Settlement of the State of Marietta, with Personal and Biographical Sketches of the Early Settlers, Narratives of Pioneer Adventurers*. Cincinnati: Robert Clarke and Co., 1869.

Walker, James. *Identity: The Black Experience in Canada*. Ontario: Ontario Educational Communications, 1979.

Walker, Timothy. "Ordinance of 1787, Historical Discourse." *Transactions Ohio History and Philosophic Society* 1 (December 23, 1837).

Wallenstein, Peter. "Race, Marriage, and the Supreme Court from *Pace v. Alabama* (1883) to *Loving v. Virginia* (1967)." *Journal of Supreme Court History* 2 (1998): 65–86.

Washington County (Ohio) Pioneer Association. *The Coming Centennial, April 7, 1888: The Ninety-eighth Anniversary of the Settlement of Ohio and the Northwest Territory,*

Celebrated at Marietta, Ohio, April 7, 1886. Marietta, Ohio: Marietta Register Power Print, 1886.

Washington, George. *Papers of George Washington.* Ed. Dorothy Twohig. 10 vols. Charlottesville: University of Virginia Press, 1993.

——. *The Writings of George Washington from the Original Manuscript Sources, 1745–1799.* Prepared under the direction of the United States George Washington Bicentennial Commission and published by authority of Congress, John C. Fitzpatrick, editor. 39 vols. Washington, D.C.: Government Printing Office, 1931–44.

Webster, Daniel. *Papers of Daniel Webster.* Ed. David G. Allen. Hanover, N.H.: University Press of New England, 1977.

——. *The Papers of Daniel Webster.* Ed. Charles M. Wiltse. 7 vols. Hanover, N.H.: University Press of New England, 1974–89.

Weeks, Louis. "John P. Parker: Black Abolitionist Entrepreneur, 1827–1900." *Ohio History* 80 (Spring 1971): 155–62.

Weisenburger, Francis. *History of the State of Ohio: The Passing of the Frontier, 1825–1850.* Columbus: Ohio State Archaeological and Historical Society, 1941.

Wesley, Charles H. *Negro Americans in Ohio: A Sesquicentennial View.* Wilberforce, Ohio: Central State College, 1953).

——. "The Participation of Negroes in Anti-Slavery Political Parties." *Journal of Negro History* 29 (January 1944): 32–74.

Wheeler, Jacob D. *A Practical Treatise on the Law of Slavery, Being a Compilation of All Decisions Made on That Subject, in the Several Courts of the United States, and State Courts.* New York: Negro University Press, 1968.

Wiecek, William M. "Somerset: Lord Mansfield and the Legitimacy of Slavery in the Anglo-American World." *University of Chicago Law Review* 42 (1974): 86–146.

——. *The Sources of Antislavery Constitutionalism in America, 1760–1848.* Ithaca: Cornell University Press, 1977.

——. "The Statutory Law of Slavery and Race in the Thirteen Colonies of British America." *William and Mary Quarterly* 34 (April 1977): 258–80.

Williams, Albert G. *The Life of Benjamin F. Wade.* Cleveland: W. W. Williams, 1886.

Williams, Frederick D., ed. *The Northwest Ordinance: Essays on Its Formulation, Provisions, and Legacy.* East Lansing: Michigan State University Press, 1989.

Williams, George Washington. *History of the Negro Race in America, 1619–1880.* Repr., New York: Arno Press, 1968.

Williams, Lou Falkner. *The Great South Carolina Ku Klux Klan Trials, 1871–1872.* Athens: University of Georgia Press, 1996.

Wilson, Carol. "Freedom at Risk: The Kidnapping of Free Blacks in America, 1780–1865." Ph.D. diss., West Virginia University, 1991.

——. *Freedom at Risk: The Kidnapping of Free Blacks in America, 1780–1865.* Lexington: University Press of Kentucky, 1994.

Wilson, Frazer Ells. *Arthur St. Clair, Rugged Ruler of the Old Northwest: An Epic of the American Frontier.* Richmond, Va.: Garrett and Massie Publishers, 1944.

Wing, George Clary, ed. *Early Years on the Western Reserve: With Extracts from Letters of Ephraim Brown and Family, 1805–1845.* Cleveland: Arthur H. Clark Co., 1916.

Winkle, Kenneth. *The Politics of Community in Antebellum Ohio.* Cambridge: Cambridge University Press, 1988.

Winks, Robin. *The Blacks in Canada: A History.* New Haven: Yale University Press, 1971.

———. "The Canadian Negro: A Historical Assessment: The Negro in the Canadian-American Relationship." Part I. *Journal of Negro History* 53 (October 1968): 283–300.

Wolinetz, Gary K. "New Jersey Slavery and the Law." *Rutgers Law Review* 50 (Spring 1998): 2227–58.

Woodson, Carter G. "The Negroes of Cincinnati Prior to the Civil War." *Journal of Negro History* I (January 1916): 1–22.

———, ed. *The Mind of the Negro as Reflected in Letters Written during the Crisis, 1800–1860.* Repr., New York: Russell and Russell, 1969.

Yanuck, Julius. "The Garner Fugitive Slave Case." *Mississippi Valley Historical Review* 40 (June 1953): 47–66.

Zilversmit, Arthur. *The First Emancipation: The Abolition of Slavery in the North.* Chicago: University of Chicago Press, 1967.

Van Camp, Enos, 249–50
Van Camp v. Logan, 249–50
Vance, Joseph, 96, 122, 135–36, 165
Vanderburgh, Henry, 13–14
Van Horn, Thomas, 79
Van Matre, Daniel, 57
Van Zandt, John, 195–96
Vinton, Samuel M., 187–90
Virginia, 14, 22–23, 43, 56, 66–67, 135,
     165, 173, 188–90, 219–20
    antimiscegenation laws, 251
    General Assembly, 64

Wade, Benjamin F., 78, 100, 102, 120,
     126, 135–36, 238
    Compromise of 1850 and, 207–8
Walker, Timothy, 228
Walton, Leroy D., 218
Watson, John L., 125, 146, 147
Wattles, Augustus, 86
Webster, Daniel, 135, 176–77, 203
Webster-Ashburton Treaty, 176–77

Weld, Theodore D., 78, 82, 98, 101
Western Anti-Slavery Society, 90, 211
Western Reserve, 118
Western Spy, 29
Whig Party, 80, 101–2, 115–18, 128, 244
White, Addison, 232–34
white slavery, 93
Wilberforce University, 148
Williams, George W., 6, 254
Williams v. Directors of School District, 86–88, 247
Wilmot, David, 143
Wilmot Proviso, 143
Wisconsin, 59–60
Wolcott, C. P., 233, 236
Wood, Reuben, 147, 208, 217
Woods, John, 26–27, 34
Woods v. Green, 107
Worthington, Thomas, 21, 24, 30, 62
Wright, Jabez, 182
Wright, John C., 106–7

Young Men's Union Society, 90